# THE GREAT AWAKENING

# THE GREAT AWAKENING.

# A HISTORY

## OF THE

# REVIVAL OF RELIGION

## IN THE TIME OF

# EDWARDS AND WHITEFIELD.

By
**JOSEPH TRACY**

**" Then shall ye return, and discern between the righteous and the wicked ; between him that serveth God, and him that serveth him not." — MALACHI III. I8.**

KALPAZ

ISBN: 978-93-5128-943-2(HB)

First Published in 1842
Indian Reprint in 2017

*Published by*

Kalpaz Publications
C-30, Satyawati Nagar,
Delhi – 110052
E-mail: kalpaz@hotmail.com
Website: kalpazpublications.com
Ph.: +91-9212142040

GWhitefield

# PREFACE.

DURING the year 1840, public meetings were held in some places, and proposed in others, in commemoration of what Edwards called "The Revival of Religion in New England in 1740." This first suggested to the author the design of the present work. No history of that revival had ever been attempted. Its importance in itself, and in its influence on the subsequent state of the churches, was universally acknowledged. Yet opinions concerning it were various and discordant, even among evangelical ministers; some thinking it worthy of unmixed eulogy in public celebrations, others speaking of it with only guarded and qualified commendation, and others doubting whether it should not be mentioned rather with censure than otherwise. For the last ten years, too, the advocates of all kinds of "measures," new and old, have been asserting that the events and results of that revival justified their several theorics and practices. There was, therefore, evident need of a work, which should furnish the means of suitably appreciating both the good and the evil of that period of religious history.

The next question was concerning its possibility. Could materials be found, for the construction of such a work? A slight investigation was sufficient to furnish an answer. The public libraries contain abundant materials, of which some account must now be given.

The leading authority is "The Christian History;

containing accounts of the Revival and Propagation of Religion in Great Britain and America." It was first suggested by Edwards, in the conclusion of his "Thoughts on the Revival of Religion in New England." The first number was issued March 5, 1743, and it was continued, in weekly numbers of eight pages, small octavo, for two years. It was conducted by Thomas Prince, Jr., son of the Rev. Thomas Prince, one of the pastors of the Old South Church. Letters from ministers, giving accounts of the progress and state of religion in their several parishes, compose the greater part of its contents. So far as is known, this was the first periodical for the diffusion of contemporary religious intelligence, ever established. Similar publications were soon after commenced in London and Glasgow. When the publication of the first volume was completed, some copies, remaining in the hands of the publisher, were bound and offered for sale. This volume is not very uncommon; and not unfrequently passes for the whole work. Both volumes are preserved, entire, in the libraries of the Boston Athenæum and the Massachusetts Historical Society. This work was published for the sake of promoting the revival, and therefore gives accounts which were then esteemed favorable, though it relates many things which no one now would commend.

Whitefield's account of his own life, his Journals and his Letters, deserve to be mentioned next. His Journals were originally published in pamphlets, of a moderate size. They appeared as often as he could find time to prepare them for the press, which was often done without sufficient care. He afterwards collected, revised, and published them as one work. In preparing this history, the original, unrevised Journals have been exclusively used; for, as the faults in the first editions produced important effects, it is necessary to know what they were. The account of his life was prefixed to the first Journal that he published, and relates only to its previous years. His letters were collected after his death, and, with some of his sermons and other works of less importance, published in four octavo volumes.

Controversial publications of that day, too numerous to be specified individually, form a third source of information. The most able and best known of these are Edwards' "Thoughts on the Revival of Religion in New England in 1740," and Chauncy's "Seasonable Thoughts on the State of Religion in New England." Besides these, about one hundred pamphlets published during the revival, or soon after, have been consulted. The greater part of them have been of service, only as aids in understanding others, by the exhibitions which they give of the spirit of the times. Something has been gleaned from the files of newspapers, preserved by the Massachusetts Historical and American Antiquarian Societies.

The records of churches ought to furnish an important class of documents; but generally, so far as the author has been able to learn, they are either lost, or were badly kept, and furnish no valuable aid. Such has proved to be the fact, in every instance, where the absence of printed documents rendered their aid peculiarly desirable. A few papers from the files of the church in Sturbridge, furnished by the kindness of its late pastor, the Rev. J. S. Clark, is all that has been obtained from such sources. More will doubtless be found, whenever the attention of the pastors of ancient churches shall be effectually drawn to the investigation.

Town histories have usually been written by men who could find but little information on this subject, or who were unable to appreciate its importance, or who supposed such matter would not be valued by those for whom they wrote. Yet they have contributed something.

Backus's "Ecclesiastical History of the Baptists in New England" is an important authority, though it furnishes little matter peculiar to itself. Backus was one of that class of Separatists which the revival brought into being, and like many others of them, became a Baptist. Of course, he gives those views of the merits of the several parties which the Separatists entertained; and yet he is honest enough to record some faults of his own party, which are not recorded by their opponents.

Trumbull's "History of Connecticut" gives a valuable account of the revival as it was in that colony, with incidental notices of it in other places. Perhaps his personal friendship for those zealous and active revivalists, Pomroy and Wheelock, with whom he was intimate, and whom he learned to venerate in his youth, may have biased his judgment on some points. Still, he is an unusually candid writer, and his personal acquaintance with the fruits of the revival gives additional importance to his narrative.

A biography of Edwards should contain almost a complete account of the revival; for in no other way can the influence of his mind on the country and on the world be fully shown. His biographers, however, seem not to have found the requisite materials. Yet the industry of the Rev. Dr. S. E. Dwight has collected matter which throws important light on some parts of it.

The author has not been able to obtain the Life of Dr. Buel, or the Life of Gilbert Tennent, which was written by his friend President Finley. A Life of Dr. Bellamy is believed to be still a desideratum. The Memoir of Wheelock despatches the history of his labors in the revival, in a single page of vague generalities. A notice of his life and character in the American Quarterly Register, by the Rev. Dr. Allen, contains valuable extracts from his diary during some of those labors. A well written and impartial history of his life and labors, with copious selections from his writings, for which materials probably exist, would be valuable. There is scarce another man of equal eminence in that age, of the peculiarities of whose character and style of promoting religion we have so little satisfactory information; and yet there is reason to suspect that those peculiarities exerted an important influence.

The Constitutional History of the Presbyterian Church, by the Rev. Prof. Hodge, of Princeton, has been a valuable assistant. It is an elegantly written work, of great historical research, and must ever remain a standard work among those to whose communion he belongs. Yet, on some points incidentally noticed, it has appeared necessary to dissent from his conclusions.

The Memoir of Whitefield, by Dr. Gillies, and Philip's Life and Times of Whitefield, have of course been consulted. The latter has furnished some valuable facts and suggestions, especially respecting the revival in Scotland.*

* Philip asks: "By the way, what became of the Mss. and books which Prince left to the Old South Church, as the New England Library? The collection was great and valuable. Can it be true that the Mss. were destroyed by the British, except by accident? I ask this question, because I find 'No,' in pencil mark, on the margin of my copy of *Amer. Biog.*" The answer, — to use language once familiar in Great Britain, — must be "More yes than no." During the siege of Boston, the Old South meetinghouse was used for a riding school. In the winter, a stove was placed in it, and the timber of the pews and galleries, except the gallery on one side, which was reserved for spectators, was used for fuel, and the library, which was kept in a room under the belfry, said to have been Prince's study, furnished paper to kindle the fires. Of course, the Mss. and pamphlets, being most convenient for that purpose, suffered most severely. Nearly all the Mss. which escaped the stove, and about 200 volumes from the library, most appropriate to such a destination, are deposited in the library of the Massachusetts Historical Society. The remainder of the library, which contains several thousands of volumes, is kept in the Parsonage. It contains many old theological and other works of great value, and is still rich in pamphlets of the times in which it was collected. It was doubtless the

A slight inspection of these multifarious documents was enough to show, that the period of "The Great Awakening" needed to be carefully studied; that some great idea was then extensively at work, breaking up established and venerated habits of thought, feeling and action, and producing a revolution in the minds of men, and thus in the very structure of society. The agitations of that day had all the characteristic marks, by which such periods of human history are distinguished. The first work of the historian, therefore, must be, to seize that great idea. He must ascertain, what was that truth, before unknown or neglected and inoperative, which, working in the minds of those who received it, and on the minds of its opposers, according to each man's situation, temperament and degree of mental and moral cultivation, produced the various phenomena of the revival. With a knowledge of that idea, we shall be able to understand the history of those times; to appreciate the motives from which men acted; to see how some were led into their errors, and others made their way to the knowledge of the truth; to ascertain the kind, and estimate the amount, of good and evil influences which the revival left behind it; to draw from a knowledge of those times, the proper lessons, both of encouragement and warning. Without it, we shall have only a labyrinth of

---

best collection of means for illustrating the religious history of Great Britain and America during those times, that ever existed.

"By the way," why does Philip call the Congregational Meetinghouses in Boston, "chapels?" The term may be needed in England, to distinguish other places of worship from those of the Established Church; but it is never used in that sense here. And why does he use *italics*, when he says, that a certain negro at Cambridge "had been *allowed*" to hear Whitefield preach? Does he suppose that there ever was a time when the few negroes in New England were not "allowed" as free access to the preaching of the gospel, as the white inhabitants enjoyed? The negro in question had probably been "allowed" to hear Whitefield preach "*in the College*," on some occasion when the public was not admitted.

facts; and though familiar with each, shall not understand their relations to each other, nor be able safely to derive one practical lesson from the whole.

The history of religious opinions and practices shows, that the most important practical idea which then received increased prominence and power, and has held its place ever since, was the idea of the "new birth," as held by the Orthodox Congregationalists of New England, and others who harmonize with them; the doctrine, that in order to be saved, a man must undergo a change in his principles of moral action, which will be either accompanied or succeeded by exercises of which he is conscious, and can give an account; so that those who have been thus changed, may ordinarily be distinguished from those who have not; from which it follows, that all who exhibit no evidence of such a change, ought to be considered and treated as unregenerate, and in the road to perdition, and therefore not admitted to the communion of the churches. This doctrine of the "new birth," as an ascertainable change, was not generally prevalent in any communion when the revival commenced; it was urged as of fundamental importance, by the leading promoters of the revival; it took strong hold of those whom the revival affected; it naturally led to such questions as the revival brought up and caused to be discussed; its perversions naturally grew into, or associated with, such errors as the revival promoted; it was adapted to provoke such opposition, and in such quarters, as the revival provoked; and its caricatures would furnish such pictures of the revival, as opposers drew. This was evidently the right key; for it fitted all the wards of the complicated lock.

If this work should fall into the hands of any who have not been accustomed to regard this doctrine with respect, perhaps a few words of explanation may enable them to understand better what it is, and to see that it deserves their attention.

In being a Christian, two things are implied; the reception of the Christian system as our creed, and the conformity of our inward and outward life to its teachings. Roman Catholic missionaries, and perhaps some others who labor among the heathen, count all as converts who adopt their creed, even though they adopt it in the gross, with no knowledge of the particular doctrines contained in it. In Christian lands, most persons grow up, of course, into this kind of Christianity, and live on, without seriously inquiring whether they live as the gospel requires. Many, in the course of their lives, some in one way and some in another, are "awakened" to this inquiry. When awakened, the very thought that they know not whether they are in the way to heaven or not; that they have lived so many years, in hourly danger of death, without once seriously considering whether they are prepared, or even preparing for it, is alarming. To noble and ingenuous minds, the thought that they have lived so long without seriously considering how they treat certain duties which many call important, and may therefore be much deeper in guilt than they ever suspected, is more alarming still. Then follows self-examination, — the deliberate comparison of their own lives, inward and outward, towards God, their neighbours and their own consciences, with the Christian standard. The result of self-examination is the discovery of guilt, or, in the technical language of practical theology, conviction of sin. The discovery that we are morally worse than we ever supposed, is an appalling discovery. To him who makes it, — if he is not hopelessly joined with apostate spirits, and ready to say, with their leader, "Evil, be thou my good," it must be a source of anxiety. It must bring up the questions, whether reformation is possible, and if so, how? And whether punishment is to be apprehended, and if so, whether it may be avoided, and how. If reformation is possible, and pardon may be obtained, the inquirer, though now a sinner, may become a holy and happy being. If not, he must be unholy and miserable for the remainder of his conscious existence,—which may be, and he has reason to suppose, will be, eternal. Such a prospect, no man, especially no one to whom it is new, can contemplate without feeling. With such views in his mind, and corresponding emotions in his heart, the inquirer seeks the solution of these questions in his Bible, from his pastor, or from others whom he believes to be truly pious; and above all, calls on the Father of spirits to enlighten him. Men may tell him that his anxiety is needless; that God is merciful, and there is no danger; but this cannot satisfy him. He must understand the remedy for himself, and see its adaptation to his newly discovered spiritual wants. He has found in himself the spiritual wants which the Bible ascribes to man, and therefore understands those parts of the Bible better than he ever did before; as the description of a plant is better understood, when read with a specimen before the eyes. He needs the same clear and satisfying view of the gospel remedy for sin and guilt, and of its adaptation to his spiritual wants; and not even the words of Scripture can give him rest, till he has it; and when it comes, it cannot fail to fill his heart with joy. He sees the way, walks in it gladly, and finds by experience that his spiritual wants are met.

Such, in substance, is the Christian experience of all real converts; modified, however, by individual peculiarities of character and circumstances. In some, the process occupies several years; in others, it is so rapid that some of the steps are seen only in their results; in others still, it is repeatedly interrupted and resumed. Varieties are caused by the varieties of intellectual character and style of thought; of errors which the inquirer is unwilling to abandon; of sins which he is unwilling to forsake; of temptations from natural temper, from pursuits in life, from social relations, and from the intentional hindrance or assistance of others. Bodily health, from its known influence over the powers of thought and emotion, cannot fail to modify the process; which, in its turn, especially in persons of a nervous temperament, may re-act on the nerves, and through them, on itself. But in all cases the essential parts of the process are substantially the same. In every case there will be, not a mere unintelligent fright, succeeded by a joy without reason; not a mere learning of things by rote, or taking of things for granted on the testimony of others; but original thought, — for self-examination must be original thought; — there will be discoveries of truth by original thinking, and emotions appropriate to those discoveries; all agreeable to the principles taught in the Scriptures, and leading to such a life as Christianity requires.

Now, will any one pretend, that persons who have been through this process themselves, cannot, by examination, form a reasonable judgment whether others have been through it or not? What teacher, what school committee man, cannot ascertain whether a boy has seen for himself and understands the nature and reason of the rule for working simple addition, or whether he has only learned it by rote? Cannot pretenders in any branch of science be detected? Cannot one who has understood and felt the power of Milton's Paradise Lost, judge whether another has understood and felt the same, or whether he only repeats, parrot-like, some of Addison's criticisms? If discrimination is possible in such cases as these, it must also, on the same principle, be possible for those who are qualified, to judge whether a man has made those discoveries of religious truth, and felt those emotions, which are essential to Christian experience.

It is doubtless true, that there can be no infallibility, with fallible judges; and that the errors of enthusiasts have done much to bring the relation of experiences into disrepute; and that some religious men have been made ashamed to show any respect for the practice, by the sneers of those who, having no religious experience themselves, hate and despise all regard for it in others; and that, for such reasons, the subject has received less attention than it deserves, and is not so well understood as it might be and ought to be. Still, it is no unimportant means of forming a judgment of Christian character; and when prejudices, arising from its abuse in days of ignorance, shall have passed away, men will be ashamed to own that they ever doubted its value.

The history of the "Great Awakening" is the history of this idea, making its way through some communities where it had fallen into comparative neglect, and through others where it was nearly or quite unknown; overturning theories and habits and forms of organization inconsistent with it, where it could prevail, and repelled by them, where it could not; working itself gradually clear in the minds of those who received it, and leading to habits of thought and practical arrangements in harmony with itself. If the reader finds a true and intelligible account of its various workings, the object for which this history ought to be written, will be accomplished.

BOSTON, December 1, 1841.

# CONTENTS.

## CHAPTER XII.



## CHAPTER XIII.



## CHAPTER XIV.



## CHAPTER XV.



## CHAPTER XVI.



## CHAPTER XVII.

CHAPTER XVIII.



CHAPTER XIX.



CHAPTER XX.

THE

# GREAT AWAKENING.

## CHAPTER I.

**INTRODUCTORY. — Previous State of Religious Opinions and Practices. — Decline of Piety. — Preaching of Edwards. — " Surprising Conversions " at Northampton, and in other places.**

THE "Great Awakening of 1740" was not confined to that year. The religious movement of which the events of that year were a conspicuous part, began at Northampton in 1734, and continued till 1742, and in many places even longer. The immediate occasion of its commencement was a series of sermons by the elder Edwards, on the doctrine of Justification by Faith; and among the most efficient means of carrying it on, were his sermons, proving that "every mouth shall be stopped" at the day of judgment, and that "nothing, at any one moment, keeps wicked men out of hell, but the mere pleasure of God." Edwards himself testified, that no discourses had "been more remarkably blessed, than those in which the doctrine of God's absolute sovereignty with regard to the salvation of sinners, and his just liberty with regard to answering the prayers, or succeeding the pains, of mere natural men, continuing such," were insisted on. These doctrines, when handled as they were by him, are always powerful; but, to appreciate the force with which they came upon the hearers then, we must consider what was then the religious state of New England, and of the world.

In the early days of New England, none but church members could hold any office, or vote at elections. This is often mentioned, as evidence of the bigotry and domineering spirit of the Puritans; but unjustly. It was so, and always had been so, throughout the Christian world, — except that, in most cases, rulers were hereditary, and nobody voted at all. Throughout Christian Europe, both Romish and Reformed, the practice was, to baptize all in infancy, and to consider them as members of the church, unless excommunicated. In childhood, they were to be taught certain forms of faith and worship, after which they were admitted to the Lord's Supper, receiving "confirmation" from the bishop, where there were bishops, and passing through an examination in the creeds and catechisms, where the government was Presbyterian. True, the officiating bishop or presbyter might require of the catechumen an experimental acquaintance with the truths of Christianity, and thus exclude from the Lord's table such as gave no evidence of regeneration. But such was not the practice. Exclusion from the Lord's table, — that is, excommunication, — was attended with the loss of certain civil rights, and, in most countries, followed by the infliction of punishment by the civil government. In England, a man appointed to any civil or military office must "qualify," by receiving the Lord's Supper in the established church; and many received it to "qualify" themselves for office, who neglected it all the rest of their lives. The clergyman who withheld the Lord's Supper from one requesting it, inflicted a civil injury, and was liable to prosecution; and, if prosecuted, must show to the court that he had good grounds for his decision, or suffer the consequences. When John Wesley, the founder of Methodism, left Georgia to return to England, a prosecution was pending against him for debarring a young lady from the Lord's Supper. Under such laws, the Lord's table must be open to all who have been baptized, who have learned the creed and catechism, and have not committed any crime which a civil court would judge "scandalous."

Such an administration of the ordinances is in perfect harmony with the doctrine of baptismal regeneration, held by the papists, and incorporated into the liturgy of the Church of England; for if baptism is regeneration, why should not all baptized persons, not excommunicated, partake of the Lord's Supper? Where this doctrine was not held, as in Scotland, for example, its place might be supplied by the habit of hoping that each communicant was a regenerate person. But in order to render such hopes possible, it must be held that the difference between the regenerate and others is not apparent to men; that regeneration, ordinarily at least, produces no apparent change, of which the teachers and rulers of the church may expect to find evidence by examination; and that, therefore, they must regard every one as regenerate, unless some scandalous offence gives evidence to the contrary. Ministers thus situated may preach on the necessity of regeneration, and on the evidence of it which every one ought to find in himself, and may express their fear that some of their people are not yet converted, and urge them to self-examination; but while they are obliged, in the most solemn offices of religion, to treat every one as a real convert, the force of such preaching is at least greatly diminished. Unconverted communicants will hope that they have passed through that imperceptible change, will come to the Lord's table, and even make their way into the ministry. The preaching can scarce fail, in the end, to come into harmony with the practice.

The New England Puritans could walk in neither of these ways. They believed, that when a man is "born again," a change is wrought in him, of which it is possible for him and others to find evidence; that the regenerate differ from the unregenerate by the possession of some substantial good qualities, which must show themselves in thought, feeling and conduct; and they felt bound to treat all as unregenerate, in whom, on examination, no evidence of Christian piety could be found. They therefore admitted none to their communion, except such as might, "in charitable discretion," be considered regenerate persons. The preface to the Cambridge Platform, published in 1648, is mostly occupied in vindicating this practice against the objections which it was expected to encounter in other parts of the Christian world.

This system of administering the ordinances laid the foundation for whatever is really characteristic of the "New England style of preaching," of which so much has been said. The preacher had before him a considerable number of men, who were in no respect regarded or treated as regenerate persons; who were regarded, both by the church and by themselves, as unrenewed, impenitent men, destitute of faith, and of every Christian grace, and in the broad road to perdition. It was not merely feared or believed that the congregation contained many such persons. The church records contained the names of those who were supposed to be in the road to heaven; and others were, by common consent, to be regarded and addressed as persons in the road to hell. Impenitence, unbelief, enmity to God, and whatever other sins are implied in these, might be, and in Christian faithfulness must be, charged home upon hearers, who would know themselves to be the persons intended, and would confess that the preacher only did his duty. Hence the New England habit of assailing hearers, either with argument or entreaty, as men who are to be brought over from opposition to agreement. Nor was this all. As their unconverted hearers were destitute of faith, had no efficient belief in the word of God, it was evidently impossible to subdue them with proof-texts and expositions of Scripture. Like Paul preaching at Athens, they must draw arguments from the nature of things, and from the consciences of their hearers. Hence that "metaphysical style," which must have come into use, even if Edwards had never lived. The manner of sermonizing must naturally be very different from this, where the preacher is required to hope well concerning each of his hearers, as a child of God.

But the New England churches had receded from their original standard. The Synod of 1662 had decided, that persons baptized in infancy, "understanding the doctrine of faith, and publicly professing their assent thereunto; not scandalous in life, and solemnly owning the covenant before the church, wherein they give up themselves and their children to the Lord, and subject themselves to the government of Christ in the church, their children are to be baptized;" though the parent, thus owning the covenant, was avowedly yet unregenerate, and as such excluded from the Lord's Supper. This practice was immediately adopted by many churches, and, after a violent controversy, became general. This was very naturally followed by a still further innovation. In 1707, "the venerable Stoddard," of Northampton, published a sermon, in which he maintained "That sanctification is not a necessary qualification to partaking of the Lord's Supper," and "that the Lord's Supper is a converting ordinance." To this, Dr. Increase Mather replied the next year; and in 1709, Mr. Stoddard published his

"Appeal to the Learned; being a Vindication of the Right of Visible Saints to the Lord's Supper, though they be destitute of a Saving Work of God's Spirit on their Hearts." The third book of the Appeal contains "Arguments to prove, that sanctifying grace is not necessary in order to a lawful partaking of the Lord's Supper." Mr. Stoddard, in his sermon, enforced his arguments with the assertion, "That no other country does neglect this ordinance as we in New England; and that in our own nation at home, [England,] so in Scotland, Holland, Denmark, Sweedland, Germany and France, they do generally celebrate the memorials of Christ's death." There had been strong tendencies towards such a practice for many years, and probably some instances of its virtual adoption; * but it now, for the first time, found an open and able advocate. It was strenuously opposed; but the desire to enjoy the credit and advantages of church membership, aided by Mr. Stoddard's influence, carried the day at Northampton, and the practice soon spread extensively in other parts of New England.

One obvious tendency of this practice was, to destroy church discipline; for unconverted members, generally, would not be strict in calling others to account for errors of doctrine or practice. But Mr. Stoddard was a Presbyterian in principle, and hoped to introduce substantially that mode of government; † under which, he probably thought, unconverted members would be less mischievous.

But this prostration of discipline was not the worst evil to which this practice tended. What must it teach the unconverted church member to think of himself, and of his prospects for eternity? He was, according to this doctrine, pursuing the very course which God had prescribed for such persons as himself: and believing this, he could not think himself very deep in guilt, or very greatly in danger. Such a man could not feel very strongly his need of conversion.

---

* Trumbull states, that some in Connecticut, as early as 1657, maintained, that "parishes, in England, consenting to and continuing meetings to worship God, were true churches; and that members of those parishes, coming into New England, had a right to all church privileges, though they made no profession of a work of faith and holiness upon their hearts." Hist. Ct. 1: 315.

The Cambridge Platform, Chap. 4: 5, expressly denies, that "cohabitation," that is, dwelling in the same parish, makes men members of the church.

† Dwight's Life of Edwards, p. 381.

And what must he suppose conversion to be? Not a change by which a man begins to obey God; for he had already begun to obey him, as he supposed, and yet was unconverted. Not a change righteously required of him at every moment; for God had given him something to do before conversion, and he was doing it. He must have thought it some mysterious benefit, which God would, in his own good time, bestow on those for whom it was appointed; but for the want of which, the obedient sinner, who was faithfully pursuing the course that God had prescribed to him, was rather to be pitied than blamed. He might, on the authority of his minister, and from the seeming force of argument, believe that he could not be saved without it; but conscience could not demand it of him, as the righteous condition of the favor of God, and he could not be much afraid that God would remove him from the world without bestowing it. Nor was this all. Being thus deceived with respect to the very nature of conversion, all his desires and prayers and labors for it would be misdirected. If aroused to effort, he would be striving after, and looking for, and endeavouring to work himself into, some new state of mind, which would do him no good if attained. And here would be a fruitful source of agonizing labor in vain, and of strange but useless changes, unhappily mistaken for conversion.

Stoddard, and many others who adopted this practice, preached the truth ably and faithfully; and their preaching did much to counteract the influence of their ecclesiastical practice. True, the doctrines which they preached, and the doctrines which were implied in their system of administering the ordinances, were in direct contradiction to each other; but they contrived to avoid seeing the contradiction, and fancied that they believed both. But in the end, the doctrines on which a church is seen to act, will prevail over those which are only uttered; and the state of feeling among the members, and ultimately the preaching itself, will conform to the theory on which the church is governed and the ordinances are administered. And this will be the more certain, because the influences which demand a certain mode of administration, must also demand a doctrine corresponding with it. So it had been now. There had been a silent and gradual increase of Arminianism. Scarce any would acknowledge themselves Arminians; but in many places, the preaching more and more favored the belief, that the unconverted might, without supernatural aid, commence and carry on a series of works preparatory to conversion, and that those who were doing it, were doing very well, and were in little danger.

It is easy to see, that this system favored the entrance of unconverted men into the ministry. If one was fit to be a member of the church; if he was actually a member in good standing; if he was living as God requires such men to live, and pressing forward, in the use of the appointed means, after whatever spiritual good he had not yet attained; if conversion is such a still and unobservable matter, that neither the candidate nor any one else can judge whether he has yet passed that point or not; and if his mental qualifications are found sufficient; why should he be excluded from the ministry? It could not be. The form of examining candidates as to their piety was still retained, but the spirit of it was dying away; and though it was esteemed improper to fasten the charge upon individuals by name, nobody doubted that there were many unconverted ministers. Stoddard, in his "Appeal to the Learned," argued from the fact, which he took for granted, that unconverted ministers have certain official duties, which they may lawfully perform. — But all these points will be made plainer by the history which is to follow.

Many think that those who expect to be saved by their works, will of course be very careful to do works by which they may expect to be saved; but, except where a corrupt clergy has invented a system of superstitious observances, to answer instead of works really good, it happens otherwise. Preparation for heaven being esteemed a matter within their own control, men choose their own time for attending to it; and, as the business and pleasures of this life demand present attention, religion is put off to a more "convenient season." And then, man's condition is not believed to be so bad, nor his escape from it so important, as is pretended by those who teach that he is wholly ruined, and entirely dependent on God for his recovery. The concerns of the soul are therefore neglected, or receive but wavering and intermittent attention; and the result is an increasing laxity of morals, without any diminution of the hope of heaven.

Such had been the downward progress in New England. Revivals had become less frequent and powerful. There were many in the churches, and some even in the ministry, who were yet lingering among the supposed preliminaries to conversion. The difference between the church and the world was vanishing away. Church discipline was neglected, and the growing laxness of morals was invading the churches. And yet never, perhaps, had the expectation of reaching heaven at last been more general, or more confident. Occasional revivals had interrupted this downward progress, and the preaching of sound doctrine had retarded it, in many places, especially at Northampton; but even there it had gone on, and the hold of truth on the consciences of men was sadly diminished. The young were abandoning themselves to frivolity, and to amusements of dangerous tendency, and party spirit was producing its natural fruit of evil among the old.

Through the influence of Edwards, there was a gradual amendment. More decency of demeanor and teachableness of spirit became apparent among the youth, and parents showed a more suitable care for the moral and spiritual good of their children. Some unseemly and unsafe habits were abandoned, some instances of conversion occurred, and several associations for religious improvement were formed.

And now the progress of Arminianism had become so manifest as to cause alarm. Its growth had been imperceptible and unacknowledged; and even at this time the charge was generally repelled as a slander. Its advocates said they were only explaining some of the doctrines of Calvinism more rationally than had formerly been done, so as to avoid certain difficulties with which the truth had been encumbered. This was natural; for there was then a horror of Arminianism, such as it is difficult now to understand. Men had not then forgotten the tremendous evils that had grown out of the doctrine of salvation by works. They remembered, that under its influence men had ceased to trust in Christ for salvation, and had learned to trust in the merits of penances and offerings prescribed by the priests. The history of popery had taught them, that the doctrine of salvation by works makes the great mass of the people slaves of the priesthood; for, as they must learn from the priests what works will save them, they are made to believe that they must do what the priests prescribe, or perish everlastingly. The same history had taught, that when a priesthood attains such power, bad men will press into it, and it will soon become corrupt and anti-christian. Hence one argument almost constantly used against Arminianism in those days was, its tendency to prepare the way for popery. Hence John Wesley, for preaching Arminianism, was even accused of being a Jesuit in disguise. And the men of that age could not regard popery as it is now regarded. Popery then never asked for toleration, or talked of the equal religious rights of different sects. It demanded and sought to enforce universal submission to the triple crown. Great Britain had just expelled a secretly popish monarch, and his heir, the "Pretender," was seeking, in alliance with France and other popish powers, to regain the throne by force of arms. Victims of popish intolerance, driven from France by the persecutions which followed the revocation of the edict of Nantes, were still living in every protestant country. The frontier settlements of New England were not yet safe from the tomahawks of savages, instigated and accompanied by French Jesuits from Canada; nor had France yet abandoned the hope of adding these prostestant colonies to her empire, and to the domain of the Romish church. The atrocities which every man remembered, and the dangers which hung over every man's head, taught all to regard popery as a false, tyrannical and murderous system, destroying the bodies of its enemies and the souls of its friends. The safety of every thing valuable, either in this world or the world to come, was felt to depend on the unimpaired maintenance of the doctrines of the Reformation. The question, therefore, whether some were departing from that faith, was one of deep interest. Men were unwilling to believe, that their newly-invented explanations were an abandonment of the faith they attempted to explain. Not only were the pious alarmed, but, Edwards informs us, "Many, who looked on themselves as in a Christless condition, seemed to be awakened by it, with fear that God was about to withdraw from the land, and that we should be given up to heterodoxy and corrupt principles; and that then their opportunity for obtaining salvation would be past; and many, who were brought a little to doubt about the truth of the doctrines they had hitherto been taught, seemed to have a kind of a trembling fear with the doubts, lest they should be led into by-paths, to their eternal undoing; and they seemed with much concern and engagedness to inquire, what was indeed the way in which they must come to be accepted of God."

This state of mind Edwards determined to meet, by preaching fully on those points on which the controversy turned. Influential friends endeavoured to dissuade him from the attempt; much fault was found with his introducing such matters of controversy into the pulpit, and the whole proceeding was ridiculed, both at Northampton and elsewhere. But it was no proof of arrogance in him, to be conscious that he understood the crisis, and the subject, and was able to say things that his people needed to hear. He commenced his series of discourses on "Justification by Faith alone," that article with which, as Luther declared, a church stands or falls. The effect of these discourses was, first, to make men feel that now they understood the subject, and had hold of the truth; and next, to sweep away entirely all those hopes of heaven which they had built upon their own doings,—upon their morality, their owning the covenant, partaking the Lord's Supper, or using any other means of grace. They were made to see, that God has not appointed any thing for men to do before coming to Christ by faith; that all their previous works are unacceptable in his sight, and lay him under no obligation, either on account of their worthiness or his promise, to grant them any spiritual favor. These discourses were followed by others, in which he taught "God's absolute sovereignty in regard to the salvation of sinners, and his just liberty with regard to answering the prayers or succeeding the pains of mere natural men, continuing such." That idea, of "God's just liberty," is an idea of tremendous power. It includes all that is meant by the doctrine of election, and expresses it most philosophically, unincumbered with forms of speech derived from human ideas of time. God is at liberty with respect to bestowing salvation. His liberty is perfect. Nothing that the "natural man" has done, or can do, while "continuing such," in any way impairs that liberty, or binds God to a favorable decision. And this his liberty is "just." It is right that it should be so. Sinners have merited and now deserve instant damnation; and God's liberty to inflict it upon them now, or defer it for the present, or save them from it wholly, according to his own pleasure, is a most "just liberty." When the sinner sees and feels this doctrine to be true, he knows that no course remains for him, but to call upon God for mercy; and he knows that when he calls upon God, there is nothing in his prayers that at all impairs God's "just liberty" with respect to hearing him, and that he has nothing to depend upon, as a ground of hope that he shall be heard, but the mercy of God in Christ. He can make no appeal to the justice of God, for that only condemns him; nor to any other attribute but mercy, which, in its very nature, is free, and not constrained. And he can find no satisfactory evidence that God is disposed to be merciful to sinners, but in the fact that he has given his Son to die for them. Here is his only ground of hope. Here he must present and urge his prayer, knowing that he deserves to be rejected, and knowing that nothing of his own, not even his prayer, diminishes God's "just liberty," to receive or reject him according to his good pleasure. And this is the point to which he needs to be brought. This is the dependence which he needs to feel, and feeling which will drive him to God in prayer.

But will not the cutting off of his hopes drive him to despair, and make him reckless? It would, but for the doctrine of "Justification by Faith," which encourages him who has no good works, to trust in "Him that justifieth the ungodly." It teaches the sinner that, in being destitute of all claim to acceptance with God, and dependent on his mere mercy, he is only like all others who have been saved through Christ, and therefore need not despair. It teaches him that there is in God an overflowing goodness, which reaches even to the salvation of those who have no claim to be saved; and it encourages him to trust in that goodness. It teaches him to resign himself to the disposal of God, sensible of God's "just liberty," and not knowing first what God will do with him; but encouraged by the goodness of God as shown in the death of his Son, to hope for acceptance and salvation. And this is faith; and faith "works by love," and transforms the whole character.

There was, then, in 1734, at Northampton and generally in New England, a special need of such sermons as Edwards preached; a special fitness in those sermons, to produce the effects which followed them.

It was in the latter part of December, 1734, as Edwards informs us,* that "the Spirit of God began extraordinarily to set in and wonderfully to work among us; and there were very suddenly, one after another, five or six persons, who were, to all appearance, savingly converted, and some of them wrought upon in a very remarkable manner."

One of these converts was a young woman who had been notorious as a leader in scenes of gayety and rustic dissipation. Edwards was surprised at the account which she gave of her religious exercises, of which he had heard no report till she came to converse with him, apparently humble and penitent. He at first feared that the appearance of the work of conversion in a person of such a character would give it a bad name, and excite prejudices which would hinder its progress; "but the event was the reverse, to a wonderful degree. — The news of it seemed to be like a flash of lightning upon the hearts of the young people, all over the town, and upon many others. — Many went to talk with her concerning what she had met with; and what appeared in her seemed to be to the satisfaction of all that did so." The consciences of men were constrained to acknowledge the goodness of the power which had wrought such a change, in such a person. "Presently upon this, a great and earnest concern about the great things of religion and the eternal world, became universal in all parts of the town, and among persons of all degrees and all ages; the noise among the dry bones waxed louder and louder; all other talk but about spiritual and eternal things, was soon thrown by. — The minds of people were wonderfully taken off from the world; it was treated among us as a thing of very little consequence. They seemed to follow their worldly business more as a part of their duty, than from any disposition they had to it. — It was then a dreadful thing amongst us to lie out of Christ, in danger every day of dropping into hell; and what persons' minds were intent upon was, to escape for their lives, and to fly from the wrath to come. All would eagerly lay hold of opportunities for their souls, and were wont very often to meet together in private houses for religious

---

* Narrative of Surprising Conversions.

purposes; and such meetings, when appointed, were wont greatly to be thronged. — And the work of conversion was carried on in a most astonishing manner, and increased more and more. Souls did, as it were, come by flocks to Jesus Christ. From day to day, for many months together, might be seen evident instances of sinners brought out of darkness into marvellous light. — Our public assemblies were then beautiful; the congregation was alive in God's service, every one earnestly intent on the public worship, every hearer eager to drink in the words of the minister as they came from his mouth. The assembly in general were, from time to time, in tears while the word was preached; some weeping with sorrow and distress, others with joy and love, others with pity and concern for the souls of their neighbours. — Those amongst us that had formerly been converted, were greatly enlivened and renewed with fresh and extraordinary incomes of the Spirit of God; though some much more than others, according to the measure of the gift of Christ. Many that had before labored under difficulties about their own state, had now their doubts removed by more satisfying experience, and more clear discoveries of God's love."

The report of the state of things at Northampton spread into other towns, where many "seemed not to know what to make of it," many ridiculed it, "and some compared what we called conversion, to certain distempers." Great numbers, however, who came to Northampton and saw for themselves, were differently affected, and not a few of them, from various places, were awakened and apparently brought to repentance. In March, 1735, the revival began to be general in South Hadley, and about the same time in Suffield. It next appeared in Sunderland, Deerfield, and Hatfield; and afterwards at West Springfield, Long Meadow, and Enfield; and then in Hadley Old Town, and in Northfield. In Connecticut, the work commenced in the First Parish in Windsor, about the same time as at Northampton. It was remarkable at East Windsor, and "wonderful" at Coventry. Similar scenes were witnessed at Lebanon, Durham, Stratford, Ripton, New Haven, Guilford, Mansfield, Tolland, Hebron, Bolton, Preston, Groton, and Woodbury. And about the same time there was an awakening in New Jersey, principally in connexion with the labors of William and Gilbert Tennent, of which a more particular account will be given in another place.

Edwards hoped that more than three hundred were converted in Northampton in half a year. They were of all ages, from the child of four years old to the man of seventy. He received about a hundred to the communion of the church before one sacramental season. Eighty of them were received at one time, "whose appearance, when they presented themselves together to make an open, explicit profession of Christianity, was very affecting to the congregation." And no wonder; for all understood that in their case the transaction had a very solemn meaning. It was the effect and avowal of their conversion. Near sixty more were received before the next sacrament. Notwithstanding the plan on which persons were here admitted to the church, the pastor thought he had "very sufficient evidence of the conversion" of those who were now added to its numbers.

The account which Edwards gives of the character of these conversions is highly interesting and instructive, but cannot be transferred to this history. One characteristic, however, is too important to be passed without remark. It would seem that in every case, the happy change came upon the sinner's mind, instead of being wrought by him. In no case, it seems, did the sinner first form to himself an idea of some volition to be put forth by himself, and then, by direct effort, put it forth, and thus become a convert. He says;

"In those in whom awakenings seem to have a saving issue, commonly the first thing that appears after their legal troubles is, a conviction of the justice of God in their condemnation, a sense of their own exceeding sinfulness, and the vileness of all their performances. In giving an account of this, they expressed themselves very variously; some, that they saw that God was a sovereign, and might receive others and reject them; some, that they were convinced that God might justly bestow mercy on every person in the town, and on every person in the world, and damn themselves to all eternity; some, that they see that God may justly have no regard to all the pains they have taken, and all the prayers they have made; some, that they see, that if they should seek, and take the utmost pains, all their lives, God might justly cast them into hell at last, because all their labors, prayers and tears cannot make atonement for the least sin, nor merit any blessing at the hand of God; some have declared themselves to be in the hands of God, that he can and may dispose of them just as he pleases; some, that God may glorify himself in their damnation, and they wonder that God has suffered them to live so long, and has not cast them into hell long ago.

"Commonly, persons' minds, immediately before this discovery of God's justice, are exceeding restless, and in a kind of struggle and tumult, and sometimes in mere anguish; but generally, as soon as they have this conviction, it immediately brings their minds to a calm, and a before unexpected quietness and composure; and most frequently, though not always, then the pressing weight upon their spirits is taken away, and a general hope arises that some time or other God will be gracious, even before any distinct and particular discoveries of mercy; and often they then come to a conclusion within themselves, that they will lie at God's feet, and wait his time; and they rest in that, not being sensible that the Spirit of God has now brought them to a frame whereby they are prepared for mercy; for it is remarkable that persons, when they first have this sense of God's justice, rarely, in the time of it, think any thing of its being that humiliation that they have often heard insisted on, and that others experience."

In some cases, their "sense of the excellency of God's justice" in their condemnation, and their approbation of it, was such that they "almost called it a willingness to be damned." But Edwards thought that this language must have been used without any clear idea of its import, and must have meant only that "salvation appeared too good for them," and that the glory of God's justice ought not to be sacrificed for their sakes. He proceeds:

"That calm of spirit that some persons have found after their legal distresses, continues some time before any special and delightful manifestation is made to the soul, of the grace of God, as revealed in the Gospel; but very often some comfortable and sweet view of a merciful God, of a sufficient Redeemer, or of some great and joyful things of the Gospel, immediately follows, or in a very little time; and in some, the first sight of their just desert of hell, and God's sovereignty with respect to their salvation, and a discovery of all-sufficient grace, are so near, that they seem to go as it were together.

"It has more frequently been so amongst us, that when persons have first had the gospel ground of relief for lost sinners discovered to them, and have been entertaining their minds with the sweet prospect, they have thought nothing at that time of their being converted. To see that there is such an all-sufficiency in God, and such plentiful provision made in Christ, after they have been borne down and sunk with a sense of their guilt and fears of wrath, exceedingly refreshes them. The view is joyful to them, as it is in its own nature glorious, and gives them quite new and more delightful ideas of God and Christ, and greatly encourages them to seek conversion, and begets in them a strong resolution to give up themselves, and devote their whole lives to God and his Son, and patiently to wait till God shall see fit to make all effectual; and very often they entertain a strong persuasion, that he will in his own time do it for them.

"There is wrought in them a holy repose of soul in God through Christ, and a secret disposition to fear and love him, and to hope for blessings from him in this way. And yet they have no imagination that they are now converted; it does not so much as come into their minds; and very often the reason is, that they do not see that they do accept of this sufficiency of salvation that they behold in Christ, having entertained a wrong notion of acceptance, not being sensible that the obedient and joyful entertainment which their hearts give to this discovery of grace, is a real acceptance of it. They know not that the sweet complacence they feel in the mercy and complete salvation of God, as it includes pardon and sanctification, and is held forth to them only through Christ, is a true receiving of this mercy, or a plain evidence of their receiving it. They expected, I know not what kind of act of the soul, and perhaps they had no distinct idea of it themselves."

Edwards informs us, that many were prejudiced against this revival, by false reports concerning impressions on men's imaginations. He did not suppose that any of the converts "imagined that they saw any thing with their bodily eyes," but only that their ideas of the torments of hell, the glories of heaven, or the dying love of Christ, or the like, excited "lively pictures in their minds." In a few instances, he was unable to account for the phenomena on natural principles; but he was not convinced that there was any thing supernatural in them, and he fully believed and taught his people, that such things deserved no confidence, as evidences of conversion.

These misrepresentations were to be expected. As we have seen, there were many in the churches, and some doubtless in the ministry, who had no personal acquaintance with such religion as then prevailed at Northampton. This was a way to heaven that they had not learned, and in which they were not walking. If this was true doctrine and true religion, their own hopes were delusive, and their souls in danger of perdition. They must of necessity think ill, either of the work at Northampton, or of the religion which they professed, and perhaps taught. It was inevitable, therefore, human nature being what it is, that evidence should be sought and found against the work at Northampton; that all real faults should be gathered up and reported; that a bad interpretation should be put upon every thing that the hearer or beholder could not understand; and that every evil report should be exaggerated, till the sum total met the wishes of those who were anxious to condemn the work, lest the work should condemn them. We shall find the same principle in vigorous operation, and on a larger scale, and with more permanent results, in following years.

About the close of May, 1735, the work began sensibly to decline. It is usually, and truly, assigned as one reason for such declensions, that the physical power to endure excitement is exhausted, and the nerves irresistibly seek repose. In the case before us, too, it is probable that nearly every person old enough to understand preaching had been excited, had been made to consider his ways, and had decided upon his course, at least for the present. Many had found peace in believing, and the rest had chosen a return to stupidity, and had their choice. New subjects were no longer to be found, by the report of whose awakening excitement could be sustained. And several events, the most important of which was the controversy that grew out of the settlement of the Rev. Mr. Breck at Springfield, diverted the minds of men to other subjects. Still, for months after the decline began, there were occasional instances of conversion, and of revival of feeling among the pious; and as late as the close of 1736, the work still continued in some places in Connecticut.

This awakening excited a lively interest among the friends of vital piety at a distance. Dr. Colman, of Boston, wrote to Mr. Edwards for an account of it. Having obtained an answer, he published it, and forwarded it to Dr. Watts and Dr. Guise in London. They told the good news in conversation, and at public religious assemblies. A request for a more complete account drew forth a letter from Mr. Edwards to Dr. Colman, dated November 6th, 1736, which was published in London, under the title of "Narrative of Surprising Conversions," with an introduction by Drs. Watts and Guise. It was circulated extensively, and with good effect, both in England and Scotland, where it gave many ministers and churches new views of what might be expected and should be sought, even in these latter days. In 1738, it was republished in Boston, with several of the sermons which had been most useful in promoting the work, and commended to the public by four of the oldest ministers of the town. It has since been published in his collected "Works," and should be attentively studied by every one, whose duty it is to understand the workings of the human mind under the convicting and converting influences of the Spirit of God.

---

## CHAPTER II.

**Revivals of 1739, 1740; at Newark, Harvard, Northampton, New Londonderry, and New Brunswick.—Remarks on the Presbyterianism of that age.**

The excitement of 1734 had passed away, but its effects remained. The churches which it had visited, were stronger, both in numbers and in piety. The morals of those towns were decidedly improved. More definite and correct views extensively prevailed, of the difference between a real and a nominal Christian, and of the great change by which that difference is produced. Extensively, the pious in other places had learned to regard awakenings like that at Northampton, as events to be desired, prayed for, and expected;

and this expectation had been kept alive by their occasional occurrence, in single parishes, in different parts of the country. In 1739, such instances began to multiply, and to grow conspicuous. The specimens which follow, will show their character.

### NEWARK, N. J.

Newark was originally a colony from New England, and must have retained much of the primitive New England feeling concerning the distinction between the church and the world.* In practice, however, that distinction appears to have been lamentably obscured. In the words of the Rev. Jonathan Dickenson, then pastor of the church in Elizabeth-

* Newark was settled in 1667 or 1668, by about thirty families from Branford, Ct. with their minister, the Rev. Mr. Pierson. Professor Hodge, of Princeton, in his excellent "Constitutional History of the Presbyterian Church," remarks, that a part of the New England Puritans were Congregationalists, and a part Presbyterians; and quotes a tradition, preserved in a manuscript "History of Newark," by Dr. McWhorter, to prove that the first settlers of Newark were Presbyterians. It may not be to the purpose, here, to refer to the notorious fact, that all who held the validity of ordination by presbyters, in opposition to diocesan episcopacy, were formerly called Presbyterians, and that the name itself was derived from that peculiarity; but it is important to remember that no part of the New England Puritans were Presbyterians in the modern sense of that word. None of them held that single churches should be governed by presbyteries composed of several churches and their pastors. Both parties held, perhaps with equal tenacity, the entire ecclesiastical independence of every "congregation of faithful men," duly associated as a church. The difference was this. The Presbyterians of New England held that each church should be governed by its own presbytery; that is, by its pastor and teaching and ruling elders; while the Congregationalists held that every adult male communicant should take part directly in the government of the church. [See President Styles's sermon of "Christian Union," and the authorities there quoted.] In this sense, the first settlers of Newark may have been Presbyterians; though there is strong reason to doubt it. The Rev. Philemon Robbins, in his "Narrative of the Proceedings of the New Haven Association," preserved in the Old South Church Library, has quoted from the town records of Branford, a preamble and resolutions adopted January 20th, 1667, in view of the emigration to Newark, from which it appears that Branford was settled "by men of Congregational principles" according to the Cambridge platform, and that those who did not emigrate, resolved to adhere to that system. If the emigrating party removed, as stated by Professor Hodge, because they were "dissatisfied with the union between the colonies of New Haven and Connecticut," they must have been Congregationalists "of the straitest sect;" for the opposition to that union was raised mainly in defence of pure Congregationalism. Davenport, of New Haven, was at its head; and the defence of the colony against the claims of Connecticut was for a time intrusted to the discretionary management of the magistrates of New Haven and Branford. [See Bacon's "Historical Discourses."]

town,—"Religion was in a very low state, professors generally dead and lifeless, and the body of our people careless, carnal and secure. There was but little of the power of godliness appearing among us, till some time in August, 1739, (the summer before Mr. Whitefield came first into these parts,) when there was a remarkable revival at Newark, especially among the rising generation.—This concern increased for a considerable time among the young people, though not wholly confined to them; and in November, December and January following, it became more remarkable, as well as more general.—This revival of religion was chiefly observable among the younger people, till the following March, when the whole town in general was brought under an uncommon concern about their eternal interests, and the congregation appeared universally affected under some sermons that were then preached to them; and there is good reason to conclude, that there was a considerable number who experienced a saving change about that time. The summer following, this awakening concern sensibly abated, though it did not wholly die away; and nothing remarkable occurred till February, 1641, when they were again visited with the special and manifest effusions of the Spirit of God."*

### HARVARD, MASS.

The Rev. John Seccomb wrote, February 20, 1744, after there had been time to test the genuineness of the revival:

"The first visible alteration among my people for the better, was some time in the month of September, in the year 1739, when several began to grow more thoughtful and serious, and somewhat reformed; more constant and diligent in attending the public worship, more attentive in hearing the word preached, more careful to sanctify the Sabbath, &c.

"Not long after this, came four young men to me under considerable awakenings and concern about their spiritual state. In December following, these same persons were taken into church fellowship, who had been of too loose a life and conversation in times past; which put many upon further thoughtfulness. From this time, the concern began to increase, and there was scarce a sacrament passed, (which is with us once in eight weeks,) without some additions to the church, from

* Christian History, Vol. I. p. 252.

that to the present time ; though twelve is the greatest number that have been received at once."

The whole number that had been admitted from September, 1739, to the date of the letter, was "near a hundred." From the details given by Mr. Seccomb, the revival appears to have been much like that at Northampton in 1734, but on a smaller scale. Through its whole continuance, it "was not carried on violently, nor by strangers." One sermon, preached in June, 1741, by an aged minister, was the only foreign aid that appeared to produce any effect. Some were awakened by hearing sermons from their pastor, which he had preached to them before without affecting them.*

### NORTHAMPTON, MASS.

Edwards shall speak for himself. His account was written December 21, 1743 :

"Ever since the great work of God that was wrought here about nine years ago, there has been a great, abiding alteration in this town in many respects. There has been vastly more religion kept up in the town, among all sorts of persons, in religious exercises, and in common conversation, than used to be before. There has remained a more general seriousness and decency in attending the public worship.—I suppose the town has been in no measure so free from vice,—for any long time together, for this sixty years, as it has this nine years past. There has also been an evident alteration with respect to a charitable spirit to the poor.—And though, after that great work of nine years ago, there has been a very lamentable decay of religious affections, and the engagedness of people's spirit in religion; yet many societies for prayer and social religion were all along kept up, and there were some few instances of awakening and deep concern about the things of another world, even in the most dead time. In the year 1740, in the spring, before Mr. Whitefield came to this town, there was a visible alteration. There was more seriousness and religious conversation, especially among young people. Those things that were of ill tendency among them were more forborne ; and it was a more frequent thing for persons to visit their minister upon soul accounts. In some particular persons, there

---

* Christian History, Vol. II. p. 13.

appeared a great alteration about that time. And thus it continued till Mr. Whitefield came to town, which was about the middle of October following."*

What followed at Northampton, belongs to a subsequent part of the history.

### PRESBYTERIANISM IN 1740.

The awakening at New Londonderry, Pa., introduces us to another class of people, the Scotch and Scotch-Irish Presbyterians, and obliges us to consider the religious bearings of their ecclesiastical polity.

It does not appear that Mr. Stoddard's doctrine concerning the Lord's Supper ever prevailed among Presbyterians, either here or in Europe. Their doctrine always has been, that saving faith is necessary, in order to an acceptable and profitable partaking of that ordinance. The preparatory lecture before each communion season seems to have been intended mainly, to call the minds of the people to the requisite qualifications, that they might not come forward unprepared, and eat and drink "unworthily." But in Scotland, the Presbyterian was the church established by law, and all, except the "ignorant" and the "scandalous," had a legal right to its ordinances. All the children born within the parish limits were to be baptized in infancy, to receive a Christian education under the care of the pastor and elders, and to be admitted to the Lord's table, when educated. To test the sufficiency of their knowledge, they must be examined by the session; that is, by the pastor and elders. The session, too, may excommunicate or suspend its offending members from the communion of the church; but all its acts are subject to revision and reversal by higher courts.

It was the design of the founders of American Presbyterianism, — at least, of such of them as were from Scotland or Ireland, — to adopt the Scottish system, as far as the different circumstances of the country would permit; or, to use the language of the Synod in 1721, "as far as the nature and constitution of this country would allow." It was not in their power to treat all born or residing within certain geographical limits, as members of the Presbyterian congregation located there. They could claim only such as volun-

* Christian History, Vol. I. p. 367.

tarily joined them. The original members of many of the congregations were doubtless received on the testimony of letters from their former pastors or sessions in Scotland or Ireland ;* and they, with pastors from the same countries, would form churches like those they left ; churches containing some converted and some unconverted members ; churches in which the necessity of regeneration was an article of faith ; while evidence of regeneration was not required in order to membership. In 1735, " Mr. Gilbert Tennent brought some overtures into the synod, with respect to trials of candidates both for the ministry and for the Lord's Supper, that there be due care taken to examine into the evidences of the grace of God in them, as well as of their other necessary qualifications." On the first of these points, the response of the synod was explicit. All the presbyteries were ordered " that they diligently examine all candidates for the ministry, in their experience of a work of sanctifying grace in their hearts ; and that they admit none to that sacred trust, that are not, in the eye of charity, serious Christians." The other point, by inadvertence or design, was evaded. " And the synod does also exhort all the ministers within our bounds, to use due care in examining those whom they admit to the Lord's Supper." † But what " care " was " due " on such occasions, and whether the candidates were to be examined as to " the evidences of the grace of God in them," was left undecided. ‡ It is probable that several ministers at that time practised according to the rule which Mr. Tennent wished the synod to establish ; but others, and probably a large ma-

* Such letters from Scotland or Ireland are even now a source of perplexity to Presbyterian pastors in America. Those who bring them, expect to be received as communicants; while perhaps neither they nor their former pastors suppose they give any evidence that they have been born again. Within a very few years, a young man who presented such a letter to a Presbyterian pastor in New York, was plainly, faithfully and affectionately told what was here required as a qualification for admission to the Lord's table, and his case was deferred. For this, he soon after expressed the warmest gratitude ; as it had been the means of his conversion.

† Professor Hodge's Const. Hist. Vol. I. p. 240. He quotes " Minutes, p. 31." Dr. Miller, in his " Life of Rogers," says it was in 1734.

‡ And there it remains, even unto this day ; every session practising according to its own views of duty. It is supposed, however, that a large majority of church sessions, among every class of American Presbyterians, now hold Mr. Tennent's views on this subject, and with greater or less strictness, practise accordingly. So far as the author has been able to learn, Mr. Tennent's overture was both the first and the last attempt to establish any uniform rule on this subject.

jority, followed the European custom, of admitting all who knew the creed and catechisms, and were not "scandalous."* Thus, though they took a different road from Mr. Stoddard, they arrived at the same practical result. Both agreed in admitting to the full communion of the church, persons who gave no evidence of regeneration. The doctrine of the new birth ceased to be regarded in the administration of the ordinances. The church bore no testimony to that doctrine at the Lord's table; and as a natural consequence, it practically slipped from the minds both of preachers and hearers.

## NEW LONDONDERRY, PA.

Keeping these remarks in mind, the reader will understand the account of the awakening at New Londonderry, given by the Rev. Samuel Blair,—justly one of the most venerated names in the history of American Presbyterianism. It is dated August 6th, 1744.

"That it may the more clearly appear that the Lord has indeed carried on a work of true real religion among us of late years, I conceive it will be useful to give a brief general view of the state of religion in these parts before this remarkable season. I doubt not, then, but there were some sincerely religious people up and down; and there were, I believe, a considerable number in the several congregations pretty exact, according to their education, in the observance of the external forms of religion, not only as to attendance upon public ordinances on the Sabbaths, but also, as to the practice of family worship, and perhaps, secret prayer too. But with these things the most part seemed to appearance to rest contented; and to satisfy their consciences just with a dead formality in religion. If they performed these duties pretty punctually in their seasons, and as they thought with a good meaning out of conscience, and not just to obtain a name for religion among men; then they were ready to conclude that they were truly and sincerely religious. A very lamentable ignorance of the main essentials of true practical religion and the doctrines nextly relating thereunto, very generally prevailed. The nature and necessity of the new

* It does not appear that the Tennents ever belonged to a Presbyterian church in Ireland. The Rev. William Tennent, sen., passed from the established (Episcopal) church in Ireland, to the Presbyterian church in America. His sons were educated here.

birth was but little known or thought of. The necessity of a conviction of sin and misery, by the Holy Spirit opening and applying the Law to the conscience, in order to a saving closure with Christ, was hardly known at all to the most. It was thought that if there was any need of a heart-distressing sight of the soul's danger, and fear of divine wrath, it was only needful for the grosser sort of sinners; and for any others to be deeply exercised this way, (as there might sometimes be before some rare instances observable,) this was generally looked upon to be a great evil and temptation that had befallen those persons. The common names for such soul-concern were melancholy, trouble of mind, or despair. These terms were in common, so far as I have been acquainted, indifferently used as synonymous; and trouble of mind was looked upon as a great evil, which all persons that made any sober profession and practice of religion ought carefully to avoid. There was scarcely any suspicion at all, in general, of any danger of depending upon self-righteousness, and not upon the righteousness of Christ alone for salvation. Papists and Quakers would be readily acknowledged guilty of this crime; but hardly any professed Presbyterian. The necessity of being first in Christ by a vital union, and in a justified state, before our religious services can be well pleasing and acceptable to God, was very little understood or thought of. But the common notion seemed to be, that if people were aiming to be in the way of duty as well as they could, as they imagined, there was no reason to be much afraid.

"According to these principles, and this ignorance of some of the most soul-concerning truths of the Gospel, people were very generally, through the land, careless at heart, and stupidly indifferent about the great concerns of eternity. There was very little appearance of any hearty engagedness in religion; and indeed the wise, for the most part, were in a great degree asleep with the foolish. It was sad to see with what a careless behaviour the public ordinances were attended, and how people were given to unsuitable wordly discourse on the Lord's holy day. In public companies, especially at weddings, a vain and frothy lightness was apparent in the deportment of many professors; and in some places very extravagant follies, as horse-running, fiddling and dancing, pretty much obtained on those occasions.

"Thus religion lay as it were dying, and ready to expire its last breath of life in this part of the visible church: and it was in the spring, An. 1740, when the God of salvation was pleased to visit us with the blessed effusions of his Holy Spirit in an eminent manner. The first very open and public appearance of this gracious visitation in these parts, was in the congregation which God has committed to my charge. This congregation has not been erected above fourteen or fifteen years from this time. The place is a new settlement, generally settled with people from Ireland (as all our congregations in Pennsylvania, except two or three, chiefly are made up of people from that kingdom.) I am the first minister they have ever had settled in the place; having been regularly liberated from my former charge in East Jersey, above an hundred miles northeastward from hence, (the Rev. Presbytery of New Brunswick, (of which I had the comfort of being a member,) judging it to be my duty, for sundry reasons, to remove from thence.) At the earnest invitation of the people here, I came to them in the beginning of November, 1739; accepted of a call from them that winter, and was formally installed and settled among them as their minister in April following. There were some hopefully pious people here at my first coming, which was a great encouragement and comfort to me.

"I had some view and sense of the deplorable condition of the land in general; and accordingly the scope of my preaching through that first winter after I came here, was mainly calculated for persons in a natural unregenerate state. I endeavoured, as the Lord enabled me, to open up and prove from his word, the truths which I judged most necessary for such as were in that state to know and believe in order to their conviction and conversion. I endeavoured to deal searchingly and solemnly with them; and through the concurring blessing of God, I had knowledge of four or five brought under deep convictions that winter.

"In the beginning of March I took a journey into East Jersey, and was abroad for two or three Sabbaths. A neighbouring minister, who seemed to be earnest for the awakening and conversion of secure sinners, and whom I had obtained to preach a Sabbath to my people in my absence, preached to them, I think, on the first Sabbath after I left home. His subject was, the dangerous and awful case of such as continue unregenerate and unfruitful under the means of grace. The text was Luke xiii. 7. 'Then said he to the dresser of his vineyard; behold these three years I come seeking fruit on this fig-tree, and find none; cut it down, why cumbereth it the ground?' Under that sermon there was a visible appearance of much soul-concern among the hearers; so that some burst out with an audible noise into bitter crying (a thing not known in these parts before.) After I had come home, there came a young man to my house under deep trouble about the state of his soul, whom I had looked upon as a pretty light, merry sort of a youth. He told me that he was not any thing concerned about himself in the time of hearing the above-mentioned sermon, nor afterwards, till the next day that he went to his labor, which was grubbing in order to clear some new ground. The first grub he set about was a pretty large one with a high top, and when he had cut the roots, as it fell down, these words came instantly to his remembrance, and as a spear to his heart, 'Cut it down, why cumbereth it the ground?' 'So' thought he, 'must I be cut down by the justice of God for the burning of hell, unless I get into another state than I am now in.' He thus came into very great and abiding distress, which, to all appearance, has had a happy issue; his conversation being to this day as becomes the Gospel of Christ.

"The news of this very public appearance of deep soul-concern among my people met me an hundred miles from home: I was very joyful to hear of it, in hopes that God was about to carry on an extensive work of converting grace amongst them. And the first sermon I preached after my return to them, was from Matthew vi. 33. 'Seek ye first the kingdom of God, and his righteousness.' After opening up and explaining the parts of the text, when, in the improvement, I came to press the injunction in the text upon the unconverted and ungodly, and offered this as one reason among others, why they should now henceforth first of all seek the kingdom and righteousness of God, viz., that they had neglected too long to do so already, this consideration seemed to come and cut like a sword upon several in the congregation; so that while I was speaking upon it, they could no longer contain, but burst out in the most bitter mourning. I desired them, as much as possible to restrain themselves from making any noise that would hinder themselves or others from hearing what was spoken ; and often afterwards I had occasion to repeat the same counsel. I still advised people to endeavour to moderate and bound their passions, but not so as to resist or stifle their convictions. The number of the awakened increased very fast. Frequently under sermons there were some newly convicted, and brought into deep distress of soul about their perishing estate. Our Sabbath assemblies soon became vastly large; many people from almost all parts around inclining very much to come where there was such appearance of the divine power and presence. I think there was scarcely a sermon or lecture preached here through that whole summer, but there were manifest evidences of impressions on the hearers ; and many times the impressions were very great and general. Several would be overcome and fainting; others deeply sobbing, hardly able to contain ; others crying in a most dolorous manner ; many others more silently weeping ; and a solemn concern appearing in the countenances of many others. And sometimes the soul-exercises of some (though comparatively but very few) would so far affect their bodies as to occasion some strange unusual bodily motions. I had opportunities of speaking particularly with a great many of those who afforded such outward tokens of inward soul-concern in the time of public worship and hearing of the word. Indeed, many came to me of themselves in their distress, for private instruction and counsel ; and I found, so far as I can remember, that with by far the greater part, their apparent concern in public was not just a transient qualm of conscience, or merely a floating commotion of the affections ; but a rational, fixed conviction of their dangerous perishing estate. They could generally offer as a convictive evidence of their being in an unconverted, miserable estate, that they were utter strangers to those dispositions, exercises and experiences of soul in religion, which they heard laid down from God's word, as the inseparable characters of the truly regenerate people of God ; even such as before had something of the form of religion ; and I think the greater number were of this sort ; and several had been pretty exact and punctual in the performance of outward duties ; they saw they had been contenting themselves with the form without the life and power of godliness, and that they had been taking peace to their consciences from, and depending upon, their own righteousness, and not the righteousness of Jesus Christ.

"In a word, they saw that true, practical religion was quite another thing than they had conceived it to be, or had any true experience of. There were likewise many up and down the land brought under deep distressing convictions that summer, who had lived very loose lives, regardless of the very externals of religion. In this congregation, I believe there were very few that were not stirred up to some solemn thoughtfulness and concern more than usual about their souls. The general carriage and behaviour of people was soon very visibly altered. Those awakened were much given to reading in the Holy Scriptures and other good books. Excellent books that had lain by much neglected, were then much perused, and lent from one to another; and it was a peculiar satisfaction to people to find how exactly the doctrines they heard daily preached, harmonized with the doctrines contained and taught by great and godly men in other parts and former times. The subjects of discourse almost always, when any of them were together, were the matters of religion and great concerns of their souls. All unsuitable, worldly, vain discourse on the Lord's day seemed to be laid aside among them. Indeed, for any thing that appeared, there seemed to be almost a universal reformation in this respect, in our public assemblies on the Lord's day.

"There was an earnest desire in people after opportunities for public worship and hearing the word. I appointed in the spring to preach every Friday through the summer when I was at home, and those meetings were well attended; and at several of them the power of the Lord was remarkably with us.—

"In some time, many of the convinced and distressed afforded very hopeful, satisfying evidence that the Lord had brought them to true closure with Jesus Christ, and that their distresses and fears had been in a great measure removed in a right gospel way, by believing in the Son of God. Several of them had very remarkable and sweet deliverances this way. It was very agreeable to hear their accounts, how that when they were in the deepest perplexity and darkness, distress and difficulty, seeking God as poor, condemned, hell-deserving sinners, the scene of recovering grace through a Redeemer has been opened to their understandings with a

3*

surprising beauty and glory, so that they were enabled to believe in Christ with joy unspeakable and full of glory. It appeared that most generally the Holy Spirit improved for this purpose, and made use of some one particular passage or other of the Holy Scripture that came to their remembrance in their distress; some gospel-offer or promise, or some declaration of God, directly referring to the recovery and salvation of undone sinners by the new covenant. But with some it was otherwise. They had not any one particular place of Scripture more than another in their view at the time. Those who met with such a remarkable relief,—as their account of it was rational and scriptural, so they appeared to have at the time, the attendants and fruits of a true faith; particularly, humility, love, and an affectionate regard to the will and honor of God. Much of their exercise was in self-abasing and self-loathing, and admiring the astonishing condescension and grace of God towards such vile and despicable creatures, that had been so full of enmity and disaffection to him. They freely and sweetly, with all their hearts, chose the way of his commandments. Their enflamed desire was, to live to him for ever according to his will, and to the glory of his name.

"There were others, that had not had such remarkable relief and comfort, who yet I could not but think were savingly renewed, and brought truly to accept of and rest upon Jesus Christ, though not with such a degree of liveliness and liberty, strength and joy; and some of those continued for a considerable time after, for the most part, under a very distressing suspicion and jealousy of their case. I was all along very cautious of expressing to people my judgment of the goodness of their states, excepting where I had pretty clear evidences from them of their being savingly changed, and yet they continued in deep distress, casting off all their evidences. Sometimes, in such cases, I have thought it needful to use greater freedom that way than ordinary; but otherwise, I judged that it could be of little use, and might easily be hurtful.

"Besides those above spoke of, whose experience of a work of grace was in a good degree clear and satisfying, there were some others (though but very few in this congregation that I knew of) who, having very little knowledge or capacity, had a very obscure and improper way of representing their case in relating how they had been exercised. They would chiefly speak of such things as were only the *effects* of their soul-exercise upon their bodies from time to time, and some things that were purely imaginary; which obliged me to be at much pains in my inquiries, before I could get any just ideas of their case. I would ask them, what were the thoughts, the views, and apprehensions of their minds, and exercise of their affections, (at such times when they felt, perhaps, a quivering come over them, as they had been saying, or a faintness, or thought they saw their hearts full of some nauseous filthiness; or when they felt a heavy weight or load at their hearts, or felt the weight again taken off and a pleasant warmness rising from their hearts, as they would probably express themselves,) which might be the occasions or causes of these things they spoke of. And then, when with some difficulty I could get them to understand me, some of them would give a pretty rational account of solemn and spiritual exercises; and after a thorough, careful examination this way, I could not but conceive good hopes of some such persons.

"But there were moreover several others, who seemed to think concerning themselves that they were under some good work, of whom, yet, I could have no reasonable ground to think that they were under any hopeful work of the Spirit of God. As near as I could judge of their case from all my acquaintance and conversation with them, it was much to this purpose: They believed there was a good work going on; that people were convinced, and brought into a converted state; and they desired to be converted too: They saw others weeping and fainting, and heard people mourning and lamenting, and they thought if they could be like these, it would be very hopeful with them; hence, they endeavoured just to get themselves affected by sermons, and if they could come to weeping, or get their passions so raised as to incline them to vent themselves by cries, now they hoped they were got under convictions, and were in a very hopeful way; and afterwards, they would speak of their being in trouble, and aim at complaining of themselves, but seemed as if they knew not well how to do it, nor what to say against themselves; and then they would be looking and expecting to get some texts of Scripture applied to them for their comfort; and when any Scripture text which they thought was suitable for that purpose came to their minds, they were in hopes it was brought to them by the Spirit of God, that they might take comfort from it. And thus, much in such a way as this, some appeared to be pleasing themselves just with an imaginary conversion of their own making. I endeavoured to correct and guard against all such mistakes, so far as I discovered them in the course of my ministry, and to open up the nature of a true conviction by the Spirit of God, and of a saving conversion.

"Thus I have given a very brief account of the state and progress of religion here through that first summer after the remarkable revival of it among us. Towards the end of that summer, there seemed to be a stop put to the further progress of the work as to the conviction and awakening of sinners; and ever since there have been very few instances of persons convinced. It remains then, that I speak something of the abiding effects and after-fruits of those awakenings and other religious exercises which people were under during the abovementioned period. Such as were only under some slight impressions and superficial awakenings, seem in general to have lost them all again, without any abiding hopeful alteration upon them. They seem to have fallen back again into their former carelessness and stupidity. And some that were under pretty great awakenings, and considerably deep convictions of their miserable state, seem also to have got peace again to their consciences without getting it by a true faith in the Lord Jesus; affording no satisfying evidence of their being savingly renewed. But, through the infinite rich grace of God (and blessed be his glorious name!) there is a considerable number who afford all the evidence that can be reasonably expected and required for our satisfaction in the case, of their having been the subjects of a thorough saving change; (except in some singular instances of behaviour, alas for them, which proceed from, and show, the sad remains of original corruption even in the regenerate children of God while in this imperfect state.) Their walk is habitually tender and conscientious, their carriage towards their neighbours just and kind, and they appear to have an agreeable peculiar love one for another, and for all in whom appears the image of God. Their discourses of religion, their engagedness and dispositions of soul in the practice of the immediate duties and ordinances of religion, all appear quite otherwise than formerly. Indeed, the liveliness of their affections in the ways of religion is much abated in general, and they are in some measure humbly sensible of this, and grieved for it, and are carefully endeavouring still to live unto God; much grieved with their imperfections and the plagues they find in their own hearts; and frequently they meet with some delightful enlivenings of soul; and particularly our sacramental solemnities for communicating in the Lord's Supper have generally been very blessed seasons of enlivening and enlargement to the people of God. There is a very evident and great increase of Christian knowledge with many of them. We enjoy in this congregation the happiness of a great degree of harmony and concord; scarcely any have appeared with open opposition and bitterness against the work of God among us and elsewhere up and down the land, though there are a pretty many such in several other places through the country. Some, indeed, in this congregation, but very few, have separated from us and joined with the ministers who have unhappily opposed this blessed work." *

NEW BRUNSWICK, N. J.

The account given by the Rev. Gilbert Tennent, dated August 24th, 1744, confirms and illustrates what has been said of the state of Presbyterian congregations, and of the means and character of the awakening among them. He says:—

"The labors of the Reverend Mr. Frelinghousa, † a Dutch Calvinist minister, were much blessed to the people of New Brunswick and places adjacent, especially about the time of his coming among them, which was about twenty-four years ago.

"When I came there, which was about seven years after, I had the pleasure of seeing much of the fruits of his ministry; divers of his hearers, with whom I had opportunity of conversing, appeared to be converted persons, by their soundness in principle, Christian experience, and pious practice; and these persons declared that the ministrations of the aforesaid gentleman were the means thereof. This, to-

* Christian History, Vol II. p. 242.

† So the Dutch pronounce *Frelinghuysen*.

gether with a kind letter which he sent me respecting the necessity of dividing the word aright, and giving to every man his portion in due season, through the divine blessing, excited me to greater earnestness in ministerial labors. I began to be very much distressed about my want of success; for I knew not for half a year or more after I came to New Brunswick, that any one was converted by my labors, although several persons were at times affected transiently.

"It pleased God to afflict me about that time with sickness, by which I had affecting views of eternity. I was then exceedingly grieved that I had done so little for God, and was very desirous to live one half year more, if it was his will, that I might stand upon the stage of the world, as it were, and plead more faithfully for his cause, and take more earnest pains for the conversion of souls. The secure state of the world appeared to me in a very affecting light; and one thing among others pressed me sore; viz. that I had spent much time in conversing about trifles, which might have been spent in examining people's states towards God, and persuading them to turn unto him. I therefore prayed to God that he would be pleased to give me one half year more, and I was determined to endeavour to promote his kingdom with all my might at all adventures. The petition God was pleased to grant manifold, and to enable me to keep my resolution in some measure.

"After I was raised up to health, I examined many about the grounds of their hope of salvation, which I found in most to be nothing but as the sand. With such I was enabled to deal faithfully and earnestly, in warning them of their danger, and urging them to seek converting grace. By this method, many were awakened out of their security; and of those, divers were to all appearance effectually converted, and some that I spoke plainly to were prejudiced. And here I would have it observed, that as soon as an effectual door was opened, I found many adversaries, and my character was covered with unjust reproaches, which through divine goodness did not discourage me in my work. I did then preach much upon original sin, repentance, the nature and necessity of conversion, in a close examinatory and distinguishing way; laboring in the mean time to sound the trumpet of God's judgments, and alarm the secure by the terrors of the Lord, as well as to affect them with other topics of persuasion; which method was sealed by the Holy Spirit in the conviction and conversion of a considerable number of persons, at various times, and in different places, in that part of the country; as appeared by their acquaintance with experimental religion, and good conversation."

Such was the character of the "Great Awakening" in its commencement, before any foreign influence was brought to mingle with it. And in many places where there was no visible movement, such as these specimens exhibit, there was a reviving of religion in secret; there was, in the pious, and especially among pastors, a sense of spiritual want; there was self-examination; there was self-abasement and mourning for discovered want of fervor and constancy in God's service; there was prayer for pardon, and for grace to be faithful, and for the divine blessing upon faithful labors; there was a better performance of pulpit and parochial duties, and a more teachable spirit, both in church members and others; and in many places, there began to be instances of manifest conversion. Such was the state and such were the prospects of New England, when George Whitefield was invited to visit Boston. As he was a member and a minister of the church of England, we must inquire what influence the institutions of that church exerted upon him, and through him upon the American churches.

---

## CHAPTER III.

**Whitefield in Early Life. His birth, education, and religious experience. His success as a preacher. — His first visit to Georgia. His return to England, opposition, and success. — Controversy with the Bishop of London. His intercourse with Watts and Doddridge. His return to America.**

In the "office for baptism" prescribed by the Church of England, the priest, after the application of water to the infant, is required to say: — "Seeing now that this child is regenerate, and grafted into the body of Christ's church, let us give thanks; — " and in giving thanks, after repeating the Lord's Prayer, he must say: — "We yield thee hearty thanks, most merciful Father, that it hath pleased thee to regenerate this infant with thy Holy Spirit, to receive him for thine own child by adoption, and to incorporate him into thy holy church." When this child dies, if he has neither been excommunicated nor committed suicide, the priest must say at his funeral:—"Forasmuch as it hath pleased Almighty God, of his great mercy, to take unto himself the soul of our dear brother here departed, therefore we commit his body to the ground; earth to earth, ashes to ashes, dust to dust; in sure and certain hope of the resurrection to eternal life, through Jesus Christ our Lord." Whatever interpretation theologians may put upon this language, its practical influence, on a large scale, cannot be doubtful.* Unless counteracted by other instructions, it must teach the member of the English church to believe, that he was made a child of God and an heir of heaven by baptism; that, if not excommunicated, he is in the road to heaven; and that for the future, he has only to avoid excommunication and suicide, to secure his admission into heaven when he dies. And such has evidently been its influence. The unthinking members of the Church of England, who are numerous, if not an immense majority, actually suppose that all who die in the communion of their church, are saved of course, and never suspect that any regeneration can be needed, except that which they received in baptism. The form of burial is doubtless soothing to the hearts of surviving friends, and it might seem cruel to withhold from them this consolation, when they so poignantly feel the need of it; but it is cruel kindness to console them by a delusion which may not improbably destroy their own souls, and which will sink deeper

* Theologians have strangely overlooked the true, original meaning of this formula, though it seems sufficiently obvious. Before the child can be baptized, it must promise to "renounce the devil and all his works, and constantly believe God's holy word, and obediently keep his commandments;" and must profess its faith in the principal doctrines of Christianity. The declaration that the child is regenerate, is based upon the supposition that this promise and profession has actually been made, understandingly and in good faith. But in fact, this has been done only by the child's sponsors, who act in its name, on account of its acknowledged inability to do these things for itself; and it needs ratifying by the child, when old enough to ratify it. The regeneration stands in the same relation to reality, as do the promise and profession on which it is predicated. Both are ante-dated, on the presumption that they will become realities in due time. If this were generally understood, the doctrine of baptismal regeneration would be comparatively harmless.

into their hearts and be more tenderly cherished, on account of the affecting circumstances under which it is administered. To deal at once tenderly and faithfully with the bereaved, doubtlesss requires some degree of manly control over one's own sympathies ; but the good of souls requires it. And we should beware of encroaching upon the prerogatives of our final Judge. We as presumptuously invade his province when we acquit, as when we condemn.

In the Church of England, religious teachers are not selected by the people, for themselves, but are imposed upon them by the king, who is the "head of the church," or by some one acting under his authority. Centuries ago, many pious and many superstitious noblemen gave funds for the support of clergymen in certain parishes, reserving to themselves and to their heirs the right of nominating, or presenting, the clergymen to be supported by them. This provision for support is called a "living." In other parishes, where the "living" is derived from some other source, the right of presentation belongs to the king, the bishop of the diocese, one of the universities, or is attached to some other public office or institution. The nobleman who has a "living" at his disposal, gives it to one of his younger sons, who has been "educated for the church," as others have been for the army or the navy ; or to a son of some relative ; or perhaps to some unprincipled sycophant, who has been his companion and assistant in vice. "Livings" at the disposal of the king, — that is, of the prime minister, — are sometimes given to those who have performed convenient drudgery in party political warfare. Those attached to the universities are sometimes the prize of laborious and successful study. It would be unjust to forget, that the right of presentation often happens to be in the hands of a pious man ; and that, by this and other means, many "livings" are bestowed on clergymen of real piety. Many, too, like Scott the commentator, are converted after they enter the ministry. Still, as every one who knows any thing of human nature must anticipate, a large proportion of the clergy of that church are utterly unfit for their places ; men who "take orders" merely for the sake of a "living" ; perhaps decently moral in their lives, and perhaps indecently dissipated ; believing, concerning preparation for heaven, just what their form of baptism and burial service naturally teach, and counting all professions of more serious religion, mere fanaticism or hypocrisy. The more decent, serious, and literary part of this division of the established clergy would naturally maintain from the pulpit and in print, that baptism is regeneration, the only regeneration possible in this world; and that baptism administered in their own "apostolic" church is "valid," and confers upon the baptized, some claim to the kingdom of heaven. Seldom, if ever, has this gloomy description been more generally applicable to the English church and its clergy, than at the time when Whitefield first appeared.

George Whitefield was born at Gloucester, England, on the 16th day of December, (old style,) in 1714. His father, Thomas Whitefield, who had been a wine merchant, but was now an inn-keeper, died about two years after his birth. From the age of twelve to fifteen, he distinguished himself among the boys at the public school by his progress in Latin, and by his speeches and dramatic performances at public examinations. His mother still kept the inn; and as a decrease of business enforced more economical arrangements, George was obliged to leave his Latin and his declamations, and assist in the drudgery of the house. He put on his blue apron, — "washed mops, cleaned rooms, and, in one word, became a professed and common drawer for nigh a year and an half."

From his childhood, he tells us, he "was always fond of being a clergyman, and used frequently to imitate the ministers reading prayers," and other exercises; and though he accuses himself of some vices not uncommon in boys of his age, his conscience seems to have been often awakened, and he "had early some convictions of sin." So strong was the bent of his mind in that direction, that while employed as a drawer, he found time to compose two or three sermons, and frequently spent the whole night in reading the Bible.

Changes in family arrangements, and the hope that he might get a servitor's place at Oxford, at length induced his mother to send him to school again. Here he was near being ruined by bad company; but his conscience was alarmed and he broke away from its influence. His narrow escape made him feel the need of religion more deeply than ever, and was followed by an external reformation, which was noticed by his friends. He overheard one of them speaking well of him, and his conscience smote him for not being so good inwardly, as he appeared outwardly. "God deeply convicted me of hypocrisy." Henceforth he became more strict and abundant in fasting, prayer, and other religious observances.

At the age of eighteen he went to Oxford, and was admitted servitor immediately. The expertness at waiting on tables and the like, which he had acquired at the inn, was now of use to him. Many of the rich students chose him for their servitor, so that his income was nearly or quite equal to his wants.

The English universities, at that time, were little else than learned dens of infidelity and dissipation. Whitefield was from the first solicited, and expected of course, to join in the revels of those around him; but he steadily refused, and they soon concluded to let him alone, "as a singular, odd fellow." His sufferings for want of a safe and well-informed religious instructor, were intense and protracted, and he run, or was led, into many errors, from some of which he escaped but slowly. Some may think that the guidance of the Holy Spirit would supply the want of human teachers; and in an important sense it was so. But the Holy Spirit leads men into truth, not in a way which renders mental effort on their part unnecessary, but in a way which rouses them to think, and brings their thoughts to a safe result. And besides; at this time, if we may trust Whitefield's own judgment, he was still unregenerate; he had not given himself up to the guidance of the Spirit of God; he was not led by the Spirit, but rather driven by the Spirit, which continually urged him onward by convictions of duty, while he was continually turning into every by-path which a carnal mind could mistake for the way of life; in short, — according to an important distinction laid down by Edwards in his "Treatise on the Affections,"— the Holy Spirit then acted *on* his mind, and not *in* it. Thus, while he was irresistibly impelled to seek the truth, and not suffered to rest without finding it, he was, in a very important sense, left to find it as he could, by his own unguided efforts, and to learn, by his own bitter experience, the folly and wickedness of many foolish and wicked devices, from which good instruction might have saved him. He had the Bible; but all the religious instruction he had received, all the books he had read, all the habits of thought, feeling, and action which had prevailed around him from his infancy, taught him to misunderstand it. Through all these influences he must break or dig his way to the truth ; to truths which the "common sense" of all around him, the common sense in which he had been brought up, condemned as nonsense. What can we expect the history of his religious experience to be, but an account of errors and extravagances by which he was injured, and of his merciful deliverance from them at last ?

An act of charity to a poor, vicious woman, who had attempted suicide, brought him to the notice of the "Methodists," as a small number of students, under the special religious guidance of John Wesley, had lately been nicknamed. Wesley was then a fellow of Lincoln College, and had been for some years in "holy orders" ; but, in his own judgment at a later period, he was still destitute of the saving knowledge of Christ, and had only been led "into the desert, to be tempted, and humbled, and shown what was in his heart." Still, he and his little company were decidedly in earnest. They avowed, that the great object of their lives was, to save their souls, and to live wholly to the glory of God ; and no company of monks ever whipped their own naked shoulders for the good of their souls and the glory of God with a more blind sincerity, than that under the misguidance of which these men were seeking salvation. One of their more harmless rules required them frequently to "interrogate themselves whether they have been simple and recollected ; whether they have prayed with fervor, Monday, Wednesday, Friday, and on Saturday noon ; if they have used a collect at nine, twelve, and three o'clock ; duly meditated, on Sunday, from three to four, on Thomas à Kempis ; or mused on Wednesday and Friday, from twelve to one, on the passion." He gladly put himself under their direction, and they led him straight forward into deep darkness. "I now began," he says, "like them, to live by rule, and to pick up every fragment of my time, that not a moment of it might be lost. Like them, having no weekly sacrament (although the rubric required it) at our own college, I received it every Sunday at Christ Church. I joined with them in keeping the stations, by fasting Wednesdays and Fridays, and left no means unused which I thought would lead me nearer to Christ. By degrees I began to leave off eating fruits and such like, and gave the money I usually spent in that way to the poor. Afterward I always chose the worst sort of food, though my place furnished me with variety. My apparel was mean. I thought it unbecoming a penitent to have his hair powdered. I wore woollen gloves, a patched gown, and dirty shoes ; and though I was then convinced that the kingdom of God did not consist in meats and drinks, yet I resolutely persisted in these voluntary acts of self-denial, because I found them great promoters of spiritual life. It was now suggested to me that Jesus Christ was among the wild beasts when he was tempted, and that I ought to follow his example ; and being willing, as I thought, to imitate Jesus Christ, after supper I went into Christ Church walk, near our college, and continued in silent prayer nearly two hours ; sometimes lying flat on my face, sometimes kneeling upon my knees. The night being stormy, gave me awful thoughts of the day of judgment. The next night I repeated the same exercise at the same place. After this, the holy season of Lent came on, which our friends kept very strictly, eating no flesh during the six weeks, except on Saturdays and Sundays. I abstained frequently on Saturdays also, and ate nothing on the other days, except Sunday, but sage tea without sugar, and coarse bread. I constantly walked out in the cold mornings, till one part of my hands was quite black. This, with my continued abstinence and inward conflicts, at length so emaciated my body, that at passion week, finding I could scarce creep up stairs, I was obliged to inform my kind tutor of my condition, who immediately sent for a physician to me." He now gave himself exclusively to religious reading ; and one of his authors having informed him, that "he that is employed in mortifying his will, is as well employed as though he was converting the Indians," Satan so imposed upon his understanding, that he resolved to shut himself up in his study, till he could do good with a single eye. When his author advised to endeavour after a silent recollection and waiting upon God, Satan told him that he must leave off all forms, and not use his voice in prayer at all. The natural consequence was, that his mind began to lose the power of action. "Whenever I endeavoured to compose my theme, I had no power to write a word, nor so much as to tell my Christian friends of my inability to do it. All power of meditating, or even of thinking, was taken from me. My memory quite failed me; and I could fancy myself to be like nothing so much as a man locked up in iron armour." His tutor kindly inquired if any calamity had befallen him, that he had twice failed to produce his weekly theme. This kindness overcame him. "I burst into tears, and assured him that it was not out of contempt of authority, but that I could not act otherwise. Then at length he said, he believed I could not; and when he left me, told a friend that he took me to be really mad. This friend, hearing what had happened from my tutor, came to me, urging the command in Scripture, 'to be subject to the higher powers.' I answered, yes, but I had a new revelation. Lord, what is man!" As further proof of the injury done to his mind, his brain, his nerves, by this discipline, he was haunted by the fear of seeing the devil. He thought the devil would appear to him every stair he went up, as servitor, at ten o'clock at night, to the gentlemen's rooms; and he was so troubled by the devil when he lay down, that for some months he scarce slept above three hours in a night. In this horrible condition, Charles Wesley was afraid to prescribe for him; and John advised him to "resume all" his "externals, though not to depend on them in the least." He did resume them; and happily, his bodily constitution broke down under them, and he was sick seven weeks. This sickness effectually interrupted his course of "externals," and his thoughts, released from the bondage in which they had willingly been held, communed with his own heart and with the word of God. He spent much of his time in reading the Greek Testament, and in prayer. He gained more clear, rational, and affecting views of his own sinfulness, and saw how hopeless was the effort to remove the sense of guilt by a series of observances. He remained in this condition, till, as he informs us, "One day, perceiving an uncommon drought and a noisome clamminess in my mouth, and using things to allay my thirst, but in vain, it was suggested to me, that when Jesus Christ cried out 'I thirst,' his sufferings were near over. Upon this, I threw myself upon the bed, and cried out, *I thirst, I thirst.* Soon after, I perceived my load to go off; a spirit of mourning was taken from me, and I knew what it was truly to rejoice in the Lord. At first after this, I could not avoid singing psalms, wherever I was; but my joy became gradually more settled, and, blessed be God, has abode and increased in my soul, saving a few casual intermissions, ever since."* Some years afterwards, in reply to objections, he said:—"My crying *I thirst*, *I thirst*, was not to put myself upon a level with Jesus Christ. But when I said those words, *I thirst*, *I thirst*, my soul was in an agony; I thirsted for God's salvation, and a sense of divine love. I thirsted for a clear discovery of my pardon through Jesus Christ, and the seal of the Spirit. I was at the same time enabled to look up to and act faith upon the glorious Lord Jesus as dying for sinners, and felt the blessed effects of it." It is not difficult, by combining these statements, to understand the progress of his thoughts. He had been driven from every ground of hope, but the mercy of God; but he had not dared boldly and without reserve to trust that mercy; and yet he had a prevailing hope that it would deliver him from his present anguish, and save his soul. His thirst, a usual symptom of fever, reminded him of the thirst of Christ upon the cross, which was near the end of his sufferings. He appears not to have inferred that it must be so with him also; but the thought arose in his mind, "Why may it not be so with me? Why may I not now receive deliverance and comfort? Why may I not now dare to trust and rejoice in the pardoning mercy of God?" There was no reason why he might not,—why he ought not. He saw nothing to forbid him. He prayed in hope, borrowing language from the fact which had suggested the train of thought,—"I thirst,—I thirst,"—for faith in pardoning love. "Lord, I believe! Help thou mine unbelief." His prayer was heard. He dared to trust in the mercy of God, as revealed in the death of Jesus Christ for sinners. He did right in trusting that mercy. Conscience bore witness that he did right. "The burden that had so heavily oppressed him," the "load" of guilt and terror and anxiety that weighed down his spirit while he sinfully and ungratefully hesitated to trust God's mercy, was gone. He saw the trustworthiness of God's mercy in Christ, and his heart rejoiced.

Though the English universities were established mainly for the purpose of educating men for the ministry, Whitefield was not likely to gain a good knowledge of theology

---

* Whitefield's "Life and Journal." Athenæum Library.

there. He took another and a characteristic course. Some time after his conversion, when he was at Gloucester, he says:—"I began to read the Holy Scriptures upon my knees; laying aside all other books, and praying over, if possible, every line and word. This proved meat indeed and drink indeed to my soul. I daily received fresh life, light, and power from above. I got more true knowledge from reading the book of God in one month, than I could ever have acquired from all the writings of men."

It does not appear that Whitefield was much inclined to compare himself with others, or to think that he was or should be a greater man than they; but he certainly looked forward to his own career in the ministry, as a great and important work; and when his friends urged him to receive ordination, he remonstrated, and insisted on more time for preparation. He intended to have a hundred sermons carefully written before beginning to preach. He had but one, and lent that to a neighbouring clergyman, to convince him that he was not yet fit to be ordained. The clergyman kept it a fortnight, preached half of it at a time to his own people, and sent it back, with a guinea for the use of it. The bishops had resolved to ordain none under twenty-three years of age, and Whitefield was but twenty-one; but Bishop Benson, who became acquainted with his talents, activity, and usefulness, told him that, notwithstanding that rule, he would ordain him whenever he should apply. His excuses being exhausted, he was ordained on the Sabbath, June 20, 1736. One week from that day, he preached his first sermon, in his native parish. Curiosity brought together a large audience; and though "some mocked," yet "most for the present seemed struck." Some one told Bishop Benson, that Whitefield drove fifteen of his hearers mad by this, his first sermon. The bishop wished the madness might not be forgotten before the next Sabbath.

This is not the place for a history of Whitefield's labors in England. It is enough for the present purpose to say, that he preached to others the doctrines on which his own soul relied for salvation; that he preached them with the full persuasion that others must receive them or perish forever; that he preached under the influence of an affecting view of the worth of the soul, and an intense desire that his hearers might be saved. In preaching that men, of all ages and conditions, must be "born again," or never "see the kingdom of heaven," though there were some in the land who believed it, he found himself practically alone, going forth as the herald of a doctrine which the public agreed to consider as new; but which, he felt, God had made known to him that he might proclaim it to others, and thus revive the power of Christianity in the land. And as God had raised him up and enlightened his mind for the work, he doubted not that God would be with him in the performance, and make his strength equal to his day. He went, therefore, fearlessly, as well as earnestly and affectionately, about his work. Moved in his inmost soul by the sight of his fellow-men, ready to perish and yet ignorant of their danger, he could not fetter himself with the rules by which ordinary men were taught to construct dull sermons; he must pour forth the desires of his heart and the convictions of his mind. And he did pour them forth, in a style natural and clear, animated and pathetic, which sometimes the intensity of pathos rendered truly sublime. He poured them forth in a voice of wonderful flexibility, compass and power, and accompanied with the most graceful, impressive and appropriate action. In look, attitude, gesture, intonation, — in all that constitutes the *manner* of an orator, the world probably never saw his superior, perhaps, never his equal. In later years, when his eloquence had excited general attention, men of powerful and cultivated minds, unmoved by the truths he uttered, — statesmen, orators, scholars, professional actors, — Franklin, Hume, Chesterfield, Garrick,* Foote, — listened, as if spell-bound, to his eloquence. But it was his ardent love for souls that were perishing, his sense of the unutterable importance of the truth, which God had raised him up to proclaim to a world that had forgotten it, and his firm assurance that God was with him to give that truth success, that was the fountain of his power. When he proclaimed that truth, and besought men to hear it and think of it, that their souls might live, they could not refuse. They were interested; they were affected; they were alarmed. They were persuaded, that they must "strive to enter in at the strait gate," or they should not avoid the road that leadeth to destruction; that, if they continued to neglect

* Garrick said, that Whitefield could make his hearers weep or tremble at pleasure, by his varied utterance of "Mesopotamia."

salvation, they should not escape final ruin. When his determination became known to go to Georgia, whither the Wesleys had invited him, rather than accept either of several eligible "livings" that had been offered him, his heroic devotedness to the good of the needy excited a new interest in his favor. Wherever he went to take leave of the congregations to which he had preached, at Bristol, at Bath, and especially at London, multitudes crowded to hear him. When, in his parting sermon at Bristol, he told them, "it might be they would see him no more," the whole assembly was drowned in tears. Many with tears followed him to his lodgings after the sermon; and the next day he was employed from seven in the morning till midnight, in conversing with those who sought his advice concerning their salvation. "The whole city," he wrote, "seems to be alarmed. Churches are as full on week days as they used to be on Sundays, and on Sundays so full that many, very many, are obliged to go away because they cannot get in." "The word was sharper than a two-edged sword; *the doctrine of the new birth made its way like lightning into the hearers' consciences.*" When he came to London to embark, those who had heard him before, obliged him to preach almost incessantly. The stewards of religious societies laid hold of him, and compelled him to preach charity sermons in their behalf. Eight pounds were contributed at a time, where the usual contributions had been ten shillings. His "mighty deeds" in the pulpit were blazoned in the newspapers. He preached nine times a week, and the people listened "as for eternity." Thousands went away from the largest churches, unable to gain admittance. Two or three of his sermons were published. And now a few of the clergy began to turn against him. Some called him a "spiritual pickpocket," and others thought he used a charm to get the people's money. Some were offended because he was on good terms with the dissenters, and some forbade him the use of their pulpits, unless he would retract a wish, expressed in the preface to his sermon on regeneration, that his brethren would preach more frequently on the new birth. The opposition, however, had not become extensive, when, having collected about a thousand pounds for charity schools, and more than three hundred for the poor in Georgia, he embarked, December 28, 1737, to cross the Atlantic.

The vessel touched and remained some time at Gibraltar. Here Whitefield's preaching was attended with its usual success. "Many," he says, "that were quite stark blind, received their sight; many that had fallen back, have repented and turned to the Lord again; many that were ashamed to own Christ openly, have waxen bold; and many saints had their hearts filled with joy unspeakable and full of glory." When this account was published in England, it called forth some remarks, which show what was then the state of many minds. As for sight being restored to the blind, the critic soberly concluded, "It seems likely to be a falsity," and that Whitefield had told the story, "to have the world think that God worked this miracle on his account." He was sadly puzzled with what Whitefield said, of enjoying the divine presence at one time and not at another, and thought that it must imply a denial of God's omnipresence. In conclusion, he recommended, "that we should go to our baptism for the date of our regeneration."

After a long voyage, in which his influence was highly salutary to his companions, Whitefield arrived at Savannah, in the month of May, 1738. He was cordially received, but found affairs in a bad condition, and prospects discouraging. The Wesleys and their associates had labored there with all their might to do good, but injudiciously, and with bad results. The temper of the colonists was not what it should be. Some, however, were converted, and Whitefield was "really happy" among them. Charles Wesley had suggested to him the design of an orphan house, which he and General Oglethorpe had contemplated. Whitefield entered into the design with all his heart, and it was thought necessary for him to visit England to procure funds for its establishment, and to be ordained as a priest. In August, he went to Charleston, S. C. to embark. The Rev. Alexander Garden, rector of St. Philip's Church, was "commissary," or deputy, of the Bishop of London for South Carolina; for the episcopal churches in these colonies were then attached to the diocese of that bishop. Mr. Garden received him very courteously, and Whitefield preached on Sabbath morning and evening in St. Philip's church. Mr. Garden thanked him for his sermons, informed him of the ill treatment which John Wesley had met with in Georgia, and promised that if the same arbitrary measures should be used against him, he would defend him with his life and fortune. On the 6th of September he embarked, and after a dangerous voyage arrived at London on the 8th of December.

The objects of the voyage were accomplished. He was ordained by Bishop Benson, January 14th, 1739, and he collected more than £1000 for the orphan house. But it had also a more important influence. It brought the great principles of the contest in which he spent the remainder of his life distinctly into action, and it fixed his mode of maintaining the conflict. The clergy had begun to perceive that either his doctrine or theirs, concerning the new birth and the way of a sinner's justification before God, must fall. True, they objected against his irregularities; but those irregularities, for the most part, grew out of this conflict of principles. The bishops received him coldly. In two days, the use of five churches was denied him. The opposition of the clergy increased the people's inclination to hear; and their crowding to hear increased the opposition of the clergy. Pamphlets were published against his sermon on regeneration, and sermons were preached against him, his doctrines, and his proceedings. But he was busy in attending prayer meetings and preaching in the few churches that were still open, and awakenings and conversions multiplied. At Bristol he had the use of the churches at first, but in a short time all were closed against him. Even at London, seeing the crowds around the doors and windows, unable to hear, he had thought of preaching to them in the open air; but both he and his friends hesitated before taking so bold a step. While at Bristol, he made the attempt. The colliers in the vicinity were numerous, rude, and ignorant. When provoked, they were the terror of the city; and at all times it was thought dangerous to go among them. Whitefield went one day to Hannam Mount, and preached to about a hundred of them. "I thought," he said, "it might be doing the service of my Creator, who had a mountain for his pulpit and the heavens for his sounding-board, and who, when his Gospel was refused by the Jews, sent his servants into the highways and hedges." The news spread rapidly among the colliers, and his audience soon increased to twenty thousand. The Gospel was indeed "good *news*" to them, for they had never heard preaching before. "Having no righteousness of their own to renounce, they were glad to hear of a Jesus, who was a friend to publicans, and who came not to call the righteous, but sinners, to repentance. The first discovery of their being affected was, to see the white gutters made by their tears, which plentifully fell down their black cheeks, as they came out of their coal-pits. Hundreds and hundreds of them were soon brought under deep convictions, which, as the event proved, happily ended in sound and thorough conversion. The change was visible to all ; though numbers chose to impute it to any thing rather than the finger of God." Besides the colliers, multitudes of all ranks came from Bristol to hear him. "The open firmament above me, the prospect of the adjacent fields, with the sight of thousands and thousands, some in coaches, some on horseback, and some in the trees, and at times all affected and drenched in tears together, to which was sometimes added the solemnity of approaching evening, was almost too much for, and quite overcame me." At the invitation of some of his hearers, he preached in a large bowling-green in the city. Much of his time was spent in giving private instruction to anxious inquirers. Having introduced Wesley to his hearers at Bristol, he travelled through Wales and the intervening parts of England to London. Here also the churches were shut against him, and he resorted to the fields. Moorfields, Kennington Common and Blackheath witnessed his repeated triumphs over audiences of ten, fifteen, twenty, and thirty thousands. Frequent excursions into the surrounding country were attended with similar results.

At length, the dignitaries of the church were obliged to take the field. On the 1st of August, the Bishop of Londen published "A Pastoral Letter to the people of his Diocese, by way of caution against Lukewarmness on one hand, and Enthusiasm on the other." Whitefield answered it on the 13th. In speaking of lukewarmness, the Bishop said, that he "who has hitherto contented himself with a bare bodily attendance upon the public worship of God, and following his daily employment on other days, and with abstaining from the more gross and notorious acts of sin, and from doing any hurt or injury to his neighbour, and has rested finally upon these, as the whole that Christianity requires of him," is "yet in a very imperfect state, or, in other words, in the number of the lukewarm ;" and he speaks of others, as having "made greater proficiency in the Christian life" than such persons have done. Whitefield replied, that such a person "is in no 'state' of Christianity at all," but "a reprobate, — at present out of a state of salvation." In speaking of enthusiasm, the Bishop said, that the ordinary gifts of the Holy Spirit "are no otherwise discernible, than by their fruits and effects, as these appear in the lives of Christians." Whitefield admitted that they were no otherwise discernible to others; but he contended that a person may feel some of them, as love, joy, peace, when there is no opportunity of discovering them to others. This was a vital point; for it involved the question whether a real Christian has an inward experience, by hearing an account of which others may form an opinion of his piety. The Bishop had expressed his hope, that when the clergy preached Justification by Faith, they explain it so "as to leave no doubt whether good works are a necessary condition of being justified in the sight of God." Whitefield showed from the Bible, and from the articles of the church, that good works are not the condition, but only the necessary consequence, of justification. The practical difference between them was palpable and important. The Bishop's doctrine sent the anxious sinner to doing good works, as a condition of justification. Whitefield's doctrine sent him directly to God for pardon, and for grace to do works truly good. The Bishop declared against the doctrine of instantaneous regeneration; and, quoting Whitefield's remark on the conversion of his friend Seward, he exclaimed: — "How it could be, that a professed Christian, who 'constantly attended the means of grace,' and 'was frequent in private duties,' did, all that while, 'know nothing of Jesus Christ,' is beyond my comprehension; and I am much at a loss to understand what was that 'saving, experimental knowledge of Jesus Christ,' for want of which he could only be reckoned among heathens and infidels." — The ideas of Whitefield and his opponents were now fairly drawn out and embattled against each other, and it was to be decided, whether a truly spiritual religion should be allowed to subsist in the church of England.

On these vital points of doctrinal and practical religion, Whitefield found sympathy among the Dissenters. He had some pleasing interviews with Watts, Doddridge, and other leading Congregationalists; but, as he preferred to labor in the church to which he belonged, and as they were afraid that his enthusiasm and irregularities would work mischief in the end, there was no public coöperation between them. Watts cautioned him against giving heed to "impressions," supposed, but not proved, to be from the Holy Spirit; warned him of the danger of delusion and imprudence, and gave him credit for sincerity and zeal, but doubted his "extraordinary call to some parts of his conduct." Doddridge called him a very honest man, but weak, and "a little intoxicated with popularity." His alliance with the Wesleys and other Methodists, who were abusing the Dissenting churches as "companies of banded formalists," probably increased their willingness to let him do good in his own way, without becoming responsible for him.

It must not be supposed that Whitefield, in these controversies and labors, was executing any great plan, which he had laid, for accomplishing great things. He was only doing his present duty, as the circumstances of each day demanded. He had come to England, to receive priest's orders, and to collect money for his orphan house. An embargo, caused by the commencement of a war with Spain, unexpectedly detained him, and he was neither willing nor permitted to be idle. He preached to a few hearers in a private room, or to thirty thousand on Kennington Common; attended a little prayer meeting, gave advice to an anxious sinner, heard good advice from Watts and Doddridge, or engaged in controversy with the Bishop of London, just as one occasion after another called him to do. And now, the embargo being raised, and the care of the colliers and some other affairs being transferred to Wesley, whom he had induced to commence field-preaching, this pastor of a little parish in Georgia embarked, August 14, 1739, for Philadelphia, on his return to the people of his charge.

---

## CHAPTER IV.

**Whitefield's Labors. His Preaching and success at Philadelphia, at New York, and in the Middle and Southern Colonies.**

Whitefield arrived at Philadelphia early in November, 1739. Gillies says, he "was immediately invited to preach in the churches, to which people of all denominations flocked as in England." His reputation had preceded him, and multitudes, such as no house could contain, crowded to hear him. He therefore frequently preached in the evening, from the gallery of the Court house in Market Street. Every word was distinctly heard on board a shallop at the wharf, four hundred feet distant, and all the intermediate space was full of hearers. Great numbers were awakened, not only in the various denominations of professed Christians, but among those who had wholly neglected religion. At the invitation of Mr. Noble, his only acquaintance in that city, he visited New York. The Episcopal commissary denied him the use of his church. Mr. Pemberton, pastor of the Presbyterian Church, was the only minister who admitted him to his pulpit. Mr. Pemberton was a native of Boston, and too much of a Puritan to be frightened at Whitefield's doctrine of the new birth. As the house of worship could not hold all that desired to hear, Whitefield preached several times in the fields; but he produced no very remarkable effect in New York, till his visit in 1764, though even now some appear to have been added to the church.

While at New York, November 16, he wrote: "God willing, in about seven months I hope to see New England in my return to Europe. An effectual door is there opened, and no wonder that there are many adversaries. Shortly I expect to suffer for my dear Master." And after his return to Philadelphia, he wrote, November 28, to the Rev. Mr. P—; "I have been much concerned since I saw you, lest I behaved not with that humility towards you, which is due from a babe to a father in Christ; but you know, Reverend Sir, how difficult it is to meet with success, and not be puffed up with it; and therefore if any such thing was discernible in my conduct, oh, pity me, and pray to the Lord to heal my pride. All I can say is, that I desire to learn of Jesus Christ to be meek and lowly in heart; but my corruptions are so strong, and my employ so dangerous, that I am sometimes afraid." *

On this journey to and from New York, Gillies informs us, "he preached at Elizabethtown, Maidenhead, Abington, Neshaminy, Burlington, and New Brunswick, in New Jersey, to some thousands gathered from various parts, among whom

* Letters, Vol. I.

there had been a considerable awakening by the instrumentality of a Mr. Frelinghuysen, a Dutch minister, and Messrs. Tennents, Blair, and Rowland. He had also the pleasure of meeting the venerable Mr. Tennent, as well as his sons, with Mr. Dickinson. It was no less pleasing than strange to him, to see such gatherings in a foreign land; ministers and people shedding tears; sinners struck with awe; and serious persons, who had been much run down and despised, filled with joy."

One of the most important incidents of this journey was, the meeting of Whitefield with Gilbert Tennent. Two powerful preachers could not well resemble each other less; and the great strength of each lay in traits in which the other was deficient. In one point, Whitefield felt and recorded his new friend's superiority. He heard Tennent preach. "Never before heard I such a searching sermon. He went to the bottom indeed, and did not daub with untempered mortar. He convinced me, more and more, that we can preach the Gospel of Christ no further than we have experienced the power of it in our hearts. I found what a babe and novice I was in the things of God." These men, having once met, could not but be friends and allies for life; and their alliance could not fail to be felt by thousands.

Both at Philadelphia and New York, printers* applied to Whitefield for sermons to publish; and two were printed. He afterwards had reason to rejoice in their influence.

The readiness which Whitefield found to aid him in sustaining his orphan house, determined him to travel by land to Savannah, while his supplies and family were sent on in a

* The leading printer of religious works at Philadelphia at this time, appears to have been "B. Franklin." In 1741 he printed Gilbert Tennent's sermon on "Justification;" at the end of which he advertised, as lately printed and for sale by himself, Ralph Erskine's "Gospel Sonnets," Finley's sermon on "Christ Triumphing and Satan Raging," Whitefield's "Journal in New England," "A Protestation to the Synod of Philadelphia," which excluded the Tennents and others, and produced the "Great Schism;" and as in press, Gilbert Tennent's "Remarks" on that Protestation; Watts's "Psalms," and Alliene's "Alarm to the Unconverted." He also printed Blair's "Vindication" of himself and others against the charges in the "Protestation" which excluded them from the Synod. His pamphlets were printed with a neatness and accuracy not usual among his contemporaries. Franklin was too shrewd a calculator to lose the chance of making money by printing such works as were about to be in demand; and his list of publications shows his judgment of the turn which the public mind was taking.

sloop purchased for him for that purpose. He left Philadelphia with his friend Seward, and nearly twenty gentlemen on horseback, for Chester. Before his arrival, two hundred more had come to meet him. A court was about to open at Chester; but the judges sent him word that they would wait till after the sermon which he was expected to preach. Nearly a thousand people had come from Philadelphia to hear it. The audience was immense, and he addressed them from a platform erected for the occasion. At Whiteclay Creek,* he became acquainted with William Tennent, well known for his extraordinary trance, in which, to speak philosophically, he continued to live and think, but as sensation was suspended, the external world had no influence upon his thoughts, and his mind, aided, perhaps, only by such divine influence as every good man experiences in health, formed to itself ideas of heaven, and its inhabitants, and its enjoyments, which seemed to be present realities, in the midst of which he was; ideas, it is not unreasonable to suppose, more vividly correct than any man could form, while under the influence of the bodily senses, and distracted by earthly sights and sounds; and showing, by actual experiment, into what state that mind would naturally pass, if released from the body.

At Charleston, Whitefield could not obtain admittance to St. Philip's Church. The commissary was absent, and his curate would not open the doors without his leave. But Josiah Smith,† the pastor of the Congregational church, opened his pulpit, and his people received a blessing.‡ So it was too at the French church. On the 11th of January, 1740, he arrived at Savannah.

In March, he again visited Charleston. The Commissary was now his decided opponent. He addressed Whitefield a letter, March 17th, attacking his doctrine of justification, and challenging him to defend what he had said concerning the Bishop of London and his clergy. Whitefield had said in his sermon, "Observe, my dear brethren, the words of the article; [the 12th article of the Church of England;] 'good works are the fruit of faith,' and 'follow after justification.' How can they then precede, or be any way the

* Not Whiteley Creek, as stated by Gillies and copied by Philip.

† Not Joseph Smith, as he is called in the late London edition of Whitefield's Sermons.

‡ Philip's "Life and Times of Whitefield."

cause of it? No, our persons must be justified, before our performances can be accepted." Commissary Garden urged in reply: "If good works do necessarily spring out of a true and lively faith, and a true and lively faith necessarily precedes justification, the consequence is plain, that good works must not only follow after, but precede justification also." Whitefield replied the next day: "I perceive that you are angry overmuch. Was I never so much inclined to dispute, I would stay till the cool of the day. Your letter more and more confirms me, that my charge against the clergy is just and reasonable. It would be endless to enter into such a private debate, as you, Reverend Sir, seem desirous of. You have read my sermon; be pleased to read it again; and if there be any thing contrary to sound doctrine, or the articles of the Church of England, be pleased to let the public know it from the press; and then let the world judge whether you or my brethren the clergy have been rashly slandered." This was all very true, and just what Garden deserved; but it was not very conciliatory, nor very decorous, when addressed by a young priest of the church of England to his ecclesiastical superior. Garden wrote and published six letters against Whitefield. About the close of the year, the Rev. Andrew Croswell wrote an answer to these letters, in his usual biting style. It was published at Boston, with an equally biting appendix, which Croswell ascribes to one of the Boston pastors; probably meaning the Rev. Joshua Gee.* Garden had maintained that good works, though not the meritorious cause, are yet the condition and means, of our justification. Croswell shows that if this be true, then it must be that a certain amount of good works is necessary for the justification of each individual; and as the exact amount is nowhere recorded, and may not be the same in all cases, no man can ever know whether he is justified or not. And then, on this plan, "a man might attain one half, two thirds, three quarters, or ninety-nine hundredths of justification;" and, he asks, "What would become of a poor sinner, that should be taken out of the world at that unhappy juncture, wherein his justification was so near being effected, that there wanted but one good wish, one *Lord have mercy upon me* more, to complete it? Shall

* Both the letters and answer are preserved in the Old South Church Library.

the man be miserable for ever for this defect? Or shall he be looked upon as justified, though he had not quite worked out his justification? Or, lastly, shall he be doomed to *purgatory* for a while, to satisfy for what was wanting, and thereby to be made meet for the inheritance of the saints in light? Lastly, I would ask, what will become of those good works which are the overplus, after a man is justified? And whether it be not from this doctrine, that the Popish priests teach, that some men may have more good deeds than they need themselves, and a little to spare for those that want?" Divines of this day will smile at Mr. Garden's argument, which rests on the assumption that a man is not justified as soon as he has faith, but only after he has had faith long enough to do a certain, or rather, perhaps, an uncertain amount of good works.

While the Commissary was writing these letters and preaching accordingly, Whitefield returned to Savannah, and on the 25th of March, laid the first brick of his orphan house, calling the institution Bethesda, the House of Mercy.

It was on the next day, March 26th, that Josiah Smith preached his celebrated Sermon on "The Character, Preaching, &c., of the Rev. Mr. George Whitefield"; of which Philip says, "I do not know of any thing written since, which defines and defends the character of Whitefield better." Mr. Smith sent a copy to his friends, Dr. Colman and Mr. Cooper, at Boston, who published it, with a commendatory preface, dated June 7, 1740. The preface concludes by bespeaking the prayers of the faithful in Christ Jesus, not only for Whitefield's preservation and general success, but "very particularly, that his purposed coming to us may be with as full a blessing of the Gospel of Christ as other places have experienced, and much more abundant, by the will of God." *

Whitefield must now go forth to solicit funds for his orphan house. Philip says, that Philadelphia was the first place where he pleaded their cause, after commencing the work. This is correct; but he had previously taken up a collection in Smith's meetinghouse in Charleston, and re-

* The publication of this sermon probably led to a controversy on Justification, in the South Carolina Gazette, fragments of which are preserved in the Library of the American Antiquarian Society at Worcester. The writers seem to have been Mr. Smith and Commissary Garden.

ceived valuable donations, both in New York and Philadelphia. Now he set forth on a journey of solicitation. The newspapers noticed his movements, and furnish almost a complete history of his present excursion. The reflecting reader will like to see how his labors, character and influence were presented to the public at the time.

The New England Weekly Journal of April 29th, 1740, copies from a Philadelphia paper of April 17th:

"The middle of last month, the Rev. Mr. Whitefield was at Charleston, and preached five times, and collected at one time upwards of £70 sterling for the benefit of the orphan house in Georgia; and on Sunday last, after ten days' passage from Georgia, he landed at Newcastle, where he preached morning and evening. On Monday morning he preached to about three thousand at Wilmington, and in the evening arrived in this city. On Tuesday evening he preached to about eight thousand on Society Hill, and preached at the same place yesterday morning and evening." Then follow his appointments daily, to April 29th, during which time he was to preach at Whitemarsh, Germantown, Philadelphia, Salem, N. J., Neshamony, Skippack, Frederick Township, Amwell, New Brunswick, Elizabethtown, and New York. May 6, the Journal copied a Philadelphia notice of April 24, that he had preached the Sabbath previous to fifteen thousand hearers, and on Monday at Greenwich and Gloucester; and that he would return to Georgia before visiting New England.

The Journal of May 20 contains a letter from Whitefield to a friend in England, dated New Brunswick, April 27. Of his visit to Charleston, he says; "A glorious work was begun in the hearts of the inhabitants, and many were brought to cry out, What shall we do to be saved? A fortnight ago, after a short passage of ten days, I landed in Pennsylvania, and have had the pleasure of seeing and hearing that my poor endeavours for promoting Christ's kingdom, when here last, were not altogether in vain in the Lord. I cannot tell you how many have come to me laboring under the deepest convictions, and seemingly truly desirous of finding rest in Jesus Christ. Several have actually received him into their hearts by faith, and have not only righteousness and peace, but joy in the Holy Ghost. In short, the word has run and been much glorified, and many negroes also are in a fair way of being brought home to God. Young ones I intend to buy, and do not despair of seeing a room full of that despised generation, in a short time, singing and making melody with grace in their hearts unto the Lord.

"An effectual door is opened for preaching the everlasting Gospel, and I daily receive fresh and most importunate invitations to preach in all the counties round about. God is pleased to give a great blessing to my printed sermons. They are in the hands of thousands in these parts, and are a means of enlightening and building up many in the most holy faith. The clergy,* I find, are most offended at me. The Commissary of Philadelphia, having gotten a little stronger party than when I was here last, has thrown off the mask, denied me the pulpit, and last Sunday preached up an historical faith and justification by works. But the people only flock the more. The power of God is more visible than ever in our assemblies, and more and more are convinced that I preach the doctrine of Jesus Christ. Some of the bigoted, self-righteous Quakers now also begin to spit out a little of the venom of the serpent. They cannot bear the doctrine of original sin, and of an imputed righteousness as the cause of our acceptance with God. I have not yet met with much opposition from the Dissenters; but when I come to tell many of them, ministers as well as people, that they hold the truth in unrighteousness, that they talk and preach of justifying faith, but never felt it in their hearts, as I am persuaded numbers of them have not, then they no doubt will shoot out their arrows, even bitter words."

A fortnight after this, the patrons of the Journal read:— "New Castle, May 15. This evening Mr. Whitefield went on board his sloop here, in order to sail for Georgia. On Sunday he preached twice in Philadelphia, and in the evening, when he preached his farewell sermon, it is supposed he had twenty thousand hearers. On Monday he preached at Darby and Chester; on Tuesday, at Wilmington and Whiteclay Creek; on Wednesday, twice at Nottingham; on Thursday, at Fog's Manor† and Newcastle. The congregations were much increased since his being here last. The

---

* That is, of the English Church.

† Fagg's Manor is now the established orthography. In publications of the day, it is also called Frogg's Manor, and Fork's Manor. Gillies has it, Frogo Maner.

presence of God was much seen in the assemblies, especially at Nottingham and Fog's Manor, where the people were under such deep soul distress, that their cries almost drowned his voice. He has collected, in this and the neighbouring provinces, about £450 sterling for his orphans in Georgia."

He arrived at Savannah, June 5th, and, immediately after, his labors with his orphans were the means of awakening many, and of the conversion of some.

Next comes a notice of a different character, in the Postboy of June 23d. It is an extract from a letter dated Philadelphia, June 5th.

"Field preaching prevails with the vulgar here so much, that industry, honest labor, and care for their families, with many, seems to be held as sinful, and as a mark of neglect for the salvation of their souls. Mr. Whitefield and his adherent ministers have infatuated [the multitude] with the doctrines of Regeneration, Free Grace, Conversion, &c., after their peculiar way of thinking, as essential articles of salvation, though inconsistent with true religion, natural or revealed, subversive of all order and decency, and repugnant to common sense. We have daily instances of the melancholy fruits of these sermons. Many, naturally timorous and of weak minds, are terrified into despair, with their threatening and denouncing eternal vengeance. Some are transported with passions which influence them to believe that they have had the beatific vision, and immediate intercourse with him who is invisible. I have informed you of this, because Mr. Whitefield intends for Boston, in the fall or autumn, where I understand he is impatiently waited for. I wish his ministry there may not be attended with the same bad effects as here, by diverting and disturbing the laboring people, who are generally too much inclined to novelties, especially in point of religion. He is the more to be guarded against, because, I can assure you, he is qualified to sway and keep the affections of the multitude."

The author of this letter may have been one of Whitefield's Presbyterian opponents; but more probably he was an Episcopalian; or most probably, from his evident theological ignorance, some purse-proud, lordly layman.

In the same paper, and also in the Journal of the next day, was another notice, which its relations to some important events invest with unusual interest: —

"Philadelphia, June 12. During the session of the Presbyterian Synod, which began on the 28th of last month, and continued to the third instant, there were no less than fourteen sermons preached on Society Hill to large audiences, by the Rev. Messrs. Tennents, Mr. Davenport, Mr. Rowland, and Mr. Blair; besides what were delivered at the Presbyterian and Baptist meetings, and expoundings and exhortations in private houses. The alteration in the face of religion here is altogether surprising. Never did the people show so great a willingness to attend sermons, nor the preachers greater zeal and diligence in performing the duties of their function. Religion is become the subject of most conversations. No books are in request but those of piety and devotion; and instead of idle songs and ballads, the people are everywhere entertaining themselves with psalms and hymns and spiritual songs. All which, under God, is owing to the successful labors of the Rev. Mr. Whitefield.

"On Sunday last, the Rev. Mr. Gilbert Tennent preached four times; at seven in the morning at Society Hill, at ten in the Presbyterian meetinghouse, at three in the afternoon at the Baptist meetinghouse, and at seven in the evening on Society Hill again; at which last sermon it is thought there were near eight thousand people."

To understand the bearings of this account, we must consider somewhat minutely the state of the Presbyterian church at that time.

---

## CHAPTER V.

Parties in the Presbyterian Church.—Different views of Regeneration, and controversies growing out of them.—Acts of the Synod in 1728, 1737, 1738, and 1739.—Meeting of the Synod in 1740.—Tennent's Nottingham Sermon.—Meeting of the Synod in 1741.—The "Great Schism."

The Presbyterian Church in America, from its very commencement, contained two classes of men, whose views, on some important points, were in direct conflict with each other. The strict Presbyterians, from Scotland and Ireland, with few exceptions, held the sentiments described on a preceding page. They insisted that all baptized persons, not convicted of heresy or immorality, should be communicants; and that such persons, regularly educated for that purpose, and possessing sufficient learning, should be regarded as qualified for the ministry. Regeneration, they held to be necessary in order to acceptance with God, both in partaking of the Lord's Supper and in performing the duties of the ministry; but a qualification not ascertainable by examination, and not requisite in order to a regular standing in the church, or in the sacred office. In short, they insisted that all should be regarded and treated as regenerate, who did not give evidence to the contrary by manifest heresy or immorality. The other party was composed of men from New England, England, and Wales, with a few from Scotland and Ireland. They held that regeneration is a change of which evidence may ordinarily be found by examination; that those in whom no evidence of regeneration can be found, should be regarded and treated as unregenerate; and that all such persons should be excluded from the Lord's Table, and from the ministry. Most of their controversies grew out of this fundamental difference, and all were more or less directly related to it.

In the Synod of 1728, the Rev. John Thompson, of Lewes-town, in Delaware, brought in an overture, which led, the next year, to what is called "The Adopting Act," by which the Westminster Confession of Faith, Catechisms, &c. were adopted as the confession of faith of the church, and all ministers and candidates for the ministry were obliged publicly to assent to them. Mr. Thompson was the ecclesiastical leader of the "Old Side," or Scotch and Irish party. His overture was opposed by many of the "New Side," or New England party. The Rev. Jonathan Dickinson wrote against it, admitting the utility of creeds "for the instruction of the ignorant," and "for a public declaration of our religious sentiments," but opposing the imposition of any human creed as a test of orthodoxy. The act was adopted with a qualification, providing that if any minister or candidate should scruple to assent to any part of the standards, the Synod should judge whether that part was essential, so that its denial implied heresy; and if not, the qualified assent should be admitted.*

* Both Mr. Thompson's Overture and Mr. Dickinson's Remarks upon it are preserved in the Old South Church Library.

In 1735, Mr. Tennent's overture, requiring candidates for the ministry to be "examined diligently as to their experience of a work of sanctifying grace on their hearts," mentioned in a preceding chapter, was adopted unanimously; but, Dr. Miller informs us, it "became a source of great uneasiness within a few years afterwards." *

In 1738, the Synod enacted, that young men be required to produce a diploma from some European or New England college, or be examined respecting their literature by a commission of the Synod, and obtain a testimony of their approbation, before they can be taken on trial by any presbytery. This brought matters rapidly towards a crisis. The elder Tennent, who was an excellent classical scholar, had erected a "log college" at his residence on the Neshamony, where he educated his four sons and several others for the ministry. This was the "New Side" Seminary, and has since grown into the College and Theological Seminary at Princeton. But several "Old Side" leaders had their academies too, and were naturally anxious to fill them with students. When this act was passed, "Mr. Gilbert Tennent cried out, that this was to prevent his father's school from training gracious men for the ministry." † He foresaw that "Old Side" men would rule the Synod's commission, and would be able to reject all candidates not educated in their own schools, and all suspected of favoring "New Side" views of religion. On the other hand, it was contended that the act was necessary, in order to prevent the introduction of uneducated men into the ministry.

This act was also opposed, as an infringement on the rights of presbyteries, to whom, it was contended, the great Head of the church has committed the entire power of licensing and ordination. And this brought up another controversy, which related to the legislative power of church courts. The "Old Side" claimed the right to enact rules, not contrary to the laws of Christ, which would be binding on the conscience, and must be obeyed on pain of ecclesiastical censure. The "New Side" contended that church courts have no legislative power whatever; that they are authorized only to administer the laws that Christ has made;

* Life of Rogers.

† Letter of the Synod to President Clap, of Yale College, quoted by Professor Hodge, from "Minutes," Vol. III., p. 17.

and that any additional rules that they may enact, are mere recommendations, which every one is bound to observe so far as he can with a clear conscience, and not further. For this, they were charged with designing "to overthrow all authority, and cast out all order and government out of the church." "These are the men," said Mr. Thompson, "who profess so much zeal for Christ's kingdom, and yet are, by one bold stroke, attempting to strike the crown from his head, by divesting his officers and courts of all governing authority." If this bold sentence means any thing, it must mean that Christ reigns over his saints on earth, only in and through church officers and courts, so that our allegiance is due to them directly, and to him only indirectly, and through them. Still, Thompson disclaimed all legislative power in the church ; though he and his party were, in the judgment of their opponents, continually exercising it.

This act was trampled under foot very soon after its adoption. The presbytery of New Brunswick took Mr. John Rowland, one of Tennent's pupils, on trial in August, without applying to the Synod's commission for testimonials, licensed him in September, and in September of the next year ordained him, and in defiance of the censures of the Synod, kept him as a member of their body, till he was regularly transferred to another presbytery.

By another act, passed in 1737 and modified in 1738, and again in 1739, ministers and licentiates were prohibited from preaching in any parishes but their own, when there appeared to be danger that their preaching would cause divisions among the people. This was regarded by the "New Side" as a device for keeping "gracious" ministers from disturbing the stupidly contented flocks of unconverted pastors. This act, like the other, was pronounced legislative, and was disregarded, wherever there was thought to be a prospect of saving souls by disregarding it.

There was also a theological controversy, the main question of which seems to have been, whether a regard for the glory of God, or for our own happiness, ought to be our ultimate principle of action. It was brought before the Synod in 1738 by Gilbert Tennent. The Synod decided, that as our own happiness can be effectually promoted only by seeking the glory of God, the two motives ought not to be placed in opposition to each other ; and forbade both Tennent and his opponent, the Rev. David Cowell, to discuss the matter publicly. When the minutes were read the next year, Tennent attempted to revive the discussion; but the Synod refused to attend to it.

All these controversies were raging, when the Synod met in 1740. During this meeting, two papers were read, which, as must have been foreseen, gave great offence. The first was presented by Blair, of New Londonderry. He proposed to read it privately, at an informal meeting. The Synod determined to hear it immediately, and in public. The reason for this decision is not stated. Perhaps it was thought that Blair would not dare to read in public, such a paper as his was supposed to be; or that if he should do it, some advantage might be taken of it, against the "New Side." But Blair was not to be thus defeated. He read his paper. Gilbert Tennent then offered and read another, prepared without concert with Blair, but of kindred character. Of their contents, Blair says:—"The papers contained an account of many things which we found great fault with in several members of the Synod. And I can truly say, for my own part, that what I aimed at was, the faithful discharge of duty, and a conscientious testimony against those evils, for the good of the brethren guilty of them, and the good of the church; and to show the reasonableness of encouraging, rather than hindering of ministers, to preach Christ's gospel as they had opportunity through the land; because I saw there was evidently too much remissness among ministers up and down, and with some, much worse than bare remissness too."* By preaching "as they had opportunity," he means, preaching in the parishes of "Old Side" ministers, without their consent. Tennent's paper charged a part of the Synod, without naming the men, with "unsoundness in some of the principal doctrines of Christianity that relate to experience and practice; as particularly in the following points: First, that there is no distinction between the glory of God and our happiness; that self-love is the foundation of all obedience. These doctines do, in my opinion, entirely overset, if true, all supernatural religion;† render regeneration a vain and need-

---

* Vindication of the Excluded Brethren. Old South Church Libary.

† For, if this be true, regeneration can be nothing but giving a better direction to self-love, by teaching the sinner a surer way to gratify it, leaving him under the dominion of the same ultimate principle of action

less thing, and involve a crimson blasphemy against the blessed God, by putting ourselves upon a level with him. Secondly, that there is a certainty of salvation annexed to the labors of natural men. This doctrine, in my opinion, supposes the greatest falsehood, viz., that there is a free will in man naturally to acceptable good. — As these opinions are contrary to the express testimony of Holy Scripture, our Confession of faith and Christian experience, they give me reason to suspect, at least, that those who hold them are rotten-hearted hypocrites, and utter strangers to the saving knowledge of God and of their own hearts."

Though Blair's proposal to read his paper in private had been overruled by a vote of the Synod, yet, as soon as the papers were read, and often afterwards, he and Tennent were severely blamed for bringing such charges in public. They were told, too, that if they knew any ministers who were guilty as set forth in these papers, they ought to have commenced processes against them before their own presbyteries. This Blair offered to do, if the Synod thought it his duty; but neither the Synod, nor his presbytery when the matter came up there, would ever pass such a vote. The Synod passed a resolution, solemnly admonishing all the ministers within their bounds, "seriously to consider the weight of their charge, and as they will answer it at the great day of Christ, to take care to approve themselves to God in the instances complained of;" and recommending to the presbyteries "to take care of their several ministers in these particulars."

At this session, the act restraining the preaching of ministers out of their own parishes was repealed, and a minute was adopted, acknowledging the existence of a work of God in the land, and giving thanks for it; which shows that party lines were not yet so strongly drawn as they were the next year.

Such were the battles, from which Tennent and his fellows went to Society Hill, to preach revival sermons. Some of the "Old Side" asked the privilege of preaching there, but were refused. They then requested the privilege for Mr. Dickinson, but this also was refused. Tennent justified

as before; so that he is not a "new man," but only the "old man," grown more expert in self-seeking. Such a change may be accounted for on natural principles, and therefore is not "supernatural."

the refusal, by saying that the platform on Society Hill had been built expressly for Mr. Whitefield, and they did not feel at liberty to depart from his directions concerning the use of it; though they would readily have admitted their "Old Side" brethren to their own pulpits.

Some may ask, how was it possible that there should be a revival, while such controversies were raging? A consideration of the subjects of controversy will show, that it was very possible. The controversies related to the doctrines by which, and the liberty of action in the use of which, the revival was sustained. When Blair and the Tennents preached, they only used the liberty and proclaimed the doctrines for which they contended in the Synod. The controversy, therefore, did not divert their attention from their great work of saving souls. Yet it certainly did much to embitter their spirits, and to tarnish the revival with a large admixture of human imperfection.

It was probably soon after this meeting of the Synod, that Tennent preached his famous Nottingham sermon, on "The Danger of an Unconverted Ministry." To understand the propriety of his choice of a subject, and the boldness of his attack, the reader must remember, that a large majority in the Presbyterian church, and many, if not most, in New England, held that the ministrations of unconverted men, if neither heretical in doctrine nor scandalous for immorality, were valid, and their labors useful. For years afterwards, this doctrine was publicly and furiously maintained.

The text was Mark vi. 34. "And Jesus, when he came out, saw much people, and was moved with compassion towards them; because they were as sheep not having a shepherd." "But what," he exclaimed, after a few words of introduction, "was the cause of this great and compassionate commotion in the breast of Christ? It was because he saw much people as sheep not having a shepherd. Why, had the people then no teachers? O, yes! They had troops of Pharisee teachers, that came out, no doubt, after they had been at the feet of Gamaliel the usual time, and according to the acts, canons and traditions of the Jewish Church. But notwithstanding the great crowds of these orthodox, letter-learned and regular Pharisees, our Lord laments the unhappy case of that great number of people, who, in the days of his flesh, had no better guides; because that those were as good as none, in many respects, in our Saviour's judgment." He then described the character of "the old Pharisee teachers," the "most notorious branches" of which he made to be "pride, policy, malice, ignorance, covetousness, and bigotry to human inventions in religious matters." "Although some of the old Pharisee shepherds had a very fair and strict outside, yet they were ignorant of the new birth. Witness Rabbi Nicodemus, who talked like a fool about it. — The old Pharisees, for all their long prayers and other pious pretences, had their eyes, with Judas, fixed upon the bag. Why, they came into the priest's office for a piece of bread; they took it up as a trade, and therefore endeavoured to make the best market of it they could." His reasons "why such people who have no better than old Pharisee teachers, are to be pitied," are in the same style. "Natural men have no call of God to the ministerial work, under the gospel dispensation. — Remarkable is that saying of our Saviour, 'Follow me, and I will make you fishers of men.' See, our Lord will not make men ministers, till they follow him. Men that do not follow Christ, may fish faithfully for a good name, and for worldly pelf; but not for the conversion of sinners to God. Is it reasonable to suppose, that they will be earnestly concerned for others' salvation, when they slight their own? — The apostle Paul thanks God for counting him faithful, and putting him into the ministry; which plainly supposes that God Almighty does not send Pharisees and natural men into the ministry; for how can these men be faithful, that have no faith? It is true, men may put them into the ministry, through unfaithfulness or mistake; or credit and money may draw them; and the devil may drive them into it, knowing, by long experience, of what special service they may be to his kingdom in that office; but God sends not such hypocritical varlets." To the objection, that "Judas was sent by Christ," he replied: — "I fear that the abuse of this instance has brought many Judases into the ministry, whose chief desire, like their great-grandfather, is to finger the pence and carry the bag. But let such hireling, murderous hypocrites take care that they do not feel the force of a halter in this world, and aggravated damnation in the next."

The "improvement" of this sermon was as might be expected. "If it be so, that the case of those who have no other or no better than Pharisee teachers, is to be pitied, then what a scrole and scene of mourning, lamentation, and woe is opened, because of the swarms of locusts, the crowds of Pharisees, that have as covetously as cruelly crept into the ministry in this adulterous generation! who as nearly resemble the character given of the old Pharisees, in the doctrinal part of this discourse, as one crow's egg does another! It is true, some of the modern Pharisees have learned to prate a little more orthodoxly about the new birth, than their predecessor Nicodemus, who are, in the mean time, as great strangers to the feeling experience of it, as he. They are blind, who see not this to be the case of the body of the clergy of this generation."

"From what has been said, we may learn that such who are contented under a dead ministry, have not in them the temper of that Saviour they profess. It is an awful sign that they are as blind as moles and as dead as stones, without any spiritual taste and relish. And, alas! is not this the case with multitudes? If they can get one that has the name of a minister, with a band and a black coat or gown to carry on Sabbath days among them, although never so coldly and unsuccessfully; if he is free from gross crimes in practice, and takes good care to keep at a due distance from their consciences, and is never troubled about his unsuccessfulness; O! think the poor fools, that is a fine man indeed; our minister is a prudent, charitable man; he is not always harping upon terror, and sounding damnation in our ears, like some rash-headed preachers, who, by their uncharitable methods, are ready to put poor people out of their wits, or run them into despair."

But what follows, though less violent in style, was really harder to bear, than all that had gone before it. "If the ministry of natural men be as it has been represented, then it is both lawful and expedient to go from them to hear godly persons. Yea, it is so far from being sinful to do this, that one who lives under a pious minister of lesser gifts, after having honestly endeavoured to get benefit by his ministry, and yet gets little or none, but doth find real benefit and more benefit elsewhere; I say, he may lawfully go, and that frequently, where he gets most good to his precious soul, after regular application to the pastor where he lives, for his consent, and proposing the reasons thereof; when this is done in the spirit of love and meekness, without contempt of any, and also without rash anger or vain curiosity."

The remainder of the sermon, which is nearly half of it, is occupied in the proof of this proposition ; and by proving it, unanswerably, Tennent wounded his opponents more deeply than by all his reproachful epithets. Ministers whose characters command no respect, and who are too ignorant, too stupid, too full of worldly cares, or too lazy to preach attractive sermons, very naturally feel their need of a divine right to a certain number of hearers ; for on what other ground shall they get audiences and support ? By proving that God does not require men to starve their own souls by hearing such preachers, Tennent offended that whole class unpardonably. And his declaration, that "the body of the clergy" of that generation were "as great strangers to the feeling experience" of the new birth as Nicodemus, was unfortunate. We may reasonably hope that it was not true, even of his own communion, the Presbyterian church ; and it certainly was impolitic thus to fix the number of those whom he condemned, and give his enemies an opportunity to convict him of hostility to the clergy in general ; an advantage which they were not slow to seize, nor indolent in using.

As to the style of the sermon, it would be gratifying to say, that Tennent understood his audience, and knew what language was necessary to make them think and feel as they ought, better than we do ; but justice forbids us to leave the matter thus. There is no sin against which a man like Tennent more needs to be on his guard, than what some call "holy indignation ;" and in his circumstances, how could he avoid it ? Personal abuse he often, and so far as history informs us, always, bore with Christian meekness ; but the abuse of his father, his brothers, his fellow-laborers in the cause of truth, and, above all, of the truth itself, and of the way of salvation, was a severer trial. That such "Pharisee teachers" as he describes were in the ministry, polluting the Presbyterian church, and leading souls to perdition, he saw and knew. They claimed a right to be there, and their claims were acknowledged and defended. They bitterly opposed the revival of religion, and ridiculed the doctrines and defamed the men by whom it was carried on. The Synod, by its solemn acts, threw its influence in their favor, and issued decrees which sustained them in their opposition to the truth. Faithful ministers, their doctrines, and their works, were industriously held up to derision and contempt, as well as odium. Should Tennent suffer all this to be done without rebuke? He felt that he understood these men, and could make others understand them; and then their power to do mischief would be at an end.

There is certainly force in these considerations. It was doubtless Tennent's duty to write and preach and print on that subject; and if his sermon had been absolutely faultless, there is no reason to believe that it would have given any less offence. As it was, its truths hurt men's feelings more than its faults. Yet he was angry, and that we may not justify; but let him who would have kept his temper better, cast the first stone at him. He overrated the number of apostates; but not so much as Elijah the Tishbite, to whom he bore no slight resemblance, had done in Israel. And though he spoke with an anger that debased his style, and wrought evil, yet he spoke truth, mainly from good motives. He spoke it in a style which he knew would command attention, and cause it to be understood and remembered. The event answered his expectations. The sermon was widely circulated, and was a topic of discussion for years. Neither friends nor enemies would let it rest. It turned the tide of popular feeling effectually against unconverted ministers; and to no other human agency, probably, so much as to this sermon, is it owing, that Presbyterian ministers at the present day are generally pious men.

The doings of the Synod the next year throw still further light on these matters, and are introduced here, though out of the order of time, for the sake of presenting this whole subject in one view.

The Synod met in 1741, exasperated by another year of clashing opinions and practice concerning the revival of religion. On the first day of June, a "protestation," signed by twelve ministers and eight elders, was presented, with the avowed intention of bringing matters to a crisis. Its authors protested, "that all our protesting brethren," that is, those who had signed certain former protests, "have at present no right to sit and vote as members of this Synod, having forfeited their right of being accounted members of it, for many reasons;" and that if they should sit and vote, the doings of the Synod should be "of no force or obligation." The reasons assigned are,

"I. Their heterodox and anarchical principles, expressed" in an "Apology," which had been published by the New Brunswick Presbytery. These principles are enumerated. Blair, in his "Vindication," already quoted, denies that they held them.

"II. Their protesting against the Synod's act in relation to the examination of candidates, together with their proceeding to license and ordain men to the ministry of the gospel, in opposition to, and in contempt of said act of Synod.

"III. Their making irregular irruptions upon the congregations to which they have no immediate relation, without order, concurrence, or allowance of the Presbyteries or ministers to which congregations belong; thereby sowing the seeds of division among the people, and doing what they can to alienate and fill their minds with unjust prejudices against their lawfully called pastors.

"IV. Their principles and practice of rash judging and condemning all who do not fall in with their measures, both ministers and people, as carnal, graceless, and enemies to God's work, and what not; as appears in Mr. Gilbert Tennent's sermon against unconverted ministers, and in his and Mr. Blair's papers of May last, which were read in open Synod: Which rash judging hath been the constant practice of our protesting brethren and their irregular probationers, for above these twelve months past, in their disorderly itinerations and preaching through our congregations; by which (alas for it!) most of our congregations, through weakness and credulity, are so shattered and divided and shaken in their principles, that few or none of us can say we enjoy that comfort, or have that success among our people, which otherwise we might, and which we enjoyed heretofore.

"V. Their industriously persuading people to believe, that the call of God, whereby he calls men to the ministry, does not consist in their being regularly ordained and set apart to that work, according to the institution and rules of the word; but in some invisible motions and workings of the Spirit, which none can be conscious or sensible of but the person himself, and with respect to which he is liable to be deceived or play the hypocrite. That the gospel preached in truth by unconverted ministers, can be of no saving benefit to souls; and their pointing out such ministers whom they condemn as graceless by their rash judging spirit, thus effectually carry the point with the poor credulous people, who, in imitation of their example, under their patrociny, judge their ministers to be graceless, and forsake their ministers as hurtful rather than profitable.*

"VI. Their preaching the terrors of the law in such manner and dialect as has no precedent in the word of God, but rather appears to be borrowed from a worse dialect; and so industriously working on the passions and affections of weak minds, as to cause them to cry out

* The bad grammar of this sentence must be credited to those very accomplished scholars, the "Old Side" leaders, who have been praised for preventing the extinction of learning in the Presbyterian church.

in a hideous manner, and fall down in convulsion-like fits, to the marring of the profiting both of themselves and others, who are so taken up in seeing and hearing these odd symptoms, that they cannot attend to or hear what the preacher says; and then, after all, boasting of these things as the work of God, which we are persuaded do proceed from an inferior or worse cause.

"VII. Their, or some of them, preaching and maintaining, that all true converts are as certain of their gracious state, as a person can be of what he knows by his outward senses; and are able to give a narrative of the time and manner of their conversion, or else they conclude them to be in a natural or graceless state; and that a gracious person can judge of another's gracious state otherwise than by his profession and life. That people are under no sacred tie or relation to their own pastors lawfully called, but may leave them when they please, and ought to go where they think they get most good."

The Presbytery of New Brunswick, the members of which were among the excluded, immediately met, and were joined by several others as corresponding members. Before separating, they adopted the following minute: "Forasmuch as the ministers who have protested against our being of their communion, do at least insinuate false reflections against us, endeavouring to make people suspect that we are receding from Presbyterian principles; for the satisfaction of such Christian people as may be stumbled by such false aspersions, we think it fit unanimously to declare, that we adhere as closely and fully to the Westminster Confession of Faith and Catechisms and Directory, as the Synod of Philadelphia in any of their public acts." So much for their Presbyterianism in profession. As to their practice, the most serious accusation was, their "irregular irruptions" into the parishes of other ministers. To this, Mr. Blair replied: "The Synod had, for a year or two before, laid, as we apprehend, an unreasonable restraint upon ministers preaching out of the bounds of their own presbyteries; and we, in those papers, [the papers read before the Synod in 1740,] signified that the necessity of our preaching abroad was great and urgent, from the soul exercises and strong desires of the people, God succeeding his word in an uncommon degree, and from the manifest unfaithfulness of sundry ministers, and their great opposition against the revival of religion. It was a grief of heart to us, that we were under any such necessity on the last mentioned account. Our design, I hope, was to attempt to propagate the kingdom of our Lord Jesus, and save the souls of men; though we were obliged indeed frequently to take occasion to vindicate the work of God's Spirit from such ministers' and others' objections and cavils, and to show the necessity of ministers' dealing searchingly and solemnly with their people. But they could never charge either of us, that I know of, with any irruptions, as they call them, into their proper congregations, that they could judicially censure; though I must observe, by the way, that had they been as friendly to a work and revival of religion as they ought to have been, they and we both would have mutually rejoiced to have had one another to preach in our several congregations. It is a vain shift for any of them, in order to clear themselves from the charge of having made an opposition to the late revival of religion, to say that they have only opposed things that were evil and irregular, which ought to be opposed. We have not been wanting ourselves to be very careful this way, as many hundreds can witness. But there is a vast difference between opposing what is evil, delusive and irregular, for the more successful carrying on of a work of divine grace, and the improving of such things by way of reproach upon it and prejudice against it. This is a real opposition to it; and this they are chargeable with. Yea, more. They lash against all high degrees of soul-distress and terror in convinced persons, as proceeding from temptations of the devil; and do lash and reproach, in unlimited terms, as the mere effects of irrational frights or delusive joys, all cryings out, or bodily faintings; when such things may be, and in numbers have been, the effects of rational, spiritual, strong exercises of the soul, from the laws of the union between the soul and body, and can only, at most, be ascribed to human infirmity, which is such in this present state, that no man can see God and live. Yea, several of them have openly and plainly enough denied that any good work more than usual has been going on, but quite the contrary."

Tennent also published a reply to the statement of the Synod.* It was written earlier than Blair's, and is less systematic and complete, but takes substantially the same grounds. One fact which he mentions, deserves special notice, as it appears to be the earliest instance of one mode of opposing the revival, which was afterwards somewhat extensively used. "Our protesting brethren," he says, "have

* Am. Antiq. Soc. and Boston Athenæum.

quite omitted any mention of the late extraordinary canon framed by the Presbytery of Donnegal, which *ipso facto* excommunicates, or deprives of church privileges, all of their people that go to hear any of the itinerary preachers." To the assertion in the fourth charge of the protest, that the "rash judging" and itinerancy of the revivalists had diminished the comfort and success of the protesters among their people, he replied: "As to comfort, we believe them; but respecting success, we thought it had been much the same as formerly; for truly, this is the first time that we ever heard of the success of most of them." He contends, that when "a number of the ministry are either unsound in doctrine, or unfaithful, or contentedly unsuccessful in their work," the ordinary rules of ministerial intercourse are suspended by the nature of the case, and it is right to preach the gospel among their people without their consent. The charge of preaching that true converts always know the exact time of their conversion, he expressly denies. In reference to the papers read in the Synod by him and Blair, he states that he offered to commence process against individual members, if the Synod thought it his duty.

By examining the several charges of the excluding "protestation," the reader will see the ground of the controversy. The fundamental question was, whether regeneration is a change, attended and followed by an experience, by which the convert and others can judge of its reality; and of course, whether those who have no such experience are to be counted as unregenerate, and therefore excluded from the communion of the church, and deemed unfit for the ministry. The Tennents and their friends maintained the affirmative, and treated all men, in the church or out of it, ministers and people, accordingly. The seventh and last of these charges is evidently a description of this doctrine, drawn by an enemy. It condemns the doctrine, that one who has felt the sanctifying influence of divine truth, can judge whether another has felt the same, by his account of his own views and feelings, or in any other way than "by his profession and his life"; that is,—for so those men used those words,—by his creed and his morals. Judging men who were orthodox and not scandalous in their morals to be unconverted, is the "rash judging" censured in their fourth reason for protesting; and "preaching the terrors of the law" so as to alarm such men, is what they caricature and condemn in the sixth. The fifth is intended to condemn the doctrine of Tennent's Nottingham sermon, that an unconverted ministry is dangerous, and ought to be forsaken for a better ; and to assert that all who have been regularly ordained and not censured, have a divine right, in virtue of their office, to be regarded and treated as true ministers of Jesus Christ, whether converted or not. The " irregular irruptions," mentioned in the second reason, consisted of preaching the gospel, at the request of those who wished to hear it, in the parishes of opposers of the revival ; of ministers supposed to be unconverted, and who defended the supposed rights of unconverted ministers. To crush the revival, many of its most ardent and active friends were protested out of the Synod, and the Presbyterian church was rent in twain. But the revival went on, and its good influences still bless the land.

Such was the school in which Tennent was trained for his labors in New England ; and such was the first acquaintance of Whitefield with American " Dissenters." It was natural that he should anticipate the necessity of telling them that they preached justifying faith without having felt its power, and should expect opposition in consequence of it. These things must be kept in mind, if we would understand the motives, conduct and influence of these men in New England. — But meanwhile, where is Whitefield ?

---

## CHAPTER VI.

Whitefield at the South. — Scenes at the Orphan House. — Visit to Charleston. — Ecclesiastical prosecution. — Conversions at and around Charleston. — Schools for Negroes. — The Bryans.

Whitefield arrived at Savannah, from Pennsylvania, on the fifth of June, 1740 ; and his labors, immediately on his return, were the means of a considerable awakening among the few on whom they were bestowed. Of his first reception he says : " Oh what a sweet meeting I had with my dear friends ! What God has prepared for me, I know not ; but surely I cannot well expect a greater happiness, till I embrace the saints in glory. When I parted, my heart was ready to break with sorrow; but now it almost burst with joy. Oh how did each, in turn, hang upon my neck, kiss, and weep over me with tears of joy! And my own soul was so full of a sense of God's love, when I embraced one friend in particular, that I thought I should have expired in the place. I felt my soul so full of a sense of the divine goodness, that I wanted words to express myself. Why me, Lord, — why me?

"When we came to public worship, young and old were all dissolved in tears. After service, several of my parishioners, all my family, and the little children, returned home, crying along the street, and some could not avoid praying very loud.

"Being very weak in body, I laid myself upon a bed; but, finding so many in weeping condition, I rose and betook myself to prayer again. But had I not lifted up my voice very high, the groans and cries of the children would have prevented my being heard. This continued for near an hour; till, at last, finding their concern rather increase than abate, I desired all to retire. Then some or other might be heard praying earnestly in every corner of the house.

"It happened at this very time to thunder and lighten, which added very much to the solemnity of the night. Next day the concern still continued, especially among the girls. I mention the orphans in particular, that their benefactors may rejoice in what God is doing for their souls."

As the result of this awakening, he mentions only four or five instances of conversion; but it was peculiarly precious to him, because it occurred at the orphan house.

On the seventh of June he wrote to a friend: — "I have brought with me a Latin master, and on Monday laid the foundation, in the name of the Lord Jesus, for an university in Georgia." Another extract from his correspondence, addressed to Mr. W. D. June 28, should be read in connexion with what he wrote from New York, in November, of the danger of being "puffed up" by success. It shows both his need of admonition, and the excellent spirit in which he received it. He wrote: "I thank you for your kind letters and friendly cautions; and I trust I shall always reckon those my choicest friends, who, in simplicity and meekness, tell me the corruptions of my heart. It is that faithfulness, which hath endeared J. S. to me. I think I never was obliged to any one so much before. For that reason, also, I find my heart knit to you. Oh my dear brother, still continue faithful to my soul; do not hate me in your heart; in any wise reprove me. Exhort all my brethren to forgive my past (I fear) too imperious carriage; and let them pray that I may know myself to be, what I really am, less than the least of them all." — We have no right to call this an affectation of humility. He did not mean to say, nor expect to be understood to say, that he was "less than the least" of his friends in eloquence or influence; for he knew that in these he was immeasurably their superior; but, filled, as he then was, with contrition and self-loathing for the sin and folly to which his friend had called his attention, he felt that he was their inferior in piety; in that, compared with which all else is worthless.

At the close of this month, Whitefield again visited Charleston, where he arrived on the third of July, and immediately commenced preaching, as on former visits. On the Sabbath, July 6th, he attended the Episcopal Church, where, he says: "I heard the Commissary preach as virulent and unorthodox, inconsistent a discourse, as ever I heard in my life. His heart seemed full of choler and resentment. Out of the abundance thereof, he poured forth so many bitter words against the Methodists, (as he called them,) in general, and me in particular, that several, who intended to receive the sacrament at his hands, withdrew. Never, I believe, was such a preparation sermon preached before. — After sermon, he sent his clerk, to desire me not to come to the sacrament till he had spoke with me. I immediately retired to my lodgings, rejoicing that I was accounted worthy to suffer this further degree of contempt for my dear Lord's sake." The next day, the Commissary issued an ecclesiastical writ against Whitefield, which, as it may be a curiosity to American readers, it may be well to give entire.

"Alexander Garden, lawfully constituted Commissary of the Right Reverend Father in Christ, Edmund, by divine permission Lord Bishop of London, supported by the royal authority underwritten. —

"Alexander Garden,

"To all and singular clerks and literate persons whomsoever, in and throughout the whole province of South Carolina, wheresoever appointed, Greeting.

"To you, conjunctly and severally, we commit, and strictly enjoining, command, that you do cite, or cause to be cited, peremptorily, George Whitefield, clerk, and presbyter of the Church of England, that he lawfully appear before us, in the parish church of St. Philip, Charleston, and in the judicial place of the same, on Tuesday, the 15th day of this instant July, 'twixt the hours of nine and ten in the forenoon, then and there in justice to answer to certain articles, heads, or interrogatories which will be objected and ministered unto him concerning the mere health of his soul, and the reformation and correction of his manners and excesses, and chiefly for omitting to use the form of prayers prescribed in the Communion Book; and further to do and receive what shall be just in that behalf, on pain of law and contempt. And what you shall do in the premises, you shall duly certify us, together with these presents.

"Given under our hands and seals of our office, at Charleston, this seventh day of July, in the year of our Lord, one thousand seven hundred and forty."

The expression of concern for the health of Whitefield's soul, appearing in this writ, is sufficiently ludicrous; but it was a necessary formality, and Garden could not avoid it. According to the theory of English law, ecclesiastical courts have no right to cite any person before them for any purpose but that of promoting their spiritual welfare,—the health of their souls; and therefore, whatever be the object of the writ, whether to punish heresy or immorality, or to collect the tithe of pigs or poultry, this motive must be set forth, representing that the soul of the person cited would be endangered, by the omission or commission for which he is summoned to answer; and the particular offence must then be stated. The sin which, according to the Commissary's writ, endangered the health of Whitefield's soul, was "omitting to use the form of prayers prescribed in the Communion Book." The undisputed matter of fact was, that he always used that form, when he could obtain an Episcopal Church to preach in; but when shut out from such pulpits, and preaching to Baptists, Presbyterians and Congregationalists in their own houses of worship, where none of the congregation had prayer books, or knew how to use them, and where the introduction of unaccustomed forms would have diverted the minds of the worshippers, perhaps produced ludicrous blunders and levity, and in every way injured the religious effect of the whole service, he omitted that form, and prayed extempore.

On the day when this writ was issued, Whitefield preached for Mr. Chanler, "a gracious Baptist minister, about fourteen miles from Charleston;" and twice on the next day "to a large audience in Mr. Osgood's meetinghouse, a young Independent minister," at Dorchester; the next day at Dorchester again, and at Charleston in the evening; the next day preached and read prayers in Christ's Church, and twice at Charleston on the next day, with great success. And now, on the 11th of July, a citation was served upon him, to appear on the 15th, as required in the writ. On the 12th, he preached and read prayers twice on John's Island.

On the 13th, which was the Sabbath, he heard the Commissary again. He says of the sermon; "Had some infernal spirit been sent to draw my picture, I think it scarcely possible that he could paint me in more horrid colors. I think, if ever, then was the time that all manner of evil was spoke against me falsely for Christ's sake. The Commissary seemed to ransack church history for instances of enthusiasm and abused grace. He drew a parallel between me and all the Oliverians, Ranters, Quakers, French Prophets, till he came down to a family of Dutartes, who lived not many years ago in South Carolina, and were guilty of the most notorious incests and murders." It was easier to censure the Commissary for attempting to excite odium against Whitefield by comparing him to the Dutartes, than to answer the argument that might be drawn from the history of their errors and crimes; for Whitefield himself, at this time, was not wholly purified from that reliance upon impulses, supposed to come from the Spirit of God, which led them to their ruin.*

* There is, prefixed to "Plain Address to Quakers, Moravians, Separatists," &c. by Robert Ross, pastor of the church in Stratfield, Ct., published in 1762, and preserved in an old "Vol. II." of "Miscellanies" in the Library of the A. B. C. F. M. an account of the Dutartes, extracted from a printed sermon of Mr. Garden; probably this very sermon. The family, it seems, consisted of father, mother, four sons, and four daughters. They received their religious impressions from Christian George, who is said to have been a Moravian. After two or three years, they withdrew from all religious association with others, believing that they alone had the true knowledge of God, and were taught by him by signs and impulses. Peter Rombert, who had married the eldest daughter, a widow, was their prophet, like unto Moses, as they thought, whom they were to obey in all things. He predicted the impending destruction of all men, except that holy family. He afterwards declared, that God commanded him to put away his wife and take her younger sister, and predicted, that after the destruction of the wicked, God would raise his wife's former husband, so

The next day Whitefield again preached twice; and on Tuesday appeared before the Commissary, according to the citation. This is said to have been the first court of the kind ever attempted in any of the colonies. The parties showed their want of familiarity with such business, and, after a series of blunders on both sides, such as an adept in canon law could not but laugh at, the court adjourned to nine o'clock the next morning, to give Whitefield time to inform himself of the extent of the jurisdiction of the Bishop and his Commissary. How intently he studied the subject, may be conjectured from the fact, that he preached twice during the remainder of the day. The next day, a Mr. Graham appeared as a prosecuting attorney, and Mr. Rutledge as counsel for the respondent. Whitefield made some mistakes; but hints from his quick-sighted advocate and his own adroitness saved him from their consequences; though once he was obliged to give the court a lecture on the meanness of catching at a word as soon as it was out of his mouth, without allowing him time to correct it. He now filed his *recusatio judicis*, that is, his objection against being judged by the Commissary, who, he alleged, was prejudiced against him. This gave rise to new questions; the court adjourned, and Whitefield went to James' Island, read prayers and preached. The next day he appeared in court; found that

---

that the whole holy family should be preserved entire. The father hesitated; but Peter gave him a sign, that, on going to another plantation, the first animal that he should see should be such an one as he mentioned. The sign came to pass, and the change was made without further ceremony. They refused to perform militia and highway duty, pretending a divine command, and threw off all obedience to the civil magistrates. Justice Simmons issued a writ for Judith Dutarte, to answer concerning the child which she was expected to bear. By direction of Rombert, the family armed, fired upon and defeated the constable and his attendants. Another attempt was made, attended by the Justice and ten or twelve men. The Dutartes fired upon the company, and killed Justice Simmons; but after a battle, their doors were forced, one, Mrs. Lesard, was found dead, six were carried prisoners to Charleston, and on the 30th of September, 1724, five were sentenced to be hanged for murder. On trial, they freely acknowledged all the facts, declared that they acted by divine command, and were about to die as martyrs, but should be raised on the third day; and, in the steadfast profession of this faith, Dutarte senior, Rombert and Boineau were executed. Daniel and John Dutarte, aged eighteen and twenty years, remained sullen till the third day was passed, when, on the failure of the prophecy, they confessed their error, and were pardoned. One of them afterwards, by pretended divine direction, killed a man with whom he had no quarrel, and was executed for it; but, in the opinion of Mr. Garden, who, as chaplain, attended on them all when under sentence, died penitent.

his exceptions were repelled, and that the arbitrators would not be appointed; appealed to the High Court of Chancery at London, declaring all further proceedings in this court to be null and void; and then read letters which refreshed his spirit, by informing him "how mightily the word of God grew and prevailed" at Philadelphia, and that Mr. Bolton, in Georgia, had near fifty negroes learning to read.

The next day, July 18th, he preached twice, and on the 19th again appeared before the Commissary, and bound himself, in a penalty of ten pounds, to prosecute his appeal at London within twelve months. The appeal was never tried. The dignitaries at London seem to have regarded the prosecution as a bad business, and contrived to let it die of neglect.

"The court being ended," says Whitefield, in his journal, "the Commissary desired to speak with me. I asked him to my lodgings. He chose to walk in a green near the church. His spirit was somewhat calmer than usual; but after an hour's conversation, we were as far from agreeing as before." "All his discourse was so inconsistent and contrary to the gospel of our Lord, that I was obliged to tell him that I believed him to be an unconverted man, an enemy to God, and of a like spirit with the persecutor Saul. At this he smiled; and, after we had walked a long while, we parted, and God gave me great satisfaction that I had delivered my soul in my private conversation with the Commisary."

The next day, July 20th, was the Sabbath. The Commissary preached in his usual style, and Whitefield preached his farewell sermon to the people at Charleston. By his advice, two or three dissenting ministers had set up a weekly lecture. Whitefield "advised the people, as the gospel was not preached in church, to go and hear it in the meeting-house." On leaving the place, he sums up the result of his labors in his journal, after this manner:

"What makes the change more remarkable in Charleston people is, that they seemed to me, at my first coming, to be a people wholly devoted to pleasure. One well acquainted with their manners and circumstances, told me, more had been spent on polite entertainments, than the poor's rate came to; but now the jewellers and dancing-masters begin to cry out that their craft is in danger. A vast alteration is discernible in the ladies' dresses. And some, while I have been speaking, have been so convinced of the sin of wearing jewels, that I have seen them with blushes put their hands to their ears, and cover them with their fans. But I hope the reformation has went* further than externals. Many moral, good sort of men, who before were settled on their lees, have been gloriously awakened to seek after Jesus Christ; and many a Lydia's heart hath been opened to receive the things that were spoken. Indeed, the word came like a hammer and a fire. And a door, I believe, will be opened for teaching the poor negroes. Several of them have done their usual work in less time, that they might come to hear me. Many of their owners, who have been awakened, resolve to teach them Christianity. Had I time, and proper schoolmasters, I might immediately erect a negro school in South Carolina, as well as in Pennsylvania. Many would willingly contribute both money and land."

Whitefield left Charleston on the 21st of July,† visiting and preaching on his way homeward. On the 23d, he arrived at Hugh Bryan's, at Good Hope; the next day he went in Mr. Bryan's boat to Beaufort; the next evening arrived at Savannah, and thinking the passage to be the lesson for the day, read and expounded what Paul says of "Alexander the coppersmith," which evidently reminded him of Alexander the Commissary. On the Sabbath, several friends from South Carolina were present, who had come to see the orphan house. He felt exhausted, and unable to preach; but was persuaded to make the attempt. "I soon found power communicated to me from above. I felt a sweet melting in my soul, and, ere I had prayed long, Mr. Bull dropped down as though shot with a gun. He soon got up, and sat attentively to hear the sermon. The power soon began to spread abroad; the greatest part of the congregation was under concern." The next day he was sent for about noon to see Mr. Jonathan Bryan, whom he found "under great concern and strong convictions of sin." After staying among scenes like these about two weeks, Bull and Bryan went home, rejoicing in the hope of reconciliation to God.

* So it reads in his original journal.

† His journal says, on "Monday, July 22;" but Monday was the 21st, and not the 22d day of the month. This erroneous reckoning continues till August 3d, which is dated correctly. Similar errors for several days in succession, sometimes backwards and sometimes forwards, are frequent in this journal.

On the 18th of August, Whitefield left Savannah, and, on arriving at Charleston, found himself able to preach only once a day; but, as he thought, with greater power and success than ever before. The Commissary was quiet. Mr. Rowe preached in his stead, and told the people that for their sins God had sent them strong delusions, that they might believe a lie. Whitefield's conscience would not suffer him to attend at the Episcopal church, because the gospel was not preached there. Mr. Bull and J. Bryan came to Charleston to see him, and to be "more established" in the right way. "Mr. Hugh Bryan they left at home, drinking deeply of the cup of God's consolations. His wife came with them to Charleston: a gracious woman. By my advice they returned home, with a resolution to begin a negro school for their slaves. A young stage-player, convinced when I was last at New York, and who providentially came to Georgia when Mr. Bryan was there, is to be their first teacher." We shall hear of these Bryans again.

Having preached a farewell sermon to four thousand hearers, Whitefield sailed for New England.

---

## CHAPTER VII.

### WHITEFIELD'S FIRST VISIT TO NEW ENGLAND.

The religious state of New England was most favorable to Whitefield's success. Local revivals were already in progress, and were multiplying; and there had been throughout the land for several years, and especially since the "surprising conversions" at Northampton, an increasing sense of stupidity, which is a very different thing from increasing stupidity. He had been invited to come, by several of the most eminent ministers and laymen; his arrival had been for some time impatiently expected, and there was a general impression on men's minds, that his coming would be followed by a great revival of religion. There is even reason to suspect, that the manifestation of a revival, which was already secretly at work in men's hearts, was kept back for several months, by the general feeling, that it would take place when Whitefield came, and not before. In short, New England was ready and waiting to be moved by him. The account of his labors shall be given on his own authority.*

He arrived at Newport, September 14. It was the Sabbath. "I think it the most pleasant entrance I ever yet saw. Almost all the morning the wind was contrary; but I found a very strong inclination to pray that we might arrive time enough to be present at public worship. Once I called the people, but something prevented their coming. At last, finding my impression increase upon me, I desired their attendance immediately. They came, with a strong assurance we should be heard. We prayed the Lord, that he might turn the wind, that we might give him thanks in the great congregation, and also that he would send such to us as he would have us to converse with, and who might show us a lodging. Though the wind was ahead when we began, yet when we had done praying and came up out of the cabin, it was quite fair. With a gentle gale we sailed most pleasantly into the harbour, got into public worship before they had finished the Psalms, and sat, as I thought, undiscovered. After service was over, a gentleman asked me if my name was not Whitefield. I told him, yes. He then desired me to go to his house, and he would take care to provide lodgings and necessaries for me and my friends. I went, silently admiring God's goodness in answering my prayers so minutely. Several gentlemen of the town soon came to pay their respects to me, among whom was one Mr. Clapp, an aged dissenting minister, but the most venerable man I ever saw in my life. He looked like a good old Puritan, and gave me an idea of what stamp those men were who first settled New England. His countenance was very heavenly. He rejoiced much in spirit at the sight of me, and prayed most affectionately for a blessing on my coming to New England." In the evening, in company with Mr. Clapp and

* A large part of it is in his own words, as indicated by marks of quotation; and in such parts as are abridged, his phraseology has been retained as far as practicable. The account is taken from his original Journal, published soon after his visit, and preserved in the library of the Athenæum. Some may think that the writer should have followed his revised Journal; but that would have shown what Whitefield *approved* some years afterwards, and not what he *was*, at the time of his first visit. And justice to his opponents requires that passages in his original Journal, which were among the causes of their opposition, should appear.

others, he visited Mr. Honeyman, the minister of the Church of England, and requested the use of his pulpit. Honeyman hesitated, and asked him what extraordinary call he had to preach on week days, which was disorderly. Whitefield told him, none, but the apostolic injunction, "As we have opportunity, let us do good to all men." After consultation, Honeyman told Whitefield, that if his preaching would promote the glory of God and the good of souls, he was welcome to use his church as often as he would, during his stay in town. Whitefield then agreed to use it at ten in the morning and three in the afternoon. After a short visit to the governor, whose plainness pleased him, he went to the house of Mr. Bowers, the man who first addressed him when coming out of church. The house was soon filled with company. He expounded and prayed about an hour, and then retired to his lodgings. Such was his first day in New England.

The next day he breakfasted with Mr. Clapp, read prayers and preached according to his appointment, to some three thousand hearers, great numbers of whom were affected. After evening service he received the following letter, dated that day at Newport.

"*Reverend Sir and beloved Brother,*

"Although mine eyes never saw your face before this day, yet my heart and soul have been united to you in love by the bond of the Spirit. I have longed and expected to see you for many months past. Blessed be God, mine eyes have seen the joyful day. I trust, through grace, I have some things to communicate to you, that will make your heart glad. I shall omit writing any thing, and only hereby present my hearty love, and let you know that I am waiting now at the post of your door for admission. Though I am unworthy, my Lord is worthy, in whose name I trust I come. I am, your unworthy brother,

JONATHAN BARBER."

"On reading it, I could not but think this was one of those young ministers whom God had lately made use of in such a remarkable manner at the east end of Long Island. I sent for him, and found he was the man. My heart rejoiced. We walked out, and took sweet counsel together; and amongst other things, he told me that he came to Rhode Island under a full conviction that he should see me there, and had been waiting for me eight days; for, he said, these words were mightily impressed upon his heart: 'Is not Aaron the Levite thy brother? I know that he can speak well, and also he cometh forth to meet thee, and when he seeth thee he will be glad in his heart; and I will be with thy mouth, and with his mouth, and will teach you what ye shall do.' What rendered this the more remarkable was, I had no intention of sailing into Rhode Island till about three days before I left Carolina; and also, I had a great desire to put in, if I could, at the east end of Long Island, to see this very person, whom the great God now brought unto me. Lord, accept our thanks, sanctify our meeting, and teach us both what we shall do, for thine own name's sake." In the evening, he exhorted a great multitude at Mr. Clapp's, who dismissed him with his blessing. The next day, he felt "a little low in the morning, but was enabled to read prayers, and preach with much flame, clearness, and power," and to larger audiences than on the previous day. The legislature adjourned, that its members might hear him. He received several invitations to visit other places, and the Newport people made him promise, by divine permission, to visit them on his return from Boston. His hearers were attentive, and many wept. In the afternoon, he conversed and prayed with several who were affected by his labors. In the evening, he says, "I went, as I thought, privately, to a friend's house; but the people were so eager after the word, that in a short time I believe more than a thousand were before the door, besides those that were within, and filled every room in the house. I therefore stood upon the threshold and spoke for near an hour on these words: 'Blessed are they that hunger and thirst after righteousness, for they shall be filled.' Blessed be God, it was a very solemn meeting. Being night, I could not see how the hearers were affected, but the Lord assisted me in speaking." He then called to take leave of Mr. Honeyman, "and had some close talk with him about the new birth."

He thought Rhode Island a place where much good might be done. The people were sadly divided among themselves. The established church (Episcopal) he found in good order as to externals, but many of the head members were exceeding great bigots. Nor was it much better in the other communions. "All, I fear, place the kingdom of God too much in meats and drinks, and have an ill name abroad for running of goods." He said to them one day in his sermon, "What will become of you, who cheat the king of his taxes?" This made them all look at each other, like men conscious of their own and each other's guilt.

On Wednesday he left Newport. About noon, he preached at Bristol, at the request of the court, which was in session there. At eight o'clock on Thursday evening, he was met, about four miles from Boston, by the governor's son, several other gentlemen, and one or two ministers, who were at a gentleman's house, waiting for him. A large funeral, and some uncertainty as to his arrival, prevented a more numerous attendance. He was conducted into Boston, to the house of Mr. Staniford, brother-in-law to Dr. Colman, who had invited him to be his guest. His heart was low, and his body weak; but at the request of several ministers, and other gentlemen who called upon him, he led their united devotions in thanksgiving for his safe arrival, and prayer for a blessing on his labors.

He slept well that night, and the next morning "perceived fresh emanations of divine light break in upon and refresh" his "soul." Several ministers and others visited him; among whom was Josiah Willard, Esq., secretary of the province, a man fearing God, with whom he had corresponded for some time. The governor, Belcher, received him with the utmost respect, and requested frequent visits. He attended public worship at the Church of England, and waited on the Commissary home, who received him very courteously. As it was a day on which that clergy met, he saw five of them together. One of them began with him, "for calling *that Tennent* and his brethren faithful ministers of Christ." He answered, that he believed they were. They questioned the validity of Presbyterian ordination, and quoted, from his journal, his own words against him. He replied, that perhaps his sentiments were altered. "And is Mr. Wesley altered in his sentiments too, said one; for he was very strenuous for the church and against all other forms of government, when he was at Boston. I answered, he was then a great bigot; but God had since enlarged his heart, and I believed he was like minded with me, as to this particular." They then went into a doctrinal discussion, which continued till Whitefield, finding how inconsistent they were, took his leave, resolving that they should not have the opportunity of denying him their pulpits. However, they treated him with more civility than any clergymen of his own church had done for a long while.

In the afternoon, he preached to about four thousand people in Dr. Colman's meetinghouse, (Brattle Street,) and, as he was told, with great success. In the evening, he exhorted and prayed with such as came to his lodgings. The next day, he preached in Dr. Sewall's meetinghouse, (the Old South,) to about six thousand * hearers ; afterwards, on the Common, to about eight thousand, and at night to a thronged company at his own lodgings.

On Sabbath morning he heard Dr. Colman ; in the afternoon preached "to a very thronged auditory, and with great and visible effect, at Mr. Foxcroft's meetinghouse." Foxcroft was senior pastor of the First Church, now in Chauncy Place. The Rev. Charles Chauncy was his colleague. The house was in Cornhill Square, not far from the Old State House, and was usually called the "Old Brick." Immediately after the sermon he preached on the Common, to about fifteen thousand ; and again at his lodging, as usual, to a greater company than before. "Some afterwards came up into my room. I felt much of the divine presence in my own soul, and though hoarse, was enabled to speak with much power, and could have spoke, I believe, till midnight."

Monday morning, he preached at Mr. Webb's meetinghouse, the "New North," at the corner of Clark and Hanover Streets. He says, there were "about six thousand hearers in the house, besides great numbers standing about the doors ;" but the house certainly could not contain more hearers than the Old South. "The presence of the Lord

---

* Whitefield was esteemed, in his day, a good judge of numbers. His estimates of his hearers were generally received by his contemporaries. It does not appear that even his enemies ever accused him of exaggeration in this respect. Yet these statements are incredible. The Old South meetinghouse is still standing, and, with its present arrangement of seats, will accommodate a larger audience than when Whitefield preached in it. According to Dickinson's Boston Almanac for 1837, a work of uncommon accuracy, it has seats, including the upper gallery, for twelve hundred and sixteen persons. With the closest "packing" of pews, aisles, porches, and stair-cases, and including all who could hear his powerful voice through the windows, his hearers must have been less than three thousand. Prince, a very safe man in such matters, estimated Whitefield's first audience at Brattle Street, at two or three thousand. Whitefield estimated the hearers of his farewell sermon on Boston Common, at thirty thousand. One of the newspapers of the day estimates it at twenty-three thousand, which, as twenty-three is not a round number, was probably the result of an attempt at computation. His estimates, therefore, though usually adopted by historians without questioning, and though given, for want of others, in this work, must be taken with considerable abatement.

was amongst them. Look where I would around me, visible impressions were made upon the auditory. Most wept for a considerable time." Webb was one of the most efficient promoters of the revival, and no church shared more largely in its blessings than this. Whitefield afterwards saw still greater things in this house. In the afternoon, he went to preach at Mr. Checkley's, in Summer Street; "but God was pleased to humble us by a very awful providence. For when the meetinghouse was filled with people, though there was no real danger, on a sudden the people were all in an uproar, and so unaccountably surprised, that some threw themselves out of the windows, others threw themselves out of the galleries, and others trampled upon one another, so that some were actually killed, and others dangerously wounded.* I happened to come in the midst of the uproar, and saw two or three lying on the ground in a pitiable condition. God was pleased to give me presence of mind, so that I gave notice, I would immediately preach in the Common. The weather was wet, but above eight thousand followed into the fields."

The next morning, he visited Mr. Walter, at Roxbury. Mr. Walter had been the colleague and was the successor of Eliot, "the apostle of the Indians." Those two men had been pastors of that church one hundred and six years. Whitefield was much pleased with him, and Walter was glad to hear, that Whitefield called *man* "half a devil, and half a beast." He preached that forenoon at Mr. Gee's meeting-house,† "but not to a very crowded auditory," because the people were in doubt where he would preach. He "preached in the afternoon at Dr. Sewall's, to a thronged auditory," and exhorted and prayed as usual at his lodgings; at neither place without effect.‡

The next day, he visited Cambridge, "the chief College for training up the sons of the prophets in all New England."

* Philip quotes, probably from the revised journal, "five were actually killed, and many dangerously wounded."

† The "Old North," in the North Square, formerly under the pastoral care of Cotton Mather. The house was taken down and burned for fuel by the British army, during the siege of Boston in 1776. The church was united with that at the "New Brick" in 1779, and called the "Second Church."

‡ Philip says, erroneously, that he preached twice at Gee's, "to immense audiences."

As his record of this visit produced important effects, it must be given entire. "It has one President, four tutors, upwards of one hundred students. It is scarce as big as one of our least colleges at Oxford; and, as far as I could gather from some who well knew the state of it, not far superior to our universities in piety and true godliness. Tutors neglect to pray with and examine the hearts of their pupils. Discipline is at a low ebb. Bad books are become fashionable among them. Tillotson and Clark are read, instead of Sheppard, Stoddard, and such like evangelical writers; and therefore I chose to preach from those words, — 'We are not as many, who corrupt the word of God;' and, in the conclusion of my sermon, I made a close application to tutors and students. A great number of neighbouring ministers attended, as indeed they do at all other times, and God gave me great freedom and boldness of speech. The President of the College and minister of the parish treated me very civilly. In the afternoon I preached again in the College yard, with particular application to the students. I believe there were seven thousand hearers. The Holy Spirit melted many hearts. The word was attended with a manifest power; and a minister soon after wrote to me, that he believed one of his daughters was savingly wrought upon at the time."

On Thursday, he preached the weekly lecture at the First Church; but, he says, "was so oppressed with such a sense of my base ingratitude to my dearest Saviour, that Satan would fain have tempted me to hold my tongue, and not invite poor sinners to Jesus Christ, because I was so great a sinner myself. But God enabled me to withstand the temptation; and since Jesus Christ had shown such mercy to me, and did not withdraw his Holy Spirit from me, the chief of sinners, I was enabled the more feelingly to talk of his love." This explanation of the workings of his own mind is as full of sound philosophy, as it is of deep and fervent piety. By such views of his own vileness, he was enabled to gain those views of the love of God, which were one principal element of his power over his hearers. That day, he and most of the Boston pastors dined with the Governor. "Before dinner, the Governor sent for me up into his chamber. He wept, wished me good success in the name of the Lord, and recommended himself, ministers and people, to my prayers. Immediately after dinner, at the Governor's motion, I prayed explicitly for them all; went in his coach to the end of the town, but had such a sense of my vileness upon my soul, that I wondered people did not stone me." He preached at Charlestown. "A gracious melting was discernible through the whole congregation, and I perceived much freedom and sweetness in my own soul, though the damp I felt in the morning was not quite gone off."

The next day he preached at Roxbury, from a little ascent, to many thousands of people, with much of the divine presence. Several came to him afterwards, telling how they were struck at the time under the word. He had a still larger audience in the afternoon, when he preached from a scaffold erected without the Rev. Mr. Byles' meetinghouse, in Hollis Street.

Saturday was a great day with him. He preached in the morning at Mr. Welsteed's meetinghouse, and in the afternoon, to about fifteen thousand people on the Common. "But oh how did the word run! It rejoiced me to see such numbers greatly affected, so that some of them, I believe, could scarcely abstain from crying out, that that place was no other than a Bethel, and the gate of heaven." He went to his lodgings. "The power and presence of the Lord accompanied and followed me. Many now wept exceedingly, and cried out under the word, like persons that were hungering and thirsting after righteousness. And after I left them, God gave me to wrestle with him in my chamber in behalf of some dear friends then present, and others that were absent from us. The Spirit of the Lord was upon them all. It made intercessions with groanings that cannot be uttered."

On the Sabbath, in the morning, he preached at the Old South, "to a very crowded auditory, with almost as much power and visible appearance of God among us as yesterday in the afternoon," and collected £555 currency for his orphan house. These herculean labors produced bodily effects, which ordinary men would have thought really frightful. He "was taken very ill after dinner; vomited violently, but was enabled to preach at Dr. Colman's in the afternoon," where he collected £470. "In both places, all things were carried on with great decency and order. People went slowly out, as though they had not a mind to escape giving ; and Dr. Colman said it was the pleasantest time he had ever enjoyed in that meetinghouse through the whole course of his life." After sermon he felt refreshed ; supped early ; had an affectionate visit from the Governor ; preached to a great number of Negroes, at their request, and with great effect ; and on his return to his lodgings, exhorted the crowd who were waiting his arrival. "My animal spirits were almost exhausted ; and my legs, through expense of sweat and vomiting, almost ready to sink under me ; but the Lord visited my soul, and I went to bed greatly refreshed with divine consolations." Such bodily effects frequently accompanied his labors.

On this day, September 28, his celebrated admonitory letter to Wesley was dated, perhaps by mistake. He had received letters from England since his arrival, some of which gave sad accounts of Wesley's Arminianism and Perfectionism. He had written to some one, September 23 : "To affirm such a thing as perfection, and to deny final perseverance,—what an absurdity is this ! To be incapable of sinning, and capable of being finally damned, is a contradiction in terms." To Wesley he wrote :

"Dear Brother Wesley. What do you mean, by disputing in all your letters? May God give you to know yourself, and then you will not plead for absolute perfection, or call the doctrine of election "a doctrine of devils." My dear brother, take heed ; see that you are in Christ, a new creature. Beware of a false peace ; strive to enter in at the strait gate, and give all diligence to make your calling and election sure. Remember you are but a babe in Christ, if so much. Be humble, talk little, think and pray much. Let God teach you, and he will lead you into all truth. I love you heartily. I pray you may be kept from error, both in principle and practice. Salute all the brethren. If you must dispute, stay till you are master of your subject; otherwise you will hurt the cause you would defend. Study to adorn the gospel of our Lord in all things ; and forget not to pray for your affectionate friend, GEORGE WHITEFIELD."

Philip says, "whatever truth there may be in this tirade, it is more than defeated by its unhallowed form. Such an appeal could only exasperate." Scarce any writer has mentioned it, but in a similar style of condemnation ; and it was certainly an improper letter to be addressed by a very young man, to a minister of the gospel, so much his superior in age and acquirements, of established reputation for piety, and who had so long been the spiritual guide of its author. Whitefield would not have written it, had he not been, — to use his own language on another occasion, — " puffed up," by his reception and success at Boston. But Wesley certainly deserved that a good part of it should be administered, in a proper style and by a suitable person ; and it is no wonder that Whitefield, when such multitudes were acknowledging his power, when such a brilliant constellation of divines were almost worshipping him, and above all, when the accomplished Belcher was courting his instructions and reproofs, should admonish him as he would any other misguided soul.

Early on Monday morning, September 29, he left Boston on an excursion to the eastward. At Marblehead, he " preached to some thousands in a broad place in the middle of the town, but not with much visible effect." At Salem, he " preached to about seven thousand people. Here the Lord manifested forth his glory. One man was, I believe, struck down by the power of the word. In every part of the congregation, persons might be seen under great concern." He went on to Ipswich, where he was " kindly entertained at the house of Mr. R——rs, one of the ministers of the place." In 1743, John Rogers, aged 77, and Nathanael Rogers, were pastors of the First Church in Ipswich ; both ardent promoters of the revival ; as was also Daniel Rogers, of the same family. Whitefield learned with deep interest, that his host was a descendant of John Rogers, the celebrated martyr. The next day, he preached there to some thousands. " The Lord gave me freedom, and there was a great melting in the congregation." At Newbury, in the afternoon, " the Lord accompanied the word with power. The meetinghouse was very large, many ministers were present, and the people were greatly affected. Blessed be God, his divine power attends us more and more." Wednesday morning, he preached at Hampton, to some thousands in the open air. The high wind made it difficult to be heard, and he had not his usual freedom. A few, however, were affected. At Portsmouth, he preached " to a polite auditory, but so very unconcerned, that I began to question whether I had been speaking to rational or brute creatures. Seeing no immediate effects of the word preached, I was a little dejected ; but God, to comfort my heart, sent one young man, crying out in great anguish of spirit,

"What shall I do to be saved?" He went on to York, in Maine, "to see one Mr. Moody, a worthy, plain and powerful minister of Jesus Christ, though now much impaired by old age." The next morning, he was much comforted to hear from Mr. Moody, that he should preach to an hundred new creatures that morning; "and indeed I believe I did; for when I came to preach, I could speak little or no terror, but most consolation." He preached morning and evening. "The hearers looked plain and simple, and the tears trickled apace down most of their cheeks." He returned to Portsmouth that night, and the next morning preached to a far greater congregation, and with much better effect, than before. "Instead of preaching to dead stocks, I now had reason to believe I was preaching to living men. People began to melt, soon after I began to pray; and the power increased more and more, during the whole sermon." A collection of £97, 7s. 6d. was taken up for the orphan house, and Mr. Shurtleff, the pastor, in remitting it, wrote that numbers were under deep religious impressions. He preached to several thousands, and collected £41, 10s. at Hampton, and to large congregations the next day at Newbury, where he collected £80, 9s., and at Ipswich. The Sabbath was spent at Salem. He preached at eight in the morning at the meetinghouse, read prayers and assisted at the sacrament at the Episcopal church, and preached again at the meetinghouse; but saw no such power as on his former visit. At Marblehead, Monday forenoon, he says: "I was upon the mount myself, and the Lord attended his word with mighty power." Two ministers had collected £70, 2s. 6d, for his orphan house. In the afternoon he preached at Malden, but with less power than in the morning, and arrived that night at Boston. His health was much improved, and he went to rest, full of peace, and desiring to be thankful to the Lord, for causing him thus to renew his strength.

Tuesday, October 7, he preached morning and evening at Brattle Street; "both times with much power." There had been a report, that he had died suddenly, or was poisoned, and the people rejoiced to see him again alive. At the New North, (Mr. Webb's,) on Wednesday, there was more of the presence of God through the whole ministration, than ever he had known at one time through the whole course of his life. He went there with the Governor, in his coach, and preached morning and evening. "Jesus Christ manifested forth his glory; many hearts melted within them; and I think I was never so drawn out to pray for and invite little children to Jesus Christ, as I was this morning. A little before, I had heard of a child, who was taken sick just after it had heard me preach, and said, he would go to Mr. Whitefield's God, and died in a short time. This encouraged me to speak to the little ones. But O how were the old people affected, when I said, — Little children, if your parents will not come to Christ, do you come and go to heaven without them. There seemed to be but few dry eyes, look where I would. — I have not seen a greater commotion since my preaching at Boston. Glory be to God, who has not forgotten to be gracious. At the same time was collected £440."

On Thursday, he preached the public lecture at the Old South. He had chosen another text, but it was much impressed on his heart, that he should preach from our Lord's conference with Nicodemus. A great number of ministers were present; and when he came to the words, "Art thou a master in Israel, and knowest not these things," he says, — "The Lord enabled me to open my mouth boldly against unconverted ministers; to caution tutors to take care of their pupils; and also to advise ministers particularly to examine into the experiences of candidates for ordination. For I am verily persuaded the generality of preachers talk of an unknown and unfelt Christ; and the reasons why congregations have been so dead is, because they have had dead men preaching to them. O that the Lord may quicken and revive them, for his own name's sake. For how can dead men beget living children? It is true, indeed, God may convert men by the devil, if he pleases, and so he may by unconverted ministers; but I believe he seldom makes use of either of them for this purpose. No, the Lord will choose vessels made meet by the operations of the blessed Spirit for his sacred use; and as for my own part, I would not lay hands on an unconverted man for ten thousand worlds. Unspeakable freedom God gave me while treating on this head. In the afternoon, I preached on the Common to about fifteen thousand people, and collected upwards of £200 for the orphan house. Just as I had finished my sermon, a ticket was put up to me, wherein I was desired to pray for a person just entered upon the ministry, but under apprehensions that he was unconverted. God enabled me to pray for him with my whole heart; and I hope that ticket will teach many others not to run before they can give an account of their conversion. If they do, they offer God strange fire." The same day and evening, he attended the funeral of one of the provincial council, preached at the Almshouse, exhorted a great number who followed him there, and conversed with many who waited at his lodgings for spiritual advice. Ever since his return from the east, he had been thronged, morning and evening, with anxious inquirers.

The next day, he went with Mr. Cooper to Charlestown, preached with much demonstration of the Spirit, collected £156 for the orphan house; preached again at Reading, to many thousands, collected £51, 5s. and observed a considerable melting in the congregation. The next day, he preached from the meetinghouse door at Cambridge to a great body of people, who stood very attentively, though it rained, and were at the latter part of the sermon much affected. Here he collected £100.

The morning of the Sabbath, October 12, was spent in conversing with those who came for spiritual advice. He then preached with great power and affection at the Old South, which was so exceedingly thronged, that he was obliged to get in at one of the windows. He dined with the Governor, who came to him after dinner, weeping, and desired his prayers. He heard Dr. Sewall in the afternoon. He was sick during and after the exercises; but went with the Governor in his coach, and preached his farewell sermon on the Common, to near thirty thousand people. Great numbers melted into tears when he spoke of leaving them. The Governor then went with him to his lodgings. He stood in the passage and spoke to a great company, both within and without the doors; but they were so deeply affected, and cried out so loud, that he was obliged to leave off praying. The Governor was highly pleased to see the power of God. The remainder of the evening was mostly spent in conversation with inquirers.

In closing his account of this day's work, he exclaims: "Blessed be God for what he has done at Boston! I hope a glorious work is now begun, and that the Lord will stir up some faithful laborers to carry it on. Boston is a large populous place, very wealthy; has the form kept up very well, but has lost much of the power of religion. I have not heard of any remarkable stir in it for these many years. Ministers and people are obliged to confess, that the love of many is waxed cold. Both, for the generality, seem too much conformed to the world. There is much of the pride of life to be seen in their assemblies. Jewels, patches and gay apparel are commonly worn by the female sex. Little boys and girls I observed commonly dressed up in the pride of life; and the little infants that were brought to baptism, were wrapped in such fine things, and so much pains taken to dress them, that one would think they were brought thither to be initiated into, rather than renounce, the pomps and vanities of this wicked world. One thing Boston is remarkable for, — the external observation of the Sabbath. Men in civil offices have a regard for religion. The Governor encourages them, and the ministers and magistrates seem to be more united, than in any other place where I have been. Both were exceeding civil to me during my stay. I never saw so little scoffing; never had so little opposition. But one might easily foresee, much would hereafter arise, when I come to be more particular in my application to particular persons; for, I fear, many rest in a head-knowledge, are close Pharisees, and having only a name to live. Boston people are dear to my soul. They were greatly affected by the word, followed night and day, and were very liberal to my dear orphans. I promised, God willing, to visit them again, and intend to fulfil my promise when it shall please God to bring me again from my native country. In the meanwhile, dear Boston, adieu. The Lord be with thy ministers and people, and grant that the remnant that is left according to the election of grace, may take root downwards, and bear fruit upwards, and fill the land."

The next day, he left Boston for Northampton, to visit Edwards and the scene of the revival of 1735. The Governor took him in his coach to the ferry, kissed him, and with tears bade him farewell. He arrived at Concord about noon, preached twice to some thousands in the open air, "and a comfortable preaching it was. The hearers were sweetly melted down." Bliss, the minister, — of whose subsequent labors more perfect accounts ought to have been preserved,—wept abundantly. On Thursday he preached at Sudbury, to some thousands, with power, and observed a considerable commotion in the assembly. He next preached at Marlborough. His heart was dead at first, and he had but little freedom ; but before he finished, the word came with such demonstration of the Spirit, that great numbers were very much melted down. Here he found Governor Belcher, who went with him through the rain that night to Worcester. Here, on Wednesday, he "preached in the open air to some thousands. The word fell with weight indeed. It carried all before it." The Governor exhorted him to go on stirring up ministers, for reformation must begin at the house of God ; told him not to spare rulers, more than ministers,—no, not the chief of them ; requested Whitefield to pray for him, that he might hunger and thirst after righteousness, and took leave of him with tears. "I have observed," he remarks, with the most amusing simplicity, "that I have had greater power than ordinary, whenever the Governor has been at public worship. A sign this, I hope, that the Most High intends effectually to bring him home, and place him at his own right hand." It was indeed "a sign" that Whitefield felt flattered by the attentions of great men, and put forth his powers with more courage and joy, when they smiled upon him, and especially when they wept before him. In the afternoon, he preached at Leicester, but with less power ; and spent the night at Brookfield. Thursday morning, he "rose in great dejection, at the consideration of indwelling sin ; retired, and wept before the Lord ; preached, not with extraordinary freedom at first, but at last the word ran, and melted many down." At Coldspring, he preached to three or four hundred people, but perceived little moving among them, except for a few minutes.

On Friday, he arrived at Hadley, "a place where a great work of God was begun some few years ago. But lately the people of God have complained of deadness, and losing their first love. However, as soon as I mentioned what God had done for their souls formerly, it was like putting fire to tinder. The remembrance of it quickened them, and caused many of them to weep sorely." *

The same day, he crossed the river to Northampton,

* Gillies applies this to Northampton, and Philip copies the error.

where he spent several delightful days. "Mr. Edwards is a solid, excellent Christian; but at present weak in body. I think I may say I have not seen his fellow in all New England. When I came into his pulpit, I found my heart drawn out to talk of scarce any thing but the consolations and privileges of saints, and the plentiful effusions of the Holy Ghost in the hearts of believers. And when I came to remind them of their former experiences, and how zealous and lively they were at that time, both minister and people wept much, and the Holy Ghost enabled me to speak with a great deal of power." That evening, he exhorted several that came to Mr. Edwards' house.

The next morning, at Mr. Edwards' request, he spoke to his little children, who were much affected; rode with him to Hatfield, where he preached, but found himself much straitened; returned, and preached at Northampton with his usual power.

On the Sabbath, he "felt wonderful satisfaction in being at the house of Mr. Edwards. He is a son himself, and hath also a daughter of Abraham for his wife. A sweeter couple I have not yet seen. Their children were dressed, not in silks and satins, but plain, as becomes the children of those who in all things ought to be examples of Christian simplicity. She is a woman adorned with a meek and quiet spirit, and talked so feelingly and solidly of the things of God, and seemed to be such a helpmeet to her husband, that she caused me to renew those prayers which for some months I have put up to God, that he would send me a daughter of Abraham to be my wife. I find, upon many accounts, it is my duty to marry. Lord, I desire to have no choice of my own. Thou knowest my circumstances." He had not yet learned, if he ever did, that God is not pleased to make such "sweet couples" out of persons who have no choice of their own.

Whitefield "preached this morning, and perceived the melting begin sooner and rise higher than before. Dear Mr. Edwards wept almost during the whole time of the exercise. The people were equally, if not more affected; and my own soul was much lifted up towards God. In the afternoon the power increased yet more and more. Our Lord seemed to keep the good wine to the last. I have not seen such a gracious melting since my arrival. My soul was much knit to these dear people of God; and though I had not time to converse with them about their experiences, yet one might see they were for the most part a gracious, tender people, and, though their former fire might be greatly abated, yet it immediately appeared when stirred up."

On Sabbath evening, Whitefield left Northampton. Edwards accompanied him as far as the residence of his father, the Rev. Timothy Edwards, in East Windsor, Ct. And here some things must be related, which do not appear in the Journal. Edwards himself was compelled to give a statement of them, by misrepresentations which were put in circulation by President Clapp, in 1744.*

It appears that Edwards purposely took an opportunity to converse with Whitefield, alone, about *impulses*, and told him some reasons he had for thinking that he gave too great heed to such things. Whitefield did not seem to be offended; but yet did not appear inclined to converse much on that subject, or to be convinced by any thing that Edwards said to him. He also conversed with Barber, (who appears to have accompanied Whitefield in all this journey, though never mentioned in the Journal after leaving Newport,) about some of *his* impulses, "dealing very plainly with him, whereby he seemed to be displeased, and replied with earnestness and zeal." He adds: "It is also true, that I thought Mr. Whitefield liked me not so well for my opposing these things; and though he treated me with great kindness, yet he never made so much of an intimate of me, as of some others." He also conversed with Whitefield, in the presence of others, about judging other persons to be unconverted. He also believed, — though it does not appear that they conversed upon it, — that Whitefield "did aim at people's forsaking unconverted ministers, and to endeavor that there should be a supply of converted ministers, as far as in him lay." Whitefield also told him of his design of bringing over a number of young men from England, to be ordained by the Tennents, in New Jersey.

From these materials, mingled, probably, with indistinct recollections of information from other sources, President Clapp, some years afterwards, constructed a frightful story of Whitefield's errors and evil intentions, and, especially, of

* See Edwards' Letters to Clapp. O. S. Ch. Lib.

his design to turn the greater part of the ministers in New England out of their pulpits, and fill their places with converted men from England.

He preached on Monday at Westfield and Springfield, and on Tuesday at Suffield, to large audiences, and with his usual power. A little below Springfield, when crossing a bridge, he was thrown from his horse, and "stunned for a while;" but was soon able to remount and proceed. At or near Suffield, he met with a minister, "who said it was not absolutely necessary for a gospel minister to be converted;" meaning, doubtless, that though conversion was necessary for his salvation, it was not indispensable to his ministerial character and usefulness. This interview gave Whitefield a subject. "I insisted much in my discourse upon the doctrine of the new birth, and also the necessity of a minister's being converted before he could preach Christ aright. The word came with great power, and a great impression was made upon the people in all parts of the assembly. Many ministers were present. I did not spare them. Most of them thanked me for my plain dealing. But one was offended; and so would more of his stamp, if I was to continue longer in New England. For unconverted ministers are the bane of the Christian church; and though I honor the memory of that great and good man, Mr. Stoddard, yet I think he is much to be blamed for endeavouring to prove that unconverted men might be admitted into the ministry. How he has handled the controversy, I know not. I think no solid arguments can be brought to defend such a cause. — A sermon lately published by Mr. Gilbert Tennent, entitled, The Danger of an Unconverted Ministry, I think unanswerable." Stoddard, in his "Appeal to the Learned," assumes, that an unconverted minister is bound to continue in the performance of ministerial duties, and infers that unconverted men may therefore be admitted to the church. This opinion prevailed extensively; though all held it desirable that a minister should be a converted man. By his attacks on this opinion, and especially by thus endorsing Tennent's Nottingham sermon, Whitefield gave great offence.

He preached that afternoon at East Windsor, spent the night with Mr. Edwards, senior, and preached "to many thousands, and with much freedom and power," at Hartford in the morning and at Weathersfield in the afternoon. Here he met Messrs. Wheelock and Pomroy, "two young, faithful and zealous ministers of Jesus Christ." From this place, he had intended to go eastward as far as Plymouth, and return by another route to Providence; and notice had been given in the newspapers, of about twenty sermons, that he would preach at the times and places specified. He was afterwards blamed for making these appointments without first consulting the pastors of the several churches, thus giving countenance, it was said, to the practice of itinerants intruding into other men's parishes without their consent. The proceeding was certainly somewhat irregular, but Whitefield was not much to be blamed for it. The details were settled and the publication made by men in whose judgment and knowledge of the customs of the country he had a right to confide; and the appointments were believed, in all cases, and doubtless known in some, to be agreeable to the parties concerned. At Weathersfield, he found himself obliged to hasten to New York, and immediately published a note, recalling these appointments. * The next day, after preaching to thousands at Middletown and Wallingford, he arrived at New Haven.

It was now Friday, October 24. He preached that afternoon, twice on Saturday, and twice on the Sabbath; besides expounding at his lodgings and conversing with individuals. The power of his preaching increased to the last. Here he saw the Rev. Jedediah Mills, of Ripton, "a dear man of God," who "talked like one that was no novice in divine things." They dined together with Mr. Clapp, Rector of the College. In one of his sermons, he "spoke very closely to the students, and showed the dreadful ill consequences of an unconverted ministry." Mills, and some other ministers, "rejoiced in spirit." He called upon the Governor, whom he had observed to be greatly affected under the word. "When I came in, he said 'I am glad to see you, and heartily glad to hear you.' But his heart was so full that he could not speak much." He wept plentifully, and said, he was thankful to God for such refreshings in the way to our rest. Having collected near £40 for his orphan house, he left New Haven that evening. Probably, this visit prepared the way for the "great and general awakening" in the college four months afterwards.

* Boston News Letter, Oct. 16 and Oct. 22, 1740. Mass. Hist. Soc. Lib.

He preached with good success at Milford on Monday morning, and with less at Stratford in the afternoon. He was still more "restrained" at Fairfield and Norwalk on Tuesday, when the weather was cold, snow had fallen, and his hearers were few. Yet he observed that some were affected, and believed the Lord never let him preach in vain. His ride to Stanford, on Tuesday evening, was dark and rainy. That night he was visited with a great inward trial, so that he was pained to the heart. He was somewhat dejected before he went out of his lodgings the next morning, and somewhat distressed for a text after he got into the pulpit. "But at length the Lord directed me to one, but I looked for no power or success, being very low by my last night's trial. Notwithstanding, before I had preached half an hour, the blessed Spirit began to move on the hearers' hearts in a very awful manner. Young, and especially many old people, were surprisingly affected, so that I thought they would have cried out. At dinner, the Spirit of the Lord came upon me again, and enabled me to speak with such vigor against sending unconverted persons into the ministry, that two ministers, with tears in their eyes, publicly confessed, they had laid hands on young men, without so much as asking them whether they were born again of God or not. After dinner, finding my heart much enlarged, I prayed, and with such power, that most in the room were put under concern. And one old minister was so deeply convicted, that, calling Mr. Noble and me out, with great difficulty, (because of his weeping,) he desired our prayers; for, said he, 'I have been a scholar, and have preached the doctrines of grace for a long time, but I believe I have never felt the power of them in my own soul.' O that all unconverted ministers were brought to make the same confession. I was much affected by his ingenuity, [ingenuousness,] and, after having by prayer earnestly recommended him to God, I took horse, rejoicing exceedingly in spirit, to see how our Lord was getting himself the victory, in a place where Mr. Davenport, a native of Stanford and a dear minister of the blessed Jesus, had been slighted and despised. 'A prophet is not without honor, save in his own country and his father's house.'" Had Whitefield been a better judge of character, he would have been more guarded in his praises of Davenport; and he would not have set down as unconverted, every man whom his heart-searching sermons led to suspect the soundness of his own hope. He proceeded the same day to Rye, in the province of New York. His reflections on leaving New England must be given entire.

"But here I think it proper to set up my Ebenezer, and, before I enter into the province of New York, to give God thanks for sending me into New England. I have now had an opportunity of seeing the greatest and most populous parts of it; and, take it altogether, it certainly on many accounts exceeds all other provinces in America, and, for the establishment of religion, perhaps all other parts of the world. Never, surely, was so large a spot of ground settled in such a manner, in so short a space as one hundred years. The towns through Connecticut, and eastward towards York, in the province of Massachusetts Bay, near the river side, are large and well peopled, and exceeding pleasant to travel through. Every five or ten miles you have a meetinghouse, and I believe there is no such thing as a pluralist or non-resident minister in both provinces. Many, perhaps most that preach, I fear, do not experimentally know Christ; yet I cannot see much worldly advantage to tempt them to take upon them the sacred function. Few country ministers, as I have been informed, have sufficient allowed them to maintain a family. God has remarkably, in sundry times and in divers manners, poured out his Spirit in several parts of both provinces; and it often refreshes my soul, to hear of the faith of the good forefathers who first settled in these parts. Notwithstanding they had their foibles, surely they were a set of righteous men. They certainly followed our Lord's rule, — sought first the kingdom of God and his righteousness; and, behold, all other things God added unto them. Their seed are now blessed, in temporal things especially; and, notwithstanding the rising generation seem to be settled upon their lees, yet I believe the Lord hath left more than seven thousand who have not bowed the knee to Baal. The ministers and people of Connecticut seem to be more simple and serious than those that live near Boston, especially in those parts where I went. But I think the ministers preaching almost universally by notes, is a certain mark they have in a great measure lost the old spirit of preaching. For though all are not to be condemned that use notes, yet it is a sad symptom of the decay of vital religion, when reading sermons becomes fashionable where extempore preaching did once almost universally prevail. When the spirit of prayer began to be lost, then forms of prayer were invented ; and I believe the same observation will hold good as to preaching. As for the universities, I believe it may be said, their light is now become darkness — darkness that may be felt ; and is complained of by the most godly ministers. I pray God these fountains may be purified, and send forth pure streams to water the city of our God. The Church of England is at a very low ebb ; and, as far as I can find, had people kept their primitive purity, it would scarce have got footing in New England. I have many evidences to prove, that most of the churches have been first set up by immoral men, and such as would not submit to the discipline of their congregations, or were corrupt in the faith. But I will say no more about the poor Church of England. Most of her sons, whether ministers or people, I fear, hate to be reformed. As for the civil government of New England, it seems to be well regulated, and I think at opening all their courts, either the judge or minister begins with a prayer. Family worship, I believe, is generally kept up. The negroes, I think, are better used, both in respect to soul and body, than in any other province I have yet seen. In short, I like New England exceedingly well, and, when a spirit of reformation revives, it certainly will prevail more than in other places ; because they are more simple in their worship, less corrupt in their principles, and consequently more easily brought over to the form of sound words, into which so many of their pious ancestors were delivered. Send forth, O Lord, thy light and thy truth, and for thine infinite mercy's sake, show that thou hast a peculiar delight in these habitable parts of the earth. Amen, Lord Jesus, amen."

---

## CHAPTER VIII.

### WHITEFIELD IN NEW YORK, AND AT THE SOUTH.

Having dined with the minister of the Church of England, preached and read prayers at Rye, spent the evening at East

Chester, preached there the next morning to about three hundred people, among whom he observed "a sweet melting," and preached to about five hundred from the steps of a public house at Kingsbridge, but without much visible effect, Whitefield arrived at New York, on the 30th of October. He told his friend Mr. Noble, on the way, that he expected but little movings at New York ; but Noble bade him expect great things from God, and told him of several who seemed to have been savingly wrought upon by his ministry when there before. "After supper the Lord filled my heart, and gave me to wrestle with him for New York inhabitants, and my own dear friends. To add to my comfort, the Lord brought my dear brother Davenport from Long Island, by whose hands the blessed Jesus has of late done great things," having given him, in his own parish, near twenty souls in about two months. "October 31, met with a bitter pamphlet wrote against me by some of the Presbyterian persuasion, and found freedom given me to answer it. I long since expected close opposition from that quarter. I believe it will be increasing daily." He also met with two volumes of sermons, published in London as delivered by him, though he had never preached from most of the texts. This "bitter pamphlet" is entitled "The Querists ; or an extract of sundry passages taken out of Mr. Whitefield's printed Sermons, Journals, and Letters, together with some scruples proposed in proper Queries raised on each remark ; by some members of the Presbyterian persuasion." The authors call themselves members of congregations belonging to the Presbytery of New Castle, and the Queries were submitted to that Presbytery at their meeting at Whiteclay Creek, September 9, 1740 ; with a request that the Presbytery would either answer them or assent to their being printed. The Presbytery thought it best to "leave it to the people to print their remarks, and Mr. Whitefield himself to answer them." They were printed at Philadelphia, and reprinted at Boston before the end of the year.* The bitterness of the pamphlet consists in its convicting him of several erroneous expres-

* The copy in the O. S. Ch. Library is of the Boston edition. There was evidently, from the commencement of the awakening, a constant correspondence, and even a close alliance, between the "Old Side" Presbyterians and Whitefield's opposers in New England.

sions ; for its language, throughout, is courteous. Whitefield thanked them for the opportunity they had furnished, of publicly correcting some errors in his printed sermons ; confessed nearly all they had charged upon him ; mentioned others that they had not noticed ; and appealed to their own hearts, whether it was right, after all they had heard of his preaching in America, to censure him for a few unguarded expressions, dropped from his pen just as he came out of the University of Oxford. He assured them, that he did not find the least resentment stirring in his soul against them. In saying this, he did not deceive himself very much, for he certainly bore their criticisms more meekly than most men would have done ; but a man who absolutely felt *no* resentment, would never have thought of *saying* that he felt none. In the morning of this day, he preached at Mr. Pemberton's meetinghouse. He never saw the word of God fall with such weight in New York before. Look where he would, many seemed deeply wounded. "At night, the word was attended with great power." The next day, he finished his answer to the pamphlet. "The Lord enabled me to do it in the spirit of meekness." He "preached twice, to very crowded auditories, and neither time without power. In the evening exercise, some fainted, and the Lord seemed to show us more and more, that a time for favoring New York was at hand. O, wherefore did I doubt! Lord increase my faith!"

"Sunday, November 2. Preached this morning with freedom and some power, but was much dejected before the evening sermon. For near half an hour before I left Mr. Noble's house, I could only lie before the Lord and say I was a poor sinner, and wonder that Christ would be gracious to such a wretch. As I went to meeting, I grew weaker and weaker, and when I came into the pulpit, I could have chose to be silent rather than to speak." This was not only a prelude, but a preparation, for the burst that was to follow. It made him feel the worth of religion, and man's need of it. It brought his mind into close and agonizing contemplation of whatever is most powerful in divine truth. It drove him to prayer, to reliance on a wisdom and strength more than human. It at once summoned, guided, and strengthened all his powers. "After I had begun, the Spirit of the Lord gave me freedom, till at length it came down like a mighty rushing wind, and carried all before it." Whitefield, according to his own explanation, felt the presence of the Spirit, only in the ideas and emotions which the Spirit gave. "Immediately the whole congregation was alarmed. Shrieking, crying, weeping and wailing were to be heard in every corner, men's hearts failing them for fear, and many falling into the arms of their friends. My soul was carried out, till I could scarce speak any more. A sense of God's goodness overwhelmed me. After I came home, I threw myself upon the bed, and, in awful silence, admired the infinite freeness, sovereignty and condescension of the love of God." Then, after witnessing the marriage of Mr. Barber, whom he met in Rhode Island, and who was going with him to Georgia, "Divine manifestations flowed in so fast"—such views of God opened to his mind,—"that my frail tabernacle was scarce able to sustain them. My dear friends sat round me on the bed sides. I prayed for each of them alternately with strong cries, and pierced, by the eye of faith, even within the veil. I continued in this condition for about half an hour, astonished at my own vileness and the excellency of Christ, and then rose full of peace and love and joy. O, how am I obliged to my enemies! God has remarkably revealed himself to my soul, ever since I have seen the pamphlet published by the Presbyterians against me."

After preaching twice on Monday, to increasing congregations, and observing, at both times, a "great and gracious melting among the people, but no crying out," he went to Staten Island. There, on Tuesday, he preached from a wagon, to three or four hundred people. "The Lord came among them." Here he met Gilbert Tennent and Mr. Cross, who told him of the progress of the good work in New Jersey and Maryland. After the sermon he rode to Newark, where he preached, as he thought, with little effect. "However, at night, the Lord manifested forth his glory. For coming down to family prayer, where I lodged, and perceiving many young men around me, my soul, as it were, melted down with concern for them. After singing, I gave a word of exhortation; with what power, none can fully express, but those that saw it. O, how did the word fall like a hammer and like a fire!"

On Wednesday, he went to Baskinridge, Mr. Cross' parish, where he found that Mr. Davenport, according to appointment, had been preaching to about three thousand people. "As I went along, I told the people my soul wept for them, and I was persuaded within myself that the Lord would in that day make his power to be known amongst them. In prayer, I perceived my soul drawn out, and a stirring of affections among the people. I had not discoursed long, but the Holy Ghost displayed his power ; in every part of the congregation, somebody or other began to cry out, and almost all melted into tears. This abated for a few moments ;" but an incident, which Whitefield seized with his characteristic skill, or rather, with an instinct of feeling, more unerring than skill, quite overpowered them. A little boy, seven or eight years old, began to weep "as though his little heart would break. Mr. Cross, having compassion on him, took him up into the wagon, which so affected me, that I broke from my discourse, and told the people the little boy should preach to them ; and that God, since old professors would not cry after Christ, had displayed his sovereignty, and out of an infant's mouth was perfecting praise. God so blessed this, that an universal concern fell on the congregation again. Fresh persons dropped down here and there, and the cry increased more and more." In the evening, Tennent preached in Mr. Cross' barn, about two miles off, "excellently well, upon the necessity and benefit of spiritual desertions." What a subject, for a sermon in a barn in the night ! It was powerfully felt. "I then began to pray, and felt the Spirit of God working in me mightily. A great commotion was soon observed among the hearers. I then gave a word of exhortation. The Lord's presence attended it in a surprising manner. One, in about six minutes, cried out, 'He is come, he is come,' and could scarce sustain the discovery that Jesus Christ made to his soul." The idea of the pardoning love of God in Christ, as ready and sufficient to satisfy all the wants of his soul, bursting at once upon his mind, that had been in agony to find some ground of hope, produced a joyful revulsion of feeling which he could scarcely bear. What wonder, if a clear, distinct image of Christ, on his cross, or crowned with thorns, or smiling from his throne, was then before his mind ! Or rather, how could it be otherwise ?

The next morning, he exhorted, sung and prayed with the people at the barn, and, after some delightful conversation, rode to New Brunswick, Gilbert Tennent's home. Here he found letters from Georgia. One of them informed him that a minister was coming over to supply his place, which rejoiced him much, as he had resolved to give up the "living." "A parish and an orphan house together are too much for me. Besides, God seems to show me it is my duty to evangelize, and not to fix in any particular place." Here William Tennent met them, and it was decided that Gilbert should go to Boston. When it was first proposed, Gilbert was unwilling to go, "urging his inability for so great a work;" for, whatever may be the propriety of the term now, Boston was then, unquestionably, the "literary emporium" of the whole country, and its ministers, as a body, were eminently holy men; and Gilbert, though never daunted at the sight of opposers, felt unfit for the station which he must occupy amongst them. But after full consultation and prayer, it was thought to be his duty to go, and he said, "The will of the Lord be done." Passing by Trenton, in company with Davenport, and having twice narrowly escaped drowning, Whitefield arrived on Saturday evening at Philadelphia.

The next day, he preached twice in the house which his friends were building for him. The roof was not yet up, but a temporary floor was laid and pulpit raised, and "several thousands" attended. "Both in the morning and evening, God's glory filled the house; for there was great power in the congregation." He stayed here more than a week, preaching daily, and talking with those who had been affected by his discourses.

"It would be almost endless," he remarked at its close, "to recount all the particular instances of God's grace, which I have seen this week past. Many that were before only convicted, now plainly proved that they were converted, and had a clear evidence of it within themselves. My chief business was now to build up and to exhort them to continue in the grace of God. Notwithstanding, many were convicted almost every day, and came unto me under the greatest distress and anguish of soul. Several societies are now in the town, not only of men and women, but of little boys and little girls. Being so engaged, I could not visit them as I would; but I hope the Lord will raise me up some fellow laborers, and that elders will be ordained in every place.

Then shall we see a glorious church settled and established in Philadelphia." The church was afterwards established, and Gilbert Tennent became its pastor.

Whitefield left Philadelphia, November 17, and, passing over into New Jersey, preached at Gloucester. His heart "was low," and he could not preach with his usual vigor. "However, there was an affecting melting, and several, who had been in bondage before, at that time received joy in the Holy Ghost." He rode on to Greenwich, where he "preached to a few, with scarce any power." The next day, in a congregation of two thousand at Pilesgrove, he "saw only a few affected;" but at night he prayed and exhorted with great power in the family where he lodged. On the 19th, at Cohansie, where Gilbert Tennent had prepared the way for him, he "preached to some thousands, both morning and afternoon. The word gradually struck the hearers, till the whole congregation was greatly moved indeed, and two cried out in the bitterness of their souls after a crucified Saviour, and were scarce able to stand." His "soul was replenished as with new wine, and life and power flew all around." At Salem, on the 20th, he preached in the morning in the court-house, and in the afternoon in the open air before the prison, to about two thousand. "Both times, God was with us." The next morning he preached in the court-house at New Castle, where he "observed some few affected, and some few scoffing." Here he was joined by Charles Tennent. As they went on they met Mr. Anderson, who had opposed him last spring at Fagg's Manor, and who proposed to have a "conference" with him. "I told him," says Whitefield, "since he had begun by sending the Queries in public, I was resolved to decline all private conversation. This, as I afterwards found, highly offended him." Perhaps he had some reason to be offended; for, so far as any public act was concerned, Blair and Charles Tennent had as much to do with sending out the Queries, as Anderson. At Whiteclay Creek, where "many thousands were waiting to hear the word," two or three more of Anderson's associates were present; and Whitefield sang, with "unspeakable comfort," the twenty-third psalm:—

> "In presence of my spiteful foes,
> He does my table spread."

Here "the melting soon began, and the power increased more and more, till the greatest part of the congregation was exceedingly moved. Several cried out in different parts, and others were to be seen wringing their hands and weeping bitterly. The stir was ten times greater than when I was here last." At Fagg's Manor he preached to "many thousands," among whom there was a "wondrous powerful moving," but not so great as on his former visit. At Nottingham he had a large congregation, notwithstanding the rain. Here his doctrine distilled "like the dew." At Bohemia, in Maryland, "preached in the afternoon to about two thousand, and have not seen a more solid melting, I think, since my arrival. Some scoffers stood on the outside, but the Holy Spirit enabled me to lay the terrors of the Lord before them, and they grew more serious." The next day, Tuesday, November 25th, he arrived at Reedy Island,* where he waited for a wind till December 1, and then sailed for Charleston. During this detention, he preached almost daily, and with good effect. He "was greatly delighted to see the captains of ships, and their respective crews, come constantly to hear the word on shore, and join in religious exercises on board."

On sailing from Reedy Island, he wrote in his journal: "But before I go on, stop, O my soul, and look back a little on the great things the Lord hath done for thee during this excursion. I think it is now the 75th day since I arrived at Rhode Island. My body was then weak, but the Lord has much renewed its strength. I have been enabled to preach, I think, one hundred and seventy-five times in public, besides exhorting very frequently in private. I have travelled upwards of eight hundred miles, and gotten upwards of £700 sterling in goods, provisions and money for my poor orphans. Never did God vouchsafe me such great assistances. Never did I perform my journeys with so little fatigue, or see such a continuance of the divine presence in the congregations to whom I have preached. All things concur to convince me, that America is to be my chief scene of action."

Whitefield, having touched and preached at Charleston by the way, reached Savannah on the 20th of December; and after rejoicing over a few instances of conversion, and having

---

* Not Rhode Island, as Gillies has it.

arranged the affairs of the orphan house, he preached his farewell sermon on the evening of the 29th, and left the place the next day, to embark for England. January 1, 1741, he was at Jonathan Bryan's, where he preached in the evening. "The Lord made it a Bethel." Hugh Bryan was present. He had lately lost his wife. Whitefield copied his letter, giving an account of her death, into his journal, with evident gratification. It shows that both Bryan and his wife, though very pious persons, perhaps, were rather weak-minded, and not very well informed, and that Whitefield immensely overrated them.

On arriving at Charleston, Whitefield found that some, of whom he had hoped well, had fallen away; but the greatest part continued steadfast, while his enemies were even more enraged than formerly. His connexion with the Bryans had furnished them with an opportunity to show it. Hugh had written a letter, in which, among other matters, "it was hinted that the clergy break their canons." At Jonathan's request, Whitefield had corrected it for the press. It was published this week. Hugh was apprehended, and on his examination, being asked, confessed that Whitefield had corrected it, and made some alterations in it.

In consequence of this confession, Whitefield received on Saturday a summons to appear and answer for having "composed a false, malicious, scandalous and infamous libel against the clergy" of South Carolina. He gave securities to appear by his attorney at the next quarter-sessions, under penalty of £100 proclamation money. "Blessed be God," he exclaimed in his journal, "for this further honor. My soul rejoices in it. I think this may be called persecution. I think it is for righteousness' sake." The next morning he preached on Herod's sending the wise men to find out Christ, professing a desire to worship him, but intending to kill him; persecution, under pretence of religion. The afternoon sermon was on the murder of Naboth; the abuse of power by men in authority. "My hearers," he says, "as well as myself, made the application. It was pretty close." No doubt it was.

From this time till Friday, when he embarked for England, he preached twice a day, and expounded in the evening, to increasing congregations, and with increasing power. "I never received such generous tokens of love, I think, from

10*

any people before, as from some in Charleston. They so loaded me with sea-stores, that I sent much of them to Savannah." Contrary winds detained him till January 24, when he passed the bar. After a pleasant voyage, he arrived at Falmouth on Wednesday, March 11, rode post to London, and on the next Sabbath preached on Kennington Common.

---

## CHAPTER IX.

**The Revival in Boston. The period from Whitefield's Departure to the Arrival of Davenport; including the Labors of Gilbert Tennent.**

The history of this period shall be given nearly in the words of the Rev. Thomas Prince, junior pastor of the Old South Church. He says: —

"Upon Mr. Whitefield's leaving us, great numbers in this town were so happily concerned about their souls, as we had never seen any thing like it before, except at the time of the general earthquake. And their desires were excited to hear ministers more than ever; so that our assemblies, both on lectures and Sabbaths, were surprisingly increased." Of the time of the earthquake, he remarks in a note: "Though people were then generally frightened, and many awakened to such a sense of their duty as to offer themselves to our communion, yet very few came to me then under deep convictions of their unconverted and lost condition, in comparison of what came now. Nor did those who came to me then, come so much with the inquiry, What shall we do to be saved, as to signify they had such a sense of their duty to come to the Lord's Table, that they durst not stay away any longer." To proceed: —

"Upon the Rev. Mr. Gilbert Tennent's coming and preaching here, the people appeared to be yet much more awakened about their souls than before. He came, I think, on Saturday, December 13th, this year; preached at the New North on both the parts of the following day; as also on Monday in the afternoon, when I first heard him, and there was a great assembly.

"He did not indeed at first come up to my expectation; but afterwards exceeded it. In private converse with him, I found him to be a man of considerable parts and learning; free, gentle, condescending; and, from his own various experience, reading the most noted writers on experimental divinity, as well as the Scriptures, and conversing with many who had been awakened by his ministry in New Jersey, where he then lived, he seemed to have as deep an acquaintance with the experimental part of religion as any I have conversed with; and his preaching was as searching and rousing as ever I heard.

"He seemed to have no regard to please the eyes of his hearers with agreeable gesture, nor their ears with delivery, nor their fancy with language; but to aim directly at their hearts and consciences, to lay open their ruinous delusions, show them their numerous, secret, hypocritical shifts in religion, and drive them out of every deceitful refuge wherein they made themselves easy, with the form of godliness without the power. And many who were pleased in a good conceit of themselves before, now found, to their great distress, they were only self-deceived hypocrites. And though, while the discovery was making, some at first raged, as they have owned to me and others, yet in the progress of the discovery many were forced to submit; and then the power of God so broke and humbled them, that they wanted a further and even a thorough discovery; they went to hear him, that the secret corruptions and delusions of their hearts might be more discovered; and the more searching the sermon, the more acceptable it was to their anxious minds.

"From the terrible and deep convictions he had passed through in his own soul, he seemed to have such a lively view of the divine majesty, the spirituality, purity, extensiveness and strictness of his law; with his glorious holiness, and displeasure at sin, his justice, truth and power in punishing the damned; that the very terrors of God seemed to rise in his mind afresh, when he displayed and brandished them in the eyes of unreconciled sinners. And though some could not bear the representation, and avoided his preaching; yet the arrows of conviction, by his ministry, seemed so deeply to pierce the hearts of others, and even some of the most stubborn sinners, as to make them fall down at the feet of Christ, and yield a lowly submission to him.

"I do not remember any crying out, or falling down, or fainting, either under Mr. Whitefield's or Mr. Tennent's ministry, all the while they were here; though many, both women and men, both those who had been vicious, and those who had been moral, yea, some religious and learned, as well as unlearned, were in great concern of soul.

"As to Mr. Tennent's preaching: It was frequently both terrible and searching. It was often for matter justly terrible, as he, according to the inspired oracles, exhibited the dreadful holiness, justice, law, threatenings, truth, power, majesty of God; and his anger with rebellious, impenitent, unbelieving and Christless sinners; the awful danger they were every moment in of being struck down to hell, and being damned for ever; with the amazing miseries of that place of torment. But his exhibitions, both for matter and manner, fell inconceivably below the reality: And though this terrible preaching may strongly work on the animal passions and frighten the hearers, rouse the soul, and prepare the way for terrible convictions; yet those mere animal terrors and these convictions are quite different things.

"Such were the convictions wrought in many hundreds in this town by Mr. Tennent's searching ministry: and such was the case of those many scores of several other congregations as well as mine, who came to me and others for direction under them.* And indeed by all their converse I found, it was not so much the terror as the searching nature of his ministry, that was the principal means of their conviction. It was not merely, nor so much, his laying open the terrors of the law and wrath of God, or damnation of hell; (for this they could pretty well bear, as long as they hoped these belonged not to them, or they could easily avoid them;) as his laying open their many vain and secret shifts and refuges, counterfeit resemblances of grace, delusive and damning hopes, their utter impotence, and impending danger of destruction; whereby they found all their hopes and refuges of lies to fail them, and themselves exposed to eternal ruin, unable to help themselves, and in a lost condition. This searching preaching was both the suitable and principal means of their conviction.

* "The same kind of searching preaching by our own ministers and others, I also observed was the most successful means of bringing people into powerful convictions, or clear and awakening views of their sinful and lost condition, and their absolute need of Christ to find and save them."

"On Monday March 2, 1741, Mr. Tennent preached his farewell sermon to the people of Boston, from Acts xi. 23, to an auditory extremely crowded, very attentive and much affected, in Dr. Colman's house of worship. It was an affectionate parting, and as great numbers of all conditions and ages appeared awakened by him, there seemed to be a general sadness at his going away.

"Though it was natural for them to resort abundantly to him by whom it pleased the sovereign God chiefly to awaken them, for advice in their soul concerns; yet while he was here, many repaired to their ministers also, and many more and oftener when he was gone. Mr. Tennent's ministry, with the various cases of those resorting to us, excited us to treat more largely of the workings of the Spirit of grace, as a spirit of conviction and conversion, consolation and edification in the souls of men, agreeable to the Holy Scriptures, and the common experiences of true believers.

"And now was such a time as we never knew. The Rev. Mr. Cooper was wont to say, that more came to him in one week in deep concern about their souls, than in the whole twenty-four years of his preceding ministry. I can also say the same as to the numbers who repaired to me. By Mr. Cooper's letter to his friend in Scotland, it appears, he has had about six hundred different persons in three months' time; and Mr. Webb informs me, he has had in the same space above a thousand.

"Agreeable to the numerous bills of the awakened put up in public, sometimes rising to the number of sixty at once, there repaired to us both boys and girls, young men and women, Indians and Negroes, heads of families, aged persons; those who had been in full communion and going on in a course of religion many years. And their cases represented were; a blind mind, a vile and hard heart, and some under a deep sense thereof; some under great temptations; some in great concern for their souls; some in great distress of mind for fear of being unconverted; others for fear they had been all along building on a righteousness of their own, and were still in the gall of bitterness and bond of iniquity. Some under flighty, others under strong convictions of their sins and sinfulness, guilt and condemnation, the wrath and curse of God upon them, their impotence and misery; some for a long time, even for several months under these convictions:

some fearing least the Holy Spirit should withdraw; others having quenched his operations, were in great distress lest he should leave them for ever: persons far advanced in years, afraid of being left behind, while others were hastening to the great Redeemer.

"Nor were the same persons satisfied with coming once or twice, as formerly, but again and again, I know not how often; complaining of their evil and cursed hearts; of their past and present unbelief, pride, hypocrisy, perfidiousness, contempt of Christ and God, and alienation from them, their love and captivity to sin, and utter impotence to help themselves, or even to believe on Christ, &c., renouncing every degree of worthiness in and utterly condemning themselves; greatly afraid of deceiving their own souls; and earnestly desirous of being searched, discovered, and shown the true way of salvation.

"The people seemed to love to hear us more than ever. The weekly Tuesday evening lectures at the church in Brattle street were much crowded and not sufficient. April 17, 1741, another lecture was therefore opened every Friday evening at the South Church; and soon after, another lecture every Tuesday and Friday evening was opened at the New North; three of the most capacious houses of public worship in town, the least of which I suppose will hold three thousand people; besides the ancient lecture every Thursday noon at the Old Church, and other lectures in other churches.

"Nor were the people satisfied with all these lectures: But as private societies for religious exercises, both of younger and elder persons, both of males and females by themselves, in several parts of the town, now increased to a much greater number than ever, viz., to near the number of thirty, meeting on Lord's day, Monday, Wednesday and Thursday evenings; so the people were constantly employing the ministers to pray and preach at those societies, as also at many private houses where no formed society met: and such numbers flocked to hear us as greatly crowded them, as well as more than usually filled our houses of public worship both on Lord's days and lectures, especially evening lectures, for about a twelvemonth after.

"Some of our ministers, to oblige the people, have sometimes preached in public and private at one house or another, even every evening, except after Saturday, for a week together; and the more we prayed and preached, the more enlarged were our hearts, and the more delightful the employment. And O, how many, how serious and attentive were our hearers! How many awakened and hopefully converted by their ministers! And how many of such added soon to our churches, as we hope will be saved eternally! Scarce a sermon seemed to be preached without some good impressions.

"As the church to which I belong—within six months from the end of January, 1741, were threescore joined to our communicants, the greater part of whom gave a more exact account of the work of the Spirit of God on their souls in effectual calling, as described in the Westminster Assembly's Shorter Catechism, than I was wont to meet with before; besides many others I could not but have charity for, who refrained from coming to the table of Christ, for want of a satisfying view of the work of renovation in them. Mr. Tennent being so exceeding strict in cautioning people from running into churches, taking the sacred covenant, and receiving the Lord's Supper, the seal thereof, until they had saving grace; that divers, brought to very hopeful dispositions, yea, some, I doubt not, to embrace the Saviour in all his offices, were through fear and darkness kept from coming into full communion. Or otherwise, many more I believe, would have entered; who, had they the like experiences a year before, I doubt not would have readily offered themselves, and we should have as readily received them, and would now, as some of the most hopeful Christians. So far did Mr. Tennent's awakening ministry shake their hopes and hinder them, that those whom I apprehended to be thrifty, and thought myself obliged to encourage, I found the impressions of his preaching had discouraged.

"By Dr. Colman's letter of June 8, 1741, it appears 'that in 1741, in April, there were nine or ten, and in May were nineteen added to his church; among whom (says the Doctor) were many of the rich and polite of our sons and daughters.'

"And the Rev. Mr. Webb, senior pastor of the New North, just now informs me with respect to his church and people, in the following words: — 'Admissions to full communion of those hopefully wrought upon in the late day of grace, about one hundred and sixty : of which one hundred and two from January, 1741, to 1742. Of the above mentioned, by far the greater part have since given hopeful signs of saving conversion. And many more give good evidences of grace ; but for the reasons in your account [above], cannot be prevailed upon to come to the table of the Lord.

"In this year 1741, the very face of the town seemed to be strangely altered. Some, who had not been here since the fall before, have told me their great surprise at the change in the general look and carriage of people, as soon as they landed. Even the negroes and boys in the streets surprisingly left their usual rudeness. I knew many of these had been greatly affected, and now were formed into religious societies. And one of our worthy gentlemen expressing his wonder at the remarkable change, informed me, that whereas he used with others on Saturday evenings to visit the taverns, in order to clear them of town inhabitants, they were wont to find many there, and meet with trouble to get them away ; but now, having gone at those seasons again, he found them empty of all but lodgers.

"And thus successfully did this divine work, as above described, go on in town, without any lisp, as I remember, of a separation, either in this town or province, for above a year and a half after Mr. Whitefield left us." Then Davenport arrived, and the aspect of things was suddenly and sadly changed. But what then occurred, must be related in another connexion.

---

## CHAPTER X.

**The Revival in New England. Natick, Wrentham, and Bridgewater. Exhorters and Raptures in Bridgewater.**

### NATICK.

The revival in this town seems to have been worthy of a more particular account than we have of it. Here convictions began before Whitefield's arrival in New England ; though they were for some time concealed from all but those who felt them. The pastor, the Rev. Oliver Peabody, wrote, July 4, 1743. *

"There have been very observable strivings of the ever blessed Spirit on the hearts of many, especially young people, in convincing and enlightening, and I hope converting them, in my neighbouring towns; as in Medfield, Dedham, Needham, Medway, and Sherbourn, &c. where the ministers have been lively and faithful. And among my little people, (I would mention it to the glory of the rich grace, and of the blessed Spirit of God,) there have been very apparent strivings and operations of the Holy Ghost among Indians and English, young and old, male and female. There have been added to our church, of such as I hope shall be saved, about fifty persons of different nations, since the beginning of last March was two years, whose lives in general witness to the sincerity of their profession. Here, we have never had any crying out in an extraordinary manner, but the Holy Spirit has been pleased to work in a more calm way; but I hope effectually. But I must mention it, although with sorrow, that for some months past, (although some are under powerful operations,) yet there has not appeared so much of the genuine operations of the Spirit as heretofore; people's minds have seemed and do seem too much taken up with disputing about persons and things; some are for one minister and some for another; and some, I think I may say, cannot bear sound doctrine; which with us has arisen, as I apprehend, from some ignorant and erroneous persons, who have spread and propagated corrupt doctrines. As a specimen of this, they say I preach dangerous doctrines, because I have preached that a person may be converted and not certainly know it."

### WRENTHAM.

Of the revival in Wrentham, the Rev. Henry Messenger, pastor of the First Church, and Rev. Elias Haven, pastor of the Second, have given a more particular account, dated August 12, 1743. †

"The people of this town, so far as we can learn, or have had opportunity to observe, have generally been externally sober and honest; have kept up a great deal of external

* Chr. Hist. Vol. I. page 183. † Ibid. 238.

religion, especially in their families, and the house of God; so that the generations that have risen up from time to time, have generally been instructed, from their very early youth, in the first principles of our holy religion. But, alas! for a long time past, the power of godliness has been evident but in comparatively few instances, till the blessed revival of religion the Almighty God has lately favored us with. And just before the descent of these late remarkable showers of divine influence, religion was plainly in a languishing condition. Even some externals of it began to be more and more neglected; insomuch that in the year 1739, there were but two in the whole town admitted to the Lord's table: and vices of various sorts were much more prevalent than before.

"The first open and public manifestation of the Lord's return to us by the power of his grace, was on the twenty-sixth of February, 1741. It was the day appointed by the government to be kept with solemn fasting and prayer throughout this province, to implore the blessings of Heaven on our nation in the war with Spain, &c. and the day in course for the public lecture preparatory to the administration of the Lord's Supper in the Second Church in this town; where on this double occasion the minister preached from Zechariah, 12: 10. There appeared, especially in the afternoon, a very uncommon attentiveness upon the word, a wonderful tenderness upon the assembly. The tokens of a very serious concern were visible on many faces. And though there is sufficient reason to believe that many persons, before this, were under considerable convictions, and abode so after the day above said, yet they kept their concern very much to themselves until some time in March following, when they could no longer conceal their distresses; they began to lament their own cases to one another, and to come frequently to their minister under soul-trouble. It was very agreeably surprising almost daily to hear of new instances of young persons (for the work of God's Spirit seemed to be chiefly on young people) in great concern, what they should do to be saved. The same thoughtfulness seemed to run from house to house, and from soul to soul; and their complaints against themselves were very much the same.

"It was but a little while after this, before the same Spirit's operations of the same kind were equally remarkable in the First Parish and congregation in the town. Particularly on the annual fast, April 23, 1741, was a very open and public display of divine grace there, very much as mentioned above, in the other congregation, when the minister preached from Jeremiah 26 : 13 ; and many were brought under strong convictions, and thenceforward many flocked to their minister, especially young people, under soul distress.

"The powerful awakenings and convictions on persons' minds spread from neighbourhood to neighbourhood, so that by midsummer there were instances in all parts of the town under great concern to know what they should do to be saved. Yea, it appeared to us, so far as we could observe in our respective parishes, that very few houses, if any in the town, were passed by and left without some observable spiritual concern on some or other of the family. Our people, in general, became much more attentive in time of public worship. Their countenances being generally solemn, listening, and tender, showed their extraordinary appetite for the word ; and it became a very common thing with us to have a great part of the assembly in tears at hearing the word, and especially when they heard the glad tidings of the gospel, and they were invited to rest their weary souls in Christ the Saviour. While we endeavoured with great plainness to show unto sinners their guilt and danger, and to open the awful contents of the law to them, these truths would often have their proper effect, in alarming guilty consciences, and filling the minds of many with great concern for their own souls ; and then the gospel news of a Saviour, and the freeness of divine grace, would marvellously melt a great part of our congregations into tears, and persuade them, by divine help, to seek the great salvation. Nor have we seen reason as yet to think any other, than that many of these earnest seekers were sure finders of the pearl of great price.

"Our people grew very desirous of lectures, that they might have more frequent opportunities for spiritual instruction, and to join in social worship ; where we found God often bestowed his blessing.

"Many of our people, living three or four miles or more from our places of public worship, are necessitated to tarry at or near about the meetinghouses, through the intermission, between forenoon and afternoon exercises ; and there used to be little else but vain and worldly talk among most. But upon the late remarkable divine influence on people's minds, there was a wonderful change in this regard among, we think, the greatest part of our people. It became a common thing for them to retire in small companies to different places, for religious conferences or reading, and sometimes these exercises were mixed. And more lately there are several societies that spend part of the intermission in praying, reading, and singing together. So that on many accounts the intermission, as well as time of public exercises of God's worship, is very remarkably holy to the Lord, esteemed honorable, and a great delight unto the more serious among us. And even the time of travel to and from our places of public worship has often been sweetly redeemed for pious discourse between two or three, as they walk in company together.

"We are satisfied that the general concern upon people's minds, which prevailed among us above two years ago, and has not ceased, did not arise from a disposition to conform to the prevailing custom of people around us; for this was the first town which was so remarkably visited and blessed by sovereign grace, within many miles. And it evidently appeared that many would be under the same concern at the same time, and would be agreeably surprised when they unexpectedly found one another uttering the same complaints relating to the state of their own souls.

"It is also very evident that this general awakening was not from the influence of travelling ministers (though we are satisfied God has made use of some of them for the revival of religion in many places); for there was but one sermon preached in the town in such a way, and that to a small auditory.

"And here it is very observable, that there was a spirit of conviction on the hearts of many, in the winter, before it was externally very evident; when, by the extremity of the winter and depth of the snow, many of our people could not for many Sabbaths together attend on the ordinary and stated exercises of religion; so clearly was it the work of God. Nevertheless, we are glad to own, that the news of many conversions in Northampton and other towns in that part of the country some years before, and of some remarkable success of the gospel in some parts of England and America, were means of stirring up thoughtfulness in many, and encouraged godly persons to pray with the more confidence for the outpouring of the Holy Ghost also on us.

"Many came to offer themselves to join in church-fellowship, whom we looked upon ourselves obliged to examine particularly of their experiences, which gave them reason to hope that they could in sincerity enter into solemn covenant with God and his people. Our times for the administration of the Lord's Supper in each church are two months apart; and into the Second Church in the town (which before consisted of sixty-three communicants, and the parish of about seventy families), just before the sacrament, May 3, 1741, were admitted twenty-four more; and between the said third of May and the first of July following, were admitted thirty-seven more; and considerable numbers afterwards from time to time.

"Into the First Church in the town (which before consisted of ninety-two communicants, and the parish of about one hundred and twenty families) were admitted, just before the sacrament, June 7, 1741, twenty more; and then before August 1, thirty-eight more; and then before October, eighteen more; and before the administration of the Lord's supper there have constantly been a considerable number admitted ever since; never less than five, except twice, and usually more at a time. In short, one hundred and thirty-six communicants are added to the First Church, and eighty-nine to the Second, since April, 1741.

"Thus greatly are the numbers of our communicants increased; and we had opportunity to discourse with each of those admitted into the respective churches under our particular watch, of the state of their souls, and with many of them several times; as well as with a considerable number who were professors before, and came to us in this remarkable day, fuller of concern about their souls than usual; and many that have been brought under some convictions, who yet stand off from the Lord's table.

"There was, about a year ago, some decay among us. But, blessed be God, among all those that we looked upon, in a judgment of charity, to be born from above, there has not one turned an open apostate, nor evidently and impenitently scandalous in their behaviour; nor have the generality of those who have been in any considerable measure awakened, returned, in this time of decay, to their former heedless and airy way of living; neither did the state of religion among us, nor the face of the town, appear to be at all the same as three years ago; and we have reason to think, that all this time conversions were more frequent than for some years before 1740.

"And the Lord, the overflowing fountain of grace, hath been pleased to visit us with another plentiful shower of grace, and so strengthen that which he had wrought for us. It is now above half a year since a second revival of religion began to be very observable in the town; first, in the First Parish in the town, and very soon after in the Second. As to the substance of the work, it appears to us to be the same as was remarkably among us above two years ago, of which there has never since been a cessation. But there are a few things observable, which are circumstances attending the work of God's grace now among us, in which there is some difference. There have not been so great numbers brought under convictions and the spirit of bondage now as before; according to our observation. Some, who have of late been under strong convictions, have been more suddenly pricked to the heart, and brought into greater distress, than before. Some, who, we have reason to hope, were sincere converts unto God before the time which we are now speaking of, have now been brought into exceeding great distress, at renewed and clearer discoveries of their own hearts, and a more bitter remembrance of their sins.

"Not a few of real Christians have been more remarkably quickened now than before, in their Christian walk.

"There have been not a very few among us within seven or eight months past, that have cried out with great agonies and distress, or with high joys on spiritual accounts, and that in time of religious exercises. But these two things we would observe relating to what we have seen of this nature, viz: First, that we are persuaded that very few, if any, among us, have cried out in such a manner while they could refrain; and we have ever cautioned persons against making any outcries in time of religious worship, if they could avoid it without doing too much violence to their nature, or turning their thoughts from divine things; though we have not thought it ordinarily proper to leave off speaking, or to have the persons so affected removed out of the house. And secondly, that we by no means account persons crying out in time of worship, falling down, or the degree of their joys or sorrows, that might occasion these effects on their bodies, to be any sign of their conversion, when separately considered;

and have carefully warned our people against such a way of thinking; though at the same time we cannot but think that most who have so manifested their sense of things, were under the operations of the Holy Ghost at the same time, which occasioned these outcries; and that their inward experiences were substantially the same as theirs who have been savingly converted to God, as we hope, and have given no such tokens of their distress or joys.

"Some among us have not been so well satisfied, nor so much delighted, with this late revival, as they seemed to be two years ago; and some, that seemed something awakened then, have appeared to look something strange upon what we take to be the same work, now it hath been attended with some uncommon circumstances. And we are concerned lest some have been prejudiced against the powerful manner in which God hath been pleased to carry on his own work, and so have lain the less open to convictions and benefit by gospel ordinances.

"We have not known trances, visions, revelations, or the like. We have had great freedom from the appearances of a censorious spirit in the subjects of this blessed work; though some tender and compassionate expressions have been misconstrued. We have not had a single instance, who hath pretended to authoritative exhorting, nor any that have pleaded for it; but Christian conference hath been much encouraged and practised among elder and younger people."

### BRIDGEWATER.

The Rev. John Porter, pastor of the church in North Precinct of Bridgewater, was one of "Whitefield's converts." His account of the revival in that town is dated October 12, 1743. After stating that "experimental religion and the power of godliness seemed to have taken their flight from Bridgewater," and that the greater part of the people who thought at all of religion, "rested in various duties, short of a saving closure with Christ," he proceeds:* "And so in general they remained, very secure and unconcerned about the great and momentous affair of securing the salvation of the soul, till sometime in the beginning of the year 1741, after the Reverend and dear Mr. Whitefield and Reverend

* Chr. Hist., Vol. I. p. 397.

Mr. Tennent had been at Boston, and through the province, preaching the everlasting gospel with such unweariedness and success. Whose names, especially the former, I shall always mention with respect and honor, whatever others may think or say of him, from the benefit one of the meanest and most unworthy of Christ's ministers hopes he received by his holy and fervent ministrations while at Boston. Be sure I knew nothing rightly of my sin and danger, of my need of a Saviour, of the way of salvation by him, neither was established in the doctrines of grace, (though a preacher, and one who endeavoured to instruct others in the way,) till I heard that man of God. And if the Lord had permitted me to have took the oversight of a flock, as I had a call to do, and had given my answer, the blind would have led the blind, and so, it is like, both would have fallen into the ditch. But he did not. Bless the Lord, O, my soul, and all that is within me, bless his holy name, for what he did for me, through the instrumentality of that man. And I was quickened and strengthened very much by Mr. Tennent's excellent sermons, and was desirous all should hear them, as I had done, and urged many to it.

"Few of the people in Bridgewater heard Mr. Whitefield, but the most did Mr. Tennent; for as this man of God, who had skill and will to win souls, was upon his return home, and passing through a neighbouring town in March, 1741, some of the Rev. ministers in Bridgewater, with myself, went to see him, in order to invite him to visit Bridgewater. Accordingly he came, and preached three sermons in the Rev. Mr. Perkins' meetinghouse in the western precinct; two in the day and one in the evening. And though the warning was short, the people in general not knowing it till that morning, and the season very difficult, by reason of the snow; yet there was a large and crowded assembly. They came from all parts of the town, and many, I believe, went away blessing God for the opportunity; though some mocked. It appears that some close hypocrites were detected, some secure awakened, and many of our young people convinced of the sin of spending away days and nights in singing and dancing, and other youthful sins, which they were much addicted to before, and greatly delighted in.

"After this, religion was more talked of in our town; particularly the great doctrines of our holy religion, were often the subject of conversation ; not for strife and contention, but information and edification.

" The people now, through the town, were very inquisitive to know how things were ; having heard of the revival of religion in some places. They appeared of a very teachable disposition ; they were swift to hear the word ; an uncommon thirst after it appeared in them. Our lectures, which were almost every week in one part of the town or another, were more generally attended than before, and with much greater seriousness and solemnity ; which encouraged us, the ministers in the town, to set up evening lectures, to be attended in all parts of the town ; which, excepting one, are upheld to this time ; besides all our lectures in private houses, which have not been a few, and occasional lectures from strangers, who come to visit us.

" Though but few, I believe, were as yet savingly converted and brought home to Christ, yet the concern on the minds of most continued and increased through the succeeding summer. The most were uncommonly thoughtful about the salvation of their precious souls. But, as I remember, in the beginning of the fall, 1741, convictions seemed at a stay, if not declining and wearing off from some.

" But upon this, two young men of Bridgewater, who had been for a time in Connecticut, (one had passed through his academical learning and was keeping school there ; the other was then a member of Yale College,) and had seen the great things God was doing for his people there, and in a judgment of charity had felt and experienced much of the power of divine grace on their own souls, returned to Bridgewater to visit their friends. And O ! the concern they appeared to have, (and we have no reason to think but it was real,) for their town's-folk, especially fellow youth, is not easily to be expressed ; which they manifested in all suitable and proper ways.

" They told our young people that on such a day, if they were willing, they would meet with them and sing and pray, and give them a relation of the great things God was doing in Connecticut, and what he had done for them since they saw them last ; to which they readily consented. When the day came, young and old went ; and I believe I should have gone, had I not been providentially absent. Accordingly, they did pray and sing with them, and gave them a friendly

Christian exhortation. And the Lord was with them, I doubt not. Some were awakened, —and those under concern, had their concern increased by means thereof. And seeing such effects following, they went on in this way for a while ; if not at the advice, yet at the connivance, of some of the ministers in the town. And whether their practice or our connivance was justifiable, as things were then circumstanced, I shall not take upon me now to say. But this I think I am obliged to say ; that if I believe the work going on so remarkably to be divine, as I most firmly do, they were greatly serviceable in promoting it in my dear charge. Here I would observe, that these were the only exhorters we have had. I think we have had no appearances of them since.

" After this, that grand and important question was in the mouths of most of my people, especially young people, What must we do to be saved ? Salvation seemed now to be the main concern of their souls, and the main business of their lives. Their secular affairs were at this time, in appearance, made a by-business. Meetings on account of religion were sought after, longed for, frequently attended, exceedingly thronged. And at almost every meeting about this time, which were very frequent, it evidently appeared God was with us in the convincing and converting and comforting influences of his Spirit. Some were awakened, many crying out under a sense of their sin and danger ; some hopefully converted, and some transported and over-borne with a sense of the love of God. I make not the least doubt, but there was joy in heaven among the angels, as well as among the saints on earth, in seeing and hearing of the glorious displays of the infinite power and sovereign free grace of God at our religious meetings. But this blessed shower did not long continue. It was not long before God, for our sin in not improving, and our ingratitude under, these showers of divine and heavenly grace, did depart from us as to the convincing and converting influences of his Spirit ; and many of those that were under good impressions, and had not received comfort in Christ, which many had, gradually lost them, and began to be somewhat careless and secure again. Now and then, it is true, I had the joy of seeing and hearing one convinced and converted, and it has been to this time ; but it is rare, like gleanings after the vintage.

" But in the judgment of charity, through the infinite compassions of God, the number is not small that have been savingly wrought upon among us in this great day of grace, and that are become real lively Christians. We have had added to the church between seventy and eighty; beside a considerable number that have owned the covenant and been baptized, that have not seen their way clear to come to the ordinance of the Holy Supper; the most of which are able to give to every one that asks them, with meekness and fear, all the satisfaction that can rationally be desired, or expected, that they are real Christians. They can give a clear, distinct account of a preparatory law-work, in all the parts of it; of their discovery of Christ, in his ability and willingness to save them in particular, and every way suited to their perishing circumstances, to make them completely and eternally happy; of their closing in with him as offered in the gospel; of the change of heart; and so consequently of principles, desires, inclinations and affections that perceptibly followed thereupon. And their lives and conversations, as far as I can observe myself, and learn from the unprejudiced, are corresponding and agreeing with their experiences.

"And now these, God is, through his abundant goodness, frequently visiting and refreshing by the gracious influences of his Holy Spirit. For although God has almost departed from us, as to the convincing and converting influences of his Spirit, yet he has not, as to the quickening, sanctifying and comforting influences thereof. Blessed be his name for it. God is verily with us in our religious meetings. It is frequent on lecture days and on Lord's days, while we are supplicating the divine Majesty, singing the high praises of God, hearing his word, celebrating the Holy Supper, that we see some of the above mentioned influences. Sometimes many of them have their frail tabernacles overborne with a sense of the great and distinguishing love of God the Father, in contriving, Son in purchasing, and Spirit in making application of redemption to their souls. Sometimes they have such a sense of the perfections of God, his holiness, justice, mercy, faithfulness, &c., as greatly weakens and overcomes the body. They have often such sweet tastes of redeeming love, and such blessed discoveries of the glories of God, beauties of Christ, holiness and happiness of heaven, as affects the body so greatly, that spectators have been ready to conclude that it would have dissolved the natural tie and union between the soul and body, and that their souls would have actually dismissed and left their bodies, and been conveyed by kind guardian angels in a chariot of love to the God and region of love. And to see the effects these discoveries have on them ; how humble, holy, heavenly, loving, and weaned from the world they are for a considerable time after, is abundantly refreshing and satisfying, and confirms further that their discoveries are true and genuine. Thus they are frequently visited and taught by the Holy Spirit ; so that they are growing Christians, in grace and knowledge. In grace, every true visit evidently transforms them more and more into the divine image and likeness. In knowledge, it is wonderful to see how their knowledge is increased, as to God, Christ, the doctrines of grace ; and as to themselves, their own hearts, the pride, envy, hypocrisy, deceit, and ingratitude of them. They see and know so much of their own vileness, that every one looks on himself as the most unworthy, and greatest miracle of mercy, and most beholden and indebted to the free grace of God. They are laboring after progressive holiness, to be perfect as their Heavenly Father is perfect. God grant their path may continue to be as the shining light, that shineth more and more unto the perfect day.

"Now of this number, many of them were, before this day of God's searching our Jerusalem with candles, as exact and strict in the performance of the externals of religion, as far as could be observed by man, as any among us, and had gained the charity of their neighbours ; but now see they built upon the sandy foundation of their own righteousness, and so had perished eternally, notwithstanding their blazing professions and the good opinion of others, had not God in mercy opened their eyes to see the way of salvation by Christ, and enabled them to embrace it.

"As to Antinomianism and enthusiastical phrensies, there are little or no appearances among us. Indeed, there is that among us that an Arminian would account Antinomianism, and one that never felt the power of divine grace on his own heart, would account enthusiasm. But this does not make it so. As far as I am capable of judging, their principles and practices are scriptural. God grant I may never have the melancholy occasion to think or say otherwise. As to trances, visions, &c., we have none, and I think have had none from the beginning."

## CHAPTER XI.

THE REVIVAL IN NEW ENGLAND. Lyme, and other places in that part of Connecticut. — The "Needful Caution in a Critical Day." — Pastors itinerating.

THE west parish in Lyme, Ct., which lies at the mouth of the Connecticut river, on the east side, opposite Saybrook, was the home of the Rev. Jonathan Parsons, who was one of the most efficient promoters of the revival. His account of the revival in his own parish, and of his labors in the vicinity, dated April 14, 1744,* is one of the most valuable documents of the time; especially when read in connexion with his sermon, delivered February 4, 1742, and entitled "a Needful Caution in a Critical Day." It should be remembered, too, that Windham and New London counties, where there were greater disorders than in any other part of New England, were near his residence, and the scene of some of his labors.

In less than six months after taking his first degree at Yale College, Mr. Parsons was invited by this church "to preach as a probationer for settlement." He arrived, February 29, 1730, and, in May following, the people invited him to become their pastor. Late in the summer, they renewed their call. He, however, was doubting about the validity of Presbyterial ordination. At length, having become convinced, "that the Scriptures make no difference between bishop and presbyter; that Christ alone is king of his church, and has given laws to it, and authority to execute them; and that no man has a right, by fines or civil force, to bind any man to worship God in this or that particular way," he consented to be ordained on the 17th of March, 1731. He then, in presence of the council and the brethren, expressly renounced the Saybrook platform of church government, and took for his rule "the general platform of the Gospel;" on which the church unanimously voted him to be their pastor, and the council proceeded to ordain him. The population of his

* Chrs. Hist. 2: 118.

parish was then "seven hundred and sixty eight souls, or thereabouts."

"The summer following my ordination, there was a great effusion of the Holy Spirit upon the people. There appeared to be an uncommon attention to the preaching of the word, and a disposition to hearken to advice; and a remarkable concern about salvation. It was a general inquiry among the middle aged and youth, What must I do to be saved? Great numbers came to my study, some almost every day for several months together, under manifest concern about their souls. I seldom went into a house among my neighbours, but they had some free discourse about religion, or were searching after the meaning of some texts of Scripture. I urged them very much to works, and gave it as my opinion (perhaps too hastily) that such awakened souls ought to attend upon the Lord's Supper, and in less than ten months fifty-two persons were added to the church. There were several whole families baptized. Many of the young people were greatly reformed. They turned their meetings for vain mirth into meetings for prayer, conference, and reading books of piety. There was a number of them kept a religious society about two years; and they not only behaved soberly, but took pains to dissuade others from levity and frothy conversation. But, although there was such a fair prospect of a considerable harvest of souls, I have no special reasons to make me think that many were savingly converted to God in that season of concern. Many, indeed, made an open profession of religion, but there were very few did it under a notion that saving grace is necessary in order to a lawful attendance upon the Lord's Supper. Nor have we, in our admissions to communion, ever acted upon that principle, but the contrary. Hence it came to pass that we found no use for relations, as they are called, but laid them by from the beginning of my ministry; though they had been of constant use in my predecessor's day."

In about three years from his ordination, he "saw cause to renounce Arminian principles, and to turn quite about in some of the most important doctrines of the Christian religion." He now felt obliged to tell his people that he could not reckon conversions by the number of those that had joined the church; that he feared few had really been converted during his ministry; that external profession and devotion, doctrinal knowledge and negative blamelessness, were not sufficient evidence of regeneration ; and that all, being spiritually dead by nature, must have a principle of spiritual life implanted, must have sensible communion with Christ, and live a life of faith, or they could not enter heaven. This his people called "censoriousness." They seem to have done little but quarrel with his doctrines for some time, till, as he says, "I was awfully deserted of God, and got into a very dull, legal frame myself ; and then some were better pleased."

This continued till the summer of 1740, when revivals, independently of each other, were beginning to appear in various parts of New England. Then, he informs us, "It pleased God to strengthen and enlarge my desires after the increase of Christ's kingdom, and to stir me up to more ardent endeavours after the eternal welfare of immortal souls.— The news of Mr. Whitefield's rising up with great zeal for holiness and souls, had a great influence upon my mind." He received an account of Whitefield's labors at Boston, from Dr. Colman, and went himself to hear him at New Haven, and some other places. "This" he says, "gave me a different turn of thought about him and his preaching, and satisfied me more fully that there were many misrepresentations of him and his views ; and I believe, served as a means to take off the prejudices that some among us had conceived against the effects of his ministry." It seems, therefore, that there were prejudices against him even then, in that region of Arminianism and ecclesiastical authority ; probably nourished by the correspondence, which is known to have been carried on, with the "Old Side" men of the Presbyterian Church. In March, 1741, he visited Hartford, to learn on the spot what he ought to believe concerning the "surprising operations" there, concerning which the country was full of reports. He returned, believing it to be a work of God.* On his return, he received letters from Dr. Colman, giving an account of the labors of Tennent, and their happy influence. All along, as he gathered information, he imparted it to one and another as he had opportunity ; and by this and other means, his people "were more generally roused up to bethink themselves, and converse about re-

* It does not appear that any account of these "surprising operations" was ever published. Church records extant at Hartford make no mention of them.

ligion." At last, March 29, he preached from Isaiah 60 : 8. " Who are these that fly as a cloud, and as the doves to their windows ?" His object was, to rectify mistakes, and give a correct history of the work of God that was begun in the land. This sermon, especially its application, had a greater visible effect upon his audience, than he had ever before witnessed. " Indeed, there were no outcries ; but a deep and general concern upon the minds of the assembly discovered itself at that time in plentiful weeping, sighs and sobs. Many told me, that they never had such an awakened sense of the danger of putting off the grand concern of their souls to a future season before, as God gave them under that sermon. They were surprised at their own past carelessness, and astonished that God had borne with them so long." Early in April, Tennent arrived, on his way home from Boston. He preached in the evening, seemed very dull, spoke with no freedom, and made only a feeble impression ; yet one of the communicants was convinced of sin, and in a few days apparently converted. The next morning he preached again, " to a very attentive and deeply affected auditory." Parsons afterwards found the effects of this sermon to have been much more extensive than he suspected at the time. Tennent went over to Saybrook, and many from Lyme followed, to hear him again. " There he preached a rational, searching sermon, suited to unconverted sinners and drowsy saints." But little effect was manifest during the delivery ; but some were very much enraged with the preacher afterwards. One man especially could not bear the sermon, it was so " censorious." He talked against it incessantly, and could not drive it from his mind, till finally " he was made to see that he was the very man to whose case it was suited, above any sermon that ever he had heard."

" After this, I observed that our assemblies were greater and more attentive at times of public worship than before. Sabbaths alone would not suffice for hearing sermons, but greater numbers still urged for frequent lectures. I was well pleased to observe such a flocking to the windows, and a hearing ear become general ; and therefore I readily consented, upon the request of the people, to preach as often as I could, besides the stated exercises of the Sabbath. Once every week I carried on a public lecture, besides several private ones in various parts of the parish. And I could not but observe about this time, that an evening lecture I had set up the winter before in a private house, for the sake of a young man that was a cripple, though at first exceeding thin (but seven persons, as I remember, besides the family) was now greatly increased, and in about a month grew up to several hundreds, so that I was obliged to turn it into a public evening lecture.

"Now it pleased God to encourage my heart, give me unusual freedom, and such a firm state of bodily health, that I could go through three times the service I had been able to endure at other times; so that I was able to study and write three sermons a week, and preach several others of my old notes (for I seldom in all the time preached without writing). Sometime in this month Mr. Griswold invited me to preach a lecture for him, and I consented. While I was preaching from Psalms 119: 59, 60, I observed many of the assembly in tears, and heard many crying out in very great bitterness of soul, as it seemed then by the sound of voices. When sermon was over, I could better take notice of the cause; and the language was to this purpose, viz., Alas! I'm undone; I'm undone! O, my sins! How they prey upon my vitals! What will become of me? How shall I escape the damnation of hell, who have spent away a golden opportunity under gospel light, in vanity? And much more of the like import. It is true, outcries were new and surprising at that time; but, knowing the terrors of the Lord, I was satisfied that they were but what might be reasonably accounted for, if sinners were under a true sense of their sins, and the wrath of a sin-hating God. And therefore I did not use any endeavours to restrain them at that time; but the greater number cried out of themselves and their vileness, the more I rejoiced in hope of the good issue. As I was satisfied that it was the truth they had been hearing, so, by their complaints, it appeared to be the force of truth that made them cry out, and threw many of them into hysteric fits. And, if I mistake not, every one that were so violently seized that night, have since given good evidence of their conversion; but that, their reverend pastor can give the best account of.

"The visible success of my ministry in that and some other lectures abroad, (though I rejoiced in the happy prospect of the advancement of the kingdom of our divine Lord,) was far from being a means to damp my hopes or slacken my

12*

endeavours at home. My heart burned with love to and pity for the people of my peculiar charge. I had constant supplies of argument flowing into my mind, and zeal to urge a speedy answer.

"By the latter end of April, our young people were generally sick of that vain mirth and those foolish amusements that had been their delight, and were formed into several religious societies for prayer and reading books of piety under my direction. Many of them were frequently in my study for advice; the bent of their souls was evidently towards the things of another world; whenever they fell into companies, the great salvation was the subject of their conversation. They were so generally displeased with themselves for past carelessness, and spending time in revels and frolics, that several, at the desire of others, came to me, and desired me to preach them a lecture upon the 14th of May (the day of our election in this Colony), which they had, for many years, accustomed themselves to spend in feasting, music, dancing, gaming, and the like. I complied with the request, and preached to a great assembly, from Matthew 24: 37, 38, 39. Upon which I observed, that Jesus Christ would certainly come to judge the world; and that, when he did come, he would find it overwhelmed in carnal security; and from these considerations I applied myself to those that had been secure and unwatchful, both among Christians and unconverted sinners, in a manner which I thought proper to awaken and convince. Under this sermon, many had their countenances changed; their thoughts seemed to trouble them, so that the joints of their loins were loosed, and their knees smote one against another. Great numbers cried out aloud in the anguish of their souls. Several stout men fell as though a cannon had been discharged, and a ball had made its way through their hearts. Some young women were thrown into hysteric fits. The sight and noise of lamentations seemed a little resemblance of what we may imagine will be when the great Judge pronounces the tremendous sentence of 'Go, ye cursed, into everlasting fire.' There were so many in distress, that I could not get a particular knowledge of the special reasons at that time, only as I heard them crying, 'Woe is me! What must I do?' And such sort of short sentences with bitter accents.

"Now those that could not restrain themselves, were generally carried out of the meetinghouse, and a second sermon was preached by Mr. Jewett to others that were able to attend; after which the assembly was dismissed, and my house soon filled with wounded souls; and I took pains to satisfy myself and others, by inquiring into the reasons of the trembling, crying, fainting, and other signs of fear that were so manifest in the assembly; and they declared in their own words, all to this purpose, viz., that a deep sense of past sensualities and careless neglects of the concerns of their souls; their slighting frequent and solemn warnings, and withstanding the calls of the gospel, together with a deep sense of their liableness, every moment, to be arrested and cast into the prison of hell, where those sinners lay that refused to hearken to the warnings given by Noah the preacher of righteousness, was truly the spring of all these various signs of distress. Some run back upon the sins of riper years (for there were several persons upwards of forty, and some of more than fifty years old, that discovered great concern by their pale countenances and tears, and trembling too). Some cried out of the hardness of their hearts, others of their unbelief. Some were crying, 'God be merciful to me, a sinner,' and others entreated Christians to pray for them. Thus they continued at my house for several hours; and after I had taken what pains with them I thought necessary for that evening, and prayed with them, they were advised to repair to their own places of abode; and accordingly, all that were able, went home.

"Now I thought the people in great danger, and especially those that were most deeply wounded. I knew, in all probability, that hell was in an uproar; the prince of darkness saw his kingdom shaking, and he was in great danger of losing many of his obedient subjects; many threatened rebellion, and were in danger of being accused of treason against his crown; and therefore, if possible, he would allure them back to former fidelity, persuade them to settle down upon the foundation of their own works, or drive them to utter despair of mercy. And therefore I dare not sit in my study the next day, (though that loudly called for me to be there,) but spent my time abroad among distressed souls, and others that fell in my way that were more lightly touched. Nor were private Christians contented in their fields or shops at home, when the fields were so white for the harvest; but some of them also, in their places, were helpers, in the work that seemed necessary to be done. The following evening a religious meeting was attended in a private house. I went to it, though I could not pretend to preach a sermon. I offered a few words of the miseries of the unconverted, the price that was now put into their hands, and the great danger of not improving it; but was obliged in a few minutes to desist, because the house was filled with outcries and bitter lamentation. The complaint was much the same with what it had been the day before.

"I continued to preach and exhort publicly, and from house to house, about six times a week through this month at home, besides attending upon distressed souls upon certain appointed days in my study. And though I spake to them with unusual moderation, in my study, (as well as in sermons about this time,) that I might have greater advantage to instruct their minds, yet I was commonly obliged to make several stops of considerable length, and intreat them, if possible, to restrain the flood of affection, that so they might attend to further truths which were to be offered, and others might not be disaffected. Some would after a while recover themselves, and others, I am satisfied, could not. I have thought since, whether I did not do wrong in endeavouring to restrain them. The pains they took with themselves to keep from outbreakings, was a greater hindrance to their hearing than their outcries were."

"I do not remember that I preached a sermon through the month, without some manifest tokens of the presence of God in our assemblies. Many were awakened, and convictions were deep. People flocked to my study daily, and in great numbers, deeply wounded, and the errand was, to lay open the state of their souls, and receive direction. Sometimes I had thirty in a day, and sometimes many more, all upon the grand affair of their souls.

"Many, with the greatest freedom, confessed that though they had a name to live, they were dead in trespasses and sins; and this not only in private, but to numbers at once. They did not think it matter of offense, if their neighbours believed them when they said it. They spake sensibly of it, as we might expect a condemned malefactor would do if he was going to the place of execution. They would solemnly declare that they never knew what real union to Christ was;

that they were strangers to sensible communion with the Father and his Son Jesus, and to the temper of the gospel, and had rested easy with merely external communion, or the form of godliness. Their distressed countenances, and free and frequent confessions that they were yet in the bonds of iniquity, together with their warnings to others, never to rest until they knew Christ was formed in them, proved awakening to many professors, and put them upon the search and inquiry into the reasons of their hope; and some were shaken off from their old foundation, supposing they had built upon the sand, whilst others had the more peace in believing.

"The like effects, sometimes more and sometimes less observable, continued through the summer. There were also many instances (and the number was daily increasing) of persons filled with great joy and comfort. It was common to hear of and to see them overcome, and fainting under high discoveries of God reconciled in Christ. Some also I have seen overcome with concern for others; and sometimes their concern terminated on particular persons, that they feared were in a state of sin.

"The conversation of the people in general, was religious. If at any time neighbours met, the great affairs of salvation were the subject of discourse. In the streets, in the fields, and in private houses, the discourse was instructive; some inquiring the way to life, others in their proper sphere endeavouring to help the distressed by their humble advice and counsel. Some, that knew the terrors of the Lord, would persuade the careless, and modestly recommend the grace of God to their acceptance, from their own experience of its sweetness. And as there were frequent inquiries about the things of infinite concern, so there was a great increase of knowledge in religious matters. According to the best observation I could make, I believe the people advanced more in their acquaintance with the Scriptures, and a true doctrinal understanding of the operations of the Holy Spirit in conviction, regeneration and sanctification, in six months' time, than they had done in the whole of my ministry before, which was nine years. Nor was this all, but many evidently looked upon sin with abhorrence. They appeared to be renewed in the spirit of their minds. Bitterness, and wrath, and anger, and clamor, and evil-speaking seemed to be put away from them, with all malice. Their fruit was unto holiness. Love to God and man, with their genuine fruits, were increasing. Rough and haughty minds became peaceful, gentle, and easy to be entreated. Lowliness, long-suffering, forbearance, a courteous deportment, beneficence, and tender-heartedness, meekness and moderation, to all appearance, seemed to increase abundantly. And to all these, we observed a delight in Christian fellowship, in breaking of bread, and in prayer. I think it cannot be expected that men, in their general course, should give clearer evidences of a Christian temper formed in them, than many did in that season. Their faith worked by love, and discovered itself in acts of piety towards God, charity and righteousness towards men, and sobriety towards themselves.

"We had some special seasons of divine influence in that time, both upon converted and unconverted, which I must not now relate; it would make the account too long; but I cannot pass over our pentecost, on the 11th day of the following October. I preached from Psalm 2: 12, upon the nature and necessity of faith in Christ; and then administered the sacrament of the Lord's Supper, to near three hundred souls, as I judge. It was a day never to be forgotten; but, I think, ought to be remembered with holy wonder and gratitude by all that were present. The house of the Lord was full of the glory of the Lord. It pierces me to the heart, that any have ever attempted to throw darkness over the rich grace of God that was so clearly discovered; or to misrepresent the gracious effects of those discoveries that were made to many. Though we had enjoyed much of the gracious presence of God in our assemblies before, yet, I think I never saw so much at any time as on that day. Especially when the Lord's Supper was administered, God poured out his Spirit in a wonderful measure. I spake a few things to the communicants, as I remember, concerning the mediatorial excellencies and love of Jesus Christ, when I came down to the communion table and began to break the bread; and then invited them all to come to him as well as to his table, and assured them, in his name, that they should be welcome to the rich treasures of his grace, which were open and free to all that would come. I had no sooner offered some things of this nature in a few short hints, but several of the church cried out in most bitter accents, of their piercing the Lord Jesus Christ by their unbelief, and showed the signs of distress in their countenances; whilst many scores were dissolving in tears. A considerable number trembled in the anguish of their souls, as though they had heard the thunderings and seen the lightnings from the thick cloud; whilst many more began to put on immortality, almost, in the look of their faces. I could not but think that the Lord Jesus was come to his table, and feasting their souls with his love, discovering his mediatorial glories to them; letting them taste of his preciousness, opening to them the mysterious wonders of his grace, and the like. But will you ask why I entertained such thoughts as these? I am willing you should know the reason. Their looks were all love, adoration, wonder, delight, admiration, humility. In short, it looked to me a resemblance of Heaven; where the shining hosts of angels and glorified saints are for ever before the throne of God, in the lowest prostration, crying 'Holy, holy, holy Lord God; thou art worthy to receive glory, and honor, and power, and blessing, and thanksgiving.' But some of those in distress, about the end of the distribution of the bread, appeared to be in a calm, and before the cup was poured, they seemed to have a delightful sense of something upon their minds. Their looks were changed from anguish to pleasure and admiration, love and humility, and the like.

"I was too much taken up with these things, and some discoveries which I trust were made to me, with the effects of them, to make any critical remarks upon any indecencies; though some few, not so well pleased with the appearances, have said, that there was one or two instances of these extraordinaries that were not decent the whole of the time of administration. One thing complained of as an indecency was, that two men embraced each other in their arms before the blessing was given. The fact, I suppose, is true; but others say it was after the blessing was given. Nor do I think it so very indecent, as some would represent it. Another thing complained of is, persons going about the meetinghouse in the sacrament time. This, I suppose, was true, that one single person, who was a subject of these influences, did go out of one pew into another upon some occasion just before the blessing was given, and some two or three others that, it seems, did not so well affect the prospect, went round the body of seats on one side of the house, and then out of doors. Blessed be God, that there was nothing further than I have related, which has been excepted against, as I remember. The general reverence and decency of behaviour in the subjects of this great grace was indeed admirable.

"Many old Christians told me, they had never seen so much of the glory of the Lord and the riches of his grace, nor felt so much of the power of the gospel before; they had never seen so clearly the infinite ocean of divine love; never been so sensible of the love of God to them, nor had such strong love so clearly in exercise to him. Several of them had the full assurance of faith, who had been seeking after it for many years, but were denied till that time. New converts were greatly refreshed and quickened. I cannot doubt whether they had the presence of the Comforter. Christ then appeared more lovely than the princes of this world. They sat under his shadow with great delight, and his fruit was sweet to their taste. They were feasted in his banqueting-house, and his banner over them was love. They could not support themselves, many of them, under the weight of it, they were so deeply affected with it. Had not Christ put underneath his everlasting arms for their support, I know not but many would have expired under the weight of divine benefits. And besides all this, I think we have a good evidence of the saving conversion of several of the communicants at the same time. The several discoveries they gave an account of, together with the effects of these discoveries, produced in a law-work and a true closure with Jesus Christ, gave me considerable hope of it; and a long time since, to observe their pious life and holy conversation, confirms my first hope that it was a reality, and no deception.

"Since that time, we have had many refreshing seasons, both in public worship and more private assemblies; and many hopeful conversions. Nor are public and private meetings the only places of these influences and effects; the closet, the field, the shop, and the kitchen, are all witnesses to them. It was no uncommon thing for Christians to be overcome in their private retirements, as they have told me of the happy seasons. In meditation at some times, and conversation at others, divine truth has been set in a clear light, and they have been made to know the truth of the gospel of the blessed God. But the work has not appeared, in a general way, so powerful since, as it did the first eight or nine months. Indeed, God gives witness to the truth of these things, at times, more or less, unto this day ; and will, I trust, until the end."

Many, who can understand how sinners should be overcome by a sense of danger, will be staggered at these accounts of intense, overpowering emotion in Christians, in view of purely spiritual objects,— of God, and the glorious truths that relate to him. But the fact that they did thus feel, and were thus overcome by their feelings, is undeniable. And the testimony is abundant, that such beholdings of the glory of the Lord did exert a transforming influence upon them, making them more humble, more kind, more patient, more ready for every good work, more entirely amiable in the eyes of all who love true goodness. It would scarce be possible to produce such effects on one of the congregations of the present day. The pulpit has labored so long, and so powerfully, to give all our religious thoughts a practical direction, to engage us in plans for accomplishing appreciable good here on earth, and we have been so thoroughly taught to expend our sensibilities in action for the good of others, that we should need a long and laborious training, to make us capable of such engrossing contemplation of objects purely spiritual. Whether we are, on the whole, the worse or the better Christians for the change, is a question not to be answered hastily. There can be no doubt that we are better than they for certain uses ; and perhaps we should be better still, if we had occasional seasons of contemplation and feeling, more like theirs.

The converts were chiefly from among the youth ; but three or four were upwards of fifty, two near seventy, and one ninety-three years of age. At the date of this account, the pastor says ; "I have reason to hope, about one hundred and eighty souls belonging to this congregation, have met with a saving change, since the beginning of the late glorious effusion of the Holy Spirit among us ; besides the frequent and more than common quickenings and refreshings of others, that were hopefully in Christ years before." In nine months, ending February 4, 1742, one hundred and fifty members were added to the church.

Still, Parsons did not pretend that all was pure in Lyme. "There have been many things amiss. I thought so from the beginning, and I think so still." Besides the opposition of enemies, "some I thought a little intemperate in their zeal at times, and for some things that it was hardly worth while to contend about. I have seen reason to alter my own conduct in several things; particularly, to treat those that opposed the work with greater candor and mildness, and to address myself to all conditions of men with more tenderness, than I did several times."

There were a few, who, for a time, inclined to favor Davenport's lay exhorters, his separate meetings, and his doctrine of impressions concerning future events; but these things never became prevalent. Two or three, who were not of the new converts, expressed their joy "several times" at religious meetings by laughing; and others, "under high spiritual discoveries," spoke out aloud during public worship, supposing that it would be as inoffensive as the crying out of the convicted; but such instances were few, and scarce any approved them. It had been reported, that "trances, visions, extraordinary missions and immediate revelations" were common among the new converts; but though he was extensively acquainted with them, and had conversed with thousands of them, he had "not met with a score who pretend to any such thing," and he doubted whether half that number could be found in Connecticut. And yet his acquaintance included the region where they were said to be most abundant.

The preservation of the converts and others at Lyme from the faults with which they were charged, was probably owing, in no small degree, to the "Needful Caution in a Critical Day." This sermon was preached February 4, 1742, about ten months from the commencement of the revival. The text was Titus 2: 8. "That he that is of the contrary part may be ashamed, having no evil thing to say of you." Its object was, to guard his people against errors in doctrine and practice, into which they were in danger of falling, and especially to urge the duty of abstaining from things which, though innocent in themselves, might lead to evil, or occasion needless reproach. After forcibly showing "the contrariety there is in men to the designs of divine grace," he urges that this "should be a strong persuasive with the children of God to improve in holiness, so that their opponents might have no evil thing to say of them." He grants that "the evil things which the happy subjects of the special grace of God are guilty of, are many times the unhappy occasion of the rising contrariety and opposition in others." The *occasion*, but not the *cause* ; for "my imperfections can no more be the *cause* of another man's sins, than my graces, if I have any, can be the cause of his goodness." But the strength of the sermon was in the "application."

"1. Let me caution and admonish all Christless sinners, whether professed opposers of the work of divine grace or not, that they do not stumble and cavil at the work of God's rich and free grace manifest at this day, from those errors and irregularities visible in the happy subjects of it. You may see by what has been offered, that I am not about to justify or excuse the sinful defects and foolish disorders of Christians. It is a matter of shame and deep abasement, (and that which hath called us together this day,) that those who were born heirs of death and immortal anguish, but are now graciously washed from their uncleanness in the blood of the blessed Jesus, and through his name have the free remission of all their sins, should be so unwatchful, so carnal in their behaviour, and such miserable patterns of humility and resignation to God, as many are. But then, dear souls, it is absurd in you to cavil against the gracious operations of the Holy Spirit, because the persons that declare the work of divine grace are guilty of some errors and defects. The saving, sanctifying influences of the blessed Spirit do not make men infallible. There is abundance of remaining blindness and corruption in the most holy men ; yea, perhaps more sin and corruption than grace and holiness in the most refined Christians. It is surely a great argument of your being blinded through lust or prejudice, that you dwell so much upon the follies of your neighbours, and would thereby hinder the success of the gospel. It is very much to be feared, at least, that you are strangers to the sanctifying influences of the Holy Spirit, when you can so easily pass over the table of rich dainties which God spreads for his own children, which while they feast upon, their souls are drawn out in rivers of pleasure and love ; and, like the crow, light upon and greedily pick every bit of filthy carrion you can meet with. By this, I do not invite you to approve of disorders ; but would humbly beseech and solemnly warn you not to be found fighting against God. Whilst you stand amazed at the rings of the wheels, as things too high and dreadful for you ; whilst you know not what to make of the effusions of the Holy Spirit, but are blundering at every thing amiss, when God is working a work of his astonishing grace before your eyes, which you will not believe; beware lest that come upon you which is spoken of by the prophet, —'Behold, ye despisers, and wonder, and perish.' Dear immortal souls, I beseech and persuade you, by the mercies of God, and the astonishing love of the Lord Jesus Christ, that you would not sacrifice the operations of the blessed Spirit to your *own* prejudice, arising from our imperfections.

"2. Let me warn and caution the children of God, now met together, to humble themselves before the Lord; that they carefully watch against every thing in principle and practice that has a tendency to bring any blemishes upon the work of divine grace, or to open the mouths of gainsayers, and be a stumbling-block in the way of their giving credit to the truth of it. Dear Christians, let me be able to bear record, that, to your power, yea, and beyond your power, you are willing to shut the mouths of the contrary part, and make them ashamed, having no evil thing to say of you. It is the reasonable expectation of God, that you give none occasion of offence to them that are without. It is the reasonable expectation of angels, who rejoice at the progress of the Redeemer's kingdom and the conversion of sinners, that you shun, to the uttermost, every folly that tends to embitter the spirits of men. Know you not that the present circumstances of the church of Christ, and the threatening aspect over it, do eminently call upon me, and all others that long for the prosperity of Jerusalem, to use great plainness of speech and holy vigilance? Especially in some of our towns, where God has shed abroad his love in the hearts of many; and so even with us, the glory of the Lord is evidently departing, and human passion and unallowed measures seem to be taking its place." Then he exhorts them, "as a means to recover the poor church from its wounds, and to prevent its being stabbed to death," to avoid several errors which he specifies. "1. Give no countenance to any mens' setting themselves up as the public teachers of the church." Brotherly exhortation, with becoming modesty, he approves, and urges as a duty; but not that laymen should set *themselves* up as teachers, and appoint meetings over which they are to preside, and in which they are to teach, like ministers. This, he contends, is unscriptural; and no fancied ability or desire to do good, or hope or supposed experience of usefulness, can justify them in attempting to do good by breaking the command of God. "2. Give no countenance to despisers of human learning in public teachers of the church." This some were prone to do, expecting such immediate revelations to teachers, as would supersede its necessity.* "3. Give no countenance to that absurd notion, of depending upon the immediate impulses of the Holy Spirit for every word you say, or every action you do. As absurd as such an opinion is, I had almost yielded to it myself, under a mistaken thought of depending upon the Lord thereby. Blessed be God, who preserved me from it. I now look upon this [as] extravagant presumption, instead of having dependence upon the Lord. I might as well, on the other extreme, command the stones to become bread for the relief of my hunger, as on this, to cast myself down from the pinnacle of the temple, and to abuse the gracious promise of God, under the imagination of being borne up on the wings of angels.—4. Give no countenance to spiritual pride and self-confidence. 5. Give no countenance to a spirit and practice of rash judging. It is a granted truth, that every man and woman, as they come into this world, are concluded under sin, and lie open to the pains of eternal damnation. Until, therefore, they give me Scripture evidence of their deliverance from the guilt of sin and the curse of the law, I should be guilty of rash judging to conclude that they were in a state of favor with God; for no evidence of such a change is sufficient, but Scripture evidence. And here suffer me to tell you, that greater occasion is doubtless given to 'the contrary part' to say some evil thing of you, and of the gracious influences of the Holy Spirit, by rashly concluding persons are converted, without good evidence of it, than by saying you have no good grounds to think those persons converted, who tender only a public profession of religion and a moral character as the evidence of it. I would in no wise, by this, encourage any rash conclusion against such men; for certainly the saving influences of God's Holy Spirit lead to a good life and a profession of Christ before men. But mere-

* The chief foundation of this error, Parsons does not notice. It was the practice of training unconverted men for the ministry, as if human learning was a sufficient qualification. This error naturally produced its opposite, entire contempt for human learning as a ministerial qualification.

ly those are not the Scripture marks of conversion ; nor do they amount to that evidence of another's conversion that I must wait for, before I may conclude him so without being guilty of rashness. And, indeed, rashly to conclude that persons are converted is of much more dangerous consequence, than rashness on the other side,—though both are to be avoided and abhorred ;" for, he argues, the false hopes of self-deceivers are strengthened by such rash decisions in their favor ; and then, when such fall away, opposers are encouraged to reproach Christianity and despise the work of God's Spirit. He had found no source of reproaches more abundant than this. "6. Be warned against justifying, excusing, or endeavouring to extenuate your known errors or irregularities, when any person puts you in mind of them. I am persuaded there is too great a readiness in some of God's dear children to justify, or at least to excuse, their own imperfections, and to suspect some ill design in those that deal plainly with them for the same. Yea, and it is too common with them, to spend that time in vain jangling, and endeavouring to excuse the very things they should condemn in themselves, which might be much better spent in their closets, begging for renewed pardons, and for grace to guard against every evil thing by which the contrary part is waiting to get some advantage."

Such were the teachings of one of the men most censured for blind enthusiasm and headlong zeal. This sermon shows that nearly all the faults charged upon the promoters and subjects of the revival really existed, and threatened to prevail ; though the vigilance, the early and prompt interference, of the pastors confined them within much narrower limits than is usually supposed. It shows, too, that Parsons himself, in the warmth of his first successful labors, strayed to the very brink of the precipice, and led his people towards the danger from which he soon had grace to recall them. But this picture is not complete without a view of the other parish in Lyme, and of Parsons itinerating.

### LYME, EAST PARISH.

The Rev. George Griswold's account of the revival in the East Parish of Lyme is dated April 3, 1744. This parish was considerably smaller than the other, containing about sixty or seventy families. Mr. Griswold's description of the previous decline of religion, of the influence of reports concerning Whitefield and others, of the increasing thoughtfulness in the winter of 1741, till the arrival of Tennent, agree substantially with that given by Mr. Parsons. After Tennent's sermons, April 1, 1741, "The concern spread and increased, and was visible in the face of the congregation on the Lord's day, and at other times of public worship; and some were distressed that they were so stupid as not to be concerned." Evening meetings were set up. At one of them, April 14, Mr. Parsons preached, as mentioned in his own account. "The word fell with great power on sundry, who were deeply wounded under a sense of sin and divine wrath. Some had fits; some fainted; and it was observable that God made use of the concern in some to create a concern in others; and some, that did not appear much concerned when the public exercises ended, yet, seeing others distressed, fell into a deep distress under a conviction of sin and the sense of divine wrath due to them. Some hours were spent in praying with and counselling the distressed. After this, cryings out at the preaching of the word were frequent. These things, being the first that had been so remarkable in any town or parish near us, were much talked of; and many persons came to see and hear," some of whom believed it to be the work of the Holy Spirit, and some knew not what to think. Mr. Griswold "was persuaded that, as to the substance of it, it was the work of God, though accompanied with some unusual circumstances;" because he found the same conviction of sin and other mental exercises that usually accompany a work of the Spirit of God. "Soon after this, there was a great concern at a private house, among about ten persons, where there had been no preaching, praying, or any thing of that nature." Mr. Griswold, passing that way, was called in to pray with and counsel them; "and some that came in to see them were struck under conviction, and the most of these persons were soon after hopefully converted. Now outcries, faintings, and fits were often in meetings; though the greater part that I hope experienced a saving change, did not make any outcries; nor did they faint or have fits under the divine influences of the Holy Spirit." By the end of June, the pastor hoped that about forty persons had "experienced a saving change." Some members of the church were among the converts. "It hath been frequent for persons to be in great distress for others, so as to be overcome thereby. Many have had such discoveries of the love of God and Christ, as to be overcome, and to lose their bodily strength thereby; which, I think, was observed to begin towards the latter end of July, 1741; after which, sometimes in public, but more especially in private meetings, this hath been frequent, not only in persons hopefully converted since this remarkable religious concern, but in those that are supposed to have been formerly converted."

From August, 1741, convictions mostly ceased till winter, when the work revived again, but less powerfully, and there were occasional conversions till the spring of 1743. As the fruits of the revival, one hundred white persons and thirteen Indians became members of the church. All but two or three of these, who merely owned the covenant and came to the Lord's table, gave satisfactory evidence of conversion; as did a few others, who had not yet united with the church. The Indians were of the Niantic tribe, for whose conversion efforts had been made for several years, but without effect, till Mr. Davenport came among them in August, 1741. Twenty or more of them were "hopefully converted." Through all this revival, Mr. Griswold had "taken care to caution persons against laying any weight on crying out, fainting, and fits, as signs or marks of conversion." There had been no separations or divisions.

### PARSONS ITINERATING.

Parsons' account of the revival in his own parish contains the following episode, which deserves to be placed under a distinct head: —

"About this time, the Rev. Messrs. Lord of Norwich, Owen of Groton, and other ministers in the eastern parts of this government, sent letters, inviting me to visit them, to see the work of the Lord, and help them also; (for it was common in that day for brethren to send for each other to preach.) After some struggles with myself, I consented to go; and accordingly set out on the 8th of June, intending to preach some few sermons before I returned. The same day I preached for Mr. Lovett of New Salem, at his desire, and there I observed a solemn attention ; concern in the countenances of some, and delight in others. I have had some acquaintance with the people in that place since that time, and believe that there is a considerable number of persons savingly converted in the late season of grace. From thence I went, the same day at evening, over to the North Parish of New London, and June the 9th preached two sermons for Mr. Jewett ; under which, but especially the first, there was a great and general concern visible in the faces of the people : weeping, sighing and the like among the aged and the youth, while many of the children of about ten, twelve and fourteen years old, cried aloud, and spake some such sentences as these, viz : 'What must I do ? I never honored this great king ! * Lord Jesus help me !' &c. From thence I hastened over to Norwich, because Mr. Lord expected me to preach a lecture for him that evening. And when I came there, there was a great assembly gathered, to which I preached from Psalm 119 : 59, 60. They gave very solemn attention ; and there was a concern apparent, by tears and sighs, in almost every corner of the house. The next day I preached another sermon for Mr. Lord, the visible effects of which were not so great as the first. I observed a great flocking of the people, not only to hear the word, but to their pastor for advice. From thence I went forward to Stonington, and, on the 11th of June, preached two sermons for Mr. Eells. There seemed to be tokens for good ; an attentive audience, and much weeping in the assembly ; but I do not remember any outbreakings in the extraordinary manner that I had sometimes heard. Yet Mr. Eells informed me afterwards in a letter, that there were many instances of particular persons, unto whom the ministry of that day was blessed. I thought when I was with him, that he had the blessing of some excellent Christians in his parish. It was formerly a place noted for profaneness and other vices, but he said (and so I thought) that there was a great reformation among them. From Stonington I returned back by the way of Groton ; and on the 12th of June preached one sermon for Mr. Owen, to a great assembly of people. It pleased God to give me greater freedom of thought and expression than I had found in all my journey before. I preached from Isaiah 61 : 1, and the people, to all appearance, were all ear and attention.

* I was preaching upon the kingly office of Christ.

There were no outcries, but the countenances of many discovered sweet refreshment; and others discovered great distress. And I had some satisfaction afterwards, by accounts from divers persons, that the spring of comforts and concern was from the Spirit of God. I could not tarry, indeed, to speak with many after sermon, because I had encouraged Mr. Croswell to preach at evening for him. But I had the company of a considerable number up to Mr. Croswell's parish, which is five miles distant from Mr Owen's. Upon the way they told what things were done, and how Jesus had been made known to them, and their hearts burned within them, while they spoke of him. Jesus seemed to be their delight, and humility their glory. At Mr. Croswell's I found great concern upon the minds of people. It was apparent, in sermon-time, by their weeping, and their looks. Some cried out, and, from after conversation, I was satisfied that many were very sensible of their sinful and undone condition, and some others were really converted. I remember two women came to me, who had made themselves easy, for some time, with the Arminian way of conversion; and had been bolstered up in it by a certain gentleman, whom they admired. They told me that they were now convinced that such a scheme of doctrines, embraced, fatally settled persons down short of Christ; and, by their embracing of them, they had gone calmly on in the way that leads down to death; but now they had an awakened sense of their sin, and of the infinite hazard they were in of perishing; yea, that they must perish, unless God was self-moved to pity and save them. From thence I returned to Norwich on Saturday, and kept Sabbath at Mr. Lord's. On June 14th, being Lord's day, I preached again to a great, very attentive and deeply affected assembly. The concern of some, and the delight of others, was manifest in their countenances; and, by conversing with many afterwards, I was satisfied they were under the influences of God's Holy Spirit. And so from time to time, upon opportunities with that people, I believe that Mr. Lord has the blessing of many souls turned to righteousness among them; a considerable number of old Christians, and many newly born, that are feeding upon the sincere milk of the word, and growing up in Christ. June the 15th, I rode out to Mr. Throop's, a new society in Norwich, and preached one sermon for him, to a full assembly. There seemed to be great listening to the word ; great concern appeared in the countenances of many ; a great number were in tears, and several cried out ; some fainted away, and one or two raged. After the sermon was over, I took pains to find out the spring of that distress which appeared in many instances, and I think, they gave grounds to judge it was from conviction of sin ; except those instances that were distressed with their outrageous passions.

"Now I had accomplished the whole of my design in this journey, both in visiting and conversing with my fathers and brethren in the ministry, and in seeing the displays of rich and sovereign grace ; and much exceeded my first design in preaching. The next laid out in my own mind was to return home as fast as I could ; but the Rev. Mr. Adams of New London sent me a letter, desiring that I would return that way, and give his people some exhortations. Having been there before in the time of the concern among the people, I was unwilling to deny his request, because I had found that there were peculiar difficulties rising up, and I feared my refusing might rather increase them than otherwise. There was a number of new converts with a flaming zeal, and jealous lest the laborers should not bear a proportion to the harvest ; and some others, from what spring I do not say, (though some have imputed it to the imprudence of these new converts,) who opposed themselves to the work going on among them. Thus the kingdom seemed to be divided against itself ;—and I was the rather inclined to gratify the venerable Mr. Adams on that account, not knowing but that I might be instrumental of some good in that respect. Accordingly I went, and on June 16th preached two sermons in that place, besides using some private endeavours to make things more easy, if it should please God to make use of me for that end ; but the success was not according to my wishes. I found mutual rising jealousies, and, as I thought, groundless surmisings in some instances, prevailing among them. These difficulties increased afterwards ; and, for want of charity and mutual condescension and forbearance, they have produced an open separation. I doubt not but that there are excellent Christians on both sides ; and there has been a very great display of divine grace among them ; but they are doubtless to be blamed for the manner of separating. What grounds they may have, I do not know, but am afraid they have gone off upon a wrong principle."

NEW LONDON.

Griswold, of East Lyme, also labored beyond the bounds of his own parish. Here is his account of some of the results: —

"Upon the report of the remarkable concern among us April, 1741, the Rev. Mr. David Jewett of the North Parish in New London, in beginning of May, came here and preached two sermons to the good acceptance of my people. And as a return for his good will, toward the latter end of May, I went and preached two sermons in his parish. Before I went, there was a seriousness on the minds of many there; though nothing of the visible appearance of a remarkable concern, like what had been among us. I observed that almost all his people came to meeting, though on a week day. And I observed a great seriousness and attention to the word preached, and many tears shed at the hearing of the word; though I did not hear of any saving effect of it on the hearts of any persons, neither was there any outcry or fainting; though, as afterward I was told, there were some that received those impressions and concern at the hearing those sermons, that stuck by them till they hopefully experienced a saving change.

"The summer and fall following, there was a concern among the people; and, as I have been told, about ten or twelve hopefully converted.

"About the latter end of July, Mr. Davenport came there, and Mr. Jewett, as I was told, refused to give him an account of his experiences of the work of God's Spirit on his heart; whereupon Mr. Davenport publicly delivered as his opinion, or at least his great fears, that Mr. Jewett was unconverted. Upon this, there arose an uneasiness among those of his people that had, perhaps, too great an esteem of Mr. Davenport; and, about the beginning of the next winter, a number of his people seemed to be got almost at the point of separation from him. Being invited by some of my brethren in the ministry to visit them and preach to their people, about the latter end of November, I set out on a small journey to preach; and almost every day preached twice a day. At this time people were exceeding greedy to hear the word, and flocked in great crowds where the word was preached. For near a fortnight I did not see much effect of my preaching that was remarkable for this day. Indeed, some cried out under the sense of sin and divine wrath, and some were overcome with joy and the sense of the love of God; but the most of them had had these impressions on them before in hearing the word; unless one or two persons, as I heard afterward, that God was pleased to make use of my ministry as a means of their saving change.

"As I returned homeward on Saturday, the thirteenth day after my going from home, I called to visit the Rev. Mr. Jewett; and in discourse with him, I found that he was desirous I should tarry and preach to his people, and he would go and preach for me. I consented; and we concluded he should preach not only to my people on the Lord's day, but also a lecture about the middle of the day on Monday; and that I should preach for him not only on the Lord's day, but on the Lord's day evening and Monday evening; and on Tuesday, Wednesday, and Thursday at some other parishes, where I thought and partly knew I was desired to preach; and on Friday, as I returned homeward, that I should preach for Mr. Jewett again in the afternoon and in the evening. I felt something of reluctancy to tarry another week from home, and in such painful service as riding from place to place and preaching twice a day, that is, once in the day and once in the evening; but I thought there was the hand of God in it, and it was not a thing of my own choosing, and composed myself to be as quiet as I could. But it seems God had some work for me, the most unworthy of his servants, to do, that I did not know of.

"On the Lord's day, which was about the 9th or 10th day of December, 1741, (it is to be noted that in the parish the people live so scattered and remote that they have but one sermon in the winter in a day,) there seemed to be considerable of concern, and the movings of the Spirit of God among the people; and about the close of the sermon, there was one negro that had hopefully a saving discovery of Jesus Christ, and received consolation. I preached a lecture in the evening of the same day; and there seemed a very great pouring out of the Spirit; many were in great distress, crying out under a sense of sin and the wrath of God; and sundry that were hopefully converted before, seemed to be filled with the Spirit, and with earnest desire for the conversion of others, and a spirit of prayer for it. After sermon was ended, about two or three hours were spent with the dis-

14

tressed, in counselling of them, and praying with and for them. This evening about three or four persons received consolation, and were hopefully brought to receive Jesus Christ.

"On Monday, I preached again at the meetinghouse ; and there seemed to be a great pouring out of the Spirit of God ; and many in distress, and one hopefully had a discovery of Jesus Christ, and received consolation. On Monday evening I preached again in the meetinghouse ; and the distress of the people was so great, among them that tarried in the meetinghouse the space between the public exercises, that I was obliged to speak to the people, to compose and still them, or I could not have had opportunity to pray with or preach to them. Though there were outcries in the time of public exercise, yet not so much as to interrupt the public worship. Within the space of about two or three minutes after the blessing was given, there seemed to be a wonderful outpouring of the Spirit ; many souls in great distress ; and those that were converted before, much concerned for the good of souls ; and about three or four hours were spent in counselling the distressed and praying with them.

"It is to be noted that the Rev. Mr. David Jewett this evening returned home, and, if I mistake not, came into the meetinghouse in sermon time ; and within a few minutes after sermon was ended and the blessing given, the Spirit of God came down on him in a wonderful manner. He seemed to be full of spirit and life from the Lord ; and this evening he spent some hours in praying with, counselling and exhorting of his people. And now they that before seemed to be at the point of separation from him, had their hearts wonderfully united to him ; and ever since, he has appeared very lively and fervent in the spirit of the Lord and in his cause. This evening about seven or eight had hopefully a true discovery of Jesus Christ, were converted, and received consolation.

"The number of them that hopefully experienced a saving change in Mr. Jewett's parish this week, either at the public meetings or in the space between, was supposed to be about twenty persons."

# CHAPTER XII.

THE REVIVAL IN NEW ENGLAND. Plymouth, Sutton, Taunton, Middleborough, Halifax, Portsmouth, Gloucester, Reading, Newcastle, Westerly, Northampton.

## PLYMOUTH.

"THE landing of the Pilgrims!" Every son and daughter of a Puritan, every enlightened friend of Christianity and of the blessings that follow in its train, will ask with interest for the history of the revival here. It shall be given in the words of the Rev. Nathanael Leonard, pastor of the First Church, who wrote November 23, 1744.*

"It pleased God to cast my lot (who am the least of all saints) in the First Church and town in the country, above twenty years ago. Religion was then under a great decay; most people seemed to be taken up principally about the world and the lusts of this life; though there appeared some serious Christians among us that had the things of God at heart, who greatly bewailed the growth of impiety, profaneness, Sabbath breaking, gaming, tavern-haunting, intemperance, and other evils, which threatened to bear down all that is good and sacred before them. We were sensible of an awful degeneracy, and kept days of fasting and prayer, year after year, that God would pour out his Spirit upon us; especially on the rising generation. At these times we invited the ministers of the county to join with us, who readily gave their assistance. The authority of this town endeavoured to put a stop to the growing intemperance, by clearing the taverns at nine o'clock in the evening, and punishing loose and disorderly persons that frequented them. But all the methods used one way and the other, proved of little effect. Iniquity prevailed, and we were in danger of losing the very form of godliness.

"The Rev. Mr. Whitefield coming into the land, and the news we presently had of his preaching and conversation at

* Christian History, Vol. II. page 313.

Boston and elsewhere, roused us a little, and we sent to him to come and preach to us. We expected him in October, 1740, but were disappointed.

"In March following, the Rev. Mr. Tennent came hither and preached eight sermons to general acceptance, which, by the blessing of God, greatly awakened this people, and many have dated such religious impressions from that time, as we have reason to believe issued in a real conversion to God. After him, several ministers of the county and others visited us, and preached with us; and we often spent whole days in prayer, singing and preaching, and had frequently three exercises in them. I often preached three times on the Lord's day myself, and sometimes three or four times in the week besides; although before this, through bodily indisposition and heaviness of spirit, I was not able to carry on the usual stated exercises, and my people had for some years provided me an assistant.

"The subjects chiefly insisted on were these following, viz: The sin and apostasy of mankind in Adam; the blindness of the natural man in the things of God; the enmity of the carnal mind; the evil of sin; the desert of it, and the utter inability of the fallen creature to relieve itself; the sovereignty of God; his righteousness, holiness, truth, power, eternity; also his grace and mercy in Christ Jesus; the way of redemption by Christ; justification, through his imputed righteousness, received by faith; this faith the gift of God, and a living principle, that worketh by love; legal and evangelical repentance; the nature and necessity of regeneration; and that without holiness no man can see God. All persons were put upon examining themselves, warned against trusting in their own righteousness, and resting in the form of godliness, without the power, &c. These things, together with pathetical invitations to sinners, to come and embrace the Lord Jesus Christ as offered in the Gospel, made a wonderful impression on the minds of all sorts of people at the first. And men, women and children were much awakened, and the out ward face of things began exceedingly to alter.

"In February, 1742, the Rev. Mr. Croswell came hither, and continued in the town about a fortnight, preaching sometimes in this, and sometimes in the other parish. At this time, I think I may say, as the apostle does to the Thessalonians: 'The Gospel came unto us, not in word only, but also in power, and in the Holy Ghost, and in much assurance. And we received the word, not as the word of man, but as it is in truth, the word of God, which wrought effectually in them that believed.' Hundreds of souls were at one time in the meetinghouse, Saturday, February 13th, crying out in the utmost concern, what they should do to be saved! and many others rejoicing in the Lord, in the sweet sense of his redeeming love and grace in Christ Jesus, as they declared. This day, and at some other times, conversions were so open and public, that we seemed to see souls, dead in trespasses and sins, revive and stand up monuments of divine grace. I do not mean that we had an intuition of their hearts, and knew infallibly the state of their souls, which is God's prerogative; but the appearance of conversion from one state to the other, and the alteration in the frame and temper of their minds, which they discovered in words and behaviour, was admirable. This day appeared to me in the time of it, and hath done so ever since, a day of great grace, for which my soul giveth thanks to God.

"After this, for some months together, you should scarcely see any body at the taverns, unless they were strangers, travellers, or some come there upon necessary business. The children forsook their plays in the streets, and persons of all denominations, except a few, gave themselves to reading the word of God, and other books of devotion, to meditation, prayer, conference, and other religious exercises, and refrained from their customary vices. And many that lived at a distance, being acquainted with this town in its former state, coming hither, beheld us now with admiration, saying, Surely the fear of God is in this place.

"Furthermore, as this present life is a state of imperfection, so there were some circumstances that attended this work, which, if they had not been, might have prevented some prejudice and offence against it.

"A violent opposition presently arose, and prevailed so far, that a number of this congregation went out from us into a distinct society, and nine of the brethren asked a dismission from us, to embody into a church by themselves. We readily granted their request, and they have lately had a minister set over them. My prayer for him and them is, 'that God would pour out his Spirit abundantly upon them, greatly enrich them with heavenly blessings, and fill them with all the fulness of God.'

"As for the subjects of this work, it hath been here as in other places. Some, that were a while under awakenings, at length got rid of them, and are now returned as the dog to his vomit. Some, that we thought at first savingly changed, have since given reason to fear that they deceived themselves as well as others. But the far greater part of them that were added to the church, behave with such meekness, humility, sobriety, and other Christian virtues, that I must say of them, as David did of the godly of his day: 'They are the excellent of the earth, in whom is my delight.' But I would not be understood to confine my good opinion to those only that have passed under a remarkable change within three or four years past. No, I am persuaded there are a number of truly godly persons among us, that experienced the new birth before these days, and even before my settlement in this town, for whom I have an equal regard.

"As to the present state of religion, the town is much reformed from what it was before these days. But Christians are not so lively as they have been; the convincing Spirit seems in a great measure withdrawn; iniquity begins to grow more bold of late; and I am afraid a day of sore declension is coming upon this place. O that God would again visit this vine, which his right hand hath planted, and hath hitherto preserved! O that he would water it every moment! Nothing but a stream of grace, from that fountain where all fulness dwells, can maintain and carry on a work of reformation against the devices of the devil, the snares of the world, and the opposition of men's hearts.

"I am so confirmed in it that this work is of God, that in my most calm and sedate seasons my prayer is, not only that God would lead me and guide me in his way, but enable me to endure all manner of ill usage in the world, rather than give up this cause, which I am fully persuaded is his, to whom be glory and praise for ever and ever. Amen."

## SUTTON.

It is not clear, from what period the awakening in Sutton should be dated; as indications of its approach appeared very early, — some months before Whitefield's arrival in New England, — though it was long in assuming a decided character. It seems to belong to the Northampton class of revivals. The Rev. David Hall's account is dated May 28,

1744. His labors among this people commenced in 1728. Within about two years, there was a very observable reformation of morals, and the number of communicants was more than doubled. After this, there appeared to be a gradual abatement of religious concern ; but it revived again in 1735. At this time, he says, "it came into my mind, and I trust it was from God, to visit the people of my charge, and to apply myself particularly to every one that was arrived to years of understanding ; that I might know the state of the flock, and make particular application to the consciences of young and old among us. This appeared to be attended with some very hopeful symptoms of success." A society of young men was formed for religious purposes ; and family meetings were established in four different parts of the town. These meetings were continued monthly ; but religious interest seemed gradually to decline for several years. At length, Mr. Hall writes, "God was pleased wonderfully to convince me of this in the latter end of April, 1740, and greatly to humble me." This was accompanied by a persuasion that he should see religion reviving, and an ardent desire to save souls for whom Christ died. He now "longed for the sanctuary," and knew, better than ever before, "what it was to preach with the spirit, and with the understanding also." There was this summer an increasing attentiveness to the means of grace, and more solemnity in the worshipping assemblies. In October, Mr. Whitefield preached in a neighbouring town on his way to Northampton. A few from Sutton were present, and were brought under conviction ; but in general, hardness of heart prevailed, and in the spring of 1741, Mr. Hall, in discouragement, began to speak of going to preach in some town where there was no minister.

"But so it was, that the very next Sabbath following, I saw considerable tokens of the goings of God in the congregation. Our assembly was generally swallowed up in tears ; and from this time I perceived a more general concern upon the countenances of the people. Sundry persons came to me under soul-concern soon after." Some of these soon gave evidence of conversion, and were added to the church. During the remainder of the year there were few instances of conversion ; but the number of the convicted increased, till at its close they amounted to at least one hundred. In January, 1742, "there appeared hopeful symptoms of a broken spirit and a bleeding heart." This was a good sign. When the anxiety that attends conviction gives place directly to joy in view of the way of salvation through Christ, we may hope the conversion will prove real ; but there will be some cases of self-deception and subsequent apostasy. When it subsides into self-abhorrence for sin and acquiescence in God's condemning sentence as just and right, every experienced pastor knows that the convert may be expected to "wear well." Soon after this, a considerable number offered themselves to the communion of the church. "They came as a cloud, and as doves to their windows." Neighbouring ministers, Parkman and Prentice, and Edwards from Northampton, preached there, and with good effect. "During all this, we were not exercised with any public outcries in time of public worship ; although there might frequently be discovered, persons under a most deep and solemn sense of the truths held forth unto them."

"It is observable * how, at this remarkable day, a spirit of deep concern would seize upon persons. Some were in the house, and some walking in the highway ; some in the woods, and some in the field ; some in conversation, and some in retirement ; some children, and some adults, and some ancient persons, would sometimes on a sudden be brought under the strongest impressions from a sense of the great realities of the other world and eternal things. But such things, as far as I can learn, were usually, if not ever, impressed upon men while they were in some sort exercising their minds upon the word of God or spiritual objects. And for the most part, it has been under the public preaching of the word, that these lasting impressions have been fastened upon them.

"Religious societies were now set up in several parts of the town, to be held weekly. And reading, praying, singing praises, and speaking one to another of their particular experiences were frequently means of enlargement of heart ; and some were by this means brought under conviction, who were before strangers to the power of godliness. Nevertheless, the imprudent conduct of a particular zealous person or two, in going beyond the proper bounds of duty and decency in some of these meetings, I do apprehend, was very hurtful to the progress of this blessed work among us.

* Christian History, Vol. II. page 166.

"We have had a considerable number visibly brought home, that were before not only destitute of the form of godliness; but also sundry who were before but a poor character in point of morals; and I have reason to think a considerable number of such were now brought home to Christ, who were before visible professors.

"In the summer of 1742, but few persons were brought under conviction; and from that time to this, conversions have not to appearance been so frequent among us. Nevertheless, in the fall of the year 1742, upon the Rev. Mr. Daniel Rogers' coming to us, we had a considerable revival of the work; at and after which, the spirit of conviction seemed for a while very powerful among our children, from eight to twelve or fourteen years of age; a small number of whom, I would hope, retain abiding impressions, but most of them, I fear, are much the same they were before under concern. Also, about this time, public cryings-out under concern became something frequent among us for some little time; though indeed seldom when we had none but our own congregation. But such things, being cautiously guarded against, have never here become common. And in my apprehension, the gospel was attended with less success afterwards, by reason of the prejudices which many among us conceived against the work, because of some public ado, that they concluded ought to have been better guarded against than they were. But however, such things, I am fully convinced, have been many times altogether unavoidable, from the overpowering views of the great reality of the eternal world; and accordingly, that it is a great fault in such persons as have conceived such prejudices against the work of the Spirit of God, because some persons under the operation thereof in strong convictions or compunction, have lost the command of their own passions, and have discovered themselves, when under the most proper concern as to the matter of it, yet through the overbearings thereof, unable to command their own faculties."

## TAUNTON.

The Rev. Josiah Crocker's account of the revival in Taunton, is dated November 24, 1744.* According to accounts which he received, confirmed by the appearances

* Christian History, Vol. II. page 231.

which he found there on his arrival, Arminianism, formality and looseness of morals had been aiding each other's growth at a fearful rate for several years ; though he appears to have felt these evils more deeply, and painted them more strongly, than most men would have done. Under the preaching of the Rev. Mr. Guild and others, there had been some reformation of morals, at least; and a sermon from Tennent, on his return from Boston, March, 1741, filled many with wonder at his strange doctrine, and permanently awakened a few. Thoughtfulness and religious conversation increased, public worship was better attended, and "there appeared to be some external reformation among many." Early in August, Mr. Crocker was invited to preach there on probation. His first sermon was on the 16th of that month. He found some degree of general seriousness, but little vital piety, and little deep and clear conviction of sin. There seems to have been a gradual increase of feeling, both in him and the people, till October, when the Rev. Daniel Rogers preached in Raynham, and the next day, at Mr. Crocker's request, at Taunton. Some were present from Middleborough and other neighbouring towns, who were in great distress. As the people in Taunton had never before witnessed such "agonies and groanings," Mr. Crocker desired them not to be frightened or disturbed by them ; and as Mr. Rogers preached, "a solemn and awful seriousness appeared among the people." The same day the Rev. Mr. Wheelock, of Lebanon, Ct., preached at Norton, and by invitation of one of the deacons, the next day at Taunton. A considerable number were awakened, and some were constrained, by the sudden and clear perception of their guilt and danger, to cry out. The first who cried out was a person who had been for some time "under some concern," but without any very clear convictions, and who had been much prejudiced against the revival on account of such things, believing that they were caused by an evil spirit, or by some sort of enchantment. However, she resolved to hear Mr. Wheelock, and while on her way, "secretly wished that if these things were right, she might partake in them." The next Sabbath, some passages in the sermon enabled her to see that Christ was a complete Saviour ; just such an one as she would have chosen, were she to choose a thousand times. She was happy. Her sins seemed to be subdued and gone ; and after this she was not angry and fretful under crosses, as she used to be before. When Mr. Crocker wrote, her conversation had continued to be as becomes the Gospel.

This was on Saturday, and Mr. Crocker was absent. When he returned at night and heard the history of the day, his thoughts became fixed upon the words, "Behold, I stand at the door and knock," as peculiarly appropriate to the state of his people. He laid aside the sermon which he had prepared, and minuted down some thoughts that evening on this text, and preached from it the next day with good effect; though he "observed no visible manifestations of their conviction of their sin, and distress of mind therefor, in the time of public exercise, other than an awful concern and solemnity, which was evident in most or all of their countenances." During the intermission, some followed him to his retirement for instruction and advice. In the afternoon, Wheelock preached a "close, searching, experimental, awful and awakening" sermon, on hypocrisy and self-deception. After a short intermission, he preached again. This was to be his last sermon in the place. As "he was delivering his discourse very pleasantly and moderately," the depth and strength of feeling increased, till "some began to cry out, both above and below, in awful distress and anguish of soul, upon which he raised his voice, that he might be heard above their outcries; but the distress and outcry spreading and increasing, his voice was at length so drowned that he could not be heard. Wherefore, not being able to finish his sermon, with great apparent serenity and calmness of soul, — he called to the distressed, and desired them to gather themselves together in the body of the seats below. This he did, that he might the more conveniently converse with them, counsel, direct, exhort them, &c." But he ought not to have done it. In the first place, he ought not to have raised his voice, for that only increased the disturbance, and hindered progressive, profitable thought. And he should have known, that people thrown into such an uproar that he could not preach to them, were not capable of receiving benefit from private, personal directions. That religious experience may be genuine, the thinking must be original, the teacher's words only serving as hints, to guide the mind of the inquirer in his search after truth. For this, Wheelock's present hearers were disqualified. They could only yield a blind submission of mind and conduct to the dictates of the preacher, in consequence of which they might think themselves converted and be very happy for a while; but "having no root in themselves," their religion would soon wither and die. He should have sent his hearers home, to engage in solitary, serious thought, in reading the Bible and in prayer. There is reason to fear that from about this time, and in the mode here exemplified, false conversions were fearfully multiplied. The number, however, on this occasion, could not have been great; for, after Wheelock's departure, Mr. Crocker found but few who had "received comfort." As yet, Mr. Crocker "found little if any open opposition among the people; though afterwards, the religious concern among some of the people wearing off, or at least abating, they began to stumble at and oppose more freely and openly these appearances." It would be interesting, were it practicable, to give a minute account of the state of Mr. Crocker's own mind at this season. He was evidently a man of very considerable power and acquirements, liable to strong excitement, and probably to great depression of spirits. He exclaims: "What a wonderful reformation was then in this town! It is impossible fully to describe it. Moreover, I labor under some peculiar disadvantages, so that I cannot give so full and particular an account of things of a religious nature, especially in the time of the greatest outpouring of the Holy Spirit, as otherwise I might have done; being but a stranger among and unacquainted with them, and not committing particular accounts of things to writing in the time of them; and laboring under many perplexities, particularly awful spiritual darkness, desertion and temptation for the most of that fall and winter; my memory being also impaired thereby. Indeed, it was a wonder of the power and grace of God, that I was carried through the service I was called unto." Still, he was carried through that service, so as to perform it, in the main, correctly and with good effect; though it is by no means sure how much the elevations and depressions of his own spirits may have affected the character and influence of his labors, and aggravated whatever was objectionable.

In November, he left Taunton for a week or two, and on his return found the attention of some of his people turned from the state of their own hearts, to disputes concerning outcries and the like; yet most who had been awakened, still continued anxious, or had found peace in believing. He accepted their call to the pastoral office, and continued preaching to them till the latter part of January ; when opposition and difficulties increasing, he went to Ipswich to consult a relative, who thought it best to exchange pulpits with him for two or three weeks. Perhaps his friends thought he needed a respite from the anxieties that oppressed him at Taunton. There was no railroad then between the two places ; travelling, in the depth of that winter, was difficult, and he remained at Ipswich till late in March ; witnessing, meanwhile, " much of the glorious work of God's grace " there, and in the vicinity. On his return, the seriousness among the people still continued, but was less general than when he left. His ordination, May 19, 1742, seems to have been followed by some reviving of the work, and there were a few instances of conversion.

As the fruits of this revival, one hundred and two persons joined the church in full communion, and some united with other churches. A few of the former communicants were awakened and apparently converted.

Mr. Crocker gives a very clear account of the exercises of these converts ; or, to speak learnedly, of the psychological phenomena of the revival. Their exercises differed circumstantially ; some being awakened suddenly, others more gradually ; some having clearer and more awful convictions than others, and continuing longer " under a spirit of bondage ;" that is, under a sense of obligation and fear of punishment, but without filial confidence in God ; and some receiving consolation more suddenly and in greater measure than others. But under all these varieties, the mental process was essentially the same. They " were convinced of their sins, original and actual," having " their sins set in order before their eyes in a clear and convincing light, and with particular application." They not only admitted that they were sinners, but saw clearly the sinfulness of particular acts and states of mind, that they were conscious of and remembered ; and from the insight thus obtained into their own characters, learned that their hearts were originally prone to evil ; that the race to which they belonged, is a sinful race. As sinners, they found themselves " under the wrath and curse of almighty God, and continually exposed to the immediate and actual execution thereof upon them in hell."

They saw also "their lost and undone estate in and of themselves, or in and of any creature;" their "utter inability to deliver themselves from this wretched state," and their need of such help as no created being could afford. But it was hard to submit to the practical inference from this appalling truth. Though convinced of their impotence, they still continued to make efforts, till, "having wearied themselves with seeking rest in and from themselves, their duties, tears, repentings, &c., and being convinced of God's righteousness, though he should cast them off for ever," they "were brought to submit to God's sovereignty," acquiescing in his right to dispose of them as he should see fit; yet not in despair, but thinking, "Who knows but God may be gracious?" "Upon their submission, they felt a calmness in their souls, having done quarrelling and disputing with the justice of God." When thus submissive, and not seeking for relief or hope in any other way, "they had a discovery of Christ, and the new covenant way of life in and through him." They "saw his glory, all-sufficiency, suitableness, and readiness to save even the chief of sinners, according to the gospel, and "had their hearts sweetly and freely drawn out to receive Christ, and rest upon him and him alone for salvation." "These discoveries were generally given them in and with some texts of Scripture;" not that the mere fact of such a text coming into their minds was a sufficient warrant for applying its comforts to themselves; but the text was the means of conveying truth to their minds, and while they meditated on a text, or perhaps when it first occurred to them, they saw in it a fulness of meaning and an applicability to themselves, which they had never seen before. And why should it not be so? They had never before so well understood themselves, and of course never were so well prepared to understand the teachings of Scripture concerning the way in which such creatures must be saved. "Or if they had no text of Scripture, as they remember, at first, there immediately came many flowing in upon their minds." They now found peace of conscience, and joy in proportion to their faith; "had their mouths filled with praises of Christ, glorying in him, and commending him to others; had their love drawn out to God, and to all mankind," but especially to Christians; "loving and forgiving their enemies, being filled with a concern for the salvation of precious and immortal souls; mourning for and hating sin as against God," and as dishonorable to him. Of course they hated and avoided sin; for on account of their sins they had pronounced themselves worthy of everlasting perdition, before they found peace. Such, for substance, though varying circumstantially, according to the strength, clearness and peculiar character of each individual mind, were the "experiences" of the converts in this revival. The fruits were, perseverance in the various duties of piety and morality.

Will any thinking man pretend, that a well-informed pastor or church member, who has himself been through such a series of exercises, and has been acquainted with others during the same process, cannot judge whether his neighbour, in telling his "experience," is telling what he has actually experienced, or is merely reciting a story that he has learned, or a fiction of his own brain? Will not the tale that has been committed to memory betray itself, by the want of individual peculiarities, in keeping with the known character of the relator? And how many men have genius enough to invent a self-consistent psychological history of their own minds during a period of excitement? In fact, judgments founded on such relations are not usually false; and in this revival at Taunton, though the occasions of self-deception were somewhat abundant, but few of the supposed converts failed to evince the reality of their conversion by persevering holiness of life.

Mr. Crocker mentions his acquaintance with the revivals in Middleborough, Plymouth, Bridgewater, Raynham, Berkely, Norton, Attleborough, Martha's Vineyard, "and other places;" adding, — "As far as I am capable of judging, the divine influence is the true spring thereof, and the revival seems to be the same for substance in every of these places."

## MIDDLEBOROUGH.

The revival in Middleborough derives unusual interest from the name of Peter Thacher, the pious pastor of that church. He was ordained there November 2, 1709, at the age of twenty-one. The church had then but twenty members, nine male and eleven female. About the year 1724, his parish was divided, and the Rev. Benjamin Ruggles ordained in the west precinct. In 1734, another division transferred a part of his flock to the church in Halifax. Yet, in the winter of 1740, his church contained about one hundred and seventy members. For some time, however, he had been compelled to lament the unfruitfulness of his ministry, and the indifference of his people. Only one person had offered to unite with the church for nearly two years. Mr. Thacher could not feel satisfied to live where he had no evidence of usefulness. He began to think that God chose to work in Middleborough by some other instrument. He talked of resigning his pastoral charge; but could find no suitable text for his farewell sermon. Tennent preached there on his return from Plymouth, in March, 1741. From reports which Mr. Thacher had heard concerning him, he felt "sensible prejudice" against his person and ministry; but a few sentences of his first prayer convinced him that Tennent was a man of God, and his prejudice vanished. Mr. Thacher laid his case freely open to his visitor, and told him of the discouragements of his ministry, expressing his apprehension that God was "about to break up his house with us." Tennent said, "No, but to revive his work." He was "glad to see the devil so vexed. It was a good sign." "The assembly," Mr. Thacher says, "was small:—no visible effect; yet from that day my people were more inclined to hear." Such was very frequently the result of a visit and a sermon or two from Tennent. Yet "some half a dozen were roused by Mr. Tennent's preaching," and they and others were still further awakened "by the ministry of the pious Mr. Rogers.* Yet, though their convictions were remarkable, they seemed to give no additional strength to the power of religion, because they were among those that had the form of godliness before. But hereby God was preparing me some sweet helpers, though the devil from this circumstance took occasion to reproach the work; so that from this time I may date the open strife between the houses of David and of Saul, that still subsists." In other words, the opposition arose from the unwillingness of church members to have their own hopes shaken.

"In the beginning of October following," he says,† "on a Tuesday I proposed a day of prayer; and spake to my brother Shaw for his assistance. This was our errand to the throne

* Rev. Daniel Rogers, of Ipswich.
† Christian History, Vol. II. p. 89.

of Grace, to ask the outpouring of the Spirit on this dry fleece. That week some of my lately awakened brethren obtained a visit from the Rev. Mr. Crocker. They appointed a lecture for him the Friday ; which pleased me to hear of on my return from my journey. He preached next morning ; one cried out ; the little assembly was struck with awe and seriousness ; which gave some hopes of a revival. He promises a visit on Monday. Of this, public notice was given the next day, the Sabbath. All that day my hearers seemed very attentive, and some meltings.

" The next day, being the 23d day of November,* 1741, Mr. Crocker came. We began about one. He preached from Romans 8 : 1. This he opened largely ; giving the characters of them that were in Christ ; and inferred the misery of those who found not the characters in themselves of their being in Christ ; there was nothing but condemnation for them ; showing what that damnation was, &c. After sermon there was an exhortation delivered.† Many now melted down. After the blessing, the people generally stayed, till some cried with terror, which flew like lightning into every breast ; I suppose, none excepted. I have written accounts of seventy-six that day struck, and brought first to inquire what they should do to escape condemnation. This inquiry awakened many. There were a number of professors of religion that day, whose lamps went out. They discovered there was no oil of true grace in them. There were four persons that this day, being left alone in the several houses to which they belong, were I suppose savingly awakened that day, by the consideration that they were left. After a stay with the distressed in public, many followed us home. Those that we had not opportunity to ask openly the state of their souls, and the reason of their outcry, repaired to us. They tell us, they see now what they never did before ; their original guilt and actual sins, and fear of the dreadful wrath of the Lord. This filled them with unutterable anguish. They seemed to be stepping into hell. This drew trembling fear and cries from them. They complain

* This date appears to be correct, though irreconcilable with some others, given both by Mr. Thacher and Mr. Crocker.

† This was delivered by Mr. Thacher himself; though he modestly forbore to mention himself, and rather chose to give the names of other instruments. — *Ed. Ch. Hist.*

of hard hearts, and blind eyes! That they should never see before! Especially unbelief! O! how dreadful to give the God of truth the lie! They now complain they cannot believe, find their hearts full of emnity to God, to Christ, to his holiness, his word, and saints. Scores, this day, told me of their hatred of me, above any one. But to hear the young people crying and wringing their hands, and bewailing their frolicking and dancing, their deriding public reproofs therefor, was affecting. O! how heavy now did their contempt and neglect of Christ appear to them, as the effect of these corrupt principles of pride, unbelief, and enmity, and vicious practices of mirth and jollity! Their mouths are at once filled with arguments to justify God in their eternal damnation, and condemn those principles and practices they had been ruled by and led into; and this from Scripture. This the peculiar work of the Spirit, to convince of sin and unbelief.

"Well, the next evening, we had another lecture. Though an excessive rain, yet many came, and the word was powerful. Thus the Lord began to hear, as soon as it was in our hearts to ask.

"From this time, there was an uncommon teachableness among my people. Scarce one word of counsel seemed lost, or a sermon in vain. From this time, they must have four sermons in a week; two Tuesdays, two Thursdays. The word of the Lord was very precious in those days. In a few days from that 23d of November, so greatly to be remembered, there appeared to be above two hundred awakened; and it was some days, and weeks, and months, before they were brought sensibly to close with Christ. Most of them tarried long in the birth; and, so far as I am capable to judge, gave as distinct and clear an account of their espousing to Jesus Christ; the means, his word of promise, and time, as they could of any action of human life. This, not all in the same manner under the preparatory work; but all came to the same espousing, closing act, when they were brought out of darkness into marvellous light; when the prison doors were opened, their captive souls set free; when set free from the oppressing burdens of guilt they so long bare; when the Lord led them into the wilderness and there spake kindly to them, saying live. Now they understood what it was to have the everlasting gates and doors of their souls set open, and the glorious king entering. How pleasantly affecting to hear them tell of their submission to God's righteousness, resigning to the hands of justice, and how sweetly and speedily in a moment they found themselves inclosed in the everlasting arms of mercy! Who would not be encouraged to come to this submission? To hear them speak of the glories of the Redeemer and his infinite fulness; how oft would they break out, O! we are sure, from God's word and our own experience, there is enough for all, every one in the world!

"This awakes professors, very moral and blameless in life, to inquire into their own standing. The most find they built on the sand, that they lived to themselves, rested in their duties, were mere hypocrites; and after a while, they joyfully tell me: 'I have found my feet on the rock. I never knew what it was to have my will subdued and heart changed and Christ there, till now. And now I know I have the witness in myself, and the Spirit in the word witnesses with my spirit. I am sure religion is real, no fable, no delusion! Christ is meat indeed, and drink indeed. I never knew what pleasure was, before Christ gave it me; and what he hath given, is better than all the world.' Such an account, I suppose, there are more than two hundred can give.

"The work grew daily; the numbers were increased; near one hundred and seventy, the following year, joined to the church."

So far Mr. Thacher had written, but not revised, for the press. In a letter to a friend, dated September 6th, 1742, he wrote:—"God's work yet prevails among us; and, blessed be God, there are yet many tokens of good in this Zion." In his own spirit, the revival never suffered any abatement, but rather grew brighter, till its light was lost among the glories of the heavenly world. During the first week in April, 1744, he preached to his own people and at Plymouth eight times; closing his last discourse, which was on the 8th of the month, by telling his people that he did not know whether he should ever see or speak to them again. Returning home, he told his wife he did not know but his work was done. He was restless that night, and rapidly declined till his death, which was on the Sabbath, April 22d. "On Wednesday afternoon," says the Rev. Mr. Prince, "was such an extraordinary confluence from the neighbouring towns, as was never seen in the place before, to attend the funeral. When the coffin was carried out, there was great weeping. —When set on the edge of the grave, it lay there some time, and they seemed to be loath to let him down ; nor did I ever see so many weepers before."

In his "Attestation," dated June 30, 1743, he wrote : — "We have not known visions, nor trances, nor revelations ; but brotherly exhorting, with more modesty and affection than hath been represented. Neither have these divine influences been attended with Anabaptistical errors. Twenty, that were before in those mistakes, have been brought off. Neither have they been attended with the errors of Familism, or Antinomianism. The Arminian errors were by the converts universally detected and detested. The doctrines of grace shine in their understandings, defended and earnestly contended for from inward and real experience. Their lives are reformed, as well as principles scripturally renewed. The drunkard is sober ; the churl peaceful ; personal feuds, that had been subsisting more than eleven years, are buried ; and love takes place and power, where envy and malice and hatred had formerly ruled."

## HALIFAX.

In Halifax, from the Rev. John Cotton's account, dated July 26, 1743,* the revival seems to have exhibited little that was peculiar. The inhabitants, he tells us, had been "a sober sort of people," among whom tavern-haunting, swearing, and such vices, had never prevailed to such a degree as in many other places ; "but the common indifference and lukewarmness in religion had too much the ascendant." In the summer of 1741, they heard many contradictory reports concerning the state of religion in other places, by which they were "set upon a gaze, and knew not what to think," and "were filled with concern, what would be the event of things." Near the close of August, they held a day of fasting and prayer for the presence of the Holy Spirit. In November, about forty or fifty of the people heard Mr. Wheelock preach at Bridgewater. "Not only myself, but almost all my people present, were fully satisfied with what they heard and saw ; they were convinced that it was God's doing. They brought home such a report as gave a wonder-

* Christian History, Vol. I. page 259.

ful turn to the course of things among us. The evil reports were banished and chased away, except a few, as bats before the light of the sun. Some few of the hearers present, who were mostly communicants, returned home under strong convictions ;" and their conversation was one of the greatest means of spreading the concern through the town.

At a private meeting at his own house one evening in November, Mr. Cotton read Mr. Edwards' "Narrative of Surprising Conversions." After the service was ended, one person cried out in great distress. When she heard a person cry out under Mr. Wheelock's preaching at Bridgewater, she had said to herself, "Ah, you are a hypocrite, and you will be discovered within this twelve-month." But though she disliked the sermon and outcries, she could not feel at ease after her return ; and her anxiety and conviction increased, till now she pronounced herself a hypocrite, and thought everybody else better than she. Mr. Cotton and others "observed her narrowly" for some time, and were convinced that she was actually overpowered by her sense of guilt and danger, and unable to conceal her emotions. After some days, she found peace.

After this, there was no considerable crying out under conviction in the public assembly during service time ; but some manifested great distress after service, at private meetings, and in their own houses. Those who cried out, however, were but a small part of the whole number of the convicted, and their mental exercises did not differ from those of others, unless in degree.

But few "received comfort" before the next spring. "Then a considerable number did ; and in about three months time there were forty-four added to the church." The whole number, before the end of that year, was sixty-two, and, by the middle of the next, sixty-nine.

In the summer of 1742, there were some instances of persons being overcome with joy, fainting, crying out, and the like. In the fall and winter they increased, "though never to such a degree as to break up public worship." Mr. Cotton was silent on this head for some time, being at a loss what to say ; but learning that some one from a neighbouring town was teaching the young people, that the more they cried out the better, if done in sincerity, he thought it time to speak. He told them, that if they cried when they could refrain from it, they acted sinfully ; though, if they actually could not refrain, he had nothing to say. After this, such " manifestations" seemed to have abated.

A few of the converts, who had been Arminians, were driven by abhorrence of their former error into Antinomianism ; but good instructions soon recovered them. They were free from "separations," and from trances and visions, except that, in the early stage of the revival, one or two were "something visionary." Lay exhorters, they allowed not ; and, in short, there were no disorders that became general, or lasted long. But few of the supposed converts fell away. During the decline of the revival, one girl " endeavoured to counterfeit the joys of others ; but she was soon detected by the friends of the reformation." New instances of conviction occurred at times till the autumn of 1742 ; and the concern of some that had been awakened, continued when the account was written.

Mr. Cotton's testimony concerning the evil reports of the day, and their authors, is of uncommon value ; as, from and even before the commencement of the revival in Halifax, he made it his business to trace back such reports to their fountain-head. He believed that a considerable number of those who had not been able to " see through the present reformation" were good men, who had not had opportunities for personal observation, or had been too much under the influence of others, or in some other way hindered from learning the truth. But asserts expressly, that " the greatest cry proceeds from those that are of Arminian principles, and of irregular lives ;" though some violent opposers were Antinomians, who "stiffly deny that ever an elect person is a child of the devil." Of the evil reports, he says : — " Some I found to be wholly groundless ; others were gross misrepresentations ; the bad circumstances of a story were picked up and related, and all the good suppressed ; and sometimes, when only one was guilty, the whole body were charged ; and when any particular person had really said or done amiss, and was soon brought to a sense of it and to repentance for it, I found that the repentance did not fly an hundredth part as fast as the sin. Those that have been most opposite to this reformation, have all along betrayed an utter aversion to examine things to the bottom. When urged, over and over, to go and discourse with the young converts, and that not only with one or two, but with many of them, and examine thoroughly into their case, they could not be prevailed with to do it, but kept aloof; so that some, that live in places where this reformation has been most prevalent, know as little of it, as if they had lived scores of miles off." This is just what a good judge of human nature would suppose, from the manifest spirit of the times; but as those reports were gathered up, thrown into newspapers, made into books, published in Europe and America, used as the basis of official action, and have produced extensive effects which still remain, it is well to have the express testimony of a man of good sense and good character, who took pains at the time to ascertain their exact value. Not that Mr. Cotton is a solitary witness, for perhaps every contemporary account or "attestation" of a revival substantially confirms his testimony; but few others, if any, seem to have examined the subject so minutely, or stated the result so clearly.

## PORTSMOUTH, N. H.

The Rev. William Shurtleff's account of the revival here, is dated June 1, 1743.* He says:—

"Mr. Whitefield's coming among us, and also Mr. Tennent's, was, I am persuaded, blessed of God; and their preaching made instrumental of putting a great many upon shaking off their heavy slumbers; and how reproachfully soever any may speak of them and their itinerancy, I must needs look upon their travelling this way as a favorable providence, and that for which we owe abundant thanksgivings to the God of all grace.

"As there had been for some time a growing concern among us, as to things of a religious nature, and a remarkable work of God's grace going on in many parts of the land; the ministers of this and some other of the neighbouring towns agreed upon observing a monthly fast, in our respective congregations, to seek for the like blessing. When the solemnity was attended in this town, which was on Wednesday, November 25, 1741, as soon as the afternoon service was ended, one cried out in a transport of joy, and others discovered a great deal of distress. The people did not care to disperse, insomuch that there was another sermon in the even-

* Christian History, Vol. I. page 383.

ing; and a great number of them, and some of the ministers with them, stayed till it was late, in the place of public worship. The next day a sermon was again preached in public, and had an unusual efficacy upon the hearers. The day after, we had two or three exercises, and the congregation, a great part of it, continued together till late at night.

"This Friday was the most remarkable day that was ever known among us. The whole congregation seemed deeply affected; and there was such a general outcry, in some from a distressing sight of their sins, and in others from a joyful sense of the love of Christ, that could not but put a great many in mind of the appearing of the Son of Man, and of the different exclamations that shall be heard from the inhabitants of the world, when they shall see Him coming in the clouds of heaven, in power and great glory."

The meeting was continued in the evening; and near its close, an event, which in other circumstances would have been trivial, greatly deepened the impression. The chimney of a neighbouring house took fire, and burnt with uncommon brilliancy. This was not seen by the worshippers; but the uncommon light, flashing at once upon the windows of the meetinghouse, without any known cause, startled some, whose consciences told them that they deserved to be arraigned and condemned immediately. It seemed to them, that the Lord Jesus was actually "revealed from heaven in flaming fire," to "take vengeance on them that know not God, neither obey the gospel." A cry was raised, that Christ was coming to judgment. Many, who knew that if he came then, they must be condemned, and that they deserved no respite, at once admitted the belief, and numbers, who before had not been greatly moved, were now filled with consternation and deep distress. The explanation of this mistake, a few minutes afterwards, instead of dispelling their fears, only showed them new reason to be afraid. If they were so evidently unprepared for judgment, as to be thrown into consternation by the light of a burning chimney, their condition was certainly full of danger, and demanded their serious and immediate attention. Mr. Shurtleff proceeds:—

"As I was called abroad the day next ensuing what I last mentioned, it was surprising to observe the seriousness that appeared in the face of almost every one I occasionally met with. It seemed as if there was hardly any such thing as entering into a house in which there was not some poor wounded and distressed soul, and where there was not a greater or less degree of concern in all belonging to it, as to their spiritual and eternal state. It was very affecting to be called into one family after another, as I was going along the street, and entreated not to leave them till prayer had been solemnly offered up to God on their behalf. A divine power was then so plainly to be seen in what had come to pass among us, that there was hardly any that durst openly and expressly deny it. As for those who, through their own prevailing corruptions, or the insinuations and persuasions of others, soon grew into a dislike of it, and have since gone so far as to pronounce the whole of it a scene of enthusiasm, and to look upon all as a delusion, their very countenance and behaviour then plainly spoke the awful apprehensions they were under of its being from God."

There was now a demand for preaching every day, and several neighbouring ministers lent their assistance. Among others, Mr. Cooper of Boston was invited. He remained nearly three weeks, preaching almost every evening, with remarkable success. So things continued through the winter. Assemblies for worship and instruction were thronged, and the number of communicants was much increased. The people were distinctly taught, from the beginning, to put no confidence in "outcries, and such like public appearances ;— that they ought always to avoid them, when it could be done without great inconvenience to themselves ;" and "that, as persons may be effectually wrought upon by the word, without any thing of this nature, so they may be put into an uncommon degree of terror, and filled with a great deal of joy, under the hearing of it, and yet continue strangers to a real, saving change."

Some members of the church were awakened and converted ; but the greater part of the converts were persons who had very little of the form of religion before. "Many of them, upon their first being brought under conviction, manifested a deep sense of their original, as well as actual sins ; complained sadly of the wickedness of their hearts, and bewailed their sin in rejecting and making light of a Saviour." The second part of this sentence is, as Biblical students say, exegetical of the first. The "original sin," of which they repented, was "the wickedness of their hearts," as distinguished from any individual sinful acts that flowed

16

from it. This sinfulness of the heart convinced them that they were the true children of apostate Adam, and justly included in his condemnation. Mr. Shurtleff remarks : —

" As was at first feared and expected, it must be confessed that so it has happened, to some that were brought under a serious concern for their souls, that they have fallen off from their good beginnings, and are the same persons that they were before ; and there are others, who, continuing under convictions, seem to have proceeded no further. But there is a considerable number who are exhibiting all the evidences that can be expected, of a real conversion to God." There are many similar expressions in the writings of that day ; indicating that the revival was held responsible, by its enemies, for the perseverance of all who were " brought under conviction." Only the most ignorant would fall into such a mistake now. As to the general character of the town, the writer says : —

" That there is an alteration in it for the better, must, I think, needs be owned by every unprejudiced observer. That there is not that profane cursing and swearing, which has formerly been usual, has been acknowledged by some who are far from being well affected to the present times. That the Sabbath is more strictly observed, is out of all manner of dispute. Family worship, where it was neglected, in a variety of instances is now set up. Some, that were manifestly of a narrow, selfish and worldly spirit, and seemed unwilling to part with any thing of what they possessed to any good and charitable use whatsoever, appear now to have their hearts much enlarged, and are ready to distribute of their substance, as the honor of God and the wants of their fellow Christians have called for it. Many, that have dealt dishonestly, have not only acknowledged the wrongs they have done, but made restitution for them."

Will those who say that morality is religion, deny the genuineness of this revival ? Another extract : —

" During the course of the spring, and so of the summer of 1742, and autumn following, though some, that had for a considerable time been under darkness and distress, were brought into light and joy, there was but now and then one that was brought under any new concern. But through the winter of 1743, instances of this nature were something more frequent, and there seemed to be a general revival of that serious concern as to eternal things, which had appeared for some time to decline.

"On the sixth of February last, which was the season of celebrating the sacrament of the Supper; among others that were wrought upon in the time of the sermon, one woman belonging to the communion, who sat in one of the galleries, was so far affected, and had her bodily frame so far weakened, that she could not come down; and though she made some signs to have the elements brought up to her, it was not perceived, and so she went without them. But she sweetly fed upon the bread of life, and told me afterwards, that it was the most blessed sacrament she ever enjoyed. Towards the close of the sacred solemnity, the aspect of most of the communicants seemed to be much changed from what it was at first; and as an uncommon joy sat upon the countenance of many of them, so, as soon as it was over, they could not forbear expressing it, in the most sweet and cheerful praises. There were but few of them that went from the house of God till the evening; and then seemed to leave it with considerable reluctancy. We were not without something of a like nature upon several of the successive communions."

### GLOUCESTER.

Of the revival here, the venerable John White wrote an account in March, 1744.* He had been settled forty-one years. At the time of his settlement, there was but one church there, of eighty-eight members. Its increase had been such, that three other churches had been formed from its members, and it still contained two hundred and sixty communicants. The additions, before this revival, had come in "one after another, and not in troops or clusters, except at two seasons. At the time of the great earthquake, the people were much frightened, especially the more rude, ignorant and wicked of them; but about a month after the first shocks, when their terrifying frights were over, it pleased God, by his Spirit, to work kindly in a way of conviction, and I trust of conversion." Afterwards, the account of the "Surprising Conversions" at Northampton led to another awakening.

"But the first most visible and powerful effusion of the Spirit was on the last Sabbath in January, 1742, and especially as

* Christian History, Vol. I. page 41.

I was preaching in the afternoon and on the evening in two religious societies in the harbour. Many were impressed, both with distress and with joy, above measure. And on Monday morning, in the school of Mr. Moses Parsons, a man disposed zealously to serve the best interests of all he has to do with, and being hired by a number of gentlemen, to train up their children in religious exercises and in singing, as well as other useful knowledge, the Spirit of God came so powerfully upon the school, that they could not attend the ordinary school exercises; but, with their joyful master, with whom I had left the care of my flock while I went a journey which I was necessitated to take, and a multitude of spectators, they prayed to and praised God, by singing spiritual hymns. And in the evening Mr. Parsons preached a lecture in the meetinghouse; and in the close of the exercise, the Spirit fell upon a great part of the congregation, to the amazement of many. And people had such an appetite to the word preached, that Mr. Parsons called in the help of the other ministers of the town. The good fruits of this visit are very apparent. No less than twenty-one had their experiences read the last Sabbath day.

"The impression was, at first, principally on the one side of the meetinghouse. And there was poured down a spirit of prayer upon young and old, especially the younger sort; and children of five, six, seven years, and upward, would pray to admiration. And in our parish, there have since been formed no less than nine distinct societies, of young and old, male and female, bond and free, (for one of them is a society of negroes, who in their meetings behave very seriously and decently. They have been greatly impressed. One of them gave a very satisfying account of his experiences, and was taken into church-fellowship. Most of them entered into covenant, and were baptized themselves, and also their issue,) who meet, several of them twice in a week, to pray and sing, as well as to read books of piety, and the rest once a week. And the younger say their catechism to the head of the meeting. And several sermons have been preached unto them.

"There has been an apparent reformation. Diversions, though lawful and innocent, have been almost wholly laid aside, and the singing of Dr. Watts' hymns is the chief recreation of Christians when they convene. There are no separations among us. Little has been said about New Lights, (which I look upon as a term of reproach, as of old the term

Puritan was,) and as little about opposers ; the mentioning of which is irritating, and tends to widen the breach, and foment divisions, contentions and separations. As to visions, we had enough of them, until such time as in a lecture sermon I declared my sentiments concerning them ; and, so far as I can understand, there has never been one since. Our congregation has been disturbed and interrupted by outcries, but I labored to suppress them.

"I would add that, as I believe there have been scores savingly wrought upon, who were strangers before that happy day, so much as to the form of godliness, so some professors who rested in the form, and were but legalists or self-righteous, have seen that they built upon a sandy foundation, and were greatly distressed under the conviction ; and, by an earnest application unto Christ for wisdom and righteousness, have had a further discovery of Jesus Christ, and have been encouraged to venture upon him for the complete salvation of their souls, and have had their hearts filled with joy in believing. So also there have been scores of persons who had truly closed with Christ in time past, but have walked in darkness, by means of the withdrawal of the Spirit, the weakness of their graces, and prevalency of their corruptions, and have been for a long time as in a wilderness. These have been anointed as with fresh oil ; their hearts have been made glad, enlarged, quickened and comforted by renewed and continued supplies of grace, have been enabled with enlarged hearts to run the ways of God's commandments."

The Rev. Benjamin Bradstreet, pastor of the church in Annisquam Parish, Gloucester, wrote, June 30, 1743*: "In my very small parish, consisting of about eighty families, we have had, in about twelve months past, (when we had before more communicants than families,) about forty added to the church, and all excepting one, by the grace of God, live to bear good fruit. Thanks be to God, we have no divisions nor separations among us ; we are without dreams, visions, and trances, (though there have been some in the neighbourhood,) nor are we troubled with exhorters. The people seem to express a greater love for their minister, and a greater desire than ever to hear the word ; and I hope their unworthy minister has a greater regard than ever for their souls."

* Christian History, Vol. I. page 187.

### READING.

The Rev. Daniel Putnam, pastor of the Second Church, wrote, June 30, 1743 :*

"Sometime in the beginning of March, 1742, under a sense of the great decay of religion among us, we kept a day of fasting and prayer, to seek to God for the pouring out of his Spirit upon us ; and God was pleased, out of his abundant grace, to give us speedy answers of prayer. For the space of five or six weeks, more or less of my people, younger and elder, came to my house every day in the week except Sabbaths ; and manifestly under a work of conviction, deeply concerned for the state of their souls, and many of them expressing themselves in these words : 'O, Sirs, what shall I do, what shall I do, to get rid of my sins ?' complaining of the load of guilt on their consciences, and of the power of sin in their souls ; of the hardness of their hearts, and of the sense of God's wrath due to them ; and some signifying to me, that they even now felt, what they only before knew as by hearsay, that the heart is so desperately wicked, and by nature so unfit for heaven. Some, when they heard mention made of Christ and of the mercy of God, I cannot relate the greatness of the distress it put them into, to consider that their sins were against such mercy, such love !

"But I will not enlarge. I know this was the work of the Spirit of God, as a spirit of bondage and fear, thus convincing and humbling them. And the most of these, we have grounds to hope, have been since as fully convinced of righteousness and of judgment, of the all-sufficiency of Christ as priest and king, as they were convinced of their sins and misery before ; and we charitably hope, have experienced by faith in him, through the merits of his righteousness and the power of his grace, that rest that he gives to such weary souls, that receive him with their whole heart. And there have been large additions to the church, considering the number of the people. And not only has this been the happy case of some that were without the visible church, but even several of the members have been very deeply concerned about the state of their own souls, and I hope it has been for their everlasting good."

---

* Christian History, Vol. I. page 181.

## NEW CASTLE, N. H.

The pastor, Rev. John Blunt, testified, July 26, 1743 :* "The parish I am settled in is small ; but God has, I hope, by the influences of his gracious Spirit, made his word and ordinances effectual to the convincing and converting a considerable number among us. The awakening in months past was almost universal. Fear seemed to fall on every soul ; and the great inquiry was, What shall I do to be saved ? And although, I have reason to fear, the impressions are in a great measure worn off from some ; yet the lasting good effects on many, I think very considerable, and for which I desire to adore the rich and free grace of God. Fifty have been added to our communion in about the space of two years ; and most of them appear to have their conversation as becometh the gospel. Some of those who were professors before this remarkable day of God's visitation, have been of late much quickened and enlivened ; and others, being convinced of their formality in times past, declare how they have felt the power of God's grace upon their souls."

## WESTERLY, R. I.

The Rev. Joseph Park's account of the revival, or, as it is called with more propriety, the propagation of the gospel, in Westerly, R. I., is of more than ordinary value. With a rare degree of honest simplicity, he exposes to our view the reasons of his ill success for several years ; and he sets before us, in their best dress, Davenport, his irregularities, and his exhorters.†

Mr. Park was sent, in May, 1733, by the Commissioners of the English Society for propagating the Gospel in New England, as a missionary to the Indians, and such English as would attend, in Westerly. He was then, as he afterwards believed, "a moral, religious person, but awfully in the dark as to the way of salvation by Christ." He "had been somewhat indoctrinated in gospel truths," and had been too much enlightened by conviction of sin to embrace Arminian principles at large ; but still secretly imagined "that there was something in men to begin with, and which gospel grace came to make perfect." He preached and labored with his own heart accordingly ; "but could not get

* Christian History, Vol. I. p. 199. † Ibid., p. 201.

to such a pitch as to think himself ripe for grace, or with any confidence lay claim to it," because he found his own works not good enough to build any such claim upon; and as for his people, he "could by no means prevail upon them to be better, but they rather grew worse." So it was for several years, till it pleased God to come closer to him, and bring all his hopes "into a ruinous heap," and to show him a way of justification by faith, without the deeds of the law. He then saw "that the way to help forward the good of mankind, was not to go to repairing and mending, but to pull down all as fast [he] could, because there was no foundation at all." He now labored to show his people "the total ruin of the first Adam, and the complete restoration in the second." They could bear to be told about their duty, so long as they could pacify their consciences with promises of future performance; but to be told that they were wholly dependent on Christ for salvation, was intolerably offensive. Though "their imaginary power" of preparing themselves for heaven, or bringing themselves into a fitness to receive divine grace, "was of no advantage to them, for they would not try to exert it;" yet the assertion that they had no such power, "stirred their indignation." Still, "Satan, and a corrupt heart," managed to take off the edge of his preaching, by an error then very common, the error of hoping, without evidence and against evidence, that his hearers were regenerate; so that, instead of "making a full and particular application to souls, by declaring what their state was," as shown by their profession and practice, he was ready to say that he hoped better things of them, and things that accompany salvation, though he thus spake. At length, God showed him his mistake on this point, and then he endeavoured to come to the conscience of every man, and bring the truth to bear upon it. "And this fretted them still more."

At length, Gilbert Tennent preached there, on his way to Boston, and again on his return, with his usual New England result, — no revival, but a disturbance of consciences, which lasted till there was one. Opposition to Mr. Park was now at its height. "Seldom above ten, twenty, or thirty souls appeared at the public assembly; sometimes not so many; and, if the weather was so as they could have any excuse, many times none at all." So things continued, till Mr. Davenport came over from Long Island.

"He preached at Stonington, adjacent to us. I went myself, and divers from this place, to hear him. I had heard many strange things of him, and strange effects of his preaching. I went to meet him some way before he came to the meetinghouse; and upon their coming in solemn procession, singing an hymn, the dread majesty of God seemed to fill heaven and earth, and a solemnity appeared in the countenances of all. He preached a plain and awakening sermon, from John 5 : 40. I heard nothing extraordinary, but the wholesome truths of the gospel, and expected no extraordinary effect; when, to my surprise, there was a cry all over the meetinghouse. I went about and inquired of one and another the meaning of their outcry. And when I came to understand the inward and secret spring thereof, viz: a deep conviction of sin, I could not but say, 'This is the Lord's doings, and it is marvellous in our eyes.' Several of our people were pricked to the heart; who heard him give another additional testimony to the truth, and saw the wonderful effects of it. And several attended his ministry longer there, and returned deeply wounded. And though the shining light seemed to darken me, as to my own experiences, yet the Lord strengthened me to plead for his truth, the witness of which I had in myself. There continued a shaking among many dry bones; and such then would generally come to hear me preach.

"There continued much of the working of God's mighty power at Stonington, and many were hopefully brought out of darkness into God's marvellous light. And several of them were moved to testify, and exhort others to fly for refuge to lay hold of the hope set before them. Upon first hearing of this, I disapproved of it in myself, and had divers objections against it.

"But providentially, a number of them came to hold a meeting at a remote part of Westerly; and one of my friends, who, I trust, had been under the saving operations of God's Spirit, informed me of his thoughts to go and hear them, and invite them to his house and hold a meeting there. I consented, provided he found them to his liking, and proposed myself to come and hear them. Accordingly, on the 21st of January, 1742, having had a lecture the night before, at a remote part of Westerly, a number of the new-born children of God came to me. Here they prayed and gave a word of exhortation. They appeared humble, and the power of God seemed to accompany them.

"I went with them to the place where they had appointed to meet in the evening. I joined with them, and began with prayer. They gave some declaration of the work of God upon their hearts, in converting them to God, and exhorted the people to come to the Lord Jesus Christ; and I gave public testimony that this was the true grace of God which they set forth, and encouraged them to bear the testimony of Jesus among the people. Many were greatly enraged at them, and at me for countenancing them; but I thought the true grace of God must not be opposed, but encouraged, wherever God was bestowing it, and however he was sending it; so that none of these things moved me. I was with them the next day likewise. The power of God appeared accompanying them; and I was myself strengthened and lifted up by their means.

"Upon the 28th day of the month, having been to Stonington to visit and assist the Rev. Mr. Fish, upon a lecture, I was accompanied home by a number of converts; and there being a considerable concourse of people, we went into the meetinghouse. We prayed, and several gave a word of exhortation; and there was somewhat of the power of God visible among the people; some crying out under a sense of their sinful and undone condition.

"Upon the 29th of January, 1742, the Rev. Mr. Eells of Stonington came and preached an awakening sermon from Amos 6 : 1; after which I declared publicly, that if any had a word of exhortation to say, they were desired to say on. Several Christians gave a word of exhortation. God began then to work more powerfully. Several were pricked to the heart. Two hopefully received light and comfort that day. The way was opened to the Father in Christ Jesus. They had a meeting in the evening at such a distance that I could not attend it. The wonderful power of God was said to be visibly manifested; several were pricked to the heart, crying out, Woe is me; and several broken hearts were healed.

"Upon the 31st, being Lord's day, some brethren from Stonington returned to keep Sabbath with us. We had a meeting also in the evening. There was great opposition; but God showed himself victorious; and several were wounded in spirit, and one negro hopefully renewed. February 1 and 2, we had meetings. The Lord was present to kill and make alive ; and in this time the number hopefully converted was fifteen souls. I continued frequent lectures, besides Sabbath exercises, among English and Indians ; had frequent help from ministers and exhorters, the Lord continuing to work salvation among us.

" Before this day of God's power, there was not, as far as ever I learned, one house of prayer in the place, in two large towns containing some hundreds of families, nor any that professed the faith of God's own operation, or the true doctrines of grace. Now, when the Lord set up his sanctuary in the midst of us, those heads of families who had been the happy subjects of his grace, immediately set up the worship of God in their houses ; reading, praying, and singing the praise of God in psalms, hymns, and spiritual songs. They were brought surprisingly to know the doctrine of the grace of God ; such as before had counted it foolishness; and their souls were thereby quickened towards God. They became earnestly engaged to come into covenant with the Lord and one another in the fellowship of the gospel. Accordingly, upon the 29th of April, 1742, a number of them set apart a day of fasting and prayer, to implore the direction and blessing of God, in settling gospel worship and ordinances among them ; and upon the 5th of May, they were formed into a church-state, by the assistance of a council of ministers and delegates from Stonington, and upon August 13, 1742, through much opposition, became an organized body ; when, by the providence of God, I was ordained to the pastoral office over them.

" The Lord has added daily to the church, such we hope as shall be saved. The number of professors first entering into the bonds and fellowship of the gospel, was fourteen souls, eight males and six females, all English ; since which time have been joined to our communion twenty-two persons, besides two that have been recommended from other churches. Of those added, six are Indians, and two negroes. They all, in some good measure, appear hopefully to continue in the grace of God, and with purpose of heart to cleave to the Lord.

" The Lord, in the beginning of his visitation, was graciously pleased to show some tokens for good towards the Indians, and singled out some of them for monuments of his free and sovereign grace. But the power of God began to be most remarkable among the body of them upon February 6, 1743, when, upon the Lord's day, a number of Christian Indians from Stonington came to visit the Indians here. I went in the evening, after the public worship of God, to meet them, and preach a lecture to them. The Lord gave me to plead with him, that his kingdom might be seen coming with power among the Indians. The Lord, I trust, began to answer, even in the time of prayer; after which we sung a hymn. The glory of the Lord was manifested more and more. The enlightened among them had a great sense of spiritual and eternal things; a spirit of prayer and supplication was poured out upon them, and a spirit of conviction upon the enemies of God. I attempted to preach from 2 Corinthians 6 : 2, but was unable to continue my discourse by reason of the outcry. I therefore gave it up, and, as I had opportunity, offered a word of exhortation, as the Lord enabled me. I spent the evening until late with them. The Indians continued together all night, and spent the most of the next day and night together; and it continued a wonderful time of God's power. And from that time, the Indians were generally stirred up to seek after eternal life. They flocked more to the house and worship of God, than they were wont to do to their frolics. They remain earnestly inquiring after God, and appear many of them hopefully to have found the Lord; and there are tokens for good that the Lord is preparing the way, and gathering numbers of them into the kingdom of his dear Son. There is now near a hundred that come very constantly, and attend very seriously, and I hope, to profit. May the Lord carry on his work to perfection."

This awakening among the Indians appears to have left permanent good effects. Within a little more than a year from February, 1743, more than sixty became members of the church, and the number increased in subsequent years. Heathenism appears to have been extinguished among them.

### NORTHAMPTON.

Here, as has been already stated, the revival had commenced in the spring of 1740. Whitefield's visit was about the middle of October. Edwards wrote, November 12, 1743:*

* Christian History, Vol. I. page 367.

"He preached here four sermons in the meetinghouse, besides a private lecture at my house, one on Friday, another on Saturday, and two upon the Sabbath. The congregation was extraordinarily melted by every sermon; almost the whole assembly being in tears for a great part of sermon time. Mr. Whitefield's sermons were suitable to the circumstances of the town; containing just reproofs of our backslidings, and in a most moving and affecting manner, making use of our great profession and great mercies as arguments with us to return to God, from whom we had departed. Immediately after this, the minds of the people in general appeared more engaged in religion, showing a greater forwardness to make religion the subject of their conversation, and to meet frequently together for religious purposes, and to embrace all opportunities to hear the word preached. The revival at first appeared chiefly among professors, and those that had entertained the hope that they were in a state of grace, to whom Mr. Whitefield chiefly addressed himself; but in a very short time, there appeared an awakening and deep concern among some young persons that looked upon themselves as in a Christless state; and there were some hopeful appearances of conversion; and some professors were greatly revived. In about a month or six weeks, there was a great alteration in the town, both as to the revivals of professors, and awakenings of others. By the middle of December, a very considerable work of God appeared among those that were very young; and the revival of religion continued to increase; so that in the spring an engagedness of spirit about things of religion was become very general amongst young people and children, and religious subjects almost wholly took up their conversation when they were together.

"In the month of May, 1741, a sermon was preached to a company at a private house. Near the conclusion of the exercise, one or two persons that were professors, were so greatly affected with a sense of the greatness and glory of divine things and the infinite importance of the things of eternity, that they were not able to conceal it; the affection of their minds overcoming their strength, and having a very visible effect on their bodies. When the exercise was over, the young people that were present removed into the other room for religious conference; and particularly that they

17

might have opportunity to inquire of those that were thus affected, what apprehensions they had, and what things they were that thus deeply impressed their minds ; and there soon appeared a very great effect of their conversation ; the affection was quickly propagated through the room. Many of the young people and children that were professors, appeared to be overcome with a sense of the greatness and glory of divine things, and with admiration, love, joy and praise, and compassion to others, that looked upon themselves as in a state of nature ; and many others, at the same time, were overcome with distress about their sinful and miserable state and condition ; so that the whole room was full of nothing but outcries, faintings, and such like. Others soon heard of it, in several parts of the town, and came to them ; and what they saw and heard there, was greatly affecting to them ; so that many of them were overpowered in like manner. And it continued thus for some hours ; the time being spent in prayer, singing, counselling, and conferring. There seemed to be a consequent happy effect of that meeting to several particular persons, and in the state of religion in the town in general. After this, were meetings from time to time, attended with like appearances. But a little after it, at the conclusion of the public exercise on the Sabbath, I appointed the children that were under sixteen years of age to go from the meetinghouse to a neighbouring house, that I there might further enforce what they had heard in public, and might give in some counsels proper for their age. The children were there very generally and greatly affected with the warnings and counsels that were given them, and many exceedingly overcome, and the room was filled with cries ; and when they were dismissed, they, almost all of them, went home crying aloud through the streets to all parts of the town. The like appearances attended several such meetings of children that were appointed. But their affections appeared, by what followed, to be of a very different nature. In many, they appeared to be indeed but childish affections, and in a day or two would leave them as they were before. Others were deeply impressed ; their convictions took fast hold of them, and abode by them ; and there were some that from one meeting to another seemed extraordinarily affected for some time, to but little purpose, their affections presently vanishing, from time to time ; but yet afterwards were seized with abiding convictions, and their affections became durable.

"About the middle of the summer, I called together the young people that were communicants, from sixteen to twenty-six years of age, to my house; which proved to be a most happy meeting. Many seemed to be very greatly and most agreeably affected with those views which excited humility, self-condemnation, self-abhorrence, love, and joy. Many fainted under these affections. We had several meetings that summer of young people, attended with like appearances. It was about that time, that there first began to be cryings out in the meetinghouse; which several times occasioned many of the congregation to stay in the house, after the public exercise was over, to confer with those who seemed to be overcome with religious convictions and affections; which was found to tend much to the propagation of their impressions with lasting effect upon many; conference being at these times commonly joined with prayer and singing. In the summer and fall, the children in various parts of the town had religious meetings by themselves for prayer, sometimes joined with fasting; wherein many of them seemed to be greatly and properly affected, and I hope some of them savingly wrought upon.

"The months of August and September were the most remarkable of any this year, for appearances of conviction and conversion of sinners, and great revivings, quickenings and comforts of professors, and for extraordinary external effects of these things. It was a very frequent thing to see a house full of outcries, faintings, convulsions, and such like, both with distress, and also with admiration and joy. It was not the manner here to hold meetings all night, as in some places, nor was it common to continue them till very late in the night; but it was pretty often so that there were some that were so affected, and their bodies so overcome, that they could not go home, but were obliged to stay all night at the house where they were. There was no difference that I know of here, with regard to these extraordinary effects, in meetings in the night, and in the day time; the meetings in which these effects appeared in the evening, being commonly begun, and their extraordinary effects, in the day, and continued in the evening; and some meetings have been very remarkable for such extraordinary effects, that were both begun and finished in the day time.

"There was an appearance of a glorious progress of the

work of God upon the hearts of sinners in conviction and conversion, this summer and fall; and great numbers, I think we have reason to hope, were brought savingly home to Christ. But this was remarkable; the work of God, in his influences of this nature, seemed to be almost wholly upon a new generation; those that were not come to years of discretion in that wonderful season nine years ago, or those that were then children. Others, that had enjoyed that former glorious opportunity without any appearance of saving benefit, seemed now to be almost wholly passed over and let alone. But now we had the most wonderful work among children, that was ever in Northampton. The former great outpouring of the Spirit was remarkable for influences upon the minds of children, beyond all that had ever been before; but this far exceeded that. Indeed, as to influences on the minds of professors, this work was by no means confined to a new generation. Many of all ages partook of it. But yet, in this respect, it was more general on those that were of the younger sort. Many that had formerly been wrought upon, that in the times of our declension had fallen into decays, and had in a great measure left God, and gone after the world, now passed under a very remarkable new work of the Spirit of God, as if they had been the subjects of a second conversion. They were first led into the wilderness, and had a work of conviction, having much greater convictions of the sin of both nature and practice than ever before, (though with some new circumstances, and something new in the kind of conviction,) in some with great distress, beyond what they had felt before their first conversion. Under these convictions, they were excited to strive for salvation, and the kingdom of heaven suffered violence from some of them in a far more remarkable manner than before. And after great convictions and humblings, and agonizings with God, they had Christ discovered to them anew, as an all-sufficient Saviour, and in the glories of his grace, and in a far more clear manner than before; and with greater humility, self-emptiness, and brokenness of heart, and a purer and higher joy, and greater desires after holiness of life, but with greater self-diffidence and distrust of their treacherous hearts.

"One circumstance wherein this work differed from that which had been in the town five or six years before, was, that conversions were frequently wrought more sensibly and visibly ; the impressions stronger, and more manifest by external effects of them ; and the progress of the Spirit of God in conviction, from step to step, more apparent ; and the transition from one state to another more sensible and plain ; so that it might, in many instances, be, as it were, seen by bystanders. The preceding season had been very remarkable on this account, beyond what had been before ; but this more remarkable than that. And in this season, these apparent or visible conversions, (if I may so call them,) were more frequently in the presence of others, at religious meetings, where the appearances of what was wrought on the heart fell under public observation.

"After September, 1741, there seemed to be some abatement of the extraordinary appearances that had been ; but yet they did not wholly cease, but there was something of them from time to time all winter.

"About the beginning of February, 1742, Mr. Buel came to this town ; I being then absent from home, and continued so till about a fortnight after. Mr. Buel preached from day to day almost every day, in the meetinghouse, (I having left to him the free liberty of my pulpit, hearing of his designed visit before I went from home,) and spent almost the whole time in religious exercises with the people, either in public or private, the people continually thronging him. When he first came, there came with him a number of the zealous people from Suffield, who continued here for some time. There were very extraordinary effects of Mr. Buel's labors ; the people were exceedingly moved, crying out in great numbers in the meetinghouse, and great part of the congregation commonly staying in the house of God for hours after the public service, many of them in uncommon circumstances. Many also were exceedingly moved in private meetings, where Mr. Buel was ; and almost the whole town seemed to be in a great and continual commotion, day and night ; and there was indeed a very great revival of religion. But it was principally among professors ; the appearances of a work of conversion were in no measure equal to what had been the summer before. When I came home, I found the town in very extraordinary circumstances, such in some respects as I never saw it in before. Mr. Buel continued here a fortnight or three weeks after I returned, there being still great appearances attending his labors ; many in their religious affections being raised far beyond what they ever had been before. And there were some instances of persons lying in a sort of trance, remaining for perhaps a whole twenty-four hours motionless, and with their senses locked up; but in the mean time under strong imaginations, as though they went to heaven, and had there a vision of glorious and delightful objects. But when the people were raised to this height, Satan took the advantage, and his interposition in many instances soon became very apparent; and a great deal of caution and pains were found necessary to keep the people, many of them, from running wild. —

"In the beginning of the summer, 1742, there seemed to be some abatement of the liveliness of people's affections in religion; but yet many were often in a great height of them. And in the fall and winter following, there were at times extraordinary appearances. But in the general, people's engagedness in religion and the liveliness of their affections have been on the decline; and some of the young people especially, have shamefully lost their liveliness and vigor in religion, and much of the seriousness and solemnity of their spirits. But there are many that walk as becometh saints; and to this day, there are a considerable number in the town that seem to be near to God, and maintain much of the life of religion, and enjoy many of the sensible tokens and fruits of his gracious presence.

"With respect to the late season of revival of religion amongst us, for three or four years past; it has been observable, that in the former part of it, in the years 1740 and 1741, the work seemed to be much more pure, having less of a corrupt mixture, than in the former great outpouring of the Spirit in 1735 and 1736. Persons seemed to be sensible of their former errors, and had learnt more of their own hearts, and experience had taught them more of the tendency and consequences of things. They were now better guarded, and their affections were not only greater, but attended with greater solemnity, and greater humility and self-distrust, and greater engagedness after holy living and perseverance; and there were fewer errors in conduct. But in the latter part of it, in the year 1742, it was otherwise. The work continued more pure till we were infected from abroad; our people hearing, and some of them seeing, the work in other places, where there was a greater visible commotion than here, and the outward appearances were more extraordinary, were ready to think that the work in those places far excelled what was amongst us ; and their eyes were dazzled with the high profession and great show that some made, who came hither from other places.

"That those people went so far beyond them in raptures and violent emotions of the affections, and a vehement zeal, and what they called boldness for Christ, our people were ready to think was owing to their far greater attainments in grace, and intimacy with Heaven. They looked little in their own eyes, in comparison of them, and were ready to submit themselves to them, and yield themselves up to their conduct, taking it for granted that every thing was right that they said and did. These things had a strange influence on the people, and gave many of them a deep and unhappy tincture, that it was a hard and long labor to deliver them from, and which some of them are not fully delivered from to this day.

"The effects and consequences of things among us plainly shows the following things, viz. That the degree of grace is by no means to be judged of by the degree of joy, or the degree of zeal ; and that, indeed, we cannot at all determine by these things, who are gracious and who are not ; and that it is not the degree of religious affections, but the nature of them, that is chiefly to be looked at. Some, that have had very great raptures of joy, and have been extraordinarily filled, as the vulgar phrase is, and have had their bodies overcome, and that very often, have manifested far less of the temper of Christians, in their conduct since, than some others that have been still, and have made no great outward show. But then again, there are many others that have had extraordinary joys and emotions of mind, with frequent great effects on their bodies, that behave themselves, steadfastly, as humble, amiable, eminent Christians.

"It is evident that there may be great religious affections, that may in show and appearance imitate gracious affections, and have the same effects on their bodies, but are far from having the same effect in the temper of their minds, and course of their lives. And likewise there is nothing more manifest by what appears amongst us, than that the goodness of persons' state is not chiefly to be judged by any exactness of steps, and method of experiences, in what is supposed to be the first conversion; but that we must judge more by the spirit that breathes, the effect wrought on the temper of the soul, in the time of the work, and remaining afterwards. Though there have been very few instances among professors amongst us, of what is ordinarily called scandalous sin, known to me; yet the temper that some of them show, and the behaviour they have been of, together with some things in the kind and circumstances of their experiences, make me much afraid lest there be a considerable number that have woefully deceived themselves; though, on the other hand, there is a great number whose temper and conversation is such as justly confirms the charity of others towards them; and not a few in whose disposition and walk, there are amiable appearances of eminent grace. And notwithstanding all the corrupt mixtures that have been in the late work here, there are not only many blessed fruits of it in particular persons, that yet remain, but some good effects of it upon the town in general. A party spirit has more ceased. I suppose there has been less appearance these three or four years past, of that division of the town into two parties, that has long been our bane, than has been these thirty years; and the people have apparently had much more caution, and a greater guard on their spirit and their tongues, to avoid contention and unchristian heats, in town meetings and on other occasions. And it is a thing greatly to be rejoiced in, that the people very lately have come to an agreement and final issue, with respect to their grand controversy, relating to their common lands; which has been, above any other particular thing, a source of mutual prejudices, jealousies and debates, for fifteen or sixteen years past. The people are also generally, of late, in some respects considerably altered and meliorated in their notions of religion. Particularly, they seem to be much more sensible of the danger of resting in old experiences, or what they were subjects of at their supposed first conversion; and to be more fully convinced of the necessity of forgetting the things that are behind, and pressing forward, and maintaining earnest labor, watchfulness, and prayerfulness, as long as they live."

## APPENDIX TO CHAPTER XII.

The two documents which follow, were written by zealous promoters of the revival, in the very midst of its excitement. They throw much light on the events recorded in this chapter, and on some events yet to be narrated. The first is from a notice of Dr. Wheelock, furnished by the Rev. William Allen, D. D. for the American Quarterly Register. The second is from a manuscript, no part of which has ever been published. *

### EXTRACTS FROM THE PRIVATE JOURNAL OF THE REV. ELEAZER WHEELOCK.

*October* 21, 1741. Had but little sleep. Arose before day. Rode with Mr. Coit and my friends to Voluntown. Courteously received and entertained by Mr. Dorrance. Went to meeting at ten. Heard Mr. Gideon Mills preach well. Preached after him. There is a great work in this town; but more of the footsteps of Satan than in any place I have yet been in: the zeal of some too furious: they tell of many visions, revelations, and many strong impressions upon the imagination. They have had much of God in many of their meetings, and his great power has been much seen, and many hopefully converted. Satan is using many artful wiles to put a stop to the work of God in this place. Good Lord, let him be confounded. Let his mischiefs fall upon his own head. At their conference at night, I mentioned some of these devices of Satan, which I apprehend they are in danger of, and heard the accounts of a number of new converts.

22. Rose this morning refreshed. A pleasant day; found my soul stretching after God. The Lord has this day in some measure fulfilled my early desires. Preached twice with enlargement, by Mr. Smith's barn, to great assemblies. Many cried out; many stood trembling; the whole assembly very solemn, and much affection; four or five converted. One woman, who came from Kingston against a great deal of opposition on purpose to hear me, came out clear and went away rejoicing in God, longing to have her husband and others taste and see with her.

23. Rose at three; somewhat indisposed. Dear Lord, I commit my body, my soul, my life, health, and all to thee. Use me as thou wilt, only let me glorify thee, and seek that as my last end. Left Voluntown about seven, accompanied by a great number of wounded and comforted. Came to Mr. Cooper's of Scituate, in the county of Providence. Preached to a considerable assembly. I am always thronged with company, and want time to talk with the tenth part of those who de-

* It is to be deposited in the library of the American Antiquarian Society, at Worcester, where some parts of it have already been placed. It contains a minute history, not only of the author's pastoral labors, but of his domestic life, even to the making of a coat, the hanging of a gate, and the killing of a wolf in the neighbourhood.

sire to converse with me. Dined, and rode with a great number of Voluntown people to Captain Angel's. Preached there. The old man and woman violently opposed; called me antichrist, etc. Came about eight to Mr. Henry's, seven miles from Providence.

24. Rose early, prayed and sang. Discoursed with some wounded; afterwards exhorted a company, who came in. Sung a hymn, prayed, and rode with a great company of Voluntown people and others to Providence. About two miles from Providence, met Mr. Knight and another man, who came out to meet us. His first salutation was, God bless you, my dear brother. Went to his house. Rev. Mr. Cotton came, invited me to preach; felt freedom and sweetness in my soul.

25. Rode with Mr. Knight into town in his calash. Preached three sermons, 2 Cor. 13: 5; Mark 1: 2; Luke 10: ult. O, the dreadful ignorance and wickedness of these parts! O, what a burthen dear Mr. Cotton has daily to bear.

26. Rode with Mr. Cotton back seven miles to Mr. Bennet's: preached at one o'clock to a numerous and affected assembly. One converted. Returned with a great number to Providence. Preached to a full assembly: many scoffers present; one man hired for twenty shillings to come into the meetinghouse and fall down; which he did, and made great disturbance; ordered all who had a real concern for the salvation of their souls, to follow me to Mr. Cotton's, in order to have a conference with them. A considerable number came, who seemed considerably moved.

27. Went with Mr. Cotton and madam over the ferry to Rehoboth, upon Mr. Greenwood's invitation; preached at one. Rode with Mr. C. etc. to Swansey.

28. Brother Finney went to deacon Kingsley, for liberty to preach in the Baptist meetinghouse, but he refused it; but deacon —— sent for the key, and I preached at one and again in the evening. O, poor, bigoted, ignorant, prejudiced people!

29. Came with Mr. Cotton and many others to Attleborough: very courteously received by Mr. Wells. Heard Mr. Turner, of Rehoboth; preached after him; a great deal of affection and sobbing through the whole assembly; had great enlargement. Exhorted in the evening at Mr. Wells'. [Quere, Weld's?]

30. Had a great sense of my own badness and unworthiness, of what a cursed heart I have. O, Lord, let me see and know more of it. Rode with Mr. Wells and many others to Norton; kindly received by Mr. Avery. Preached to a full assembly; much affection and sobbing through the whole assembly. Rode to Raynham with Mr. Wales and brother Byram.

*November* 1. Preached in the forenoon to a full assembly; one cried out, many affected. Advised those who belonged to the assembly, not to follow me to Taunton, but stay and hear their own preacher. Went with Brother Byram to Taunton; preached there. One or two cried out. Appointed another meeting in the evening. I believe thirty cried out. Almost all the negroes in town wounded; three or four converted. A great work in the town. Dear brother Crocker, a true servant of Jesus Christ, preaches here upon probation. I was forced to break off my sermon before it was done, the outcry was so great: continued the meeting till 10 or 11 o'clock.

2. Rode with Mr. Crocker to the tavern, to see Capt. Leonard's negro, (a slave;) found him under a very clear and genuine conviction. Dear brother Rogers came to see me here. Rode with a great number to Bridgewater. Preached to a full assembly in Mr. Shaw's meetinghouse.

3. Rode with a great number to Mr. Perkins' meetinghouse; a very full assembly. After sermon, the lecture was appointed at Mr. Anger's; but so many wounded that I could not leave them. Therefore preached again to a full assembly. A great outcry: four or five converted.

4. Rode to Mr. Porter's. A great multitude. Preached upon a stage. One converted in sermon. After dinner, rode with Mr. Belcher, and a great multitude, to Easton. Brother Rogers preached. A very great outcry in the assembly. I preached after him. Four or five converted.

5. Came to Mr. Niles', of Braintree. Preached with great freedom. Present, Messrs. Eells and Hancock; Mr. Worcester came in the evening.

6. Set out for Boston. Met by dear Mr. Prince and Mr. Bromfield about eight miles from Boston. Came in to Mr. Bromfield's. Soon after my arrival, came the Hon. Josiah Willard, Secretary, Rev. Mr. Webb and Mr. Cooper, and Major Sewall, to bid me welcome to Boston. At six o'clock, rode with Mr. Bromfield in his chaise to the north end of the town, and preached for Mr. Webb to a great assembly. After sermon, returned to dear Mr Webb's; pleased with the conversation of dear Mr. Gee.

8. Went to Dr. Coleman's meeting; preached with considerable freedom. Dined with the Dr. Went with Mr. Rogers to Mr. Prince's. Preached to a full assembly. After meeting, was followed by a great throng of children, who importunately desired me to give them a word of exhortation in a private house, which I consented to do, though I designed to go and hear Mr. Prince, who, being by, desired that I would have it publicly, which I consented to.

9. Visited this morning by a great number of persons under soul trouble. Refused to preach, because I designed to go out of town. Just as I was going, came Mr Webb, and told me the people were meeting together to hear another sermon. I consented to preach again. A scholar from Cambridge being present, who came to get me to go to Cambridge. hastened to Cambridge, and, by a little after six, a great part of the scholars had got to Boston. Preached to a very thronged assembly, many more than could get into the house, with very great freedom and enlargement. I believe the children of God were very much refreshed. They told me afterwards, they believed that Mather Byles was never so lashed in his life. This morning, Mr. Cooper came to me, in the name of the Hon. Jacob Wendell, Esq., and earnestly desired a copy of my sermon, preached in the forenoon of the Lord's day, for the press. O, that God would make and keep me humble.

## EXTRACTS FROM THE PRIVATE JOURNAL OF THE REV. EBENEZER PARKMAN, OF WESTBOROUGH, MASS.

*January* 7, 1742. Cold day; but I rode over to the private meeting at deacon Forbush's, and preached on John 3: 36; after which I had a brief exercise of prayer and exhortation to the society of young women. It is agreeable to see how readily and gladly many receive the word.

26. Catechetical exercise to young women.

28. There being at Leicester very considerable awakenings among some of the people, they set apart this day for fasting and prayer, for obtaining a plentiful effusion of the Holy Spirit upon them; and they having sent for me to assist on that occasion, I went up. Mr. Edwards, of Northampton, was there, and preached a very awakening sermon on Rom. 9: 22—"Vessels of wrath." I preached in the afternoon on Zech. 12: 10. In the evening, Mr. Hall preached on Isa. 54: 13. N. B. Some stirrings.

29. Mr. Edwards preached on John 12: 23, a peculiarly moving and useful sermon. May God bless it to me, to draw my heart effectually to Jesus Christ, by his love, by his bitter and ignominous sufferings on the cross for me! I prevailed on Mr. Edwards, before we went out of the pulpit, to come by divine leave next week to Westborough.

31. I cannot help remarking what a wonderful time was now appearing; for there are great movings upon the hearts of the people of the country, in one part thereof and another. O! that I and mine might be stirred up earnestly and seasonably to put in for a share! The Lord grant us this mercy, and let us not be left behind!

*February* 1. It was a rainy day, but I rode to Grafton and Sutton. Mr. Edwards was come from Leicester. Mr. Edwards preached to a large assembly on Ps. 18: 25. At evening, in a very rainy, stormy time, I preached to a considerable assembly on Ps. 68: 8. Religion has of late been very much revived in Sutton, and there is a general concern about their souls.

2. A rainy morning. Mr. Edwards put on resolution and came with me to Westborough. Mr. Edwards preached to a great congregation on John 12: 32, and at eve at my house on Gen. 19: 17. N. B. Mr. James Fay was greatly wrought on by the sermon on John 12: 32. So were Samuel Allen and Ezekiel Dodge, who manifested it to me; and doubtless multitudes besides were so. *Deo Opt. Max. Gloria.*

6. Mr. James Fay, who thinks he sees things in a new light, and that he is now converted, was here to see me and discourse with me.

9. Mr. James Fay came for me to go and see Isaiah Pratt, who lay in a strange condition at his house, not having spoke nor been sensible since nine o'clock last night. I went to him, and seeing him lie so insensible, and his pulse *exceeding slow*, I advised them to send for Dr. Gott, to bleed him; but sitting by him and rousing him, by degrees he came to. Many were present, and were astonished. When he regained his senses, he said he had not been asleep, had seen hell, and seen Christ; and said Christ told him his name was in the book of life, &c. When he had taken some slender food, he yet further revived, and spake more freely. We gave thanks and prayed, and I gave

some exhortation. N. B. One of the deacons of the church was there, who took me aside to lament to me his dullness and backwardness in the things of the kingdom of God. These things are now (blessed be God) more frequent, which heretofore were very rare. May God increase them, and furnish me abundantly for his work, in every part of it!

10. By agreement with Mr. Cushing, this day was kept in a religious manner at my house, as a time of humiliation and supplication, but as privately as we could. And I sent a letter last week to the neighbouring ministers to join with us, in that we might unitedly implore divine direction in such an extraordinary day as this is, and that we might obtain the outpouring of God's Spirit upon us and our respective charges; but none came but Mr. Cushing.

11. Mrs. Pratt with her son were here according to my appointment, to acquaint me further with what he had seen, or apprehended he saw, in the time of his trance or reverie the other night. He having informed me of his seeing (as he thought) the devil, who met him as he seemed to be in the way towards heaven, and told him that there was no room for him there; of his seeing hell, and hearing the most dreadful noise of roaring and crying; his seeing heaven, so wondrously happy a place as nobody could tell but those that were there; and Christ, who looked more pleasant than ever he had seen any man, and who had a great book before him, and in turning over the leaves of it, told him that his name was there, and showed it him; and that he had seen a great many more things, which were such great things that he could not speak of them; — I told him that these things were not to be depended upon, but that the apostle Peter has cautioned us, saying, that we have a more sure word of prophecy, to which we should do well to take heed, &c. I endeavoured further to instruct, direct, and comfort him, and lay the charges of God upon him. P. M. I preached at Mr. James Fay's, on Luke 19: 9, to a great multitude, and it pleased God to give it some success. As soon as the exercise was over, Deacon Fay broke forth with a loud voice, with tears of joy, and blessed God that he saw this day, &c.; desiring that I would in due time have an exercise at his house; and bore a message from his brother, old Mr. Samuel Fay, that I would have one at his also,— which it was a cheerful thing to hear, considering his temper and conduct for some years past. The rest of the people seemed so inclined to religious matters, that they did not freely go away. Many tarried to discourse of the affairs of their souls, and hear of the experiences of one another.

12. At eve. Mr. Stephen Fay was here in great distress concerning his spiritual state, fearing that all he had done in religion was only to still conscience. I directed him to read what was most awakening still, and most searching; and particularly Mr. Alliene's Alarm and Mead's Almost Christian.

*March* 9. N. B. Mr. Pattershall informs me of Mr. Croswell's irregular zeal at Charlestown.

11. Fast in this place, on account of the extraordinary dispensations of God's grace in the land; that we might on the one hand implore the gift of the Holy Spirit, and divine direction, that we be not carried away by the many snares, temptations, and delusions to which we are greatly exposed.

15. Very cold day. Yet I rode to Mr. Charles Rice's, and preached to the society of young women on Ps. 119: 59.

20. Rainy. Mr. Buel and three young men with him here. I found him willing to submit to any examinations concerning his doctrines, or opinions, or life; whereupon I made several inquiries, to which he made ready answers, and told me he had made up with Mr. Noyes at New Haven above a month after commencement, and was examined and licensed by the ministers of that association to preach. I urged him to preach; but he said he was under such obligations to preach at Concord, that he must proceed thither.

21. On 2 Cor. 6: 2.—I hope there was some good success of the word to-day, through the blessing of God. O may it prove an accepted time and a day of salvation to us all!

22. Catechised boys A. M. at the meetinghouse. P. M. Girls at my own house.

23. P. M. Catechetical exercise with the young women. I preached on John 13: 17. At Ensign Maynard's at evening, to remove his stumbling at my slippers.

27. N. B. Mr. James Fay and Mr. Francis Whipple here. P. M. A great deal of discourse about the assurance of every new convert.

29. N. B. The world full of Mr. Buel's preaching at Concord. In the judgment of some, great success; in the judgment of others, great confusion.

30. I proceeded to Cambridge.—Visited Mr. Appleton. N. B. Various accounts from Ipswich, of the state of religion there. The people are greatly enlivened and awakened there. At evening I was at Charlestown. Mr. Buel preached on Gen. 6: 3. N. B. Mr. Croswell lies sick at Charlestown, after zealous preaching there for some time.

*April* 1. Mr. Hooper at the public lecture, on 1 John 4: 13. N. B. Great disgust given by Mr. Barnard's sermon last Thursday, and now continued among some by Mr. Hooper; as appeared to me at evening at Mr. Cooper's.

9. Mr. Beriah Rice here to join the church. Neighbour Thurston here at evening. N. B. His experience of extraordinary grace, the months past. His discourse very savory and very free.

10. Mr. Williams here P. M. to join the church.

13. [He went with his daughter to Cambridge.]

14. Rainy; but yet Molly and I rode to Boston, and were at the ordination of the Rev. Mr. Andrew Eliot, at the New North Church. Dr. Sewall prayed, Mr. Eliot preached 1 Cor. 4: 2, Mr. Webb the charge, Mr. Appleton the right hand. N. B. A vast assembly, and a glorious time of God's grace.

15. [He returned home with Sarah Sparhawk, of whom more hereafter.]

20. Catechetical exercise No. 5, at the meetinghouse. Above thirty young women, I suppose, were present. N. B. Mary Bradish with me afterwards, being in some spiritual difficulties.

21. Mr. Samuel Williams here about his spiritual state, and desirous to join the church. I took pains in examining him, and hope God is doing a good work in him.

22. I had sent to Mr. Stone and to Mr. Cushing, fruitlessly, to as-

sist me. I sent a verbal message to Mr. Burr, and, though it was a rainy day, he came and preached my lecture; a good, useful sermon on Rom. 10: part of the 14th and 15th verses, and the 17th, against exhorters among the people, &c., with a moving application.

25. Administered the Lord's Supper. Repeated on 2 Cor. 11: 27, 29. P. M. on Eph. 5: 14. I was in much fear and trembling, but cast myself on God. I chose to repeat in the forenoon. that I might deliver the latter part of that discourse, and likewise that I might deliver my sermon in the afternoon more entirely by itself, it not admitting to be divided, but it being the quantity of two sermons. I was much above an hour. Some number of Southborough people at meeting, and some of Hopkinton.

26. [Went to Rutland, to attend a council and fast.]

30. Mr. Grow here in spiritual distress, and Mr. Jesse Brigham's wife.

*May* 1. Stephen Fay here upon soul accounts.

2. On Eph. 5: 14. Mrs. Bathsheba Pratt here, being greatly distressed for the hardness of her heart, notwithstanding that she had been a member in full communion above twenty years.

6. Mr. Paterson, an Irishman from Stoddardtown, here. N. B. He had been one of those that had fallen into a stange fit by the pressure of his distress at hearing the word preached. P. M. I preached at Capt. Fay's, on Eph. 5: 14, sermon II. — N. B. I repeated that sermon, because of divers people being at a great loss about the doctrine held forth therein.

7. Mary Bradish with me on account of her spiritual troubles. Cousin Winchester also.

11. Mr. Bliss here, on his journey to Grafton and Sutton. I rode Mr. Benjamin How's horse to Shrewsbury, and preached to the society of lads there, on 2 Cor. 6: 2.

13. I rode Mr. Burns's horse to Marlborough, and preached the lecture on Eph. 5: 14.

14. Mr. [or Mrs.] Williams here again, — Sarah Bellows, — Daniel Stone and his wife, — all of them candidates for the communion.

17. Phineas Forbush with me upon his soul distresses. N. B. News from Grafton, that Mr. Philemon Robbins preached there yesterday, and twenty or more persons fell down with distress and anguish.

18. Exercise to young women on Ps. 73: 24. — Mrs. Edwards from Northampton, and Searl, a Freshman of New Haven College, here, and lodged here.

19. Sweet converse with Mrs. Edwards, a very eminent Christian. At half after eleven I left home and rode to Sutton Falls. Preached there on Eph. 5: 14. After meeting, an elderly woman, one Mrs. White, whose husband is a Baptist, so overcome that she was led into Mr. Hall's. She seemed to be in great distress, but she had much joy and love.

21. My wife rode with me to Stephen Fay's, where I preached on Mat. 3: 10. The assembly somewhat considerable, being there was a town meeting at the same time to choose a representative. Ensign Maynard chosen, but refused. Town then concluded not to send. I had a great cold.

23.—At eve, called at Ensign Maynard's, to visit Mrs. Wheeler of Concord, (heretofore Rebecca Lee,) who was under a grievous melancholy and mingled despair and distraction.

[25. Rode to Boston.]

26.—Mr. Appleton preached excellently to the Court, from Ps. 72: 1, 2. P. M. When I went to Dr. Sewall's, there was but a thin appearance of ministers; upon which I heard Mr. John Caldwell, at the French meetinghouse. The drift was against false prophets, and not without bitterness, mixed with his wit and sense. I sat very uneasy, and went out as soon as it was done. Went up to Mr. Chauncy's, the convention being adjourned. Some number of ministers there, congratulating him upon his being made Doctor of Divinity by the University of Edinburgh. Our conversation was upon assurance; the ground of it, the manner of obtaining it, and the special operation of the Holy Spirit therein. A very useful conversation; Mr. Barnard and others having talked very judiciously and piously upon it. Sought Mrs. Edwards fruitlessly.

27. Mr. Loring preached to the ministers from 2 Cor. 2:16, last clause. The contribution, I understand, amounted to £230.—P. M. I went to Dr. Chauncy's, where was a very considerable number of ministers in conversation upon the present state of things with respect to religion.

28. [Returned home.]

29. Mrs. Edwards, and young Searl with her, in her journey to Northampton.

30. On Song, 2: 16. N. B. Mrs. Edwards' conversation very wonderful,—her sense of divine things.

31. I rode with Mrs. Edwards to Shrewsbury, but could not proceed to Worcester, as I had purposed.

*June* 8. Mr. Wheeler at evening, opposing my late doctrine from Eph. 5: 14,—that the natural man can do nothing but what is sinful.

15. Much interrupted in the morning with Mr. Joseph Wheeler, who takes exceptions against the doctrines I deliver one Sabbath after another. I rode to Mr. Loring's of Sudbury, where the association met. There were Mr. J. Prentice, Mr. Cushing, Mr. N. Stone, and Mr. Buckminster. Mr. Buckminster offered himself to be examined. He was so, and he delivered a sermon on Luke 10: 41, 42. At eve, I asked advice respecting the doctrine I had lately delivered from Eph. 5: 14, and Rom. 8: 8, and on that question,—"Are there not some promises made to humble, fervent strivers, that they shall obtain the grace of God?"—N. B. Council at Concord, called by Ezekiel Miles and others, dissatisfied with Mr. Bliss.

16. Very useful and profitable conversations upon several heads of divinity, especially referring to the great article of conversion. Comparing several of Mr. Stoddard's writings. I also read a large paper of the experiences of a young woman, a member of the church in Westborough, which I had from her own Mss.

20. I preached at Shrewsbury, A. M. and P. M. on Eph. 5: 14.

22. My sixth exposition of the catechism, to thirty-eight young women. N. B. Elizabeth Chamberlain and Mr. Joseph Green, upon soul affairs.

24. I rode over to the north of Shrewsbury, and preached to a young society there on 1 Thess. 1: 10.

28. I rode over to Hopkinton, at the request of Isaac How, who lay in a low languishment. His state of mind I feared to be very dreadful, because of his insensibility of the amazing wrath of God, and being so comfortable in the apprehensions of death, notwithstanding his impenitence. Many had expected me to preach; but I received no hint of his desiring any thing of that; besides, that there was no intimations from Rev. Mr. Barrett especially, of any thing of it.

29. Mrs. Snell was with me about her owning the covenant; as was also Mr. Jonathan Brigham and his wife.

30. [Received a request from the Rev. Mr. Barrett and Isaac How, to preach to How to-morrow.]

*July* 1. I rode over to Hopkinton, and Isaac How being yet alive and an assembly gathered, at the house of Mr. Josiah Rice, I preached there on 1 Tim. 1 : 15; followed with a moving and awakening address to the poor dying man, who seemed to take it in some suitable manner, to outward appearance; but I fear he has not really an apprehension of his astonishing danger, but is in a false peace. The assembly were very attentive, and some number affected.

6. Rode to Charlestown; made a visit to Mr. Davenport, who kept at Major Jenner's.

8. I rode to Boston. Mr. Hooper's public lecture on 1 John, 5 : 3. P. M. I was at Dr. Chauncy's, where was Mr. Barnard of Marblehead and his lady. Afterwards came Mr. Hooper, and Mr. Malcolm, Episcopal minister of Marblehead. The conversation turned upon Mr Davenport, who is the subject everywhere. But few among the wise and worthy, but judge he is touched in his brain. Mr. Malcolm and I walked down to the North End, and up Snow Hill, to hear him. There had been a thunderstorm, and there were little showers in time of exercise. The sermon was from Rev. 22 : 17; a very fervent exhortation, and to unconverted ministers in special. Said he was then in the experience of the Divine Spirit's influences. Said he was then ready to drop down dead for the salvation of but one soul, &c. After sermon, a considerable number of ministers went to Mr. Webb's, who gave us an account of the disorders in that neighbourhood last night, by people's being so late at Mr. Procter's; (where Mr. Davenport lodges, and which is right over against Mr. Webb's;) and he also informed us of his discourse with Mr. Davenport this morning, concerning his conduct and actions, (in running out into the street among the crowd, and crying out to them in an indecent voice, gesture &c.,) but to no purpose. he supposing himself to be under the immediate impressions and directions of the Divine Spirit. In a word, Mr. Webb concludes him to be crazed.

9. [Returned home. — From about this time, the "throat distemper" prevailed, and was often fatal.]

25. Mr. Jacob Amsden's wife came to meeting, who has never been at the public worship till now, ever since I was first in this town.

*August* 10. [He was called to Cambridge and Boston by his mother's sickness.]

19. The great disturbance last night, by means of Mr. Davenport's condemning the ministers of Boston as unconverted; and Dr. Colman, Dr. Sewall, and Dr. Chauncy, by name.

20. Mr. Davenport condemned by name nine more of the ministers.

Grand Jury, I hear, have sat, and have found a bill against him as a disturber of the peace.

24. The association met at my house.

25. N. B. The account Mr. Weld gave of the remarkable work of God among them [at Attleborough].

30. Mr. Nathaniel Smith of Hopkinton here, for advice respecting his son Nathaniel, who was so oppressed and overcome with the affairs of his soul and another world, that he would not attend to the necessary supports of life.

*September* 10. N. B. Mr. Davenport at Capt. Fay's, going upwards.

12. On 1 Thess. 5: 19. The congregation much moved. At noon, Molly Gurfield of Shrewsbury greatly distressed, being awakened by the forenoon sermon, earnestly desired prayers P. M. for her.

13. N. B. Mr. Daniel Rogers of Ipswich, Dr. Gott, and Mr. Dodge came and dined with us. Mr. Rogers had preached three times at Marlborough.

18. Mr. Parsons of Lyme made me a kind visit, and I persuaded him to stay and keep Sabbath here.

19. I preached at Marlborough. I rode up home at eve. Found Mr. Parsons preaching with great fervency to young people, on the gathering manna in the morning. It made great impression. But the most remarkable signs were immediately after the blessing was pronounced. Mr. Stephen Fay's wife cried out, and cousin Winchester presently upon it, both of whom strove what they could to contain themselves, but burst forth with great agony of soul. Sarah Shattuck and Betsey Fay discovered also their inward distress. But Sarah Sparhawk was unbounded, and like one deprived of her reason. A great tumult ensued. Mr. Parsons advised me to compose them, and either pray or sing a psalm. I requested him to direct to a psalm. After singing, I spoke strongly to the people, advising and beseeching them to retire to private meditation and prayer; and it had success. Sarah Sparhawk was brought away home by some young men. A number of the distressed and others came to my house, but went home about nine o'clock. Sarah Sparhawk was however often crying out, and striving much in her fits for an hour or two;—then went to bed and slept well.

20. Mr. Parsons took leave. Sarah Shattuck and Betty Chamberlain here to take advice upon their spiritual concerns, and Sarah Bellows was very helpful in family business, instead of Sarah Sparhawk, who was still feeble and pensive, and could do little.

21. P. M. I preached to a number that gathered together and requested it, but no public notice had been given. I repeated, as I was desired, my last sermon on 1 Thess. 5: 19. N. B. Sarah Sparhawk cried out again, and was in much distress.

30. My wife rode with me to Hopkinton. Mr. Moody of York was to preach A. M., but at 11 o'clock Mr. Barrett with a message and the Bible to me, that I must preach. Mr. Barrett prayed before sermon. I preached on Eph. 5: 14. P. M. Mr. Stone prayed, and Mr. Moody preached on Prov. 1: 23. At evening Mr. Barrett was requested to suffer Mr. Bliss to preach an evening lecture; but he would not allow of its being publicly in the meetinghouse. He gave way to its being at a private house.

*October* 4. Stephen Fay here, in various religious disquietments. His brother James here at evening; and while some young women, Sarah Shattuck, Mary Graves, and Sarah Bellows, were receiving instructions from me in singing, Mr. Fay was in much spiritual commotion; but while we were singing the 63d psalm, he was in a peculiar manner rapt in spiritual delight, and panted with the overbearing joy and admiration of the divine greatness and condescension to us, and his patience towards us; and his expressions of these things were very becoming and noticeable.

13 [Went to Boston and Cambridge.]

15. At Deacon Sparhawk's, to discourse with them concerning Sarah, and apprized them of my unwillingness to keep her. I returned home.

20. Mr. Hall preached a moving sermon on John 5: 40. No crying out in the meetinghouse; but, as I was going home from the meetinghouse, Mrs. Ruth Fay, in anguish of spirit, burst out and went into my house. I took her into my study, and gave her what instructions I could. In the mean time Sarah Sparhawk was crying and screaming upon her bed in another part of the house. Many people were in the house below. Mr. Edwards of Northampton was come, and both he and Mr. Hall assisted me in ministering to these distressed souls, and others that needed. It was an evening of great engagement.

21. Mr. Hall and Mr. Edwards went, the one to Sutton and the other to Boston.

23. N. B. I have understood there are various commotions on religious accounts among brethren on the south side of the town.

56. Mr. Secomb went with me to the Association at Marlborough. A considerable number of ministers and candidates. The conversation turned mostly of all upon the times. Mr. Marsh of Wachusett very full of his stories, to discredit those who were zealous in promoting convictions, &c.

27. N. B. Mr. Loring's angry rebuke directed to me at dinner, for opposing Mr. Marsh.

28. We have the utmost reason to celebrate the divine patience and long suffering, inasmuch as he has not only waited three years upon this church, and upon me their unworthy pastor, seeking fruit upon us; nor only three times three; but this day it is no less space than twice three times three years. O may we be humbled for our manifold defects and unprofitableness! O might I, in peculiar, who have the greatest need! And may God, of his infinite mercy, grant us grace, and to me in special, that, henceforth, we may bring some fruit to his glory! *Jejun. Priv.*

31. On Hab. 6: 7, 8; in which I endeavoured to improve the divine admonitions and instructions to our quickening and awakening. See the 28th day.

*November* 16. N. B. Mr. Stephen Fay here, and tarried and dined with me; was with me all the afternoon, and some part of the evening. He revealed several wonderful experiences which he had, both last spring and lately. He told me he had a weighty, pressing concern for two souls. I found he meant his own and mine. I asked him what he had discovered in me, that gave him reason to suspect me. He told me, my preaching and conversation; for that if I had a true sight of eternal things, he thought I should be more zealous and fervent; for, for his part, he felt as if he could cry out, &c. I confessed my dullness; yet made some appeal to my sermons, especially of late delivered. I spoke of the different tempers of men; the diversities of gifts, but the same spirit; the different frames which both speakers and hearers are in at different times; professed, however, my need of divine grace and the supply of the Spirit, to revive and quicken and furnish and assist me, and of his prayers, (and asked them,) that I might obtain the presence and Spirit of God with me; and whatever God should afford, should give in to me, I would endeavour to give out to them. We parted in great peace and love. May the Lord sanctify the admonition to me, and hereby stir up in me a spirit of care and jealousy over my own soul; and enliven me with respect to the souls committed to my care! O might it please God to impress me deeply with the worth of immortal souls, and my tremendous account in the day of Christ, of those of this flock, and of all my charge!

18. Mr. Cushing here P. M. He came on the business of Sarah Sparhawk's living here, that he might write to her grandfather about her. But she grows so untoward, that we drew up determinations to put her away, unless she will reform.

22. P. M. came Mr. Samuel Streeter, of Hopkinton, and gave me some account of himself and his spiritual state for some years past, but especially of his darkness and trouble till the fast at Hopkinton last December 29, and (to God the sole glory) the help he received by my sermon on Ps. 63: 8.

26. Mr. Prentice of Grafton came to see me. I inquired whether he had sought reconcilement with Mr. Loring of Sudbury, as he had engaged at Rutland. He could not say he had. He brought me his church's desire and his own, to assist them in a fast next Thursday come sennight. But I insisted upon his reconcilement with Mr. Loring. N. B. Mr. Hall had told him and his wife, that at his late visit to me, I received him but coldly.

*December* 4. [Returned home from Boston, late, and in bad weather. Took cold, which brought on rheumatism and fever, from which he was slowly recovering Dec. 20.]

9. A fast at Grafton. — Sarah Sparhawk very intolerable in insisting to go to Grafton, though there was nobody at home but she to take care of the business of the house, my wife waiting on me.

18. I had sent a letter to Mr. Joseph Sparhawk, but no return. The ways heavy yet, but sent Ebenezer with Sarah to said Mr. Sparhawk at Sutton.

## CHAPTER XIII.

EDWARDS.—The Revival at Enfield.—Outcries, Faintings, and Convulsions.

IT cannot be said that, during all these transactions, Jonathan Edwards was the presiding mind of New England. His reputation and influence had indeed been increasing rapidly, both in America and in Europe; and perhaps there was no other man in New England whom the friends of piety esteemed so highly, or from whom they expected so much. But New England never, at any period of her history, had a presiding mind. Even among the Orthodox Congregational clergy, there has never been a man who could procure the adoption of his own views, without the aid of others who agreed with him substantially, and who did not borrow their views from him. Edwards, indeed, had done more than any other man to awaken the ministry and the churches in the first instance, and to produce the movement which had now become general. But it was a movement of minds that thought for themselves. No one man, therefore, could guide it. Many would be sure to throw in the influence of their peculiarities, — their wisdom, their folly, and their passions, — to modify the result. Whitefield had shot across the land like a meteor, flashing light, and creating astonishment and admiration. Tennent, from the revival school in New Jersey, which, though harmonious and in correspondence with that at Northampton, was not derived from it, had taken his own way, and perhaps having contracted something of a tone of defiance from the warfare in which he had been engaged, he, unlike Edwards, sometimes irritated the wicked without overawing them. The fervid Parsons, who was a safe man only because he learned so readily by experience, and retreated so quickly from the borders of error, had enkindled a spirit like his own around the mouth of the Connecticut. Wheelock and Pomroy had spread wide an impulse, generally in the right direction, but not sufficiently discriminating. And finally, the learned, orthodox and pious clergy of Boston were still regarded as the chief depositaries of influence; and though they gladly borrowed thoughts from all, and most readily from their esteemed friend at Northampton, could give themselves up to the guidance of none. The character of the revival, then, was derived from many independent sources, each imparting characteristic traits, which prevailed according to the power from which it sprung. The influence of Edwards made no forced marches, but was steadily advancing to the occupation of the whole country; and it continued to advance, while he lived and after his death.

Still, he was perhaps the most efficient preacher in New England, even if judged by the immediate effect of his sermons. Many think of him as an intellectual giant, indeed, but as a giant wholly composed of intellect, and suppose that his power consisted entirely in the cold conclusiveness of his unimpassioned logic. A greater mistake is scarce possible. Besides his logic, there was his strong and realizing faith. God, heaven, hell, the sinfulness of sin, the beauty of holiness, the glory of Christ and the claims of his gospel, were as substantial realities to his mind and heart, as the valley of the Connecticut or the mountains of Berkshire. He spoke of them accordingly, and made them seem real to his hearers. He was perhaps as remarkable for his power and habit of deep and strong and tender feeling, as for his powers of argumentation. Take a specimen, from his own personal narrative.

"Sometimes, only mentioning a single word, caused my heart to burn within me; or only seeing the name of Christ, or the name of some attribute of God.—The sweetest joys and delights I have experienced, have not been those that have arisen from a hope of my own good estate; but in a direct view of the glorious things of the gospel. When I enjoy this sweetness, it seems to carry me above the thoughts of my own estate. It seems, at such times, a loss that I cannot bear, to take off my eye from the glorious pleasant object I behold without me, to turn my eye in upon myself, and my own good estate."

"Once, as I rode out into the woods for my health, in 1737, having alighted from my horse in a retired place, as my manner commonly has been, to walk for divine contemplation and prayer, I had a view, that for me was extraordinary, of the glory of the Son of God, as mediator between God and man, and his wonderful, great, full, pure and sweet grace and love, and meek and gentle condescension. This grace, that appeared so calm and sweet, appeared also great above the heavens. The person of Christ appeared ineffably excellent, with an excellency great enough to swallow up all thought and conception;—which continued, as near as I can judge, about an hour; which kept me the greater part of the time in a flood of tears, weeping aloud. I felt an ardency of soul to be, what I know not how otherwise to express, emptied and annihilated; to lie in the dust, and to be full of Christ alone; to love him with a holy and pure love; to trust in him; to live upon him; to serve and follow him; and to be perfectly sanctified and made pure, with a divine and heavenly purity. I have several other times had views very much of the same nature, and which have had the same effects."

Such a man must have felt strongly when he preached. He must have been powerfully moved with compassion for the souls of his hearers, and with desires for their salvation. And besides this, he must have preached with an ardent zeal for the glory of God; with an intense anxiety that the divine object of his affections should not be wronged, by the withholding of that love and trust and reverence which are his due.

The traits already mentioned imply a powerful imagination; and in this respect he has seldom had a superior. Heaven and holiness were too heavenly and holy, in his apprehension, to be set forth by earthly imagery; yet he has left us some bright specimens of the beautiful.

"Holiness, as I then wrote down some of my contemplations on it, appeared to me to be of a sweet, pleasant, charming, serene, calm nature; which brought an inexpressible purity, brightness, peacefulness and ravishment to the soul. In other words, it made the soul like a field or garden of God, with all manner of pleasant flowers; enjoying a sweet calm, and the gentle, vivifying beams of the sun. The soul of a true Christian, as I then wrote my meditations, appeared like such a little white flower as we see in the spring of the year; low and humble on the ground, opening its bosom to receive the pleasant beams of the sun's glory; rejoicing, as it were, in a calm rapture; diffusing around a sweet fragrancy; standing peacefully and lovingly in the midst of other flowers round about, all in like manner opening their bosoms to drink in the light of the sun."

What delicate imagery is here! What exquisite personification of the flowers of the garden, endowing them with life, and consciousness, and moral beauty! How naturally these lovely musings "move harmonious numbers," so that his very words flow sweetly as he utters them!

But the most wonderful displays of his imagination were put forth in describing the imminent danger of the wicked, and the awful scenes that await the enemies of God. There is nothing of the kind in the great masters of English poetry, or of any other uninspired poetry, that equals, in imaginative power, many passages in his sermons. Read his sermon on the Punishment of the Wicked, or that on the Eternity of Hell Torments. Or rather, read that entitled "Sinners in the hands of an angry God;" of the preaching and effects of which we have an account.

It was preached at Enfield, July 8, 1741. "While the people in the neighbouring towns were in great distress for their souls," says the historian,* "the inhabitants of that town were very secure, loose, and vain. A lecture had been appointed at Enfield ; and the neighbouring people, the night before, were so affected at the thoughtlessness of the inhabitants, and in such fears that God would, in his righteous judgment, pass them by, while the divine showers were falling all around them, as to be prostrate before him a considerable part of it, supplicating mercy for their souls. When the appointed time for the lecture came, a number of the neighbouring ministers attended, and some from a distance. When they went into the meetinghouse, the appearance of the assembly was thoughtless and vain. The people hardly conducted themselves with common decency." Edwards preached. His plain, unpretending manner, both in language and delivery, and his established reputation for holiness and knowledge of the truth, forbade the suspicion that any trick of oratory would be used to mislead his hearers. He began in the clear, careful, demonstrative style of a teacher, solicitous for the result of his effort, and anxious that every step of his argument should be clearly and fully understood. His text was, Deut. 32 : 35. "Their foot shall slide in due time." As he advanced in unfolding the meaning of the text, the most careful logic brought him and his hearers to conclusions, which the most tremendous imagery could but inadequately express. His most terrific descriptions of the doom and danger of the impenitent, only enabled them to apprehend more clearly the truths which he had compelled them to believe. They seemed to be, not the product of the imagination, but, — what they really were, — a part of the argument. The effect was as might have been expected. Trumbull informs us, that "before the sermon was ended, the assembly appeared deeply impressed and bowed down with an awful conviction of their sin and danger. There was such a breathing of distress and weeping, that the preacher was obliged to speak to the people and desire silence, that he might be heard. This was the beginning of the same great and prevailing concern in that place, with which the colony in general was visited."

---

* Trumbull's History of Connecticut, Vol. II. p. 145. Trumbull learned the particulars from Wheelock, of Lebanon, who was present.

Edwards was often called to preach beyond the limits of his own parish; and "whithersoever he turned himself," he seems to have prospered. In the winter of 1742, he spent some weeks, by invitation, at Leicester, of which we only know that his labors were attended with distinguished success.* There is no reason to doubt that scenes much like those at Enfield occurred in many places under his preaching. Those who understand the force of his sermon at Enfield will not wonder, that men who were awakened and convinced by it, were unable to conceal their anguish, and "cried out" in bitterness of spirit. Edwards was right in doubting whether those who blamed such outcries, would behave much better, if they had equally clear views of their own guilt and danger. We must remember, too, that the sentiments and usages of society, a century ago, did not require that universal repression of feeling, which is now expected in all well-educated people. The Puritans of the first generation were by no means scandalized, when their people felt so strongly that they could not conceal their emotions. Of Thomas Shepard, the holy minister of Cambridge, it was said, "that he scarce ever preached a sermon, but some or other of his congregation were struck with great distress, and cried out in agony, what shall I do to be saved?" This was so much expected, that those who had been detained from worship used to ask, "Who hath been wrought upon to day?" In the time of Edwards, audible expressions of feeling by the hearers in public worship had begun to be considered indecorous; for hearers were not expected to be overcome by strong emotions; but the demand of public sentiment for silence was much less imperative then than now.

It was a time, too, of agitable nerves. There had been two centuries of tremendous nervous excitement. There had been the Reformation, the peasant's war, and the religious wars in Germany; the Reformation, the rise of Puritanism, the republic, and the times of the Covenanters in Great Britain; the rise of Protestantism, the religious wars, and the persecutions of the Huguenots in France, ending with the appearance of the "French prophets" in the Cevennes, some of whom were still holding forth among their followers

* The appendix to Chapter XII. shows that he spent a part of the time in other towns.

in London. New England sprung out of some of the strongest, deepest, and most permanent of these excitements; and, to say nothing of her religious history, her contest with boisterous seas, and gloomy, unexplored forests, and savage foes, the arrow from an unseen hand by day and the warwhoop that startled her sleepers by night, had kept her spirit ready for excitement. Though not to be frightened, she was easily roused, even to an unnatural intensity of feeling and action.

The presence and agency of the spiritual world were much more real to men's minds than they are now. The discussions which grew out of the Salem tragedy, had shown the fallacy of those principles of evidence, on which persons had, up to that time, been condemned and executed for witchcraft in every nation of Christendom; * but the British statute for punishing witchcraft with death was still in force, and the belief in its reality was still general. Spirits, good and bad, were then expected, by multitudes, occasionally to produce sensible effects on the visible world, and especially on sentient bodies. And as the influence of the mind and the nerves on each other and on the whole human system had not been investigated as it has since, many phenomena were naturally referred to supernatural agency, which now would be referred at once to well known laws.

With these facts in view, the reader of Edwards' Enfield sermon cannot be surprised at its visible and audible effects. Nor can it be thought surprising that some, constitutionally accessible to such influences, fainted, fell down, or were thrown into convulsions on similar occasions. Nor is it stranger than dreaming, while their bodies were thus overcome, the activity of their minds should continue; that the train of thought which had subdued them, should keep possession of them; that their imaginations should give to the objects of their thoughts, the appearance of bodily form; in short, that there should be trances and visions. Nor is it at all incredible that these trances and visions should help them forward in the knowledge of the truth. If the trains of thought that overcame them were advancing in the right direction, that intense nervous excitement might increase their power, and enable them to see truths which, in the calm of

* Had the fallacy of those principles been exposed in any other part of the world? Or has New England the honor of first showing, that the ordinarily admitted evidence of witchcraft was insufficient?

ordinary health and unimpassioned meditation, would have been beyond their reach. And then, in every time of revival, there are some who remain wilfully unmoved and unconvinced. Where this required strong and protracted effort, the mental and nervous excitement which that effort cost, increased the liability to fainting and convulsions. And when they came on, and the man found himself mastered by an invisible power, which he could neither resist nor understand, but which, in some mysterious way, accompanied the arguments that he was wilfully and wickedly resisting ; when the power of divine truth over him had become manifest to all, and his perverse pride of character, as an unmoved despiser of religious terrors, was prostrate, so that his motive for concealment was gone ; it was natural that he should yield to the arguments which had before loudly demanded his assent.

Still it will be said, that men who were thus impelled to cry out, who fainted, fell, and had convulsions, were under an awful delusion ; that the gospel addresses men kindly, and bids them hope ; that, if they had been taught and had understood and believed its messages of mercy, they would have been filled with joy and peace ; that, therefore, the terrific view of their condition, which filled their minds and overcame their hearts, was an erroneous view, such as men under the gospel ought not to entertain ; and that their teachers should have striven to fill their minds with the comforts which the gospel offers. This is all true; and Edwards and his friends knew it, and acted accordingly. These alarmed, convicted sinners *were* under an awful delusion, and that delusion was what kept them from peace, and from rejoicing in God their Saviour ; but their delusion shortly before, while they were sinning thoughtlessly and carelessly, was still more awful. They had left the path of duty and of safety, and in proud self-reliance had wandered forth upon the dark mountains, despising what they esteemed idle tales of danger. At length, the lightnings of the gathering storm show them where they are, — on the brink of a fatal precipice. They start back and gaze around with horror. Before them and below them, are bones, and putrid corpses, and mangled bodies writhing death. Above them are the fires and thunders of the tempest. Behind them and around them are the howling winds, and the rising, rushing floods, and the falling trees, and the roar of lions, seeking whom they may devour. There is a safe path, and the voice of the guide is heard behind them, saying "This is the way; walk ye in it;" but they have learned to regard it as the voice of a fool, or a madman, or of one that would lead them into perpetual gloom; and they neither understand nor heed it. They see nothing, hear nothing, think of nothing, but what threatens instant ruin. They are under an awful delusion, which fills them with terror, and, unless soon dispelled, will plunge them into destruction. But blame not the flash of light which showed them where they stood. Without it, the next step would have been into perdition. Now, they may perish in their consternation; but it may also be, that they will hear the voice that calls them to safety, and their souls will live.

It is very true, that "preaching hell cannot frighten men into religion;" but it may frighten them into serious thought, and secure to religious truth that attention, without which it cannot save the soul. After all that can be said of the power of love and of kindness, and the winning accents of mercy, and the like, it remains an awful truth, that men will not give any efficient attention to these things, till they have been first brought to see their need of them. Till then, all that they hear about the mercy of God, only gives them courage to neglect him.

But these views, though true and conclusive, do not go to the bottom of the subject. These sinners were not merely alarmed, but convicted. They not only were told of their danger, but were made to see their guilt; and it was the sight of their guilt, that fastened upon them the conviction of their danger. Examine the accounts given by Edwards, by Prince, by Crocker, and by others, of the exercises of the convicted. These men understood what they were writing of, and carefully observed the distinction between the mere alarm of a frightened man, and the rational conviction of one who feels remorse for sins which he knows he has committed. They examined the awakened diligently on this very point, and made no account of any awakening which was not clearly of the latter kind. To condemn the whole, therefore, as the effect of irrational fright, is to show a culpable disregard of well-attested facts Where they found this clear and rational conviction, Edwards and his fellow-laborers were right in pronouncing the work genuine, notwithstanding any irregularities or strange effects upon the body, that might attend it.

Still, such "outward manifestations" are exceedingly to be deprecated. They imply a state of the nerves, in which the mind does not operate safely. It acts with increased vigor, and may do more and better than at other times; but its liability to error is increased. Strong hopes or fears may give an apparent conclusiveness to false reasonings. Vivid impressions on the fancy may be mistaken for clear perceptions of truth. And among the more ignorant, the bodily agitations themselves may come to be counted valuable; and then men will trust in them, and seek after them, and learn to produce them voluntarily; and thus religion may be degraded into a mere system of nervous excitement. These "manifestations," therefore, though they do not prove the work in which they commence, to be spurious, are a fearful sign that it will soon become so; and as they prevail, false conversions will be sure to multiply.

Occasional instances of this kind will occur, wherever religion appeals with sufficient force to the heart. Persons sometimes involuntarily "cry out," fall down, faint, or go into convulsions, on occasions of unexpected joy or grief, as the arrival or death of a friend; and whenever a religious consideration moves a person susceptible of such influences with equal force, and especially with equal suddenness, the same effect naturally follows. Where they are understood and treated as the result of human or individual weakness, they amount to little more than an inconvenience to the persons afflicted, and to a few immediately around them. But where they are valued and cultivated, another principle comes in, — that of sympathy, or involuntary imitation, and they grow into what may be called, with the strictest propriety, an epidemic disease. The process has never been fully explained, but is illustrated by many analogous facts. A man may walk without difficulty on a plank six inches wide, laid on the ground. But let him attempt to walk on that same plank, one hundred feet from the earth, and his head swims. The thought of falling "from such pernicious height" makes a strong impression on his mind, takes away his sense of safety, deprives him of the control of his own muscles, and, in the end, makes him fall. So the expectation or the dread of being thrown into convulsions, or any other feeling which fixes the thoughts strongly upon it, even if it be a feeling of strong unwillingness, may be the means of bringing them on.

There have been many instances, more or less extensive, of such epidemics. On this principle, Mesmer, the author of animal magnetism, produced many of the phenomena that appeared in great companies of patients. The poor-house at Haerlem was pervaded, for a time, by convulsions, frequently recurring, and propagated from one to another by sight. But though their occasions have been various, they have more frequently attended religious excitements, than any other single concomitant. One of the most remarkable examples attended the great "Kentucky revival," which commenced in 1800. Of this we have accounts from able and learned men, physicians, divines, and others, who were eyewitnesses and careful observers;* but the most graphic and instructive seems to be that of the shrewd, though eccentric, Lorenzo Dow. He preached in the Court-house at Knoxville, Tennessee, in 1805, when about one hundred and fifty of his hearers were exercised with "the jerks"; that is, with violent spasmodic contractions of the muscles, which sometimes turned the head quickly from right to left and back again; and sometimes threw the person on the ground, where he flounced like a live fish. He says, "I have seen all denominations of religion, exercised with the jerks, gentleman and lady, black and white, young and old, without exception. I have passed a meetinghouse, where I observed the undergrowth had been cut for a camp meeting, and from fifty to a hundred saplings were left, breast high, on purpose for the people who were jerked, to hold on by. I observed, where they had held on, they had kicked up the earth, as a horse stamping flies. A Presbyterian minister told me, while he was preaching, the day before, some had the jerks. I believe it does not affect those naturalists, who wish and try to get it to philosophize upon it; and rarely those who are the most pious; but the lukewarm, lazy professor is subject to it. The wicked fear it, and are subject to it; but the persecutors are more subject to it than any, and they have sometimes cursed and swore and damned it, while jerking." The remark concerning naturalists is

---

* The account given by the Rev. Dr. Alexander may be found in the Connecticut Evan. Mag. Vol. II. p. 354.

what might be expected. Franklin and his fellow commissioners, appointed by the king of France to investigate the claims of animal magnetism, could not get the "jerks" which Mesmer inflicted upon his patients, "to philosophize upon," with all the assistance the magnetizer could render. The deep, established peace of mind of "the most pious," too, was generally a protection. Dr. Robertson, an eyewitness, says, in his Inaugural Essay before the Medical Faculty at Philadelphia: — "It attacks both sexes, and every constitution; but evidently more readily, those who are enthusiasts in religion;" that is, Dow's "lukewarm, lazy professors," when heated; for enthusiasts are usually of that class. Dr. Alexander says, that the phenomena "were common to all ages and sexes, and to all sorts of characters." Dow says, that "persecutors" had it, without relaxing their open hatred of religion. Others testify that they have been thrown into "the jerks" by hearing a description of the jerking of others, and without any religious impression, either attending or following the attack.*

It is evident, therefore, that in this instance, although these spasmodic contractions of the muscles, in the beginning, had their rise from strong religious excitement, they soon became a genuine epidemic; a distinct matter from the revival; as really distinct as the cold and cough, which a person may take by attending worship, is from his devotion while worshipping. It thenceforth subsisted independently of the cause that produced it; spread itself by its own laws, and was connected with the revival only by subsisting at the same time and in the same place, and affecting, in many instances, but not in all, the same subjects.

Towards the close of the Great Awakening of 1740, these "manifestations" began to assume the character of an epidemic; though by no means so clearly as in the "Kentucky revival." The various steps of the process are not so clearly marked, as the reader would desire. No one seems to have made them the subject of calm physiological observation. Men looked upon them and wrote about them, merely in their bearing on the genuineness of the revival;

* This subject is ably illustrated in an "Essay upon the Influence of the Imagination on the Nervous System, contributing to a False Hope in Religion, by Rev. Grant Powers." It was published at Andover, by Flagg & Gould, in 1828, and has furnished several of the facts here mentioned.

some alleging them as proof of its spuriousness, and others adducing them as marks of its divine origin; while sound divines, generally, considered them as the results of human weakness under the powerful operations of the Holy Spirit, and thus as the measure of the amount of divine power exerted on the several subjects.

Insulated cases, but not unfrequent, occurred from the commencement of this awakening. They appeared under the preaching of Blair, in Pennsylvania, in 1739. Blair, as appears by his own account, in a former part of this volume, was peculiarly suspicious of the soundness of the spiritual work in such as were thus affected, and examined them with unusual closeness; though, when he found the spiritual part as it should be, he was too good a philosopher to condemn the work on account of the state of the body. The Scotch Presbyterians, among whom Blair preached, might have seen such things before their emigration; for there had been not a few instances of the kind in their father land, many years before. Whitefield had seen them in England. Among the Methodists, they first appeared under the preaching of the Wesleys. John received and valued them as proofs of the divine presence, and they increased under his labors. Charles discouraged them, and in one instance, at least, recorded his suspicion of hypocrisy. Whitefield was incredulous; and when at last some, who had been John Wesley's hearers, fell down under Whitefield's preaching, Wesley thanked God for it, thinking that Whitefield would then be convinced. The argument seems to have failed; for when Whitefield saw the same "manifestations" under his preaching in Pennsylvania and New Jersey, in 1740, he ascribed them to diabolic influence. "Satan now begins to throw many into fits."* Our accounts from this region are very defective. Gilbert Tennent, who had the best opportunities for observation, kept no journal. Blair's account of the revival among his people, already quoted, and a few incidental remarks of Whitefield and others, are our only sources of information. Mr. Dickinson, in his account of the awakening at Elizabethtown, June, 1740, writes: "There was no crying out, or falling down, *as has elsewhere happened.*" William Tennent states, that under the ministry of his brother John, who was

---

* Letter from Reedy Island, May 19.

ordained at Freehold, N. J. November 19, 1730, and died April 23, 1732, "it was no uncommon thing to see persons, in the time of hearing, sobbing as if their hearts would break, but without any public outcry: and some have been carried out of the assembly, (being overcome,) as if they had been dead." Gillies * mentions faintings, so that a number were carried out in a state of insensibility, under the preaching of Rowland, in a Baptist church, probably at Philadelphia; but he gives no date. Gilbert Tennent was present; and at his suggestion, Rowland changed the style of his discourse, and the faintings ceased. In Finley's Nottingham sermon, "Christ triumphing and Satan raging,"—"wherein is proved that the kingdom of God is come unto us at this day," which was printed at Philadelphia, Boston, and London in 1741, † we are told that opposers of the revival, "without observing the deep concern that souls seem to be under,—only ask about the fits and convulsions that their sorrow throws them into." In New England, some instances of fainting and falling attended the "Surprising Conversions" at and around Northampton in 1735; but, so far as appears, without convulsions.

We may conclude, therefore, with little hazard of error, that the nervous diathesis, as physicians say, of the age was favorable to such phenomena; that sporadic cases were more frequent then than now; that when one happened under some alarming or exciting sermon, other individuals, already predisposed, and strongly moved by the preaching, would be more readily affected in the same way; and that, on this side of the Atlantic, they first became prevalent, so as to be a common, though not constant attendant on revivals, in New Jersey and Pennsylvania. How were they made prevalent in New England?

Here, as everywhere, the nervous diathesis favored their production; and the wonder with which they were viewed, increased the predisposition. They occurred in considerable numbers, under the preaching of Parsons, at Lyme, and of others, in other places. Ministers who saw such effects produced by preaching the truth with prayer and singleness

* Life of Whitefield, p. 39; note.

† A copy of the Boston edition of 1742, is in the O. S. Ch. Lib. It is a tremendous discourse, scarcely less scorching than Tennent's Nottingham sermon.

of heart; who, by careful examination, found that they were accompanied with rational conviction, and followed by sound conversion, dared not treat them otherwise than gently. They never ascribed these bodily agitations to divine influence directly, as was slanderously reported; but to those convictions, hopes, and fears, which divine influence had imparted, and which produced the same effects as equally violent feelings concerning wordly things might have done. This distinction they carefully and clearly made and abundantly urged; and their adversaries committed sin in wilfully overlooking it. But after all, the lenity with which these "manifestations" were treated, though natural, was too great, and the ignorant took occasion to consider them as parts of the revival, — of that process by which their souls were to be saved. A more decided discouragement of them would have saved a vast amount of evil. "As to visions," says good old father White, of Gloucester, "we had enough of them, until such time as in a lecture-sermon, I declared my sentiments concerning them; and, so far as I can understand, there has never been one since." It would have been well, if others had taken the same course.

Edwards published copiously on the subject; and it will not be an easy task to point out an error in all his reasonings. Yet it must be admitted, that, in the practical application of his own principles, he was too indulgent to these bodily agitations. Several reasons concurred to make him so. Under many of his most effective sermons, — those which actually accomplished most in the promotion of holy living, — numbers of his hearers were deprived of self-command, and forced to "cry out," and to weep aloud, as at Enfield. A little more would have produced fainting in some, and convulsions in others. He, himself, in some of his best frames, had been nearly overcome, so as to spend he knew not how much time in loud weeping; and he knew that such seasons promoted his own piety. But there was another, — a domestic reason, the exhibition of which will give to many a new idea of the character of Edwards.

In 1723, when he was about twenty years of age, he wrote on a blank leaf of some book:

"They say there is a young lady in ———, who is beloved of that Great Being who made and rules the world; and that there are certain seasons, in which this Great Being, in some way or other, invisible, comes to her and fills her mind with exceeding sweet delight, and that she hardly cares for any thing, except to meditate on him; — that she expects after a while to be received up where he is; to be raised up out of the world, and caught up into heaven; being assured that he loves her too well to let her remain at a distance from him always. There she is to dwell with him, and to be ravished with his love and delight for ever. Therefore, if you present all the world before her, with the richest of its treasures, she disregards it and cares not for it, and is unmindful of any pain or affliction. She has a strange sweetness in her mind, and singular purity in her affections; is most just and conscientious in all her conduct; and you could not persuade her to do any thing wrong or sinful, if you would give her all the world, lest she should offend this Great Being. She is of a wonderful sweetness, calmness, and universal benevolence of mind; especially after this Great Being has manifested himself to her mind. She will sometimes go about from place to place, singing sweetly, and seems to be always full of joy and pleasure, and no one knows for what. She loves to be alone, walking in the fields and groves, and seems to have some one invisible always conversing with her."

This young lady was Sarah Pierrepont, and about four years after this was written, she became his wife. She was not only a person of eminent piety, of rare intellect, and accomplished education, but uncommonly beautiful. After all that moralists can say, insensibility to beauty is an imperfection, as really as the want or dormancy of any other faculty of the soul. A great and important part of education consists in developing the taste, — the power of appreciating beauty. In Edwards, as we have already seen, it was highly developed; and he could not but feel exquisitely the loveliness of one, on whose moral beauty he had so long indulged such rapturous musings. It would be a great mistake, to think this an illusion, which a few years of reality would dispel. The celebrated Hopkins, who came to study theology at Northampton when she was the mother of seven children, pronounced her beautiful. Still more would she appear so to her husband. Beauty loses its power, only when experience proves it to be a cheat, and shows that the soul is not, as was expected, fit to dwell in the lovely form which it animates. Edwards had made no such discovery. His wife had always been to him, all that his young imagination had promised. He, therefore, would be the last man to perceive that the more unimportant part, the outward sign of her loveliness, had begun to fade. He was, while he lived, — as the Bible required him to be, — "ravished always with her love." If any thing had been wanting to complete his ravishment, her devoted attachment to him must have supplied the deficiency.

Mrs. Edwards continued to enjoy, after her marriage, and at least till the time of this awakening, those occasional visits of the "Great Being, who made and rules the world," with which she had been favored in her childhood; especially near the close of 1738, in the summer of 1740, and again in January, 1742, — of which last, at her husband's request, she wrote a particular account.* At these seasons, her views of spiritual objects appear to have been most delightful, and absolutely overpowering. Of their "very great effects on the body," Edwards mentions, "nature often sinking under the weight of divine discoveries, the strength of the body being taken away, so as to deprive of all ability to stand or speak; sometimes the hands clenched, and the flesh cold, but the senses still remaining; animal nature often in a great emotion and agitation, and the soul very often, of late, so overcome with great admiration and a kind of omnipotent joy, as to cause the person, (wholly unavoidably,) to leap with all the might, with joy and mighty exultation of soul; the soul at the same time being so drawn towards God and Christ in heaven, that it seemed to the person as though soul and body would, as it were of themselves, of necessity mount up, leave the earth, and ascend thither." Edwards testifies expressly and minutely, that these visitations were followed by manifest improvement in practical holiness.

The influence of these things on his opinions is not a matter of mere conjecture. A great part of her account of her exercises in January, 1742, he transcribed, partially changing the phraseology, concealing the name and even the sex of the person, and adding some particulars from his own knowledge, into his "Thoughts on the Revival of Religion in New England;" where he used it to prove that the influence which produced such bodily effects was good, and of salutary tendency. Thus we have his own word for it, that what he saw in her, helped to give him, or at least to confirm him in, the views which he entertained concerning these "extraordinaries." What he saw in her, in connexion with her holiest and most improving exercises, he could not but view with some partiality, when he saw it occur as a result of his own

* It may be found in Dwight's Life of Edwards, p. 170.

most faithful labors, or heard of it as occurring under the labors of some of the best men in the land. He did not regard these outcries, faintings, and the like, "as certain evidences of a work of the Spirit of God on the hearts" of men, nor esteem them "to be the work of God, as though the Spirit of God took hold of and agitated the bodies of men;" nor did he know any who held such views. But he avowed his belief that they were "probable tokens of God's presence, and arguments of the success of preaching. And therefore," he said, "when I see them excited by preaching the important truths of God's word, urged and enforced by proper arguments and motives, or consequent on other means that are good, I do not scruple to speak of them, and to rejoice in them, and to bless God for them, as such. I confess that when I see a great crying out in a congregation, in the manner that I have seen it, when those things are held forth to them that are worthy of their being greatly affected by, I rejoice in it, much more than in an appearance of solemn attention and a show of affection by weeping; and that, because when there have been those outcries, I have found from time to time a much greater and more excellent effect. To rejoice that the work of God is carried on calmly, without much ado, is in effect to rejoice that it is carried on with less power, or that there is not so much of the influence of God's Spirit. For though the degree of the influence of the Spirit of God on particular persons is by no means to be judged of by the degree of external appearances, because of the different constitutions, tempers and circumstances of men; yet, if there be a very powerful influence of the Spirit of God on a mixed multitude, it will cause, some way or other, a great visible commotion." Some thought, that "when any in a congregation are strongly seized, so that they cannot forbear outward manifestations of it, they should be removed, that others' minds may not be diverted." He thought otherwise. "The unavoidable manifestations of strong religious affections tend to a happy influence on the minds of bystanders, and are found by experience to have an excellent and durable effect; and so to contrive and order things that others may have opportunity and advantage to observe them, has been found to be blessed, as a great means to promote the work of God." *

* The ancient Romans decided a similar question more judiciously. They

Such opinions, coming from such a man, could not fail to produce a vast increase of "these bodily effects." They made preachers more willing to see them, and people more willing to suffer them. They promoted a state of mind, in which unintelligent excitement produced a fearful harvest of mistake, extravagance, and false conversions. It was probably well that another influence hastened the evil to a crisis; but of that in another chapter.

---

## CHAPTER XIV.

DAVENPORT.—His Rise, Progress, Excesses, Recovery, and "Retractations."—His posthumous influence.—The Eleventh Congregational Church in Boston.—Note, on the Catastrophe of Hugh Bryan.

REPEATED mention has been made, in the course of this history, of the Rev. James Davenport, of Southold, Long Island. He was a favorite of Whitefield, who met him in New Jersey, and had stood high in the opinion of the Tennents. The Rev. Andrew Croswell, in a pamphlet in his defence, produced numerous testimonies in his favor; for example:—"Mr. Whitefield declared in conversation, that he never knew one keep so close a walk with God as Mr. Davenport. Mr. Tennent, in my hearing, affirmed Mr. Davenport to be one of the most heavenly men he ever was acquainted with. Mr. Pomroy, who is acquainted with both, thinks he doth not come one whit behind Mr. Whitefield, but rather goes beyond him, for heavenly communion and fellowship with the Father and with the Son Jesus Christ. Mr. Parsons of Lyme told me the other day, [this was July 16, 1742,] that not one minister whom he had seen, was to be

---

had observed that the excitement of the *Comitia*, or public meetings of the citizens for the election of officers and other purposes, sometimes produced "seizures" of this kind, and that when one fell and was convulsed, the sight threw others into similar convulsions. These "seizures" were called the "Morbus Comitialis," or, as we should say, if they appeared at such of our meetings as most resemble the Comitia, "the Convention distemper." Their occurrence was not thought favorable to the safe transaction of public business; and it was made a standing rule, that whenever one was seized, the Comitia should immediately adjourn.

compared to Mr. Davenport for living near to God, and having his conversation always in heaven.* Mr. Owen, also, of Groton, said that the idea he had of the apostles themselves scarcely exceeded what he saw in Mr. Davenport. In brief, there is not one minister in all Connecticut that is zealously affected in the good cause of God at this day, but instead of slighting him, is apt to think more highly of him than we ought to think of men, and to receive him almost as if he was an angel from heaven." This is the statement of an honest partisan, — so far as a partisan can be honest; not false, but too highly colored. Davenport had certainly produced wonderful effects, and collected a large tribute of veneration. He rode, — to use language of a more modern date, — "on the very top wave of the spirit of the age." More than any other man, he embodied in himself and promoted in others, all the unsafe extravagances into which the revival was running; and those whose zeal outran their knowledge, saw in him, what they proudly hoped soon to become. In admiring the "spirit of the age," as it appeared in him, men admired their own spirit, full grown. Such a man could not fail to have a popularity, violent in his favor and vindictive against all opposers. As he went foremost in the wrong direction which the revival had begun to take, he was regarded by multitudes as its model man, by comparison with whom all others were to be judged. As appears from the concurrent testimony of all parties, his influence, mainly, brought the revival to a crisis. He led it so deeply into such errors, that it ought to stop, and provoked the opposition which brought it to an end. A knowledge of his character and proceedings is therefore of the first importance to one who would understand the history of his times; and it is to be regretted that we have not as full and minute accounts of his whole life, as we have of some parts of it. It is also to be regretted, that nearly all we have, except indefinite praise, comes to us through his decided opponents. Still it seems possible, by omitting all facts concerning which prejudice might mislead the witnesses, to make out a well authenticated history of his proceedings, sufficiently complete to show their true character.

For an account of the commencement of his career, we

---

* Parsons, however, did not approve of all his measures, as appears by his own statements.

are indebted to the Rev. William Hart, pastor of the First Church in Saybrook. Mr. Hart appears to have been a man of good character, moderately Calvinistic, and had been condemned by Davenport as unconverted. He learned many of the particulars from Davenport himself, and others in Southold, which he visited, perhaps for that very purpose. The account was addressed to Dr. Chauncy, and appears in his work on the "State of Religion in New England."

It seems, that when the reports concerning Whitefield's labors and success first reached Long Island, both Davenport and Barber, of Oyster Ponds, "received him as an angel of God," and were confident that a glorious revival of religion was about to pervade the land. They betook themselves to special prayer, that God would hasten the work, teach them what he was about to do, and make them eminent instruments in promoting it. From their subsequent career, it appears neither unreasonable nor uncharitable to suppose that their prayers were inspired, in part by a sincere zeal for God and for the salvation of souls, and in part by pleasing visions of their own future greatness, as "eminent instruments of its promotion;" though of this last element of their feelings, they probably were not aware. After some time, the words in Habakkuk 2 : 3,—"For the vision is yet for an appointed time, but at the end it shall speak and shall not lie : though it tarry, wait for it; because it will surely come, it will not tarry," were strongly impressed on Barber's mind; which he took as a divine intimation that their expectations should be fulfilled. He informed Davenport of the impression, on whom it had a similar effect. Soon after,—it must have been about the beginning of March, 1740,—Barber sat up all, or nearly all, of Saturday night, meditating on these things; and at family worship the next morning, as he was reading Ps. 102, the 13th verse was impressed upon his mind. The words are, "Thou shalt arise and have mercy upon Zion; for the time to favor her, yea, the set time, is come." This he took as an intimation from heaven that the great revival which he had been expecting, should immediately commence, and as an order to begin his labors without delay. He fainted; but recovered so as to attend public worship at the usual hour. He spent about a week in visiting and exhorting his people, telling of the wonderful discoveries that God had made to him, and how he had fainted at the vision.

He then left Oyster Ponds, to go forth and proclaim the gospel abroad. Intending to obey a scriptural direction, he took no money, nor change of apparel, nor yet shoes, but was shod with *boots*. He declared that he had laid aside all premeditation, being taught on every occasion by the Holy Ghost, what he should say, and where he should go. He came first to Davenport, at Southold, whose mind had been impressed with the words of Psalm 115 : 12 – 14 : "The Lord hath been mindful of us : he will bless us : he will bless the house of Israel : he will bless the house of Aaron : he will bless them that fear the Lord, both small and great. The Lord shall increase you more and more, you and your children." Davenport assembled his people, and Barber addressed them in his usual style. After visiting all parts of Southold, Barber went about twenty miles, to Oldmans. Having delivered his message here, he ceased to receive the usual directions as to his course, and could do nothing "while the cloud abode upon the tabernacle." He refused to preach when requested. Some of his own people visited him, to urge his return ; but in vain. Here he remained in idleness for several months, till he grew fat and ragged. At length, after a few excursions in the vicinity, he returned to Oyster Ponds, and soon proceeded to Rhode Island, to meet Whitefield. The account of their meeting has already been given, in Whitefield's own words. Whitefield took him to Georgia, and made him superintendent of spiritual affairs in his orphan house.

After Barber's visit to Southold, Davenport commenced his extraordinary labors, but at first, only among his own people. He assembled them at his lodgings, and addressed them for almost twenty-four hours together. The effort overcame his strength, and he was confined for several days to his chamber. It is not improbable that the febrile state of body which afterwards certainly affected the soundness of his mind, had already commenced. His church seems to have been, like many others, in a bad condition, containing many unconverted members. At least, he thought so, and began to make distinctions accordingly in his public treatment of them, calling those whom he esteemed regenerate, "brother," and the others, "neighbour." He soon forbade the "neighbours" to come to the Lord's table. This produced no little excitement ; but, as he believed, the divine

20*

blessing attended his preaching and measures, and about twenty of his people were converted. He came very near attempting to work a miracle. A woman in an adjoining parish had been long insane, and for some time dumb. Davenport fasted and prayed for her recovery, and gave out that she would recover on a certain day that he named. On that day, she died. He claimed the event as an answer to his prayer, as she was relieved from her infirmity by being taken to heaven. This was in the summer of 1740; not far from the time when Whitefield saw him in New Jersey, and was so much pleased with his piety.

Of the commencement of his itinerations, the date is wanting; but we have his own account of the principal facts, as he related them to the Boston pastors in 1742. One of his brethren proposed to him to go forth and preach beyond the bounds of his own parish; but he made no reply at the time; not knowing the will of the Lord concerning it. He, however, made it a subject of prayer; and after some time, on opening his Bible, though he had no thought of turning to that passage, his eye fell on the account of the attack which Jonathan and his armor-bearer made on the Philistines. As he read, he saw every line, every word, in a new light. The Lord caused it to make a strong impression on his mind. As Jonathan and his armor-bearer went to the camp of the Philistines, so the Lord called him and the man just mentioned to go to Easthampton, where they should convert as many as Jonathan and his armor-bearer slew; but as Jonathan had a sign, — that he should not attack the garrison unless the Philistines called him, "come up hither," — so he must wait till he was invited to Easthampton. At length, some of the people in Easthampton said they should like to have him come and preach to them. He went, with his friend before mentioned, up to their knees in snow, as Jonathan and his armor-bearer climbed up the hill to the Philistines, on their hands and knees. The result was according to their expectation, for twenty were converted. This same man generally accompanied him in his future itinerations, and was called by Davenport and by others throughout the country, his armor-bearer.

The reader must not set aside this account as a caricature. True, Dr. Chauncy was the reporter; but Davenport told the story in the presence of at least a dozen witnesses, ministers of Boston and Charlestown, many of whom were staunch friends and active promoters of the revival; so that Chauncy could not have dared materially to alter the facts, even if he had been wicked enough to desire it. And the facts are of such a character, that no choice of language can essentially change their appearance.

In June, 1740, during the session of the Presbyterian Synod, we find him at Philadelphia, preaching at Society Hill, with the Tennents and others.

In the autumn, he joined Whitefield, who wrote in his Journal, October 30, on arriving at New York:—"To add to my comfort, the Lord brought my dear brother Davenport from Long Island, by whose hands the blessed Jesus has of late done great things." Having parted, they met again, November 5, at Baskinridge, New Jersey, where Davenport had been preaching to Mr. Cross' parishioners. From this place, they travelled together towards Philadelphia. Here we lose sight of him till the next spring or summer.

It was on or near the 14th of July, 1741,* that Davenport came from Long Island to Stonington, Connecticut. Here, it was said, near one hundred persons were struck under conviction by his first sermon, and about that number converted in eight days, including about twenty Indians; and that many were left under "hopeful convictions." From Stonington, he visited Westerley, Rhode Island. Of his labors there, a favorable account, by Park, the missionary, has been given in a preceding chapter. The history of subsequent years shows that a considerable part of these supposed conversions among the Indians were genuine. In many of the towns in that region, he condemned the ministers as unconverted, and exhorted their people to leave them. Among those whom he condemned, was the venerable Eliphalet Adams, of Windham, Connecticut, whose faithful labors had been a principal means of preserving the flame of piety in that region from extinction, and under whom there had been a happy revival in 1721, the period of deepest darkness in New England. Here his influence in producing alienations and divisions is said to have been peculiarly unhappy, though no particulars are given; and the report of the injustice done to a man so extensively known and revered, and

* Boston Postboy, Aug. 10, 1741. Mass. Hist. Soc. Lib.

of the injury done to his people, produced a deep sensation throughout the country. At Lyme he was received with a qualified approbation by Parsons and Griswold, but produced no very remarkable effects.

On the 25th of August, he called on Mr. Hart, of Saybrook, and asked if he was willing that he should preach in his pulpit. Mr. Hart, before answering, asked him if it was his practice, as reported, publicly to condemn ministers as unconverted. He replied that it was. Mr. Hart asked, on what evidence he condemned them. Instead of answering that question, he stated the object for which he did it, — which was, for the purification of the churches, and the discovery of the unconverted, that they might be avoided. In answer to other questions, he avowed that he encouraged the establishment of separate meetings of the converted, and the labors of itinerant exhorters. After a vain attempt to procure some concession from him, Mr. Hart refused him the use of his pulpit. He then said to his attendants, — "Come, let us go forth without the camp, after the Lord Jesus, bearing his reproach. O, 't is pleasant to suffer reproach for the blessed Jesus! Sweet Jesus!" The next day, four ministers, the Rev. Messrs. Worthington, Nott, Beckwith and Hart, called upon him, to converse with him on his mode of proceeding; but it was found impossible to converse with him. He commenced a vehement discourse to them, and would not be interrupted; lecturing them as unconverted men, blind guides, wolves in sheep's clothing, and the like; then offered a prayer, partly for their conversion and partly against them; and then left them, to attend a meeting which he had appointed, refusing to decide whether he would grant them an interview at any future time. He had given out, before his arrival, that he had a great work to do at Saybrook; but the event seems to have fallen short of his expectation.

He continued his course to New Haven, calling on ministers by the way, demanding of each an account of his religious experience, and condemning all who refused to give it, or whose accounts were unsatisfactory, or who in any way opposed his movements, as unconverted. He seems to have considered himself specially commissioned for this work; for he declared at Stonington, that God had promised to call a number of unconverted ministers, by impressing on his mind the words, "He will bless the house of Aaron."

He arrived at New Haven in September. Here a general revival had commenced the preceding winter, and its influence still remained. His descent from the famous John Davenport, the first pastor of that church, his consanguinity with several respectable families, and especially his reputation for uncommon sanctity and usefulness, procured him a favorable reception. Mr. Noyes, the pastor of the church, admitted him to his pulpit, and there appears to have been no visible opposition, till he pronounced Mr. Noyes an unconverted man. On this, Mr. Noyes called a meeting of several friends, September 21, among whom were the principal officers of Yale College, to whom Davenport gave some very frivolous reasons for believing that Mr. Noyes was unconverted. The result was, that he was thenceforth excluded from the pulpit. How long he continued there, is uncertain ; but after his departure, and before the end of the year, his followers organized a separate church, which, after several years of controversy, numerous councils, and some confessions, came to be acknowledged as a regular church, and still subsists and flourishes.* While here, there were a few instances of trances and visions among his adherents. He probably spent the winter at Southold.

Among those who suffered temporary injury from the influence of his labors at New Haven, the celebrated missionary, David Brainerd, ought probably to be mentioned. Brainerd dated his conversion from July 12, 1739. He became a member of Yale College in September of that year. During the revival of 1741, he "was much quickened," and used to meet frequently with a few religious friends, for unreserved and confidential religious intercourse. In the winter of 1742, a woman told President Clapp, that a Freshman told her, that he heard Brainerd say of somebody, "He has no more grace than this chair ;" and he guessed that Brainerd was speaking of some of the Faculty. The words had been uttered in the Hall, where Brainerd and two or three others of his religious circle were conversing, and the listener was in an adjoining room. Clapp sent for the Freshman, ascertained who were conversing with Brainerd, called them, and extorted from them the fact, that the words were used in reply to a question, "What do you think of

* Bacon's Historical Discourses.

tutor Whittelsey ?" Mr. Whittelsey was a man whose piety there was no good reason to question. Brainerd deserved to be privately reprimanded, and made to confess his fault before those who heard him commit it. But he was required to make a public confession. Disgusted with the harshness of the sentence, and with the meanness of thus ferreting out a private conversation, he refused, was expelled from College, and, though powerful influence was used in his favor, never permitted to rejoin his class. He had also once attended a meeting of the Separatists, when forbidden by the Rector; and it was reported, but not proved, that he had said he wondered the Rector did not expect to drop down dead, for fining the scholars who followed Mr. Tennent to Milford. There can be no doubt, that he was guilty of improprieties of which we have no account; for he afterwards burned his diary for thirteen months, including the time of his expulsion, "inserting a notice at the beginning of the succeeding manuscripts, that a specimen of his manner of living during that entire period would be found in the first thirty pages next following, except that he was now more refined from some imprudences and indecent heats than before." * He died, October 9, 1747. Edwards thought him less careful of life and health, than duty required; and the inquiry deserves attention, how far the false views of duty into which this revival led him, and which led him into "imprudences and indecent heats," continued to influence him, and hurried him to his grave. The question derives additional interest, from the failures of health of foreign missionaries, in about the same length of time from the great revivals of 1831–1834.

On the 29th † of May, 1742, two persons, Captain Blacklatch and Samuel Adams, of Ripton parish, in Stratford, Connecticut, came to Hartford, where the General Assembly was in session, and filed their complaint with the Secretary, stating that James Davenport had arrived there about ten days before, and Benjamin Pomroy soon after, and that, with certain illiterate persons, [exhorters,] they were collecting assemblies of people, mostly children and youth, and, under pretence of religious exercises, were inflaming them with a

* Edwards' Life of Brainerd.

† Boston News Letter, No. 1997. Massachusetts Historical Society Library. This date is nearly obliterated; but appears to be the 29th, which corresponds well with the other parts of the account.

bad spirit, and with doctrines subversive of all law and order; by which the peace of the town was greatly disturbed. A warrant was therefore issued, and Davenport and Pomroy were brought before the Assembly on the first of June. The investigation of the case occupied a considerable part of two days. It appeared from the testimony, that he preached, prayed and exhorted with even more than his usual vehemence of language and gesture, denounced ministers as unconverted without reserve, and urged the duty of all to sustain "the work," in defiance even of the commands of parents or the laws of the colony. The Assembly, at this very session, had enacted a law "For regulating abuses, and correcting disorders, in ecclesiastical affairs." This law was intended to repress, by civil penalties, the practices of itinerants and exhorters. It was a high-handed infringement of the rights of conscience, and in a few years fell, and buried the party which enacted it in its ruins. This was the law which he exhorted his hearers to set at defiance; and seldom, it must be acknowledged, has a more plausible occasion been found in New England, for preaching disregard of law. He also professed to have been taught by the Spirit, that the end of the world was near. He knew not the exact time, but it was very near.

At the close of the first day of his examination, when the Assembly adjourned in the evening, as the sheriff was conducting him to his lodgings, he stopped on the front door steps of the meetinghouse, where the session seems to have been held, and began to exhort the great crowd that had collected. The sheriff took hold of his sleeve, to lead him away. He exclaimed, "Lord, thou knowest somebody's got hold of my sleeve. Strike them, Lord, strike them!" Pomroy cried out, "Take heed how you do that heaven-daring action!" Their partisans rushed in to resist the sheriff. Others refused to aid him, when called upon. For a while, the crowd and the tumult increased, and it seemed that the sheriff would be overpowered; but taking advantage of a little relaxation of the pressure, he effected his retreat with his prisoners; the disappointed multitude saying as they went, "We will have five to one on our side to-morrow." A mob collected around the gentleman's house where the prisoners were lodged, and it was two hours before the magistrates could disperse it. Sounds of excited devotion were heard in all parts of the town, nearly all the night; and in the morning, a militia force of forty armed men was ordered out, to protect the Assembly from insult and interruption. This guard was kept on duty till this business was concluded, and seems to have prevented any further public disturbance.

On the third day of June, which was also the third day of these proceedings, the Assembly decided, that "the behaviour, conduct, and doctrines advanced by the said James Davenport, do, and have a natural tendency to, disturb and destroy the peace and order of this government. Yet it further appears to this Assembly, that the said Davenport is under the influence of enthusiastical impressions and impulses, and thereby disturbed in the rational faculties of his mind, and therefore to be pitied and compassionated, and not to be treated as otherwise he might be." They therefore ordered him to be sent home to Southold. On hearing their decision, he said, "Though I must go, I hope Christ will not, but will tarry and carry on his work in this government, in spite of all the power and malice of earth and hell." About four o'clock, P. M. the sheriff, with two files of men armed with muskets, conducted him to the bank of the Connecticut, and put him on board a vessel, the owner of which agreed to carry him to his home.

Pomroy, who seemed "almost orderly and regular" in comparison, was discharged.*

* All these things, of course, operated against the reputation of Whitefield, who was considered the most prominent leader in the present excitement, who had so highly and so publicly eulogized Davenport and Barber, and who was known himself to give religious heed to impulses, and to texts of Scripture impressed upon his mind. Another story, which went through New England about the same time, must have increased the unfavorable impression. The reader will recollect Hugh Bryan, of South Carolina, whom Whitefield praised so highly in his Journal, and by correcting whose letter he brought upon himself a prosecution for a libel. Hugh at length imagined himself a prophet, and, among other mad freaks, sent twenty closely written sheets of his journal, containing predictions and the like, to the Speaker of the House of Commons of the colonial legislature. It was also rumored, that he was encamped in the wilderness, and was gathering multitudes of all sorts of people about him, especially negroes; and that he had even procured firearms to be sent from Charleston, for some secret and dangerous purpose. Warrants were issued for his apprehension; but before they could be served, he discovered his delusion, and addressed a letter to Speaker Bull and the other members of the House of Commons, confessing his errors, and asking pardon. His letter is dated March 1, 1742. He begins: — "It is with shame, intermixed with joy, that I write you this. I find that I have presumed, in my zeal for

Davenport stayed but a short time at Southold. He determined to visit Boston. He arrived at Charlestown on Friday evening, June 25. On the Sabbath, he attended public worship in the forenoon, and partook of the Lord's Supper. In the afternoon he stayed at his lodgings, from an apprehension that the minister was unconverted. This "greatly alarmed" the ministers in the vicinity; and well it might; for it was an indication that whatever they had heard against him was true.

On Monday afternoon, he came to Boston. The association of ministers was then in session. What was done, appears from their "Declaration with regard to the Rev. Mr.

---

God's glory, beyond his will, and that he has suffered me to fall into a delusion of Satan, — particularly in adhering to the impressions on my mind; thought not, to my knowledge, in my reflections and other occurrences of my journal. This delusion I did not discover till three days past, when, after many days' converse with an invisible spirit, whose precepts seemed to be wise, and tending to the advancement of religion in general, and of my own spiritual welfare in particular, I found my teacher to be a liar, and the father of lies; which brought me to a sense of my error, and has much abased my soul with bitter reflections on the dishonor I have done to God, as well as the disquiet which I may have occasioned to my country. Satan, till then, appeared to me as an angel of light, in his spiritual conversation; but since I have discovered his wiles, he has appeared a devil indeed, showing his rage." It seems, he still believed he had been conversing with an invisible spirit. After some details of confession, not worth transcribing, he concludes, and adds: "P. S May we all keep close to the law and to the testimony of our God, and hearken to no other revelation for divine truth, and watch and pray, that we enter not into temptation, is a further prayer of your most unworthy servant, H. Bryan." This was published, by order of the Commons House of Assembly, passed March 3, 1742. As published in the Boston Postboy of May 3, it was accompanied with a statement on the authority of his brother, — perhaps Jonathan, of the means by which he was undeceived. The invisible spirit bade him go, by a direct course, and without looking on the ground, to a certain tree, and take thence a rod, with which he must smite the waters of the river, and they should be divided, so that he should go over on dry ground. He started to obey; and after several falls from not looking at the ground, found the tree and procured the rod. With this he began to smite the river, and press forward towards the farther bank, till he was up to his chin in the water, and his brother, who had followed him as fast as he could, but just saved him from drowning. His brother then urged him to go home; but the spirit had assured him that, if he went home that night, he should be a dead man before morning. However, the sharp weather and his wet jacket at length prevailed. He went home; and, finding himself alive in the morning, concluded that the spirit, which had lied to him twice, must be the "father of lies." The account is found in the second edition of "A letter from a gentleman in New England to his friend in Glasgow," on "the state of Religion in New England since the Rev. Mr. George Whitefield's arrival there." O. S. Ch. Lib.

James Davenport and his conduct," which was published on the first of July.

"We, the associated pastors of Boston and Charlestown, in the Province of Massachusetts Bay, in New England, being assembled June 28, in our stated course of meeting, and being then informed that the Rev. Mr. James Davenport, pastor of the church of Christ in Southold, L. I., was come to town, sent two of our brethren to inform the said Mr. Davenport that we were then assembled, and should be glad to see him.

"Whereupon he presently came to us; and after a respectful greeting, we desired him to inform us of the reasons of his leaving his flock so often, and for such length of times as we had heard of; as also concerning his assuming behaviour in the places whither he had gone; more especially in judging the spiritual state of pastors and people, and too positively and suddenly declaring concerning one and another, that they were in a converted or unconverted estate; thereby stumbling the minds of many, and alienating the hearts of others from their ministers and brethren, even to such a degree that some had withdrawn from the ministry and communion to which they belonged.

"Whereupon Mr. Davenport, in a free and ready manner, gave us such an account of the manner of God's working upon him from his early days, and his effectual calling in riper years, as that he appeared to us to be a man truly pious; and we hope that God has used him as an instrument of good unto many souls.

"Nevertheless, also, it appears to us, that he is a gentleman acted much by sudden impulses, upon such applications of the Holy Scriptures to himself, and his particular friends, desires and purposes, as we can by no means approve of or justify, but must needs think very dangerous and hurtful to the interests of religion.

"And in particular, by the account he gave us of his judging some reverend ministers of the gospel on Long Island and in New England to be in an unconverted state, it did by no means appear to us that he had reason and righteousness on his side in so doing. Nor do we see into his Scripture warrant for thinking himself called of God to demand from his brethren from place to place, an account of their regenerate state, when or in what manner the Holy Spirit of God wrought upon or renewed them.

"We judge also, that the Rev. Mr. Davenport has not acted prudently, but to the disservice of religion, by going with his friends singing through the streets and high ways, to and from the houses of worship on Lord's days and other days; and by encouraging private brethren to pray and exhort in larger or smaller assemblies of people gathered for that purpose; a practice which we fear may be found big with errors, irregularities and mischiefs.

"We judge it therefore to be our present duty, not to invite Mr. Davenport into our places of public worship, as otherwise we might readily have done, so that we may not appear to give countenance to the forementioned errors and disorders; against which we bear this testimony, both in faithfulness, love and care to the churches of Christ, and also to our said brother, whose usefulness in the church is likely to be still more obstructed by his being deeply tinctured with a spirit of enthusiasm.

"And though we are not satisfied that the Rev. Mr. Davenport has a call to preach in the fields from day to day, as he has done of late, yet we think it our duty to bear a testimony against all those disorders, and that profaneness, which have been promoted by any who have lately gone forth to hear him.

"Upon the whole, we humbly beseech the great Lord and Head of the church, to lead us, and all his ministers and churches, into all the paths of truth, righteousness, peace and spiritual edification, for his name's sake. And we take this opportunity to repeat our testimony to the great and glorious work of God, which of his free grace he has begun and is carrying on in many parts of this and the neighbouring provinces; beseeching him to preserve, defend, maintain and propagate it, in spite of all the devices of Satan against it, of one kind or other; that, however it may suffer by the imprudence of its friends, or by the virulent opposition of its enemies, yet it may stand as on the rock, and the gates of hell may never prevail against it."

This was signed by Benjamin Colman, Joseph Sewall, Thomas Prince, John Webb, William Cooper, Thomas Foxcroft, Samuel Checkley, William Wellsteed, Joshua Gee, Mather Byles, Ellis Gray and Andrew Eliot, of Boston, and by Hull Abbot and Thomas Prentice of Charlestown. Dr. Chauncy appears to have been present at the conversations with Davenport; but his name is not annexed to the Declaration; probably, because he would not sign any paper containing testimony in favor of the revival.

It appears from the newspapers of the day, that on being excluded from the pulpits, Davenport repaired to the Common, where he preached repeatedly, but to decreasing audiences. Here, and at Copp's Hill and its vicinity,* the disorders occurred, to which the last paragraph but one of the Declaration refers.

"Upon publishing this Declaration on Friday," says Mr. Prince,† "many were offended: and, some days after, Mr. Davenport thought himself obliged to begin in his public exercises to declare against us also; naming some as unconverted, representing the rest as Jehoshaphat in Ahab's army, and exhorting the people to separate from us: which so diverted the minds of many from being concerned about their own conversion, to think and dispute about the case of others, as not only seemed to put an awful stop to their awakenings, but on all sides to roil our passions and provoke the Holy Spirit, in a gradual and dreadful measure, to withdraw his influence.

---

* See Mr. Parkman's account, append.x to Chapter XII.

† Christian History, Vol. II. p.408.

"Now a disputatious spirit most grievously prevailed amongst us; and, what almost ever attends it, much censoriousness and reflection; which had a further tendency to inflame and alienate, and whereof many of every party were sadly guilty. It was indeed a lamentable time."

These evils could not fail to be aggravated by a "Reply" to the Declaration, from the pen of the Rev. Andrew Croswell, of Groton, Ct. whose reply to Commissary Garden has already been mentioned. It was dated at Groton, July 16, and printed at Boston, doubtless without delay. On reading the Declaration, Croswell says: "I was so astonished that I could scarce believe my own eyes; nor could once reading sufficiently convince me that all their names were really subscribed to it." He first notices what is said of Davenport's absences from his own parish, which he attempts to justify by the examples of Whitefield and Tennent. But the cases were not parallel. Whitefield first left his parish on their business,—to take up collections for their benefit; and when he determined to continue his itinerations, he resigned his charge. The accusation had been brought against Tennent, during his absence at Portsmouth.* On his return, he published a reply, stating what arrangements had been made before he left home, for the supply of his pulpit during his absence.† With respect to Davenport, the case was different. At an ecclesiastical council, held at Southold, October 7, 1742, —about three months after his visit to Boston,—one of the complaints brought against him by his people was, "His leaving his congregation, at several times, for a great while together, at his will and pleasure, without leave or consent of the church or society." And the council said in their result: "We think that his congregation have just cause to complain of his leaving them, at several times, for so long a space as he has done, without their consent; whereby he has not only left them destitute of gospel ordinances, but has been too unmindful of the obligation he lies under by his pastoral relation, to them who are his peculiar charge." In fact, his only excuse was, some impression upon his mind, which he took to be a command from the Holy Ghost; or, as he expressed it in conversation with the Boston pastors, "The Lord sent me."

* Postboy, Dec. 28, 1740.
† N. E. Weekly Journal, Jan 27, 1741, Mass. Hist. Soc. Lib.

Passing over some pages, we come to a truly instructive passage.

"The Reverend gentlemen do indeed say in the next clause, 'that they hope God hath used him as an instrument of doing good unto many souls.' And why are they not willing that God should use him as an instrument of doing good unto more souls? Can any thing be more inconsistent, than to acknowledge him to be a man whom the Lord delights to honor, and yet to dishonor him themselves at the same time? To own him to be one God hath much employed in gathering in his elect, and yet in the same breath give him such a setting out as tends to make people run away from him, and keep out of reach of his ministry?

"The honored Association having been constrained to own him to be a truly pious man and a very useful minister, they go to butting and bounding him in the following manner. 'He is a gentleman,' they say, 'much acted by sudden impulses, upon application of the Holy Scriptures to himself,' &c. To which I reply: What if he holds ten thousand times ten thousand impulses, which others cannot so well see through; yet if it appears plain that the great God, who sends by whom he will send, improves him in saving many souls from hell, each of whom is worth more than the whole world, for God's sake let no one dare to do any thing which hath a tendency to render his ministry contemptible, lest they kick against the pricks, and be found fighters against God. But rather let all who love the prosperity of Zion, wish him God speed, and besiege the throne of grace night and day, that the blessings of more souls ready to perish may come upon him. However, regarding impressions is no new thing peculiar to Mr. Davenport. Those that have walked most humbly with God, and had their affections the most entirely set on things above, have generally laid the greatest stress upon them. I remember that Mr. Whitefield looks upon the impression that was occasioned on Mr. Barber's mind by the application of a passage of the Holy Scriptures to himself and Mr. Whitefield, to be really from God. Nor have Mr. Davenport's impressions done him any harm as yet: and to expect danger from that quarter, is fearing where no fear is; especially if we consider the uncommon sanctity of the man, and his trembling at the appearance of evil."

So it is apt to be. If a preacher appears zealous, pretends uncommon holiness, and succeeds in producing a considerable number of apparent conversions, no one must say a word to guard people against the influence of his errors, however gross and dangerous they may be; no one may oppose any of his measures, be they ever so unscriptural, or even withhold his coöperation, on pain of being counted an enemy of revivals, and hindering the work of God. He may denounce and slander whom he pleases, wounding the hearts and ruining the influence of better men than himself; but no

21 *

one may say a word of him, but by way of commendation, lest it should diminish his influence.

It has been said, by a writer from whose opinions it is not often safe to dissent,* that this Declaration concerning Davenport was injudicious, and that if he had been neglected, his influence would have been less. Perhaps it would. It is doubtless a general rule, that extravagances die soonest if neglected; yet there are exceptions. There are fanatical doctrines, both in religion and politics, to which a considerable part of every community are constitutionally predisposed, and which, if zealously urged by a skilful agitator, will be sure to take hold of many minds. They would do no harm, if nobody would attend to them, just as the smallpox or the plague would do no harm if none would take the infection. In either case, the neglect with which the danger may be treated by the healthy and the wise, will not save others from becoming its victims; and in the treatment of moral epidemics, it requires great practical wisdom to know when and how their progress may be checked by protests and explanations. The state of men's minds at Boston, when Davenport arrived, may have been such as called for the Declaration which the ministers put forth; such that, had they been silent, affairs would have taken a still worse course than they did. Nor is it certain that silence and neutrality were in their power. Conscientious agitators, like Davenport, have strange ways of making all men take sides. Sometimes they assert, that a certain pastor is on their side; and he must contradict the assertion, or his whole flock will be carried over by this unauthorized use of his influence. Sometimes all who will not actively coöperate, are denounced as enemies, and are obliged either to come over publicly and avow themselves friends, or be regarded and treated as enemies. When such tactics are used, the force of the agitating party is commonly brought to bear on one man at a time; and it may be good policy for those who do not wish to be conquered, to take their stand early and unitedly in defence of the truth and of their rights against the aggressors. But for this Declaration, Davenport might, perhaps, have demanded admission to some pulpit, the occupant of which could not safely refuse him on his own responsibility, and without the pledged support of his brethren. His admission into one might have

* Bacon's Hist. Discourses.

increased the difficulty of excluding him from another. Thus they might all have been conquered in detail, and he might have used the influence of the Boston pastors to commend him and his vagaries, first to their own people, and then to all other churches throughout the land.

But the case was not left to the action of the ministers alone. The Grand Jury took it up, and in their presentment, Thursday, August 19, set forth, that "one James Davenport, of Southold, — under pretence of praying, preaching and exhorting, at divers places in the towns of Boston and Dorchester, and at divers times in July last and August current, — did, — in the hearing of great numbers of the subjects of our Lord, the King, maliciously publish, and with a loud voice utter and declare many slanderous and reviling speeches against the godly and faithful ministers of this province, but more particularly against the ministers of the gospel in the town of Boston aforesaid, — viz: that the greatest part of the said ministers were carnal and unconverted men; that they knew nothing of Jesus Christ, and that they were leading their people, blindfold, down to hell, and that they were destroying and murdering souls by thousands; the said James Davenport, at the same time, advising their hearers to withdraw from the said ministers, and not to hear them preach; by means whereof, great numbers of people have withdrawn from the public worship of God and the assemblies by law required."

Among the witnesses before the Grand Jury, H. V. testified, that Davenport said, in July, on Copp's Hill: "Good Lord, (or O Lord,) I will not mince the matter any longer with thee; for thou knowest that I know, that most of the ministers of the town of Boston and of the country are unconverted, and are leading their people blindfold to hell." N. T. heard him say: "Good Lord, thou knowest the most of them are unconverted. Pull them down; turn them out, and put others in their places." A juror heard him say, that "they, (the ministers,) knew nothing of Jesus Christ;" but no testimony to that effect was offered. There were twenty-three jurors, only six of whom were from Boston. Twenty-one sustained the indictment; one was an ignorant exhorter, and the other was a Quaker, who said it was all true, but his conscience forbade him to vote on such a matter. On Saturday, Davenport was arrested, and refusing to give bail, though two gentlemen offered to be his sureties, was committed for trial. The sheriff offered him perfect liberty till the day of trial, if he would promise so to conduct, that he should receive no damage ; but he refused to promise, and was kept in comfortable quarters. On Tuesday, August 24, the Rev. Messrs. Colman, Sewall, Checkley, Welsteed, Byles and Gray addressed a note to the court, then in session, entreating that no severity might be used on their account, and that the matter might be conducted with all the gentleness and tenderness which their honors might judge consistent with justice and the public peace. The verdict was, "that the said James Davenport uttered the words laid in the presentment, except those words, 'that they, (viz. the ministers,) knew nothing of Jesus Christ ;' and that, at the time when he uttered these words, he was *non compos mentis*, and therefore that the said James Davenport is *not guilty*."

It does not appear how long Davenport continued at or near Boston, or how extensively he itinerated in the vicinity. August 6, he visited Ipswich, where he remained some days. August 9, he was at the house of the Rev. Nathaniel Rogers, pastor of the First Church. Rev. Theophilus Pickering, pastor of the Second Church, had heard that some of his people had invited Davenport to preach in his parish, and wrote him a letter, expressing his disapprobation.* The warrant for his apprehension was issued at Boston on the 21st, and he was probably arrested the same day. The council at Southold, which censured his irregular absences from his charge, was held on the 7th of October, at which, we may presume, he was present. He probably spent the winter with his people.

Meanwhile, the spirit which he had been a chief means in exciting, was raging in the eastern part of Connecticut. By invitation of a company of his partisans, he arrived at New London, March 2, 1743, to organize them into a church. Immediately on his arrival, in obedience to messages which he said he had received from God in dreams and otherwise, he began to purify the company from evils which prevailed among them. To cure them of their idolatrous love of worldly things, he ordered wigs, cloaks and breeches, hoods, gowns, rings, jewels and necklaces to be brought together

* O. S. Ch. Lib.

into his room, and laid in a heap, that they might, by his solemn decree, be committed to the flames. To this heap he added the pair of plush breeches which he wore into the place, and which he seems to have put off on being confined to his bed, by the increased violence of a complicated disease. He next gave out a catalogue of religious books, which must be brought together and burned, as unsafe in the hands of the people. March 6, in the afternoon, all things being ready, his followers carried a quantity of books to the wharf and burned them, singing around the pile, "Hallelujah," and "Glory to God," and declaring that, as the smoke of those books ascended up in their presence, so the smoke of the torment of such of their authors as died in the same belief, was now ascending in hell. Among the authors were Beveridge, Flavel, Drs. Increase Mather, Colman, and Sewall, and that fervid revivalist, Jonathan Parsons of Lyme. The next day, more books were burned, but one of the party persuaded the others to save the clothes.*

This is the last recorded outbreak of Davenport's fanaticism. From this time, he disappears from the publications of the day, till the summer of 1744, when he published his "Retractations" of his errors. This paper was forwarded by the Rev. Solomon Williams, of Lebanon, Ct. to the Rev. Mr. Prince, of Boston, for publication. Mr. Williams says, in his letter enclosing it, "He is full and free in it, and seems to be deeply sensible of his miscarriages and misconduct in those particulars, and very desirous to do all he possibly can to retrieve the dishonor which he has done to religion, and the injustice to many ministers of the gospel." As originally published, the document reads thus:—

"THE REV. MR. DAVENPORT'S RETRACTATIONS.

"Although I do not question at all, but there is great reason to bless God for a glorious and wonderful work of his power and grace in the edification of his children, and the conviction and conversion of numbers in New England, in the neighbouring governments and several other parts, within a few years past; and believe that the Lord hath favored me, though most unworthy, with several others of his servants, in granting special assistance and success; the glory of all which be given to Jehovah, to whom alone it belongs:

* This was probably John Lee. of Lyme, who, according to Trumbull, told them that his "idols" were his wife and children, whom he could not burn, as the word of God forbade it, and that idolatry could be suppressed only by a change of heart.

"Yet, after frequent meditation and desires that I might be enabled to apprehend things justly, and, I hope I may say, mature consideration, I am now fully convinced and persuaded that several appendages to this glorious work are no essential parts thereof, but of a different and contrary nature and tendency; which appendages I have been in the time of the work very industrious in, and instrumental of promoting, by a misguided zeal: being further much influenced in the affair by the false Spirit; which, unobserved by me, did (as I have been brought to see since) prompt me to unjust apprehensions and misconduct in several articles; which have been great blemishes to the work of God, very grievous to some of God's children, no less ensnaring and corrupting to others of them, a sad means of many persons' questioning the work of God, concluding and appearing against it, and of the hardening of multitudes in their sins, and an awful occasion of the enemies blaspheming the right ways of the Lord; and withal very offensive to that God, before whom I would lie in the dust, prostrate in deep humility and repentance on this account, imploring pardon for the Mediator's sake, and thankfully accepting the tokens thereof.

"The articles which I especially refer to, and would in the most public manner retract, and warn others against, are these which follow, viz.

"I. The method I used, for a considerable time, with respect to some, yea many ministers in several parts, in openly exposing such as I feared or thought unconverted, in public prayer or otherwise; herein making my private judgment, (in which also I much suspect I was mistaken in several instances, and I believe also that my judgment concerning several was formed rashly and upon very slender grounds,) I say, making my private judgment, the ground of public actions or conduct; offending, as I apprehend (although in the time of it, ignorantly) against the ninth commandment, and such other passages of Scripture as are similar; yea, I may say, offending against the laws both of justice and charity; which laws were further broken,

"II. By my advising and urging to such separations from those ministers whom I treated as above, as I believe may be justly called rash, unwarrantable, and of sad and awful tendency and consequence. And here I would ask the forgiveness of those ministers, whom I have injured in both these articles.

"III. I confess I have been much led astray by following impulses or impressions as a rule of conduct, whether they came with or without a text of Scripture; and my neglecting, also, duly to observe the analogy of Scripture. I am persuaded this was a great means of corrupting my experiences and carrying me off from the word of God, and a great handle, which the false Spirit has made use of with respect to a number, and me especially.

"IV. I believe, further, that I have done much hurt to religion, by encouraging private persons to a ministerial and authoritative kind or method of exhorting; which is particularly observable in many, such being much puffed up and falling into the snare of the devil, whilst many others are thus directly prejudiced against the work.

"I have reason to be deeply humbled that I have not been duly careful to endeavour to remove or prevent prejudice, (where I now believe I might then have done it consistently with duty,) which appeared remarkable in the method I practised, of singing with others in the streets, in societies frequently.

"I would also penitently confess and bewail my great stiffness in retaining these aforesaid errors a great while, and unwillingness to examine into them with any jealousy of their being errors, notwithstanding the friendly counsels and cautions of real friends, especially in the ministry.

"Here may properly be added a paragraph or two, taken out of a letter from me to Mr. Barber at Georgia; a true copy of which I gave consent, should be published lately at Philadelphia: '—I would add to what brother T—— hath written on the awful affair of books and clothes at New London, which affords grounds of deep and lasting humiliation; I was, to my shame be it spoken, the ringleader in that horrid action; I was, my dear brother, under the powerful influence of the false Spirit, almost one whole day together, and part of several days. The Lord showed me afterwards, that the spirit I was then acted by, was in its operations void of true inward peace, laying the greatest stress on externals, neglecting the heart, full of impatience, pride and arrogance; although I thought, in the time of it, that it was the Spirit of God in a high degree; awful, indeed! my body, especially my leg, much disordered at the same time,* which Satan and my evil heart might make some handle of.'

"And now may the holy, wise and good God be pleased to guard and secure me against such errors for the future, and stop the progress of those, whether ministers or people, who have been corrupted by my words or example in any of the above mentioned particulars; and, if it be his holy will, bless this public recantation to this purpose. And O! may he grant, withal, that such, as by reason of the aforesaid errors and misconduct, have entertained unhappy prejudices against Christianity in general, or the late glorious work of God in particular, may, by this account, learn to distinguish the appendage from the substance or essence, that which is vile and odious, from that which is precious, glorious and divine, and thus be entirely and happily freed from all those prejudices referred to, and this, in infinite mercy through Jesus Christ: and to these requests, may all God's children, whether ministers or others, say Amen.

"JAMES DAVENPORT.

"July 28, 1744.

"P. S. Inasmuch as a number, who have fallen in with and promoted the aforesaid errors and misconduct, and are not altered in their minds, may be prejudiced against this Recantation, by a supposition or belief, that I came into it by reason of desertion or dullness and deadness in religion, it seems needful, therefore, to signify, what I hope I may say without boasting, and what I am able, through pure rich grace, to speak with truth and freedom, that for some months in the time of my coming to the abovesaid conclusions and retractations, and since I have come through grace to them, I have been favored, a great part of the time, with a sweet calm and serenity of soul, and rest in God, and sometimes with special and remarkable refreshments of soul,

"* I had the long fever on me and the cankry humor, raging at once."

and these more free from corrupt mixtures than formerly. Glory to God alone. J. D."

August 30, he addressed a note to Mr. Williams, containing the following corrections: —

"Upon the Rev. Dr. Colman's observing, that the use of a word in the first edition of these Retractations is liable to be understood in a sense different from what I intended in the use of it, I desire, if they be printed again, that instead of what is now in the third page between these words, 'I am now fully convinced and persuaded, that'; and those words, 'much influenced in the affair by the false Spirit': the following words may be inserted, viz: 'Several things, which in the time of the work I was very industrious and instrumental in promoting, by a misguided zeal, were no parts of it, but of a different and contrary nature and tendency; and that I was' — And in page 7, instead of those words, 'the appendage from the substance or essence': let these be put, viz: 'what is no part of the work, from the work itself.'"

It will appear in a subsequent chapter, that Dr. Colman had good reasons for his scrupulousness in respect to phraseology.

Davenport's recovery from his errors is commonly ascribed to the Christian labors of the Rev. Messrs. Williams and Wheelock. Their arguments were doubtless useful, and he calls them "the greatest means" of convincing him of his errors. But other causes conspired.

He had twice been judicially pronounced insane; once by the Colonial Assembly at Hartford, and once by the jury that acquitted him at Boston. During a great part, if not the whole, of his itinerations, he was lame with some kind of inflammatory ulcerations, so that he needed the assistance of his "armor-bearer" in walking; and there are other evidences of a febrile state of body. This fever predisposed him to unnatural and unhealthy mental excitement; and on the other hand, his splendid dreams, sleeping and waking, of himself as a great reformer and a special favorite of God, his want of sleep while he spent whole nights in prayer, his excessive pulpit labors and the mental efforts they required, the sight of the multitudes that gathered around him, and of the effect which he produced upon them, their outcries, faintings and convulsions, all bearing witness to his power, — all these things acted through his mind upon his nerves, or upon his nerves directly, and kept up the fever. Such excitement inconceivably increases the power of the mind, and especially the power of moving others; but, in the same proportion, renders it uncertain what the man will do with that power. At New London, when the books were burnt, the disease seems to have reached its crisis, and the mental disturbance amounted to a clearly defined insanity. He was at least partially aware of this, when he wrote his "Retractations;" for he states that his body, especially his leg, was much disordered, which Satan and his evil heart might make some handle of. Here he speaks of the disease as past; as what *was*. As health returned, he recovered the power of calm reflection, and became inclined to be convinced of his errors, and to return to sobriety of measures. At length, he applied to Williams and Wheelock for arguments against his former course. Williams commences his letter, "You desire my thoughts." "In answer to your question," was the beginning of Wheelock's. Their letters contain merely a plain, well-written statement of the common arguments, which he must often have met in the course of his career; but now, when he was convalescent, and seeking health in the right direction, they had new power with him. They convinced him, — as he, whether he was aware of it or not, hoped they would. His history should teach the excitable, whether leaders or followers, a salutary lesson. He soon after removed to New Jersey, where he appears to have labored faithfully and usefully; but he was frequently in trouble, often obliged to change residence, and lived but a few years. The influence of his errors did not cease with his recantation, or even with his life. Among the Separatists, of whom he was the leader, and the sects in which they finally became merged, his most mischievous disorders, and even the tone and manner of public speaking which Trumbull ascribes to him, have been preserved, even to this day. "With his unnatural and violent agitations of the body," says Trumbull, "he had a strange singing tone, which mightily tended to raise the feelings of weak and undiscerning people, and consequently to heighten the confusion among the passionate of his hearers. This odd, disagreeable tuning of the voice in exercises of devotion, was caught by the zealous exhorters, and became a characteristic of the Separate teachers. The whole sect was distinguished by this sanctimonious tone."* The use of this tone in devotional exercises, the excited and disorderly worship, the occasional appearance of

* History Conn., Vol. II. pages 160, 161.

"the power" under which people cry out and fall down, the regard for unaccountable "impressions," the pretense of preaching from the immediate suggestion of the Holy Spirit, the habit of condemning all ministers who do not favor such things as cold formalists, destitute of piety and incapable of usefulness, and of laboring to destroy their influence and break up their churches, have greatly diminished within the last thirty years, but are not yet extinct.

Of the result of Davenport's labors in Boston, little is recorded. Prince says: "A small number from some of our churches and congregations, (some had been communicants formerly, and some added lately,) withdrew, and met in a distinct society;" and having just mentioned events that occurred in December, he says: "Sometime after, a man of the Separate society became a Saturday Baptist; who, being dipped in the country, and having hands laid on him, thought himself a minister, drew five women after him, and proceeded to dip them; yet they have all since deserted him. But six males of the said society, with one in Brookline, — went on to associate as a church, — and have not yet returned to the several churches whence they went out." But he had heard of none of the Separatists who had fallen in any "censurable evil," besides their separation, except one from the Old South Church and a few from the New North. This church appears to have been short lived; but its history is unknown. In February, 1748, some members of the Congregational Churches in Boston "embodied themselves" as the Eleventh Congregational Church. October 5, of the same year, Croswell, the defender of Davenport, was installed as their pastor. The Old South Church refused to unite in the installing council, regarding the formation of the church as a bad precedent, tending to "crumble the churches in pieces." The French Protestant Church being disbanded about this time, the new church obtained possession of their meetinghouse in School street, where Croswell continued to be their pastor till he died, April 12, 1785, aged 76, and having been blind for several years. The house then passed into other hands, and the building on its site is now occupied by a society of Universalists. The records of this church are lost.*

* History of Boston, p. 231.

The influence of Davenport's errors was most severely felt in the eastern part of Connecticut. The events that occurred there, demand a distinct consideration; but we must first glance at Whitefield's labors in Great Britain.

---

## CHAPTER XV.

WHITEFIELD in England.—His breach with Wesley.—The Revival in Scotland.

WHITEFIELD arrived at Falmouth, on his return from America, March 11, 1741. "On the following Sabbath," says Philip, "he was again on Kennington Common, but with "not above a hundred to hear him." It was not quite so bad as that. Whitefield says, that on Sunday his congregation was about as large as usual, but on week days he had not more than two or three hundred. But this was not all. "One," he says, "that got some hundreds of pounds by my sermons, refused to print for me any more. And others wrote to me that God would destroy me in a fortnight, and that my fall was as great as Peter's. Instead of having thousands to attend me, scarce one of my spiritual children came to see me from morning to night. Once, on Kennington Common, I had not above a hundred to hear me."

Among the causes of this loss of popularity, he mentions "two well-meant, though ill-judged letters against England's two great favorites, 'The Whole Duty of Man,' and Archbishop Tillotson, who, I said, knew no more about religion than Mahomet." He condemned them for their Arminianism; and for these letters, "the world was angry" at him. A more powerful cause was his controversy with Wesley. Before Whitefield left England, Wesley had threatened to "drive John Calvin out of Bristol;" and some one had charged him with not preaching the gospel, because he did not preach the doctrine of election. Whitefield besought him not to preach against that doctrine,—as he, though he believed it, never preached in favor of it,—lest they should become divided among themselves. Wesley solemnly appealed to God for direction, by drawing lots. His lot was "preach and print." He preached; but Whitefield begged him not to print, and he did not, till after Whitefield's departure. Whitefield reluctantly wrote a reply, from "Bethesda, in Georgia, Dec. 24, 1740," hoping that the perusal of it would have such an effect on Wesley's mind, as would render its publication unnecessary; but, contrary to his intention, it was soon published in England by some of his officious friends. Wesley was formed for a leader, and could ill bear opposition, even from the man who had raised the present excitement and put him at the head of it. The letter, too, contained some arguments, which it was easier to be offended at, than to answer. But the arguments were not the most galling part of its contents. In his preface, Wesley had informed his followers, in terms sufficiently intelligible to them, that he published his sermon by special divine direction. Those who believed this, of course could not question the correctness of the doctrine; for certainly God would not direct Wesley to publish error. In order to obtain an impartial consideration of his own arguments, Whitefield must do away this impression. He therefore told how Wesley received his divine direction to "preach and print;" and reminded him of his neglect to inquire of God, in the first place, whether the doctrine was true. In a note, he added another instance of Wesley's sortilege. "The morning I sailed from Deal for Gibraltar, Mr. Wesley arrived from Georgia. Instead of coming on board, to converse with me, though the ship was not far off the shore, he drew a lot, and immediately set forwards to London. Behind him he leaves a letter for me, in which were words to this effect: 'When I saw God, by the same wind which was carrying you out, brought me in, I asked counsel of God. His answer you have enclosed.'" This was a piece of paper, in which were written, these words: "Let him return to London." Whitefield states that he was surprised at a message so contrary to what appeared his plain duty, betook himself to prayer, and the account of the prophet that was slain by a lion, for turning back, contrary to divine direction, at the word of another prophet, was powerfully impressed upon his soul. He continued his voyage, and Wesley afterwards acknowledged that God gave him a wrong lot then, though he had never given him a wrong one before. Whitefield concluded that God gave him a wrong lot, justly, because he tempted God in drawing one. When this letter was published and distributed among their followers, Wesley commented upon it in one of their meetings, and saying, "I will just do what I believe Mr. Whitefield would, were he here himself," he tore it in pieces. All present followed his example. But Wesley could not forgive the author. Whitefield confessed his error in publishing a private transaction, begged pardon, and entreated his old friend to be reconciled; but Wesley reminded him, that *for betraying secrets, every friend would depart.* The insolent language in which he professes his kindness, shows his resentment. "The general tenor, both of my public and private exhortations, when I touch thereon at all, as even my enemies know, if they would testify, is,—'Spare the young man, even Absalom, for my sake.'" He seems not to have been aware how accurately these words describe his treatment of Whitefield. Meanwhile, the war went on between Wesley and the leading Calvinistic Methodists. It was managed in a bad spirit on both sides; but the high standing and superior tactics of Wesley carried the day, and almost the whole body submitted to his dictation. The Moravians, too, made inroads upon Whitefield's societies, and turned his printer against him.

Such was the state of things, when Whitefield returned to London. "At the same time," he writes, "I was much embarrassed in my outward circumstances. A thousand pounds I owed for the orphan house. Two hundred and fifty pounds bills drawn on Mr. Seward, were returned upon me.* I was also threatened to be arrested for two hundred pounds more. A family of a hundred to be maintained, four thousand miles off, in the dearest part of the king's dominions.

"Ten thousand times would I rather have died, than part with my old friends. It would have melted any heart, to have heard Mr. Charles Wesley and me weeping, after prayer, that if possible the breach might be prevented. Once, and no more, I preached in the Foundry, a place which Mr. John Wesley had procured in my absence. All my work was to begin again."

He began to preach in Moorfield on week days, under one of the trees; where he saw numbers of his spiritual children

* Seward was dead, and had not, as was expected, left him any thing by his will.

running by him without looking at him, and some of them putting their fingers in their ears, that they might not hear one word he said. "A like scene opened at Bristol, where I was denied preaching in the house I had founded." It was the Kingswood schoolhouse, built for the children of the colliers. Whitefield had first dared to preach to them, and persuaded them to hear the gospel; had originated the school, procured the building lot, laid the corner-stone, and put up the walls with money he had raised for that purpose, and then transferred the whole to Wesley; and now he was not suffered to preach in it.

We must not, as we are tempted to do, exclaim against the cold-hearted selfishness of Wesley. The man who spent his life in labors for the good of others, who acquired and gave away in charity, many thousand pounds, and lived and died poor, must not be called selfish. But Wesley had extensive and well-defined plans for doing good; and he had a heart which could deliberately sacrifice every interest and every feeling, either of himself or his friends, that stood in the way of their accomplishment. Whitefield could not have done it. He could and did sacrifice himself for the good of others; but he could not sacrifice his friends. Emotions of love towards every human being whom he saw or thought of, governed the life of Whitefield. Cool, calculating benevolence on a large scale, was the characteristic of Wesley.

But Whitefield could not long be kept down. His friends built a new house and opened a new school at Kingswood. Some "free grace dissenters," as Gillies calls them, procured the loan of a building lot in London, on which they erected a large temporary shed, which he called the Tabernacle. Here his congregations immediately increased, and he addressed them with his usual power and success. At the desire of his hearers, he sent for some of his Calvinistic friends from other places, to come and assist him in gathering the spiritual harvest. Invitations soon poured in from the country, and even from places where he had never been. At a common near Braintree, he had more than ten thousand hearers, and at many other places, congregations were large, and much affected. "Sweet," he says, "was the conversation which I had with several ministers of Christ; but our own clergy [of the established Church] grew more and more shy, now they knew I was a Calvinist." In about four months from his arrival in London, he not only had triumphed in England, but was triumphing in Edinburgh. Events in that region have a closer connexion with the "Great Awakening" in America, and must be narrated at greater length.

When Presbyterianism was established in Scotland by act of Parliament, it was intended as a religion for the whole people. The Directory for Worship takes for granted that all children will be baptized, taught the catechism, and at a suitable age, having shown their doctrinal knowledge in an examination, and not being heretical in their opinions or scandalous in their lives, will be admitted to the communion. The doctrine of the church is, that none but the regenerate can partake of the Lord's Supper acceptably, and some pastors have, at their examinations, required evidence of an experimental knowledge of saving truth ; but the formularies of the church allow the sessions to hope that every candidate who is neither heretical nor scandalous, is regenerate, and to admit all who, after suitable admonition to examine themselves, choose to come ; and such seems to have been the prevailing practice. As might be expected, the gospel was faithfully preached by many of the clergy, and there were conversions and revivals ; while many unrenewed men, of decent morals, were admitted, first to the communnion, and then, having been educated at the Universities, to the ministry. The law of patronage existed there, as well as in England ; and when a parish became vacant, the patron, if unconverted, would be very likely to nominate an unconverted minister. In many cases, the presentee would be received without gainsaying. In others, the parish would "reclaim," or protest against his induction into office. What should be done in such a case, is a question which has never been put at rest, and which is now shaking the Church of Scotland to its centre ; the General Assembly having decided that such candidates shall not be ordained, and the civil government having decided that they have a right to ordination, and that the Presbyteries must and shall ordain them.

Christ is certainly the sole head of his own church. It is the duty of his church, through its appropriate organs, to maintain and promulgate those moral truths which are binding on all men ; and it is the duty of all men in office, to be governed by those truths in all their official conduct ; and if a civil ruler, being a member of a church, receives bribes to pervêrt justice, or is guilty of any other violation of Christian principle, either in his private conduct or his official acts, he is as much amenable to the discipline of the church, as any other person. But the theory always contended for by a part of the Church of Scotland, and now embraced by the General Assembly, goes further. It assumes, that Christ has established two kinds of government on earth ; civil, to take care of worldly concerns, and ecclesiastical, to take care of all matters pertaining to religion ; that he has established church courts, to act in his name on all ecclesiastical questions ; and that the civil government may never reverse the decisions of these courts, but must always execute them, whenever force is necessary for their execution. This was the leading thought in the " Solemn League and Covenant," by which the Scotch Presbyterians bound themselves to procure and maintain, by force of arms if necessary, the establishment of the church according to the order of the gospel, under Christ as its sole head.

But who shall decide what questions are civil and what are ecclesiastical? And what shall be done with questions, numerous in Great Britain and all Europe, which are partly ecclesiastical, and yet affect important civil rights and privileges? Here are difficulties which have never been surmounted ; for if the church may determine the extent of its own jurisdiction, it may make the civil government its mere tool, as the Popedom has done ; and to this, no Protestant government can submit. The state, therefore, takes the liberty to interfere in all questions that affect civil rights. Ordination is clearly ecclesiastical ; but it gives a right to a salary, which is a civil right. The right of presentation to a parish is a civil right. It is worth money, more or less, according to the income of the parish, and the certainty that the presentee will be ordained. The civil government, in order to protect these and other civil rights, is obliged to bring the church into subjection. But to this, the church can never submit. These two governments can never act harmoniously over the same people. One or the other must be abolished, or become the submissive tool of the other, or they must be at war.

But the Church of Scotland was also divided against itself, — as every church must be, which is composed of such heterogeneous materials. To a great extent, the unconverted clergy took sides with the state against their more spiritual brethren. They loved the arrangement to which they owed their offices and salaries. They loved to study ecclesiastical polity better than theology, and felt more at home in church courts than in prayer meetings. They gained influence in the General Assembly, and used that influence to strengthen their party, to discourage all efficient discipline, and to give prevalence to a rationalizing Arminianism, that disturbed no man's conscience and alarmed no man's fears. With the aid of such good men as they could manage, they passed several acts, which some of the more pious deemed subversive of the authority of Christ, the liberties of his people, and the interests of religion. The minority were not allowed to protest, on the minutes of the Assembly, as they thought it their right and their duty to do. They therefore protested in their own pulpits; and for a public condemnation of some of the doings of the Assembly, process was commenced against Ebenezer Erskine in 1732. The next year, he and three others were suspended from the exercise of the ministerial office. This sentence was afterwards recalled, but they refused to return, and in 1740, the Assembly dissolved their connexion with their congregations and with the national church. They, however, with others, had formed the "Associate Presbytery;" and after their deposition they continued their ministerial labors among their people, and many, of the agricultural population especially, adhered to them. Yet far the greater part of the pious clergy, and even of those who thought the Seceders abused, remained in connexion with the General Assembly. The state of religion among them is thus described by the Rev. James Robe, of Kilsyth:

"There hath been a great and just complaint amongst godly ministers and Christians of the elder sort, who had seen better days, that for some years past, there hath been a sensible decay as to the life and power of godliness. Iniquity abounded, and the love of many waxed cold. Our defection from the Lord and backsliding increased fast to a dreadful apostasy. While the government, worship and doctrine established in this church were retained in profession, there hath been an universal corruption of life, reaching even unto the sons and daughters of God." Of the controversy raised by the Seceders, he says : — "This unhappily filled the heads and mouths of most professors to such a degree, as to mind and converse about nothing, even on the Lord's day, but ministers, church judicatures, and other disputable things, far from the vitals of religion. The state of their souls was much forgotten, and they were either disaffected to their worthy ministers, and the Lord's ordinances dispensed by them ; or if they attended, they were diverted by those things from a concern about their regeneration, conversion, and amending their ways and doings which were not good. Wherever our lamentable divisions prevailed, serious religion declined to a shadow."

Meanwhile, events abroad, as well as the declension at home, were calling the attention of ministers, both of the Kirk and Secession, to the revival of vital piety. Edwards' Narrative of "Surprising Conversions" at Northampton had excited attention. The awakening in England under Whitefield could not but move the minds of Christians in the sister kingdom. The Seceders had strong hopes that piety would revive under their labors ; and Ralph Erskine, in August, 1739, wrote of some late sacramental meetings : — "The Spirit of God was sometimes remarkably poured out, and I hope the power of the Lord was present to heal many souls. Enemies gnash with their teeth, as they do with you ; but the Lord carries on his work." This was written to Whitefield, in answer to a letter from him, inquiring about the Associate Presbytery, for sympathising with whom he had been blamed. Their sympathy was natural, for both parties were zealous for the promotion of vital piety, both were protesting against the corruptions of their own church, and both were opposed by an overwhelming majority of their own brethren. The correspondence continued, and the Seceders invited Whitefield to Scotland. In June, 1741, Ebenezer Erskine wrote :

"We hear that God is with you of a truth, and therefore we wish for as intimate a connexion with you in the Lord as possible, for building up the fallen tabernacle of David in Britain ; and particularly in Scotland, when you shall be sent to us. This, dear brother, and no party views, is at the bottom of any proposal made by my brother Ralph, in his own name and in the name of his associated brethren. All intended by us at present is, that when you come to Scotland, your way may be such as not to strengthen the hands of our corrupt clergy and judicatories, who are carrying a course of defection, worrying out a faithful ministry from the land, and the power of religion with it. Far be it from us to limit your great Master's commission to preach the gospel to every creature. We ourselves preach the gospel to all promiscuously who are willing to hear us. But we preach not upon the call and invitation of the ministers, but of the people, which, I suppose, is your own practice now in England; and should this also be your way when you come to Scotland, it could do the Associate Presbytery no manner of harm. But if, besides, you could find freedom to company with us, to preach with us and for us, and to accept of our advices in your work, while in this country, it might contribute much to weaken the enemy's hand, and to strengthen ours in the work of the Lord, when the strength of the battle is against us."

This is perfectly honest. They wished for the promotion of piety, for Whitefield's aid in promoting it, and for the increase of credit, influence and numbers which his coöperation would give them; and they were unwilling that any part of these advantages should be enjoyed by their opponents, who, they believed, were corrupting the church and destroying piety from the land. Ralph Erskine had written, April 10, 1741.

"Come, if possible, dear Whitefield, come, and come to us also. There is no face on earth I would desire more earnestly to see. Yet I would desire it only in a way that, I think, would tend most to the advancing of our Lord's kingdom and the reformation work among our hands. Such is the situation of affairs among us, that unless you come with a design to meet and abide with us particularly of the Associate Presbytery, and to make your public appearances in the places especially of their concern, — I would dread the consequences of your coming, lest it should seem equally to countenance our persecutors. Your fame would occasion a flocking to you, to whatever side you turn; and if it should be in their pulpits, as no doubt some of them would urge, we know not how it would be improved against us. I know not with whom you could safely join yourself, if not with us."

Whitefield wrote to both these brothers, that he could not join himself to any one denomination of Christians; that he could visit Scotland only as an occasional preacher, "to preach the simple gospel to all who are willing to hear." "I write this," he says, "that there may be no misunderstanding between us."

Meanwhile, there was probably some increase of spiritual life in the national Church of Scotland, though little to that effect has been recorded. Robe, of Kilsyth, informs us, that in 1740 he began to preach on regeneration; its necessity, its nature, and its effects. He then saw no fruit of these sermons, except some increased seriousness among the pious while hearing them; but he afterwards found that they were the means of some instances of conviction and conversion. Similar events, we may presume, occurred in a few other parishes; but there was no movement of sufficient power and extent to attract public notice, or secure a place in history.

Whitefield arrived at Leith, July 30, 1741. As the Erskines had foretold, he was urged to preach in Edinburgh. He declined, and went the next day to Dunfermline, to see Ralph; for, as the Seceders had invited him to Scotland, he felt bound to make his first public appearance among them. Here he preached, to the satisfaction, and even delight, of both ministers and people. The next day, Erskine accompanied him to Edinburgh, where he preached in the Orphan House Park, to a large concourse of hearers, with good effect; and afterwards in some of the churches. August 5, he met the Associate Presbytery at Dunfermline, the members having been called together "by a letter from Mr. Ralph Erskine, who had formed the tryst with Mr. Whitefield." There are several imperfect accounts of this conference, all agreeing, however, in the most important particulars. Whitefield, in a half humorous, half pathetic letter to his friend Noble, of New York, says: "They soon agreed to form themselves into a Presbytery, and were proceeding to choose a moderator. I asked them, for what purpose? They answered, to discourse, and set me right about the matter of church government and the Solemn League and Covenant. I replied, they might save themselves that trouble, for I had no scruples about it; and that settling church government, and preaching about the Solemn League and Covenant, was not my plan." After some further remarks, he says, "I then asked them seriously, what they would have me to do. The answer was, that I was not desired to subscribe immediately to the Solemn League and Covenant, but to preach only for them till I had further light. I asked, why only for them? Mr. Ralph Erskine said, 'they were the Lord's people.' I then asked, whether there were no other Lord's people but themselves? and supposing all others were the devil's people, they certainly had more need to be preached to, and therefore, I was more and more determined to go out into the highways and hedges; and that if the Pope himself would lend me his pulpit, I would gladly proclaim the righteousness of Jesus Christ therein." The company soon broke up; one of them preached a sermon against prelacy and its appendages ; Whitefield retired, wept, prayed, preached in the fields, dined with the Presbytery, and took his final leave.

According to a minute by Ebenezer Erskine, it was proposed to discuss Whitefield's opinion, that the Scriptures allow the toleration of all sects. E. Erskine reminded him that God had made him the instrument of converting many souls ; that he ought to consider how that body was to be organized and preserved ; that this could not be done without ordaining elders over them, in which he must have the assistance of "some two or three, met together in a judicative capacity, in the name of the Lord." "Unto all which Mr. Whitefield replied, that he reckoned it his duty to go on, in preaching the gospel, without proceeding to any such work."

Whitefield had some further correspondence with the Erskines, but the breach could not be healed. He would not bind himself to preach in no pulpits but those of the Associate Presbytery, and therefore they would have no connexion with him. August 13, he wrote to a son of E. Erskine: "The treatment I met with from the Associate Presbytery, was not altogether such as I expected. It grieved me, as much as it did you. I could scarce refrain from bursting into a flood of tears. I wish all were like minded with your honored father and uncle. Matters would not then be carried with so high a hand." And again : "I doubt not but their present violent methods, together with the corruptions of the Assembly, will cause many to become Independents, and set up particular churches of their own. This was the effect of Archbishop Laud's acting with so high a hand ; and whether it be presbytery or episcopacy, if managed in the same manner, it will be productive of the same effects. Blessed be God, I have not so learned Christ." He remarked to a lady, that the Associate Presbytery were building a Babel, which would soon fall down about their ears. Subsequent events have shown his sagacity. The Seceders quarrelled among themselves, on some minute ecclesiastical matter, and became divided, in 1747, into Burghers and Anti-Burghers, between whom there was a long and bitter controversy. And many have become "Independents." "The Congregational Union of Scotland" is now a large and efficient body of Christians.

Whitefield returned to Edinburgh, where the clergy of the established church received him with the heartier welcome, because they had heard of the conference at Dunfermline, and knew that his powerful influence would now operate in their favor, and against the Seceders. He, however, cared little what ecclesiastical party gained or lost by his labors, if he could only win souls to Christ. August 14, he wrote to Howel Harris, his friend in Wales: "It would make your heart leap for joy to be now at Edinburgh. I question whether there are not upwards of three hundred in this city, seeking after Jesus every morning. I have a constant levee of wounded souls, and many quite slain by the law. God's power attends me continually, just as when I left London. At seven in the morning, we have a sweet lecture in the fields, attended, not only by the common people, but by persons of great rank. Our congregations consist of many thousands. Never did I see so many Bibles, nor people looking into them with more attention. Plenty of tears flow from their eyes, and their concern appears in various ways. I preach twice daily, and expound at a private house at night, and am employed in speaking to souls in distress, a great part of the day." So it was for several weeks. One day he preached seven times.

At Glasgow, he preached ten sermons; and some months after, fifty persons were known, who appeared to have been converted by means of them; and the evident change in them, had awakened others. He wrote from Aberdeen, October 9: "At my first coming here, things looked a little gloomy; for the magistrates had been so prejudiced against me by one Mr. Bisset, that when applied to, they refused me the use of the kirk yard to preach in. This Mr. Bisset is colleague with one Mr. O., at whose repeated invitation I came hither. Soon after my arrival, dear Mr. O. took me to pay my respects to him. He was prepared for it; and immediately pulled out a paper, containing a number of insignificant questions, which I had neither time nor inclination to answer. The next morning, it being Mr. O.'s turn, I lectured and preached. The magistrates were present. The congregation was very large, and light and life fled all around. In the afternoon, Mr. B. officiated. I attended. He began his prayers as usual; but in the midst of them, naming me by name, he entreated the Lord to forgive the dishonor that had been put upon him, by my being suffered to preach in that pulpit. And, that all might know what reason he had to put up such a petition, about the middle of his sermon, he not only urged that I was a curate of the Church of England, but also quoted a passage or two, out of my first printed sermons, which he said were grossly Arminian. Most of the congregation seemed surprised and chagrined, especially his good-natured colleague, Mr. O., who, immediately after the sermon, without consulting me in the least, stood up and gave notice that Mr. Whitefield would preach in about half an hour. The interval being so short, the magistrates returned to the Sessions house, and the congregation patiently waited, big with expectation of hearing my resentment. At the time appointed, I went up, and took no other notice of the good man's ill-timed zeal, than to observe in some part of my discourse, that if the good old gentleman had seen some of my later writings, in which I had corrected several of my former mistakes, he would not have expressed himself in such strong terms. The people being thus diverted from the controversy with man, were deeply impressed with what they heard from the word of God. All was hushed, and more than solemn. On the morrow, the magistrates sent for me, expressed themselves quite concerned at the treatment I had met with, and begged me to accept the freedom of the city. But of this, enough." "This triumph," says Southey, "Whitefield obtained as much by that perfect self-command, which he always possessed in public, as by his surpassing oratory." "Mr. O." (the Rev. James Ogilvie,) gives substantially the same account, except that he omits whatever was discreditable to his colleague.*

Few other ministers of the established church, if any, treated Whitefield so rudely as Bisset; but many of them opposed him. Willison, of Dundee, testified: "He is hated and spoken against, by all the Episcopal party; and even the most of our clergy do labor to diminish and expose him. This is not to be much wondered at, seeing his incessant labors for Christ and souls is such a reproof to them. Besides, what he says publicly against the sending out of unconverted ministers, and their preaching an unknown Christ, this must be galling to carnal men."† However glad some

* Christian History, Vol. I. p. 281. † Ibid., p. 282.

others may have been at first, to have Whitefield draw crowds to the kirk, rather than to the Seceders, it was only the more pious that were his enduring friends; and doubtless some, even of them, feared the consequences of his measures, and lent their influence to his opposers. "But for him," as Philip well observes, "the moderate party would have held the ascendant" in the established church; vital piety would have been obstructed by acts of the Assembly, and sneered into obscurity, and that church would have been thoroughly corrupted. At least, nothing but an influence like that which he exerted, could have prevented such results.

About the end of October, he left Edinburgh, and passing through Wales, where he was married, reached London early in December. He spent the winter and spring in England, in his usual labors, and with his usual success. Meanwhile, greater things than he had seen there, were taking place in Scotland.

February 18, 1742, an "extraordinary outpouring of the Holy Spirit" commenced at Cambuslang, a little parish about four miles southeast from Glasgow, of which the Rev. William McCulloch, a correspondent and admirer of Edwards, "a man of considerable parts and great piety," was pastor. "This concern," says Rev. John Hamilton, "appeared with some circumstances very unusual among us; to wit, severe bodily agonies, outcryings and faintings in the congregation. This made the report of it spread like fire, and drew vast multitudes of people from all quarters to that place; and I believe, in less than two months after the commencement of it, there were few parishes within twelve miles of Cambuslang, but had some more or fewer awakened there to a very deep, piercing sense of sin; and many to a much greater distance." Robe, of Kilsyth, says: — "The bodies of some of the awakened are seized with trembling, fainting, hysterisms in some few women, and with convulsive motions in some others, arising from that apprehension and fear of the wrath of God, [which] they are convinced they are under and liable to, because of their sins. They have a quick apprehension of the greatness and dreadfulness of this wrath, before they are affected." He believed, too, that these effects of conviction were not altogether new in Scotland; having attended the great revival in the west of Scotland in

1625 – 1630. It was estimated that these bodily effects did not appear in more than one fifth, some said not more than one eighth, of the awakened. As no difference could be discovered between the mental exercises of those who were thus overcome and those who were not, the ministers friendly to the revival supposed them to be only the natural effects of strong feeling, operating on persons whose constitutions were peculiarly susceptible. As the revival advanced, they became less frequent, and nearly disappeared.

The awakening next appeared in Kilsyth, a parish of "above eleven hundred examinable persons," about nine miles northeast from Glasgow, where Mr. Robe had been settled in 1713. "The most part of them," he says, "have attended upon public ordinances and means of instruction as well as any about them. The most of them who are about or under forty years, have attained such a measure of knowledge of the principles of religion, as renders them inferior to few of their station and education." On hearing of the revival at Cambuslang, he sometimes spoke of it to his congregation, and, as he afterwards learned, not without some good fruit; though few of his people went there, and none of them were manifestly awakened. There was, however, an increasing seriousness, and proposals for reviving societies for prayer, which had been intermitted. On Saturday morning, April 16, the Rev. John Willison, of Dundee, preached at Kilsyth on his return from Cambuslang, where he had been spending about a week. Several, as it afterwards appeared, were awakened by the sermon. The next day, Mr. Robe preached on the desirableness of regeneration. He felt "more than ordinary tenderness in reading the text, and could scarce do it without tears and emotion." He saw much seriousness among his hearers. During the last week in April, he visited the families in a part of the parish where there appeared to be more than ordinary seriousness, and about the same time, heard that several young girls, from ten to sixteen years of age, had been observed meeting for prayer in an outhouse. May 9th, which was the Sabbath, he found that two of his people were awakened. On the 12th, he preached at Cambuslang, where he saw "a great day of the Mediator's power." Returning by a shorter but unfrequented way, he found a manufacturing family with which he was unacquainted, in which six of the servants had been awakened at Cambuslang; and while he was there, six others were seized with deep and pungent convictions. May 16, Mr. Robe continued his course of sermons on regeneration; and while urging its importance in the afternoon, "an extraordinary power of the Spirit from on high accompanied the word preached." About thirty were found to be awakened, many of whom were constrained by their distress to cry out. After the sermon, the exercises were prolonged, Mr. Robe sang and prayed, and then attempted to address them, but his voice was drowned in their cries and groans. He directed that they should be brought to his closet, one by one, while the precentor and some of the elders sang and prayed with those in the kirk, where, to cut off occasion for reproach, he directed that no exhortation should be given. Wednesday, May 19, he says, "We had a sermon for the first time upon a week day. I preached, as did the Rev. Mr. John Warden, minister of the gospel at Campsie, and the Rev. Mr. John McLaurin, minister of the gospel at Glasgow, who had come hither the night before at my invitation. The number of the awakened this day, were as many as were upon the Lord's day. The greatest number was from the parish of Kirkintillock. There were also some from the parishes of Campsie and Cumbernauld. The number of the awakened belonging to this parish, amounted this week to forty."

Meanwhile, similar blessings were descending on other parishes. At Kirkintillock, deep impressions were made on many minds in April, by the fact that a company of children had begun to meet in a barn for prayer. The Rev. James Burnside inquired carefully into their case, and frequently met with them. May 20, he, Mr. McLaurin and Mr. Robe all preached, and many were awakened. At Auchenloch, in the parish of Calder, four miles northwest from Glasgow, fourteen were awakened, and "there was a great cry in the congregation," May 11, under the preaching of the pastor, the Rev. James Warden. At Badernock, which lies north and west from Calder, where there was no pastor, James Forsyth, the pious schoolmaster, began in February to labor with new diligence for the conversion of his pupils. His exhortations soon began to take effect; some of the older people were awakened by observing the seriousness of the children; others, by visiting Cambuslang and other parishes;

and in a short time there was manifestly a revival there. Indeed, in every parish for some distance around Glasgow, there were more or less awakened, and hopeful beginnings in other parts of Scotland ; and wherever it had commenced, it was going on with increasing power, when Whitefield returned from London.

He arrived at Leith on the third of June, and proceeded directly to Edinburgh. "He was received," says Gillies, "by great numbers, and by some persons of distinction, with much joy, and had the satisfaction of seeing and hearing more and more of the happy fruits of his ministry. He continued to preach twice a day, as usual, in the Hospital Park, where a number of seats and shades, in the form of an amphitheatre, were erected for the accommodation of his hearers." He also heard other sounds than those of joy, or of penitence. June 6, which was the Sabbath after his arrival, Adam Gib, one of the Seceders, in the New Church at Bristow, Edinburgh, publicly warned his hearers "against countenancing the ministry of Mr. George Whitefield." He, however, paid no attention to his opposers, but continued his triumphs at Edinburgh, and at other places to which he was invited. The revival, too, continued to spread and gain strength, in places which he never visited. McCullock invited him to Cambuslang. He went, and having preached to a vast assembly at Glasgow in the morning, preached three times at Cambuslang the first day. The last of these sermons he commenced at nine o'clock at night, and concluded at eleven. McCullock then preached till past one, "and even then they could hardly persuade the people to depart. All night in the fields might be heard the voice of prayer and praise."* Mr. McCullock wrote, July 14,—"It is not yet quite five months since this work began in this place ; and in that time I have reason to think that above five hundred souls have been awakened here, and brought under deep

* Such "night meetings" may grow very naturally out of high religious feeling, and are not to be condemned as necessarily sinful. They are certainly much less objectionable than "night meetings" in theatres, ballrooms, and the like. Yet there is always danger that long continued excitement and want of sleep will produce a feverish state of the brain and nerves, in which the mind will not act soberly or safely. Experience has taught the judicious friends of revivals in New England, to be very decided in guarding against unseasonable hours. Few would allow meetings to continue much later than nine o'clock.

convictions of sin, and are now mostly, I believe, savingly brought home to God. I do not in this number include those that have been pretending to be under spiritual distress, and have been discovered to be mere counterfeits ; nor those that appeared to have nothing in their exercises but a dread of hell, which, you know, when it goes no further, never comes to any saving issue. Nor do I include those who have been awakened by means of Mr. Whitefield's sermons in this place, because I cannot pretend to compute them. He has preached seventeen sermons here since he came last to Scotland. He and Mr. Webster * assisted at dispensing the Lord's Supper here last Lord's day,† and the day before and after, and were both much assisted and countenanced in their sermons and exhortations, and a more than ordinary concern appeared among the people all along ; and particularly the time of Mr. Whitefield's sermon on Monday, there was a very great weeping and mourning among the auditory." The audience was estimated at twenty thousand. "The whole work was without doors, in the open air. There were two tents, and two ministers employed in speaking in different places all day ; except in the evening, when Mr. Whitefield preached alone to all the vast multitude then present. The tables, or services, were seventeen in number, each, except the last, which was not quite full, containing about one hundred or more." Whitefield says, "On Saturday I preached to above twenty thousand people. In my prayer, the power of God came down and was greatly felt. In my two sermons, there was yet more power. On Sabbath, scarce ever was such a sight seen in Scotland. There were undoubtedly upwards of twenty thousand people. A brae, or hill, near the manse of Cambuslang, seemed formed by Providence for containing a large congregation. Two tents were set up, and the holy sacrament was administered in the fields. The communion table was in the field. Many ministers attended to preach and assist, all enlivening and enlivened by one another. When I began to serve a table, the power of God was felt by numbers ; but the people so crowded upon me, that I was obliged to desist, and go to preach at one of the tents, whilst the ministers served the rest of the tables. God was with them and with his

---

* Of Edinburgh. † July 11.

people. On Monday morning I preached to near as many as before; but such a universal stir I never saw before. The motion fled as swift as lightning from one end of the auditory to another. You might have seen thousands bathed in tears; some at the same time wringing their hands, others almost swooning, and others crying out, and mourning over a pierced Saviour. But I must not attempt to describe it. In the afternoon, the concern again was very great. Much prayer had been previously put up to the Lord. All night, in different companies, you might have heard persons praying to and praising God." Such was the happiness and spiritual benefit of this occasion, that though the communion was usually observed only once a year in the same parish, Mr. Webster proposed, and Mr. Whitefield desired, to hold another communion season in a few weeks. McCullock and his elders, after some deliberation, consented, and August 15 was appointed for that purpose.

The Associate Presbytery were filled with consternation. Whitefield's labors, in the pulpits of the established church, and at the invitation of its ministers, were producing the very effects that the Erskines had predicted, — drawing men away from the Seceders, and giving influence to their opponents. Men were fast forgetting them and their "testimony" against the corruptions of the church, and learning to regard that corrupt church as God's favored channel of spiritual blessings. Something, they thought, must be done, or the cause of reform would sink into obscurity and be ruined. They met at Dunfermline, and on the 15th of July, published their "Act anent a Public Fast." This act sets forth, that Scotland stands indispensably bound, by the word of God and sundry covenants, to preserve entire the reformed religion of the Church of Scotland; that the present generation, like their fathers, abjure and burn those covenants, invade the rights of the Lord's people by the act restoring patronages, refuse to give an explicit testimony to the great truths of God that are now impugned, and even censure those who have testified doctrinally and judicially against their sinful proceedings, and do what they can to bury a testimony for the cause of Christ, by pretending to depose several ministers of this Presbytery for opposing the corruptions of the church; that infidelity, atheism, and immorality abound and are increasing; that, "therefore, it is no wonder that the

Lord hath, in his righteous displeasure, left this church and land to give such an open discovery of their apostasy from him, in the fond reception that Mr. George Whitefield has met with, notwithstanding it is notourly known that he is a priest of the Church of England, who hath sworn the oath of supremacy, and abjured the Solemn League and Covenant; endeavors, by his lax toleration principles, to pull down the hedges of government and discipline, which the Lord has planted about his vineyard in this land; and, in the account he gives of his life, makes a plain discovery of the grossest enthusiasm and most palpable error and delusion touching his own experience, with reference to the effectual application of the redemption purchased by Christ; yet, because he is found a fit tool for bearing down a testimony for the reformation principles of this church, he is highly commended and extolled by several ministers in their printed letters, and likewise received into full communion with them; and thus, because they would choose their own way, in opposition to our known principles, the Lord hath also chosen their delusions, in permitting the minds of multitudes, through the land, to be corrupted from the simplicity that is in Christ, by departing from the faith, and giving heed to seducing spirits, who, by good words and fair speeches, deceive the hearts of the simple;" that people are imposed upon by ministers, who, "notwithstanding all the ordinary symptoms of a delusion attending the present awful work upon the bodies and spirits of men, yet cry it up as a great work of God," thus attempting "to deceive, if it were possible, the very elect, out of the profession of their faith, and a testimony for our covenanted reformation principles, as if it were nothing but bigotry and party zeal," the promoters of the work being "as far from acknowledging the former and present sins of this church and land, as they were before this work began;" that "bitter outcryings, faintings, severe bodily pains, convulsions, voices, visions, and revelations, are the usual symptoms of a delusive spirit;" that there is nothing in this work to distinguish it "from the common operations of the Spirit of God upon hypocrites, or from the delusions of Satan," but, on the contrary, it produces "the warmest opposition and aversion to a testimony" in favor of the truths for which the Seceders were contending, "contrary to the practice of scripture converts and the experience of the saints of God in this land, who, upon their conversion, still espoused the testimony of their day, and contended for the present truth." For these, "and many weighty causes and considerations," the Presbytery appointed Wednesday, August 4, "to be observed as a day of solemn humiliation in all their congregations, and by all under their inspection, earnestly beseeching and obtesting all and each of them" to examine themselves, and to pray, among other things which are mentioned, that God "would revive a covenanted work of reformation, and direct this Presbytery in essaying to lift up a testimony for the same; that he would preserve all the lovers of Zion from being soon shaken in their minds by the spirit of error and delusion that is now gone abroad amongst us, and determine them to mark those that cause divisions and offences by crying up a boundless liberty of conscience in all sects, contrary to the doctrine we have learned from the word of God and sworn in these lands, and avoid them; that he would purge his church of a corrupt ministry," "be merciful to his witnessing remnant," and "preserve them from dividing amongst themselves," about unimportant matters.*

Robe pronounced this act "the most heaven-daring paper that hath been published by any set of men in Britain, these three hundred years past." "You declare," he says, "the work of God to be a delusion, and the work of the grand deceiver. Now, my dear brethren, for whom I tremble, have you been at due pains to know the nature and circumstances of this work? Have you taken the trouble to go to any of these places where the Lord has appeared in his glory and majesty? Have you so much as written to any of the ministers to receive information of it? Is it not amazing rashness, without inquiry or trial, to pronounce that a work of the devil, which, for any thing you know, may be the work of the infinitely good and Holy Spirit?"

They, however, felt no need of any such inquiries as Robe urged upon them. Their principles enabled them to decide beforehand, that the work could not be of God, but must be of Satan. They believed that the work of God must begin with the reformation of the church, and that he would carry it on only "in a way of solemn covenanting," as in the days of their ancestors. Ralph Erskine argued, that "aversion

* Whitefield Tracts. O. S. Ch. Lib.

from, or opposition to, the testimony of the time," was opposition to God, and that a conversion which "draws men off from any of the ways of God," must be "a false conversion." "The testimony of" that "time," they were confident, was the testimony which the Associate Presbytery was bearing in favor of the Solemn League and Covenant, and against the corruptions of the church; and therefore the conversions under Whitefield, which drew men away from that Presbytery, to worship in the churches of the corrupt establishment, must be false conversions, and the whole work must be opposition to God.

But Adam Gib, though he said no more than is implied in the Act anent a Fast, or in Erskine's sermons, made himself the most notorious of the Seceders. He published* his "Warning against countenancing the Ministry of Mr. George Whitefield," with a preface, and an appendix, "wherein are shown," the titlepage declares, "that Mr. Whitefield is no minister of Jesus Christ; that his call and coming to Scotland are scandalous; that his practice is disorderly, and fertile of disorder; that his whole doctrine is, and his success must be, diabolical; so that people ought to avoid him, from duty to God, to the church, to themselves, to their fellowmen, to posterity, and to him." The main strength of the work lies in the appendix, in which he argues:

"That Mr. Whitefield is no minister of Christ, appears from the manner wherein that office he professes to bear is conveyed to him. He derives it from a diocesan bishop, who derives his office from the king, and the king professes not to be a church officer.—The manner of conveyance is merely human, and so distinct from, and opposite unto, a conveyance from Jesus Christ, according to his institution." "Mr. Whitefield, in swearing the oath of Supremacy, has sworn that Christ is not the supreme and sole head of his church; and, in this condition, he cannot possibly be a minister of this glorious head." "He who professes to preach in the name of Jesus Christ, and declares not the whole counsel of God, but, on the contrary, discredits and condemns part of it, and declares and promotes the counsel of Satan, to the ruin of souls and the subversion of the kingdom of Christ; it cannot but be unwarrantable, provoking to God, and a path to swift perdition, to countenance his ministry, and drink in his doctrine. But this charge, in all its parts, lies against Mr. Whitefield; and therefore the

---

* Philip speaks as if this was done before Whitefield's first visit to Cambuslang; but he was there at the great communion season, July 11, and Gib's preface is dated July 23. Gib indeed says, that his Warning was "published" in the Bristow church, June 6; but his preface shows that it was then only published orally, from the pulpit.

conclusion obtains in the present case." "He condemns not bigotry and party zeal, merely as set in opposition to a due concern about the appurtenances of Christ's visible kingdom of grace, but as he sets it in opposition to a concern about the invisible grace of Christ. It is in this light that he condemns it; which shows us that, under the names of bigotry and party zeal, schismatical and seditious, Mr. Whitefield condemns all concern and duty anent the visible kingdom of the Mediator, as such. This, then, is what he calls earthly, sensual, devilish. —If this be not a discrediting and condemning of the counsel of God, there never was such a thing. If this be not a declaring and promoting the counsel of Satan on earth, it was never declared nor promoted in hell." "As divine revelation, so whatsoever is thereby intimated and ordained, concur unto both these noble ends, the salvation of men, in subordination unto the glory of God. And it is God Mediator, into whose hands this revenue of glory doth immediately come. Whatsoever glory he acquires, is a kingly glory. The glorifying of his priesthood must respect him as a *priest upon his throne.* Zech. 4: 13. The glorifying of his prophetical office must respect him as *one having authority.* Mat. 7: 29. For, when he stands and feeds, (with knowledge,) it is in the *majesty* of the name of the Lord his God. Micah. 5: 4. Thus the glory of his other offices is gathered unto his kingly office, and all concurs unto a kingly glory; whence it is evident, that any glorifying of him whatever, that is not ultimately aimed at his kingly office, is nothing better than a hypocritical show, that cannot meet with acceptance. Moreover, this kingly glory is twofold, according to his twofold mediatorial kingdom, visible and invisible. Though his visible kingdom is to continue but for a set time, yet, during that time, there can be nothing more indispensable than the affairs of church government. Let men revile these externals never so much, they are of no small account with Zion's king. The doctrine and maintenance of church government is of as essential necessity to the Mediator's glory in the church,* as the doctrine of grace is unto the salvation of men. And which is of the highest importance, the divine glory, or the salvation of all men? It will not believe with me, that any are rightly concerned about the salvation of themselves or others, while contemning the visible glory of the Mediator; while contemning the doctrine, being and exercise of church government, that promote the same. It is not the salvation of *God* that those men do mean. That salvation which is not actually subordinate unto the divine glory, is a cheat. And that salvation which reconciles not men unto the doctrine and maintenance of church government, in so far renounces subordination to the divine glory." "His errors communicate diabolical corruption unto those very truths he reserves, as to their immediate influence." "The doctrine of grace that Mr. Whitefield retains, cannot possibly discover the true Christ, because his back is towards him, in flouting away the doctrine that discovers Christ a king of a visible kingdom. It avails nothing to say that the doctrine of grace, by itself, may discover Christ in his invisible kingdom; for his kingly character, with respect to both his visible and invisible king-

* By "the Mediator's glory in the church," Gib means, the gloriousness of church courts.

doms, is, during the gospel day, one character, indivisible, and if any clip it through, he spoils it all. But Mr. Whitefield uses the doctrine of grace to discredit one half of that character, one half of that king; and therefore, as Christ cannot be divided, seeing Mr. Whitefield's doctrine directly fights against him in part, it is not possible that it can truly discover him at all. Mr. Whitefield and his followers have much talk about Christ; but what Christ must it be? His doctrine cannot discover the true Christ, who died at Jerusalem, as we have seen. It must therefore be a notional Christ. Yes, every Christ that is not Christ a king, in a visible kingdom, must be a notional Christ. O, then, how does the scene cast up? The doctrine of grace, that Mr. Whitefield publishes, is carried off from its true posture, connexion and use, and applied to a diabolical use, viz: to create a Christ in people's imaginations, as a competitor with the true Christ." "The doctrine of grace, as diabolically perverted through Mr. Whitefield, is versant about such a Christ as is merely a Saviour; and it hurries men off in quest of such spiritual influences, convictions, conversions, consolations and assurances, as are unconcerned with and hostile unto the Mediator's visible glory.* But such a Christ, such influences, convictions, conversions, consolations, assurances, are not of God. They can be no better than idols set up in men's imaginations. Hence it is, that as those who hear Mr. Whitefield, do thereby approve the satanical cast of his doctrine, and expose themselves unto its influence, so therein, at best, they but hunt after and worship idols. It is therefore to be fearfully expected, that God will, in judgment, answer them accordingly, and send them an idol Christ, idol conversions, &c. according to their lust." "But how is it that this judgment of God must be accomplished? Certainly, it must be by a spirit. The Spirit of God it cannot be; and the spirit of man can be only the melancholy subject, and not the author, of such operations. It remains, then, that God's great executioner, Satan, must be employed in the producing of such effects. And what other can be expected, from the justice of God, than that a diabolical doctrine should become the channel of a diabolical spirit and influence?" Satan "can enter no further into a man, than his imagination. It is peculiar to the divine Spirit, to penetrate into the soul. When a man, under this satanical influence, is affected by any word of Scripture, it can hit only his imagination. It is not faith that brings in the word to his soul, but the devil brings it in, with hurry, into his fancy.—His horrors must be blind, as they will be more glaring than what the divine Spirit occasions, just because they are on the fancy, and must kindle it. The miserable man, under such satanical influence, can have no sight of the true Christ, in the word without him, by a calm and quiet faith. The only Christ he can see, is formed by Satan on his imagination; or Satan gives himself out there for the true Christ. And, as the poor man's fancy may be thus so kindled as to craze his brain, gathering his animal spirits in a hurry, to attend the angel of light that possesseth his fancy, what can he then imagine, but that he is converted, and in high communion with God; and can he fail to be extatic and

* That is, the gloriousness of his visible church, as seen in church judicatories.

rapturous in his consolations? Can he fail to have his imagination filled with assurance, when thus under strong delusions?" "The divine Spirit doth improve human nature in its general condition, as he works in a way agreeable to our frame; but the satanical spirit must operate the reverse of all this. And how can it be otherwise, seeing the imagination is the first seat of his influence? Hence he must torture the animal frame; as the divine Spirit, on the other hand, tames the soul; and as our Lord, in the days of his flesh, sent forth his Spirit to chase out devils from racking men's bodies. Hence also, Satan, while kindling men's fancies, must carry them out under strong, sudden and blind impulses, frights, freaks, raptures, visions, revelations, boastings, blunders." "Satan cannot make use of the whole truth. He only deals with a part of it, and that for discrediting the whole. And therefore, wherever a person falls under Satan's use of the truth, he will soon cast up to be unconcerned about the public dishonors done to Jesus; he will pretend regard to him in his invisible grace, that he may smother regard to him in his visible kingdom." "And now, though men should write a thousand volumes upon the fine, the holy and evangelical-like appearances of that success which attends the doctrine we have been considering; yet, after all, they no way vindicate it, till they overturn the arguments proving that it must be devilish." "The diabolical set of the whole complex scheme is what he [Whitefield] cannot be privy to, or sensible of, in this world, till God mercifully, if ever, break Satan's blinding snare. The proper and designing author, then, of this scheme, whom we are ultimately to consider, is not Mr. Whitefield, but Satan: and thus our contendings against Mr. Whitefield must be proportioned, not to his design, but Satan's, while hereof he is an effectual, though blinded tool." "As it appears that God hath sent him strong delusion, that he should believe a lie, I look not upon human argument as a means of God's appointment for rolling off the weight of that judgment. I expect not that he is capable of being undeceived, but immediately by God; and therefore I see no duty that men owe him, in the present case, but to avoid him, and pray for him." *

Such were the arguments by which the Seceders justified to their own consciences, and attempted to justify to others, their opposition to Whitefield. Gib does not deserve the "bad eminence" among them, which most writers have awarded him. The assertions and arguments of the "Act anent a Public Fast" are as bad as any thing from the pen of Gib; and if the language is less virulent, it is made so by the brevity and formality required in an official document, and not by any dissent of the Associate Presbytery from any of the views set forth in the "Warning" and its appendix. Yet the members of this Presbytery were some of the most excellent men of the age in which they lived. Their feelings

* Whitefield Tracts, O. S. Ch. Library.

and conduct on this occasion were at variance with their general character.* Fraser declares, that "they themselves lived to repent of the rancor into which the heat of controversy had at first betrayed them."† Gib, on his deathbed, wished that there were no copies of his pamphlet on the face of the earth, and said that if he could recall every copy, he would burn them. The whole history is a lamentable but instructive specimen of the unchristian absurdities into which even a good man may be betrayed, and in defence of which he may become most conscientiously zealous, when a single idea gets entire possession of his head, and "being alone there, has every thing in its own way."

The Seceders were made the subjects of special prayer by the good people at Cambuslang, when they met to pray for the divine blessing on the approaching sacramental season. McCullock has given an account of that season, in a letter to a friend: ‡

"The ministers that assisted at this solemnity were, Mr. Whitefield, Mr. Webster from Edinburgh, Mr. McLaurin and Mr. Gillies from Glasgow, Mr. Robe from Kilsyth, Mr. Currie from Kinglassie, Mr. Kneight from Irvin, Mr. Bonner from Torpichen, Mr. Hamilton from Douglass, and three of the neighbouring ministers, viz., Mr. Henderson from Blantyre, Mr. Maxwell from Rutherglen, and Mr. Adam from Cathcart. All of them appeared to be very much assisted in their work. Four of them preached on the fast day, four on Saturday, on Sabbath I cannot well tell how many, and five on Monday, on which last day it was computed that about twenty-four ministers and preachers were present. Old Mr. Bonner, though so frail that he took three days to ride eighteen miles from Torpichen to Cambuslang, yet his heart was so set upon coming here, that he could by no means stay away, and when he was helped up to the tent, preached three times with great life; and returned with much

* Philip says: "It would be wrong, after having quoted so often from Ralph Erskine's sermons, were I not to say, even of the sermons which are most disfigured with tirades against Whitefield and the revivals, that they are full of evangelical truth, and flaming with love to immortal souls, and as faithful to the conscience, as any that Whitefield preached at Cambuslang. Indeed, had they been preached on the *brae-head*, at the great sacrament there, Erskine would as surely have slain his hundreds, as Whitefield did his thousands."

† Quoted by Philip.

‡ Christian History, Vol. I. 297; Glasgow W. History, No. 39.

satisfaction and joy. Mr. Whitefield's sermons on Saturday, Sabbath, and Monday, were attended with much power, particularly on Sabbath night about ten, and that on Monday; several crying out, and a very great but decent weeping and mourning was observable through the auditory. On Sabbath evening, while he was serving some tables, he appeared to be so filled with the love of God, as to be in a kind of extasy or transport, and communicated with much of that blessed frame. Time would fail me, to speak of the evidences of the power of God coming along with the rest of the assistants.

"The number of people that were there on Saturday and Monday, was very considerable. But the number present at the three tents on the Lord's day was so great, that, so far as I can hear, none ever saw the like since the revolution, in Scotland, or even anywhere else, at any sacrament occasion. Some have called them fifty thousand; some, forty thousand; the lowest estimate I hear of, with which Mr. Whitefield agrees, who has been much used to great multitudes and forming a judgment of their number, makes them to have been upwards of thirty thousand.

"The number of communicants appears to have been about three thousand. And some worthy of credit, and that had proper opportunities to know, gave it as their opinion, that there was such a blessed frame fell upon the people, that if there had been access to get tokens, there would have been a thousand more communicants than what were.*

"This vast concourse of people, you may easily imagine, came not only from the city of Glasgow, and other places near by, but from many places at a considerable distance. It was reckoned there were two hundred communicants from Edinburgh, two hundred from Kilmarnock, a hundred from Irvin, a hundred from Stewarton. It was observed, that there were some from England and Ireland here at this occasion. A considerable number of Quakers were hearers. A great many of those that had formerly been Seceders were

* Every baptized person, not under ecclesiastical censure, and having passed examination as to doctrinal knowledge, has a legal right to the communion in that church; and the amount of pious feeling in a place is very naturally estimated by the number who come forward to claim the privilege. The applicant, however, must previously appear before the Church Session, and obtain a "token" of his fitness, which he is to present and return at the Table.

hearing the word, and some of them were communicants. A youth that has a near view to the ministry, and had been for some time under great temptations that God's presence was no more to be enjoyed, either in the Church or among the Seceders, communicated here, and returned with great joy, full of the love of God.

"There was a great deal of outward decency and regulation observable about the tables. * Public worship began on the Lord's day just at half past eight in the morning. My action sermon, I think, was reasonably short. The third or fourth table was serving at twelve o'clock, and the last table was serving about sunset. When that was done, the work was closed with a few words of exhortation, prayer and praise, the precentor having so much daylight as to let him see to read four lines of a psalm. The tables were all served in the open air, beside the tent below the brae. The day was temperate; no wind or rain in the least to disturb. Several persons of considerable rank and distinction, who were elders, most cheerfully assisted our elders in serving the tables.

"But what was most remarkable was, the spiritual glory of this solemnity; I mean, the gracious and sensible presence of God. Not a few were awakened to a sense of sin, and their lost and perishing condition without a Saviour. Others had their bands loosed, and were brought into the marvellous liberty of the sons of God. Many of God's dear children have declared, that it was a happy time to their souls, wherein they were abundantly satisfied with the goodness of God in his ordinances, and filled with all joy and peace in believing."

"Besides Edinburgh and Glasgow," Gillies says, "it is really wonderful to think how many places in the west of Scotland he [Whitefield] visited within a few weeks, preaching at every one of them. And when he retired for a day or two, it was on purpose to write letters, and prepare pieces for the press." For this last mentioned employment, his American opposers helped to create the necessity.

Foulis, the celebrated University Printer at Glasgow, had published a pamphlet, entitled, "The State of Religion in New England, since the Reverend George Whitefield's arri-

* The Presbyterians of Scotland, and many in America, sit around a table to receive the Lord's Supper.

val there: in a Letter from a Gentleman in New England to his friend in Glasgow. To which is subjoined an Appendix, containing Attestations of the principal Facts in a Letter, by the Reverend Mr. Chauncy, Pastor of the First Church of Christ in Boston, Mr. John Caldwell, in New Londonderry, Mr. John Barnard, Pastor of a Church in Marblehead, Mr. Turell, Mr. Jonathan Parsons, Minister at Lyme, and Dr. Benjamin Colman, Minister in Boston." The Letter was merely a denial that any good had been done, an exaggerated account of all the disorders that had appeared since Whitefield's arrival, and some stories that seem to be absolute fictions. Of the "Attestations" in the appendix, the last three were garbled extracts, applied as their authors never intended, and all of them fell far short of sustaining "the principal facts in the letter." The author "desired and insisted that his name should not be mentioned," professing "apprehensions of the fury this account might raise against himself among some of the high pretenders to a Christian spirit" in New England. He had good reason to fear the ruin of his reputation for veracity. Foulis, however, assures us that he was a layman, and Whitefield inferred, from his commendation of the Episcopalians in Boston, who had nothing to do with the revival, that he was one of them. The letter was dated "May 24, 1742." Whitefield's answer is dated "Cambuslang, August 31, 1742." Philip says, "He proved pretty fully, although without bringing home the fact to any one, that the pamphlet was altered in Scotland, to suit a purpose. And there are dates of Scotch publications in it, which could not have been known in Boston when it was written." The affair is worth examining, for a lesson which it teaches. Whitefield's whole argument reads thus:—

"There is one thing in the letter which makes me shrewdly suspect that the letter itself is not genuine; at least, that there has been some additions made to it since it came to Scotland. For the supposed writer says, 'In the preface to the sermon published by Mr. Edwards of Northampton, which, I see, is reprinted among you.' Now, how this gentleman, May 24, could see at Boston, that Mr. Edwards' sermon was reprinted in Scotland, which was not done till June following, I know not. If it be said, that by the words '*among you*' he means *in Britain*, I see that the printed advertisement in the London Weekly History, of the publication of Mr. Edwards' sermon in England, is dated May 1, and says, 'This day is published.' I myself was one that was chiefly concerned in publishing of it. I sent the first copy to Scotland, and, to my certain knowledge, it was never published in Britain till May 1. Is it probable that people at Boston should know this, May 24?"

This looks like a strong case; but the proof is insufficient. Foulis shows, in his second edition, that the London Weekly History of April 10 contained an advertisement of the Sermon as "in the press," and as "earnestly recommended by Mr. Whitefield;" and that even in March, a bookseller at Glasgow had been requested to procure some of them from London when printed. From these facts Foulis argues, that Whitefield must have known that the intention of reprinting the sermon had been known in Britain, long enough to reach Boston before the date of the letter; and on this he grounds a charge against Whitefield of "Jesuitical dissimulation," in bringing forward an implied charge of forgery, which he must have known to be false. That there was time for the news to cross the Atlantic, is certain. His Majesty's ship Dover arrived at Boston May 17, 1742, in five weeks from Plymouth.* She must have sailed, therefore, April 12, and brought London dates as late as April 11, the day after the date, and probably two days after the printing, of the advertisement. There was also, before the 27th, and probably before the 24th, another arrival in five weeks.* The disgrace of forgery, therefore, cannot be fixed upon the editor of the pamphlet. Nor ought any one to desire it. The disgrace of publishing it is enough. Neither was Whitefield guilty of "Jesuitical dissimulation," but only of inconsiderate haste in charging a scandalous crime upon his opponents. He did not stop to think, as he ought to have done, that a person writing on the 24th of May, would very naturally say of a sermon which he knew to have been "in the press" five weeks before, "which, I see, *is* reprinted among you." He understood it strictly, as an assertion, that the writer had seen some notice of its actual appearance in the market; and this, he knew, was highly improbable. Many of the irritating charges of that day, on both sides, arose from a similar want of deliberate investigation, and not from any design to misrepresent. In the midst of such high and general excitement, it could hardly be otherwise. Excited men cannot wait for the slow move-

* Boston News Letter, May 20 and May 27, 1742, Lib. Mass. Hist. Soc.

ments of patient investigation. They assert, with undoubting confidence, what they believe to be true, but what the other party confidently believes to be false; and thus they destroy their own reputation as honest men. The controversy concerning this pamphlet doubtless confirmed each party in the belief, that the other was deliberately dishonest. This must be remembered, if we would do justice, either to Whitefield, to his friends, or to his opponents.

There were many other publications, for and against Whitefield and the revival. The Arminianizing clergy of the national church were all against him; as were also some of the most thorough Calvinists. Among the latter, John Bisset, Ogilvie's colleague at Aberdeen, who preached against Whitefield on his first visit, published, October 26, a letter of one hundred and twelve pages, "On Communion with a Priest of the Church of England." He heartily belabors all parties; the Seceders, for first inviting Whitefield to Scotland, and then disguising the fact, instead of frankly confessing the sin, in their "Act anent a Fast;" a part of the clergy of the church, for using Whitefield to break down the Seceders; and all parties in that church, for not testifying against the inroads of false doctrine. He quotes respectfully a passage from Adam Gib's pamphlet, which, he says, he has preserved from the flames, to which Webster of Edinburgh had sentenced the whole edition.

Meanwhile, Whitefield had returned to London,* where, Gillies says, "he found a new awakening at the Tabernacle, which had been much enlarged." But the revival continued in Scotland. In several parishes, awakenings commenced in July and August, 1742, and in others about the beginning of 1743. March 30, 1744, Mr. Hamilton wrote from Glasgow to Mr. Prince: "The state of religion in our country is much the same as when I wrote you last. The strong sensible awakenings are in a great measure ceased; and indeed it could not be expected they should continue long; but the effects of them, with great numbers, I hope will never cease. There are still many instances of persons awakened and hopefully converted in a more silent way. The ordinances continue to be more frequented than formerly; a more close attention to the preaching of the word, and a greater power

* He was at Glasgow, October 20, and at London, November 6.

accompanying it; and especially sacrament occasions have of late been remarkably blessed for the quickening and comfort of sincere Christians. Our societies for prayer and conference are likewise in a flourishing condition in many parts."

Yet even then intelligence had just been received, of awakenings in the north of Scotland, where the revival seems to have been attended with fewer objectionable circumstances than at Cambuslang and Kilsyth. There was a revival, too, in the remote Highlands. It was in the parish of Lockbroom, the largest in Scotland, being more than one hundred miles in circumference. It had no pastor; but Hugh Cameron, the pious schoolmaster, travelled from place to place, gave personal instruction, formed societies for conference and prayer, and was the means of enlightening many souls.

The benefit of this revival extended even to Holland. Accounts of the awakenings at Cambuslang and Kilsyth were translated into the Dutch by the Rev. Mr. Kennedy, of the Scots Congregation at Rotterdam. Some of the clergy recommended the work from their pulpits. Several editions were sold, and it was made "a means of quickening, enlightening and consolation to many."

## CHAPTER XVI.

The Revival in New England. — Conventions and Testimonies.

The General Convention of Congregational Ministers in Massachusetts obtained its form and official character gradually. It grew out of the custom of visiting Boston on the day of the opening of the colonial legislature. As many pastors were then in Boston, it became a custom for them to meet together, to converse on matters of general interest, hear a sermon from some one of their number previously appointed, and take up a collection for some pious object, commonly the support of missions among the heathen. Sometimes, if not always, they had a moderator and a clerk, but kept no record of their proceedings.* The declaration

* The vote directing the purchase of a book for records, was passed in 1748. It is still preserved, on a loose piece of paper, as originally written.

Joseph Sewall.

of its opinions, however, especially when unanimous, or nearly so, could not fail to exert a powerful influence; and it was determined to bring that influence to bear against the revival. The result of the effort was published in the following words:

"The TESTIMONY of the Pastors of the Churches in the Province of Massachusetts Bay, in New England, at their Annual Convention in Boston, May 25, 1743, against several Errors in Doctrine and Disorders in Practice, which have of late obtained in various Parts of the Land; as drawn up by a Committee chosen by the said Pastors, read and accepted, paragraph by paragraph, and voted to be signed by the Moderator in their name, and printed.

"We, the pastors of the churches of Christ in the province of Massachusetts Bay, in New England, at our Annual Convention, May 25, 1743, taking into consideration several errors in doctrine and disorders in practice that have of late obtained in various parts of the land, look upon ourselves bound, in duty to our great Lord and Master, Jesus Christ, and in concern for the purity and welfare of these churches, in the most public manner to bear our testimony against them.

"I. As to errors in doctrine; we observe that some in our land look upon what are called secret impulses upon their minds, without due regard to the written word, the rule of their conduct; that none are converted but such as know they are converted, and the time when; that assurance is of the essence of saving faith; that sanctification is no evidence of justification; with other Antinomian and Familistical errors which flow from these; all which, as we judge, are contrary to the pure doctrines of the Gospel, and testified against and confuted in the Acts of the Synod of August, 1637; as printed in a book entitled 'The Rise, and Reign, and Ruin, of Antinomianism, &c., in New England.'

"II. As to disorders in practice, we judge,

"1. The itinerancy, as it is called, by which either ordained ministers or young candidates go from place to place, and without the knowledge, or contrary to the leave of the stated pastors in such places, assemble their people to hear themselves preach,—arising, we fear, from too great an opinion of themselves, and an uncharitable opinion of those pastors, and a want of faith in the great Head of the churches, is a breach of order, and contrary to the Scriptures, 1 Pet. 4: 15; 2 Cor. 10: 12, to the end, and the sentiments of our fathers expressed in their Platform of Church Discipline, chap. 9, sect. 6.

"2. Private persons of no education and but low attainments in knowledge and in the great doctrines of the gospel, without any regular call, under a pretence of exhorting, taking upon themselves to be preachers of the word of God, we judge to be a heinous invasion of the ministerial office, offensive to God, and destructive to these churches; contrary to Scripture, Numb. 16: 1 Cor. 28, 29, and testified against in a 'Faithful Advice to the Churches of New England' by several of our venerable fathers.

"3. The ordaining or separating of any persons to the work of the evangelical ministry at large, and without any relation to a particular charge, which some of late have unhappily gone into, we look upon as contrary to the Scriptures, and directly opposite to our Platform, chap. 6 sect. 3, and the practice of the Protestant churches; as may be seen in 'The order of the Churches Vindicated,' by the very Reverend Dr. Increase Mather.

"4. The spirit and practice of separation from the particular flocks to which persons belong, to join themselves with, and support lay exhorters or itinerants, is very subversive of the churches of Christ, opposite to the rule of the gospel, Gal. 5: 19, 20; Jude 19; 1 Cor. 12: 25; 1 Cor. 3: 3, and utterly condemned by our Platform, chap. 13, sect. 1, 5, and contrary to their covenant engagements.

"5. Persons assuming to themselves the prerogatives of God, to look into and judge the hearts of their neighbours, censure and condemn their brethren, especially their ministers, as Pharisees, Arminians, blind and unconverted, &c., when their doctrines are agreeable to the gospel and their lives to their Christian profession, is, we think, most contrary to the spirit and precepts of the gospel and the example of Christ, and highly unbecoming the character of those who call themselves the disciples of the meek and lowly Jesus. John 13: 34, 35; 1 Sam. 16: 7; Mat. 7: 1; Rom. 14: 10.

"6. Though we deny not that the human mind, under the operations of the Divine Spirit, may be overborne with terrors and joys; yet the many confusions that have appeared in some places, from the vanity of mind and ungoverned passions of people, either in the excess of sorrow or joy, with the disorderly tumults and indecent behaviour of persons, we judge to be so far from an indication of the special presence of God with those preachers that have industriously excited and countenanced them, or in the assemblies where they prevail, that they are a plain evidence of the weakness of human nature; as the history of the enthusiasms that have appeared in the world, in several ages, manifests. Also, 1 Cor. 14: 23, 40. At the same time we bear our testimony against the impious spirit of those that from hence take occasion to reproach the work of the Divine Spirit in the hearts of the children of God.

"Upon the whole, we earnestly recommend the churches of this country to the gracious care and conduct of the great Shepherd of the sheep, with our thankful acknowledgments for his merciful regard to them in supplying them with faithful pastors, and protecting them from the designs of their enemies, and advancing his spiritual kingdom in the souls of so many, from the foundation of this country to this day; and where there is any special revival of pure religion in any parts of our land at this time, we would give unto God all the glory. And we earnestly advise all our brethren in the ministry carefully to endeavour to preserve their churches pure in their doctrine, discipline and manners, and guard them against the intrusion of itinerants and exhorters, to uphold a spirit of love towards one another, and all men; which, together with their fervent prayers, will be the most likely means, under God, to promote the true religion of the holy Jesus, and hand it, uncorrupt, to succeeding generations.

"Signed, NATHANIEL EELLS, Moderator,
in the name and by order of the Convention."

This was forthwith published, without note or comment, and was copied by Dr. Chauncy into his work on the "State of Religion in New England," and has been published elsewhere, in the same style. Happily, something may be known of its secret history, though not so much as seems desirable.

The Rev. Joshua Gee, pastor of the Second Church in Boston, is represented by Dr. Chauncy as a man of more genius than any other of the Boston ministers, and one who might have been a great man, but for his indolence and love of talking. A newspaper satirist of the day, describes him as one who never loved to do any thing himself, but was excellent at setting others at work. His name scarcely appears in the history of the revival, till this movement in the Convention. This seems to have fairly roused him, and he talked and set others to work to some purpose. He addressed a printed letter, dated June 3, to Mr. Eells, moderator of the Convention, which called forth replies from the Rev. Benjamin Prescott of Salem, and Rev. John Hancock of Braintree. These letters furnish what information we have, concerning the adoption of this Testimony.*

The Convention met, May 25. What preliminary consultations had been held, does not appear. Hancock says, that he had "reason to think that multitudes in those places that had been rent with them, [disorders,] as well as others, had great expectations of receiving such a faithful Testimony" from the Convention. Gee intimates his suspicion, that it was intended to carry out the designs of a party. Prescott states, that "upon the motion of some members of the Convention, that they would take into consideration, and give their advice upon some melancholy accounts then given, which related to the state of religion in the land, and specially in some particular parts of it," it was proposed, and voted without opposition, to appoint a committee, to report the next morning, immediately after the Convention sermon, which was to be at nine o'clock. After the sermon, the convention retired to Dr. Sewall's, who was one of the committee, but had not met with them. He had but just time to glance at the report, before it was presented. Gee says,

* All these letters are preserved in the Athenæum Library, and those of Hancock and Prescott in that of the Old South Church.

that when the report was presented, Dr. Sewall "declared his judgment that it ought to have contained an attestation to a revival of religion in many parts of the land, by such a work as an assembly of pastors at their annual convention should publicly acknowledge to his praise, and that this ought to have preceded the testimony against errors and disorders;" and that it ought to testify against Arminianism, as well as Antinomianism. A debate arose, and finally three were added to the committee, and the report was recommitted. The committee met at Dr. Sewall's, after dinner. Prescott, who was one of them, says, that in relation to Arminianism, it was observed, that in the statements which had led to the appointment of the committee, nothing was said of its prevalence, or of disorders arising from it, and as they could not be expected to testify against all errors, there was no reason for testifying against that in particular; so the matter was dropped, except that the word "Arminians" was added after the word "Pharisees" in the fifth article. The last sentence of the sixth article was added, and the words, "and where there is special revival of pure religion in any parts of our land, we would give unto God all the glory," were inserted in the concluding paragraph.

When the report, thus amended, was brought in, an attempt was made to adopt it entire, by a single vote; but the Convention decided first to consider the articles separately. The first five articles passed with little or no opposition; some, however, refusing to vote, because the Testimony did not contain an open acknowledgment of the revival. On the sixth article, a very earnest debate arose. During this debate, Gee attempted to speak. Dr. Chauncy objected, that eight years before, Gee had, by a written instrument, withdrawn from the Convention, and urged that he should now be asked whether he spake as a member. Gee refused to answer, and was not permitted to speak. Several urged the duty of testifying fully that there had been a glorious work of divine grace in the land. It was replied, that as the revival had not appeared in all places, many pastors, who had not seen it, could not join in testifying its reality. But, it was said, neither had errors and disorders appeared in all places, and the Convention might as well rely on information concerning one, as concerning the other. Webb, of Boston, then gave an account of the revival among his people, and others were ready to follow him. Gee says, "they were interrupted in a rude manner, and treated with open contempt;" that "many earnest pleas for their being heard were stifled in clamor and opposition; that the Rev. Mr. W——s of W——n,* who was one of the committee, testified against the bad spirit of the assembly, and the ill-treatment given to pastors who desired to speak; and that he declared openly, that "he had seen much of the gracious work of God, in a late revival of religion among his people, and this, without any appearance of the errors and disorders mentioned in the Testimony;" that others wished to speak, "but saw it was in vain to desire and wait for a patient hearing." Hancock admits, that there was too much warmth on both sides; but says those who wished to speak, "to the best of my remembrance, were generally treated with respect and decency." Prescott gives a sketch of this part of the debate. It was said, against hearing any more statements, that the Convention did not need to hear them, "there having been abundant publication, already, of these things." When it was urged that these accounts should be believed, as well as accounts of errors and disorders, the reply was, that equal credit was given to the facts, in both cases; but in one case, the facts were such as evidently amounted to errors and disorders, but in the other, they were not such that the hearer could testify that there had been a revival of religion. It was then urged, that, if the acknowledgment of the revival were omitted, the Convention would not give that glory to God which was his due. The reply was, that "God would certainly have the glory of his grace in every instance wherein it was displayed;" that every convert would praise him for his own conversion, and that every church where there was a revival, — Mr. Webb's, for instance, — would thank him for that revival, so that the whole would be acknowledged; but the praises of those who were not personally acquainted with the facts, it was argued, could serve no important purpose. But the great argument was, that "if the Convention should give so full and enlarged a testimony for a glorious work of divine grace," the disorderly and erroneous "would be led to apply it to themselves, and take it for granted, that, however they might be chargeable with some

* Probably, Williams of Weston.

errors and disorders, yet, in the judgment of the Convention, they had experienced that which was an evidence of a remarkable divine influence," and therefore would "but little regard our testifying against errors and disorders." That is, the Convention did not dare to tell the whole truth and risk the consequences, lest it should defeat the good object they had in view.

At length, the question on the adoption of the whole paper, was put and carried. The vote was disputed, and a count was ordered. The moderator counted thirty-eight votes in the affirmative, which he pronounced to be a majority; and that number was entered on the minutes by Mr. Prince, the scribe. Gee suggests a doubt whether there would have been a majority, without the votes of ministers from other colonies. Hancock and Prescott think there were more than thirty-eight affirmative votes, and that the moderator counted only that number, because no more were necessary to decide the question. The mode of subscription was then to be decided. Gee writes to Eells, "I am sensible you plainly told the assembly, you could not subscribe it for yourself personally, upon which there was a vote for your signing it as moderator." On this, Prescott says nothing. Hancock wrote to Eells, to know if it was true, and whether he would testify that there were only thirty-eight affirmative votes; but he received no answer. Eells was a cautious man. Hancock says, he was "the most famous of any in these parts, for a steady opposer of the very errors and disorders mentioned in the Testimony."

Gee regretted that the proposal for a personal subscription did not prevail; for then it would have appeared that the Testimony was voted by less than one fifth of the ministers of Massachusetts. He thought the Testimony, as it was, "powerfully tended to unhappy effects, both among those who live at a great distance from us, and among our own churches," and that nothing "could be better calculated and contrived to confirm the fallacious accounts of the 'State of Religion in New England,' which had lately been sent over to Scotland by some virulent opposers" of the revival.

This same Convention furnished another important "Testimony." It was contained in the election sermon, by the Rev. Nathaniel Appleton, pastor of the first church in Cambridge; a man famous for his extreme care, if any care can be extreme, always to speak the exact truth. He said: —

"I cannot but think there are many things at this day that have a plausible appearance at first view, and yet are of a dangerous tendency; which I think, ministers, if they would be a light to their people, should instruct and warn them about, with the meekness and gentleness of Christ.

"As, particularly, ministers leaving their own particular charges, and going from place to place, without any regular call or desire, intruding themselves into other men's parishes; whereby they are in danger of exciting and gratifying their own pride, stirring up itching ears in the people, and leading them away from love and esteem of their own faithful ministers.

"So, again, ministers setting up to preach without premeditation and study, looks plausible to the weak and ignorant, but is of dangerous tendency.

"Again, encouraging illiterate persons publicly to exhort, which, by speaking freely and boldly upon some points, lead the people to think they have more of the Spirit of God than their ministers; by which means such novices are in danger of being lifted up with pride themselves; and the end of it with respect to the people, if it should go on, would be ignorance and error; for many of the gross errors and corruptions of the church of Rome have come in at the door of ignorance.

"Again, pretending to immediate impulses of the Spirit, and taking them for their guide, rather than the Holy Scriptures, or pretending by such impulses to explain the Holy Scriptures. So all disparaging speeches about the Scriptures, as if they were useless to the unconverted, and as if the converted had the Spirit in such a degree as in any measure to supersede the use of the word; pretending, also, that none but the saints have any understanding of the Scriptures, and as if they could understand all Scriptures without any help of human study and learning. Those are very dangerous things, that must be pointed out, and the people enlightened in, that are in danger of being carried away with them.

"Again, false notions about faith, as if assurance was of the essence of saving, justifying faith. Or the refining faith in such a manner as to separate it from good works, and pleading for such a faith as the apostle says is dead. So the speaking too slightly of good works, and leading people into an apprehension of the needlessness of them, and making them careless about them, are dangerous points.

"Again, leading people to think it is of necessity for them to know the particular time of their conversion.

"So, again, their uncharitableness towards others; a freedom in judging men's state, even though they are regular and blameless in their lives; and a pretending it is an easy thing to judge whether men are in a state of grace or not; and a denying, at the same time, that sanctification is any evidence of justification.

"Now these and such like are stumbling-blocks; yea, some of them dangerous rocks, that ministers must be as a light unto their people about, and must hold the light of God's word to them, that they may see and avoid them.

"But then there are stumbling-blocks on the other hand, yea, most dangerous rocks, which ministers, if they would be as lights unto the world, must point out, and warn seasonably and earnestly against.

"Thus, the denial of there having been a glorious work of God in the land of late; and the speaking disparagingly of those convictions, and all that serious concern that has been stirred up in multitudes, as if there was nothing of the Spirit of God in any of them; and as if all the religious commotions had been the work of the devil, or had been wrought in a mere mechanical way; and the ridiculing and reproaching such persons in general and without distinction, and discouraging rather than encouraging any concernedness of soul, and so the lulling men asleep in their carnal security again, that began to be roused up, and the settling them in their natural, unconverted state; these, I say, are dangerous things, and ministers must hold up the light of God's word, and show people the danger hereof."

It was from hearing this sermon, of which they requested a copy for the press, that the Convention went to Dr. Sewall's, and engaged in the debates which have just been described.

The next day, Friday, May 27, some friends of the revival met, and agreed to hold another Convention. Accordingly, the following notice appeared in the Boston Gazette of May 31:

"It is desired and proposed by a number of ministers, both in town and country, that such of their brethren as are persuaded there has of late been a happy revival of religion, through an extraordinary divine influence, in many parts of this land, and are concerned for the honor and progress of this remarkable work of God, may have an interview at Boston, the day after the approaching commencement; to consider whether they are not called to give an open conjunct testimony to an event so surprising and gracious; as well as against those errors in doctrine and disorders in practice, which, through the permitted agency of Satan, have attended it, and in any measure blemished its glory and hindered its advancement: and also to consult the most likely methods to be taken, to guard people against such delusions and mistakes as in such a season they are in danger of falling into, and that this blessed work may continue and flourish among us.

"But if any gentlemen who heartily concur in the end and design of this proposal, may be hindered in providence from giving their presence at this designed interview, it is earnestly desired they would send their attestations, and communicate their thoughts seasonably in writing: though at the same time it is hoped, none will suffer small difficulties to prevent their attendance on an affair of such importance to the interest of Christ's kingdom, both here and in other parts of the world."

The official account of this Convention reads as follows:—

"Agreeable to this invitation, a considerable number of ministers met at Boston on Thursday July 7, in the forenoon: when the Rev.

Mr. White of Gloucester, opened the assembly with prayer. They had some discourse; and then adjourned (in order to attend the public lecture) to half an hour past two in the afternoon.

"In the afternoon they met, to the number of ninety, chose Dr. Colman moderator, Dr. Sewall assistant, and Mr. Prince and Mr. Hobby, scribes. But Dr. Colman excusing himself, Dr. Sewall acted as moderator.

"They then proceeded to read letters from twenty-eight who were absent, bearing their testimony to this remarkable work of God in the land. And after further inquiries, declarations, discourses and debates, a little after eight in the evening, was read, proposed and put, without any objection, the following vote, viz.

"We, pastors of churches in the provinces of the Massachusetts Bay and New Hampshire in New England, met at Boston this seventh day of July, 1743, being persuaded there has of late been a happy revival of religion, through a remarkable divine influence, in many parts of this land, and apprehending it our duty to give an open conjunct testimony, to the glory of God, to an event so surprising and gracious, as well as against those errors in doctrine and disorders in practice, which, through human frailties and corruptions and the permitted agency of Satan, have attended it, and in any measure blemished its glory and hindered its advancement; came to the following resolution: that a committee be chosen to consider the premises and make a report to-morrow morning at nine o'clock. Voted in the affirmative, generally.

"And chose the Rev. Dr. Sewall, Mr. Wigglesworth, Prince, Adams, Cooper, Nathaniel Rogers, Leonard and Hobby, to be said Committee.

"The Rev. Mr. Moody prayed; and they adjourned to meet to-morrow morning at nine o'clock.

"*Friday* morning, about ten, they met again, to the number of about seventy. Dr. Sewall prayed, and then presented the Committee's report. First we read the whole throughout; then began again, and read the introduction; then read and severally considered the following paragraphs; and after divers amendments, proceeded to subscribe.

"*Voted*, That Mr. Prince, Cooper and Gee be a Committee to take care of publishing the subscribed Testimony and Advice, together with suitable extracts from the letters communicated to us.

"Rev. Mr. Baxter returned thanks and prayed; and about three in the afternoon, we dissolve.

"A true account, according to the minutes.

"THOMAS PRINCE, Scribe.

"THE TESTIMONY AND ADVICE of an Assembly of Pastors of Churches in New England, at a meeting in Boston, July 7, 1743, occasioned by the late happy Revival of Religion in many parts of the Land.

"If it is the duty of every one capable of observation and reflection, to take a constant religious notice of what occurs in the daily course of common providence; how much more is it expected that those events in the divine economy, wherein there is a signal display of the power, grace and mercy of God in behalf of the church, should be observed with sacred wonder, pleasure, and gratitude! Nor should the people of God content themselves with a silent notice, but publish with the voice of thanksgiving, and tell of all his wondrous works.

"More particularly, when Christ is pleased to come into his church in a plentiful effusion of his Holy Spirit, by whose powerful influences the ministration of the word is attended with uncommon success, salvation-work carried on in an eminent manner, and his kingdom, which is within men, and consists in righteousness and peace and joy in the Holy Ghost, is notably advanced, this is an event which, above all others, invites the notice and bespeaks the praises of the Lord's people, and should be declared abroad for a memorial of the divine grace; as it tends to confirm the divinity of a despised gospel, and manifests the work of the Holy Spirit in the application of redemption, which too many are ready to reproach; as it may have a happy effect, by the divine blessing, for the revival of religion in other places, and the enlargement of the kingdom of Christ in the world; and as it tends to enliven the prayers, strengthen the faith, and raise the hopes, of such as are waiting for the kingdom of God, and the coming on of the glory of the latter days.

"But if it is justly expected of all who profess themselves the disciples of Christ, that they should openly acknowledge and rejoice in a work of this nature, wherein the honor of their divine Master is so much concerned; how much more is it to be looked for from those who are employed in the ministry of the Lord Jesus, and so stand in a special relation to him, as servants of his household, and officers in his kingdom! These stand as watchmen upon the walls of Jerusalem; and it is their business not only to give the alarm of war when the enemy is approaching, but to sound the trumpet of praise when the King of Zion cometh, in a meek triumph, having salvation.

"For these and other reasons, we, whose names are hereunto annexed, pastors of churches in New England, met together in Boston, July 7, 1743, think it our indispensable duty, (without judging or censuring such of our brethren as cannot at present see things in the same light with us,) in this open and conjunct manner to declare, to the glory of sovereign grace, our full persuasion, either from what we have seen ourselves, or received upon credible testimony, that there has been a happy and remarkable revival of religion in many parts of this land, through an uncommon divine influence; after a long time of great decay and deadness, and a sensible and very awful withdraw of the Holy Spirit from his sanctuary among us.

"Though the work of grace wrought on the hearts of men by the word and Spirit of God, and which has been more or less carried on in the church from the beginning, is always the same for substance, and agrees, at one time and another, in one place or person and another, as to the main strokes and lineaments of it, yet the present work appears to be remarkable and extraordinary,

"*On account of the numbers wrought upon.* We never before saw so many brought under soul concern, and with distress making the inquiry, What must we do to be saved? And these persons of all characters and ages. *With regard to the suddenness and quick progress of it.* Many persons and places were surprised with the gracious visit together, or near about the same time; and the heavenly influence diffused itself far and wide like the light of the morning. *Also in respect of the degree of operation*, both in a way of terror and in a way of consolation; attended in many with unusual bodily effects.

"Not that all who are accounted the subjects of the present work, have had these extraordinary degrees of previous distress and subsequent joy. But many, and we suppose the greater number, have been wrought on in a more gentle and silent way, and without any other appearances than are common and usual at other times, when persons have been awakened to a solemn concern about salvation, and have been thought to have passed out of a state of nature into a state of grace.

"As to those whose inward concern has occasioned extraordinary outward distresses, the most of them, when we came to converse with them, were able to give, what appeared to us, a rational account of what so affected their minds; viz., a quick sense of their guilt, misery, and danger; and they would often mention the passages in the sermons they heard, or particular texts of Scripture, which were set home upon them with such a powerful impression. And as to such whose joys have carried them into transports and extasies, they in like manner have accounted for them, from a lively sense of the danger they hoped they were freed from, and the happiness they were now possessed of; such clear views of divine and heavenly things, and particularly of the excellencies and loveliness of Jesus Christ, and such sweet tastes of redeeming love, as they never had before. The instances were very few in which we had reason to think these affections were produced by visionary or sensible representations, or by any other images than such as the Scripture itself presents unto us.

"And here we think it not amiss to declare, that in dealing with these persons, we have been careful to inform them, that the nature of conversion does not consist in these passionate feelings; and to warn them not to look upon their state safe, because they have passed out of deep distress into high joys, unless they experience a renovation of nature, followed with a change of life, and a course of vital holiness. Nor have we gone into such an opinion of the bodily effects with which this work has been attended in some of its subjects, as to judge them any signs that persons who have been so affected, were then under a saving work of the Spirit of God. No; we never so much as called these bodily seisures, convictions; or spake of them as the immediate work of the Holy Spirit. Yet we do not think them inconsistent with a work of God upon the soul at that very time; but judge that those inward impressions which come from the Spirit of God, those terrors and consolations of which he is the author, may, according to the natural frame and constitution which some persons are of, occasion such bodily effects; and therefore that those extraordinary outward symptoms are not an argument that the work is delusive, or from the influence and agency of the evil spirit.

"With respect to numbers of those who have been under the impressions of the present day, we must declare there is good ground to conclude they are become real Christians; the account they give of their conviction and consolation agreeing with the standard of the Holy Scriptures, corresponding with the experiences of the saints, and evidenced by the external fruits of holiness in their lives; so that they appear to those who have the nearest access to them, as so many epistles of Christ, written, not with ink, but by the Spirit of the living God, attesting to the genuineness of the present operation, and representing the excellency of it.

"Indeed, many, who appeared to be under convictions, and were much altered in their external behaviour when this work began, and while it was most flourishing, have lost their impressions, and are relapsed into their former manner of life. Yet of those who were judged hopefully converted, and made a public profession of religion, there have been fewer instances of scandal and apostasy than might be expected. So that, as far as we are able to form a judgment, the face of religion is lately changed much for the better in many of our towns and congregations; and together with a reformation observable in divers instances, there appears to be more experimental godliness and lively Christianity, than the most of us can remember we have ever seen before.

"Thus we have freely declared our thoughts as to the work of God, so remarkably revived in many parts of this land. And now, we desire to bow the knee in thanksgiving to the God and Father of our Lord Jesus Christ, that our eyes have seen and our ears heard such things. And while these are our sentiments, we must necessarily be grieved at any accounts sent abroad, representing this work as all enthusiasm, delusion and disorder.

"Indeed, it is not to be denied, that in some places many irregularities and extravagances have been permitted to accompany it, which we would deeply lament and bewail before God, and look upon ourselves obliged, for the honor of the Holy Spirit, and of his blessed operations on the souls of men, to bear a public and faithful testimony against; though at the same time it is to be acknowledged with much thankfulness, that in other places, where the work has greatly flourished, there have been few, if any, of these disorders and excesses. But who can wonder, if at such a time as this, Satan should intermingle himself, to hinder and blemish a work so directly contrary to the interests of his own kingdom? Or if, while so much good seed is sowing, the enemy should be busy to sow tares? We would therefore, in the bowels of Jesus, beseech such as have been partakers of this work, or are zealous to promote it, that they be not ignorant of Satan's devices; that they watch and pray against errors and misconduct of every kind, lest they blemish and hinder that which they desire to honor and advance. Particularly,

"That they do not make secret impulses on their minds, without a due regard to the written word, the rule of their duty: a very dangerous mistake, which, we apprehend, some in these times have gone into. That to avoid Arminianism, they do not verge to the opposite side of Antinomianism; while we would have others take good heed to themselves, lest they be by some led into, or fixed in, Arminian tenets, under the pretence of opposing Antinomian errors. That laymen do not invade the ministerial office, and, under a pretense of exhorting, set up preaching; which is very contrary to gospel order, and tends to introduce errors and confusion into the church. That ministers do not invade the province of others, and in ordinary cases preach in another's parish without his knowledge, and against his consent; nor encourage raw and indiscreet young candidates, in rushing into particular places, and preaching publicly or privately, as some have done, to the no small disrepute and damage of the work in places where it once promised to flourish. Though at the same time we would have ministers show their regard to the spiritual welfare of their people, by suffering them to partake of the gifts and graces of able, sound and zealous preachers of the word, as God in his providence may give opportunity therefor; being persuaded God has in this day remarkably blessed the labors of some of his servants who have travelled in preaching the gospel of Christ. That people beware of entertaining prejudices against their own pastors, and do not run into unscriptural separations. That they do not indulge a disputatious spirit, which has been attended with mischievous effects; nor discover a spirit of censoriousness, uncharitableness, and rash judging the state of others; than which scarce any thing has more blemished the work of God amongst us. And while we would meekly exhort both ministers and Christians, so far as is consistent with truth and holiness, to follow the things that make for peace; we would most earnestly warn all sorts of persons not to despise these outpourings of the Spirit, lest a holy God be provoked to withhold them, and instead thereof, to pour out upon this people the vials of his wrath, in temporal judgments and spiritual plagues; and would call upon every one to improve this remarkable season of grace, and put in for a share of the heavenly blessings so liberally dispensed.

"Finally, we exhort the children of God to continue instant in prayer, that He with whom is the residue of the Spirit, would grant us fresh, more plentiful and extensive effusions, that so this wilderness, in all the parts of it, may become a fruitful field; that the present appearances may be an earnest of the glorious things promised to the church in the latter days; when she shall shine with the glory of the Lord arisen upon her, so as to dazzle the eyes of beholders, confound and put to shame all her enemies, rejoice the hearts of her solicitous and now saddened friends, and have a strong influence and resplendency throughout the earth. Amen! Even so. Come, Lord Jesus; come quickly!

"After solemn repeated prayer, free inquiry and debate, and serious deliberation, the above Testimony and Advice was signed by

Samuel Moody, pastor of the First Church in York.

John White, pastor of the First Church in Gloucester.

Joseph Sewall, pastor of the South Church in Boston.

Samuel Wigglesworth, pastor of a church in Ipswich.

Ames Cheever, pastor of the church in Manchester.

Thomas Prince, a pastor of the South Church in Boston,—to the substance.

John Webb, a pastor of a church in Boston.

John Cotton, pastor of the church in Newton.

Joseph Adams, pastor of the church in Newington, New Hampshire.

James Allin, pastor of the church in Brookline.

John Chipman, pastor of a church in Beverly, to the substance, scope, and end.

William Cooper, a pastor of a church in Boston.

Thomas Foxcroft, a pastor of the First Church in Boston.

Joshua Gee, pastor of the Second Church in Boston.

Joseph Emerson, pastor of the First Church in Malden, to the scope and substance.

Henry Messinger, pastor of the First Church in Wrentham.
James Bayley, pastor of the Second Church in Weymouth.
Nathanael Leonard, pastor of the First Church in Plymouth.
Thomas Smith, pastor of the First Church in Falmouth.
Nathanael Rogers, a pastor of the First Church in Ipswich.
Josiah Cotton, pastor of a church in Providence, to the general scope and tendency.

Habijah Weld, pastor of the church in Attleborough, to the substance, scope and end.

William Hobby, pastor of the First Church in Reading.
James Pike, pastor of the church in Summersworth, New Hampshire.

John Warren, pastor of the church in Wenham.
Nathan Webb, pastor of the church in Uxbridge.
Jedediah Jewet, pastor of the First Church in Rowley.
John Emerson, pastor of the church in Topsfield, to the scope and substance.

John Moorhead, pastor of a church in Boston.
Solomon Prentice, pastor of the church in Grafton.
James Chandler, pastor of the Second Church in Rowley.
Othniel Campbell, pastor of the Second Church in Plympton.
John Seccomb, pastor of the church in Harvard.
Ward Cotton, pastor of the First Church in Hampton, New Hampshire.

Amos Main, pastor of the church in Rochester, New Hampshire.
John Cotton, pastor of the Church in Halifax.
James Diman, pastor of a church in Salem, to the substance, scope, and end.

Phineas Hemmingway, pastor of the church in Townshend.
David Goddard, pastor of the church in Leicester, to the substance.

Samuel Bachellor, pastor of the Third Church in Haverhill.
Daniel Bliss, pastor of the church in Concord.
Samuel Tobey, pastor of the church in Berkley.
Elias Haven, pastor of the Second Church in Wrentham.
Thomas Balch, pastor of a church in Dedham.
Samuel Chandler, pastor of the Second Church in York.
Samuel Hill, pastor of the church in Marshfield.
Joshua Tufts, pastor of the church in Litchfield, New Hampshire.

Samuel Veazie, pastor of the church in Duxborough.
John Porter, pastor of the Fourth Church in Bridgewater.
Jonathan Ellis, pastor of the Second Church in Plymouth.
Josiah Crocker, pastor of the church in Taunton.
Daniel Emerson, pastor of the Second Church in Dunstable.
Francis Worcester, pastor of the Second Church in Sandwich.

"We, whose names are underwritten, concur with the Testimony for the substance of it, excepting that article of itinerancy, or ministers and others intruding into other ministers' parishes without their consent, which great disorder we apprehend not sufficiently testified against therein.

Benjamin Colman, a pastor of a church in Boston.

JOSEPH BAXTER, pastor of the church in Medfield.
NATHANIEL EELLS, pastor of the Second Church in Scituate.
JOSEPH DORR, pastor of the First Church in Mendon.
SAMUEL CHECKLEY, pastor of a church in Boston.
BENJAMIN BASS, pastor of the church in Hanover.
HULL ABBOT, a pastor of the church in Charlestown.
EZRA CARPENTER, pastor of the church in Hull.
EBENEZER TURELL, pastor of the church in Medford.
EBENEZER PARKMAN, pastor of the church in Westborough.
THOMAS PRENTICE, a pastor of the church in Charlestown.
SIMON BRADSTREET, pastor of the Second Church in Marblehead.
JOHN FOWLE, pastor of the Second Church in Hingham.
ANDREW ELIOT, a pastor of a church in Boston.
THADDEUS MACCARTY, pastor of the church in Kingston."

The Attestations published by the Committee were from the Rev. John Rogers, of Ipswich; Jeremiah Wise, of Berwick, Me.; Peter Thacher, of Middleborough; William Shurtleff, of Portsmouth; Jonathan Russel, of Barnstable; Benjamin Allen, of Falmouth, Me.; William Thompson, of Scarborough, Me.; Samuel Jefferds, of Wells, Me.; John Hovey, of Arundel, Me.; Nicholas Loring, of North Yarmouth, Me.; Moses Morrill, of Biddeford, Me.; John Rogers, of Kittery Me.; Stephen Williams, of Springfield; Peter Raynolds, of Enfield; Jonathan Edwards, of Northampton; Samuel Allis, of Somers; John Woodbridge and David Parsons, of Hadley; Edward Billing, of Coldspring; Timothy Woodbridge, of Hatfield; Chester Williams, of Hadley; Daniel Putnam, of Reading; Oliver Peabody, of Natick; John Tucke, of Gosport, N. H.; David Hall, of Sutton; Benjamin Bradstreet, of Gloucester; John Wales, of Raynham; Ivory Hovey, of Rochester; Nathaniel Appleton, of Cambridge; Jonathan Parker, of Plympton; David McGregore, of Londonderry, N. H.; Joseph Meacham, of Coventry, Ct.; Benjamin Lord, of Norwich, Ct.; Hezekiah Lord, of Preston, Ct.; Solomon Williams, of Lebanon, Ct.; Daniel Kirtland and Jabez Wright, of Norwich, Ct.; John Owen, of Groton, Ct.; Samuel Mosely, of Windham, Ct.; Jonathan Parsons, of Lyme, Ct.; Eleazer Wheelock, of Lebanon, Ct.; Benjamin Pomroy, of Hebron, Ct.; David Jewett, of New London, Ct. Attestations were afterwards received and published, from the Rev. John Blunt, of Newcastle, N. H. and Benjamin Ruggles of Middleborough. The number of signers at the meeting was 68; attestors by letter, 45; total, 113. But this was by no means the whole number of those who were of the same sentiments, even in Massachusetts.*

Concerning the statements and views of those that attended the meeting, the Rev. Mr. Prince testified :—

"That very few of the ministers present in the late venerable assembly, complained of errors or disorders in the parishes they belonged to: that several declared they had none from the beginning; but in the extraordinary revival of religion among their people, the work had been carried on with great seriousness and regularity: that others declared, that where there had been some disorders and mistakes at first in some, through the great numbers suddenly and mightily awakened, the great distress of some in their convictions, the great joy of others upon their laying hold on Christ and finding a wondrous change within them, the frailties of some and the surprise of all; yet in a little while they saw and owned their mistakes, came into a more settled way of thinking, speaking and behaving, and the disorders ceased: declaring also, that both errors and disorders had been greatly magnified and multiplied above what they really were in the congregations they belonged to: and that, as far as they could learn, the greatest errors and disorders were in those places where the ministers opposed the work, and thereby lost much of their respect and influence."

He also explained the qualification annexed to his own signature, and to that of some others. They objected to the clause, "That ministers do not invade the province of others, and in ordinary cases preach in another's parish without his knowledge and against his consent." They do not seem to have questioned its correctness, when rightly understood; but they thought it "in danger of being construed and perverted to the great infringement of Christian and human liberty of conscience."

---

## CHAPTER XVII.

**Opposition to the Revival in Connecticut.—Pains and Penalties.—The Separatists.**

As early as 1741, some of the clergy of Connecticut determined to call in the aid of the civil government, to prevent

* An attestation was also sent by the Rev. Messrs. Anthony Stoddard, John Graham, Joseph Bellamy and Reuben Judd, of Woodbury; Samuel Cook, of Stratfield; Hezekiah Gold, of Stratford; Jedidiah Mills, of Ripton; Ebenezer White, of Danbury; Benajah Case, of New Fairfield; David Judson, of Newton, Ct, and Elisha Kent, of Philippi, N. Y.; but, falling into careless or unfriendly hands, it was detained till near the close of 1744.

and punish disorders. In the latter part of that year, certain ministers near New Haven obtained an Act of the General Assembly, calling a "Grand Council," or Convention, at Guilford, to consist of three ministers and three lay delegates from each association. The Consociation of New Haven county met at New Haven, to appoint delegates, on the 10th of November. The Rev. Mr. Whittelsey, of Wallingford, proposed that the delegates should receive instructions, which was voted. He then wrote down three questions, the first of which was, "whether a number of ministers going abroad, and preaching and administering the seals in another parish, without the consent of the minister of the parish, be not disorderly." Voted in the affirmative. — This question may have been suggested by events in Mr. Whittelsey's own parish. There was a Baptist church there, the members of which had, some years before, been under his ministry. Near the close of the year, the since celebrated Bellamy preached to them, as their elder, John Merriman, says, "to very good satisfaction and success on several persons," some of whom were yet members of Mr. Whittelsey's congregation; so that it seemed to be the desire of both denominations, to hear other Congregational ministers of similar views and spirit. Not improbably, there were symptoms of such a state of things earlier than November. The Convention at Guilford met November 24. They resolved, among other things: — "That, for a minister to enter another minister's parish, and preach or administer the seals of the covenant, without the consent of, or in opposition to, the settled minister of the parish, is disorderly: notwithstanding, if a considerable number of people in the parish are desirous to hear another minister preach, provided the same be orthodox, and sound in the faith, and not notoriously faulty in censuring other persons, or guilty of any other scandal, we think it ordinarily advisable for the minister of the parish to gratify them, by giving his consent upon their suitable application to him for it, unless neighbouring ministers should advise him to the contrary."*

* Robbins' "Plain Narrative of the Proceedings" against him. O. S. Ch. Lib. Trumbull has copied a large part of this pamphlet into his "History of Connecticut," and added some facts that occurred after its publication. — It is believed that no account can be found of the doings of the Convention at Guilford, or of the instructions given at New Haven to the delegates, except what Robbins has preserved, which is here given.

The legislature, at their next session, which was in May, 1742, passed "An Act for regulating abuses and correcting disorders in ecclesiastical affairs." The preamble sets forth, that the Assembly did formerly, by law, establish and confirm the Platform of church government agreed upon at Saybrook in 1708, under which peace and quietness had been enjoyed, till, of late, sundry persons had been guilty of certain disorders; whereupon the Assembly directed the calling of a general convention at Guilford in November last, at which an attempt was made to prevent growing disorders; notwithstanding which, divers ordained ministers and licentiates still continue to go into the parishes of settled ministers without any lawful call, and there preach and administer the seals; and illiterate persons, who have no ecclesiastical character, set up as exhorters, by which they create disorder in the churches, and are the means of introducing unqualified men into the ministry, especially where one association meddles with affairs that by the Platform belong to another.

Here the Assembly seem to take it for granted, that the Saybrook Platform had been imposed by law upon all the churches, as the ecclesiastical law of the colony. The fact was far otherwise. The act referred to was entitled "An Act in approbation of the Agreement of the Reverend Elders and Messengers of all the Churches in this Government, made and concluded at Saybrook, in 1708." It declares "their great approbation of such a happy agreement," and ordains, "that all churches within this government that are or shall be thus united in doctrine, worship and discipline, be, and for the future shall be, owned and acknowledged established by law;" and it contained a proviso, "that nothing herein shall be intended or construed, to hinder any society or church that is or shall be allowed by the laws of this government, from exercising worship and discipline in their own way, according to their consciences." Accordingly, many churches, already organized according to the Cambridge Platform, still adhered to it, and others were organized on the same plan. These were sometimes called "Congregational" churches, by way of distinction. For years, no one suspected that the Saybrook Platform was binding on any church which had not voted to accept it. Besides, the Assembly had, in 1730, expressly declared that, besides churches on the Saybrook Platform, Congregational and Presbyterian churches were allowed and protected by law.

The first section of the act of 1742 enacted, "that if any ordained minister or other person licensed as aforesaid to preach, shall enter into any parish not immediately under his charge, and shall there preach or exhort the people, he shall be denied and secluded the benefit of any law of this colony made for the support and encouragement of the ministry; except such ordained minister or licensed person shall be expressly invited and desired so to enter into such other parish, and there to preach and exhort the people, either by the settled minister and the major part of the church of said parish, or, in case there be no settled minister, then by the church or society in said parish."

The second section enacted, that if any association of ministers "shall undertake to examine or license any candidate for the ministry, or assume to themselves the decision of any controversy, or to counsel and advise in any affair, that by the Saybrook Platform is within the province and jurisdiction of any other association; then, and in such case, every member that shall be present in such association so licensing, deciding or counselling, shall be, each and every of them, denied and secluded the benefit of any law of this colony, made for the support and encouragement of the ministry."

The third section prescribed the mode of inflicting punishment; for punishment was to be inflicted without trial. The minister of the parish in which any such offence should be committed, or the civil authority, or any two of the committee of the parish, were to send an information thereof in writing, under their hands, to the clerk of the offender's own parish; and then the clerk was to stop all legal proceedings for collecting the offender's salary. No provision was made for cases in which false information might be sent to the clerk, either by mistake or design.

The fourth section was directed against "exhorters," who were forbidden to hold forth, unless invited as required in the first section.

The last section enacted, "that if any stranger or foreigner, that is not an inhabitant within this colony, including as well such persons that have no ecclesiastical character or license to preach, as such as have received ordination or license to preach by any association or presbytery, shall presume to preach, teach, or publicly to exhort in any town or society within this colony, without the desire and license of the settled minister and major part of the church, town or society, or at the call and desire of the church and inhabitants of such town or society, provided that it so happen that there is no settled minister there; that every such teacher or exhorter shall be sent, as a vagrant person, by warrant from any one assistant or justice of the peace, from constable to constable, out of the bounds of this colony."*

This was the law against which Davenport declaimed so violently; and this was the session at which he was brought before the Assembly and sent home to Southold, as before related. At the same session, the Assembly advised the faculty of the college at New Haven, that all proper care should be taken to prevent the students from imbibing the errors that prevailed among the Separatists, and that those who would not be orderly and submissive, should be expelled.

The General Association met at New London, June 15, 1742, soon after this act was passed. Trumbull furnishes the following extract from its records:

"This General Association being of opinion, that the God of all grace has been mercifully pleased to remember and visit his people, by stirring up great numbers among us to a concern for their souls, and to be asking the way to Zion, with their faces thitherward, which we desire to take notice of with great thankfulness to the Father of mercies: being also of opinion, that the great enemy of souls, who is ever ready with his devices to check, damp and destroy the work of God, is very busy for that purpose: we think it our duty to advise and entreat the ministers and churches of this colony, and recommend it to the particular associations, to stand well upon their guard, in such a day as this, that no detriment arise to the interests of our great Lord and Master, Jesus Christ:

"Particularly, that no errors in doctrine, whether from among ourselves or foreigners, nor disorders in practice, do get in among us, or tares be sown in the Lord's field:

"That seasonable and due testimony be borne against such errors and irregularities as do already prevail among some persons; as particularly, the depending upon and following impulses and impressions made on the mind, as though they were immediate revelations of some truth or duty that is not revealed in the word of God; laying too much weight on bodily agitations, raptures, extasies, visions, &c.; ministers disorderly intruding into other minister's parishes; laymen taking it upon them, in an unwarrantable manner, publicly to teach and exhort; rash censuring and judging others; that the elders be careful to take heed to themselves and their doctrine, that they may save themselves and those that hear them; that they approve themselves in all things as ministers of God, by honor and dishonor, by

* See the Act, entire, in Trumbull's "History of Connecticut."

good report and evil report; that none be lifted up by applause to a vain conceit, nor any be cast down by any contempt thrown upon them, to the neglect of their work; and that they study unity, love and peace among themselves:

"And further, that they endeavour to heal the unhappy divisions that are already made in some of the churches, and that the like may for the future be prevented; that a just deference be paid to the laws of the magistrate, lately made to suppress disorders; that no countenance be given to such as trouble our churches, who are, according to the constitution of our churches, under censure, suspension or deposition, for errors in doctrine or life."

The consociation of New Haven county met September 28, thanked the legislature for passing the act against disorders, and prayed that it might continue in force.

At their session in May, 1743, the Assembly repealed the "Act for the Relief of Sober Consciences," as it was usually called. That act was passed in 1708, the year in which the Saybrook Platform was adopted. It provided that such as soberly dissented from the prevailing worship and belief, might, on taking certain oaths required in the English act of toleration, be exempt from taxation for the support of the ministers from whom they dissented. Now, as this act was repealed, sober dissenters had no longer any mode of relief, except by applying severally to the Assembly, for a special act to meet each individual case; and the Assembly was growing continually more averse to granting any such indulgence. At the same session, an order was passed for the arrest of the Rev. John Owen of Groton, for uttering hard speeches against the laws and officers of the colony; but the secretary neglected to issue the writ.

There was a church at Milford, which declared itself Presbyterian, put itself under the care of the New Brunswick Presbytery, and applied to that body to send them a preacher. They sent the Rev. Samuel Finley, afterwards president of the college at Princeton. He came, but was sent out of the colony as a "vagrant." He afterwards returned, and preached to a Congregational church at New Haven; probably, that which had been gathered after Davenport's first visit. He was arrested, and sentenced to be again transported from the colony; but through the negligence, perhaps intentional, of some officer, the sentence was but partly executed, and he returned and preached a third time. Both these churches had been legally recognised as churches, under the laws of the colony. His preaching, it was said, "greatly disquieted and disturbed the people," and was the principal motive for an additional act, passed by the Assembly in October, 1743. This additional act required, that every person transported under the former, should pay the costs of his transportation; and if he should return again and offend in the same way, it was made the duty of any assistant or justice of the peace, on information, to cause him to be arrested, and to give bonds in the penal sum of one hundred pounds, lawful money, for his peaceable and good behaviour till the next county court in that county, and that he would not thus offend again; and the next county court might, if they should see cause, further bind him during their pleasure.* The Association of New Haven county also took up the matter, and formally resolved that no member of the Presbytery of New Brunswick should be admitted into any of their pulpits, till satisfaction had been made for sending Mr. Finley to preach within their bounds.†

At this same session, the Assembly ordered the arrest of the Rev. John Owen, of Groton, and Benjamin Pomroy, of Hebron, but it was not executed till the next session. They carried proscription into the affairs of government. Justices of the peace, and other subordinate officers who were deemed "New Lights," were removed from office, and men of different views were put in their places. This policy was rigidly maintained till 1748, when some, at least, of the displaced "New Light" justices were restored.

These laws were not allowed to remain a mere dead letter. Both civil and ecclesiastical authorities joined to enforce them. A few instances of their execution, which Trumbull has preserved, may serve as specimens of many.

Soon after the first of these laws was enacted, the Rev. Mr. Pomroy, of Hebron, received an invitation from some of the people of Colchester, to preach to them. From the habits of intimate and friendly intercourse which existed between them, he never suspected that it could be otherwise than agreeable to Mr. Little, the pastor, and made the appointment accordingly. Contrary to expectation, Mr. Little

---

* See "The Essential Rights and Liberties of Protestants. A Seasonable Plea for Liberty of Conscience and the Right of Private Judgment in matters of Religion, without any control from Human authority." O. S. Ch. Lib. Backus says, that Col. Elisha Williams, afterwards president of Yale College, and "the best president they ever had," was its "undoubted author." The true doctrines of liberty have seldom been so well exhibited and defended, even in 1776.

† Trumbull.

objected, and forbade him to preach in his meetinghouse. A great concourse of people had assembled, from several towns. Mr. Pomroy preached to them in a grove. A certificate of this fact was lodged with the clerk of his society, which of course annulled the legal contract between him and his people, for his support, and during the next seven years, he was dependent on the voluntary contributions of his hearers.

The orders for his arrest, and that of Mr. Owen of Groton, have been mentioned. They were brought before the Assembly in May, 1744. Mr. Owen made such concessions, that he was released on paying the costs. Mr. Pomroy also made some concessions; but he had said some hard things against these laws, which, as he knew them to be true, he could not retract. He was sentenced to pay costs, £32, 10*s.* 8d, and to give bonds in the sum of £50 for his good behaviour till the next May.

Many of the leading clergy were accused of Arminianism. They indignantly denied the charge. The truth seems to have been, that they were moderate Calvinists in their doctrinal discussions, but Arminian in their "practical applications." They discussed the doctrines of original sin, regeneration and justification by faith, like Calvinists; but advised and exhorted their people just as Arminianism would have taught them to do. They led their hearers to believe, that by a certain round of duties, performed while still impenitent, they might insure their regeneration; that regeneration would probably come in a still, quiet way, so that neither they nor others would perceive any very decided change at any one time; and that the proper course for a sinner to take was, to go steadily about the duties which God has appointed for impenitent sinners to perform before conversion, and leave the event with God. Whatever they meant, such was the state into which they threw the minds of their followers. It was, practically, Arminianism. If any one preached Calvinism thoroughly, to the very end of his sermon, maintaining that God has made no promise to such as industriously perform certain duties while impenitent; that nothing done during impenitence counts at all towards the justification of the doer; that deferring repentance and faith, and doing something else first, is flat rebellion against God; all such preaching was said to make people think lightly of good works, and was condemned as "Antinomian." And it must be confessed that some, in their zeal against the prevalent theology, did become really Antinomian, and others were sometimes led, in the heat of argument, to use Antinomian language. It was the policy of the Arminianizing clergy, to strengthen their party by ordaining young men who adopted their views, wherever they could, even over churches where there were strong opposing minorities; and they were accused of doing it, even where the dissentients were the majority. This was one principal ground of the "separations," of which so much was said. As early as 1738, the Rev. Samuel Whittelsey, son of Mr. Whittelsey of Wallingford, was ordained at Milford, against the remonstrance of a large minority. A part of the people seceded and formed the Presbyterian church, for preaching to which Mr. Finley was transported from the colony. These Presbyterians were compelled, by legal processes, to pay taxes for the support of Mr. Whittelsey.

The church at Canterbury was strictly Congregational, being organized on the Cambridge Platform. During the revival, its members were divided into parties. Some of them seem to have become decidedly Antinomian and fanatical. One party, acting in the name of the church, gave a call to Mr. James Cogswell, to become their pastor. This was probably in the summer of 1744. The other party pronounced Mr. Cogswell an unconverted man, refused to hear him, and maintained separate meetings. They asserted that they were a majority of the church, and therefore were the church. The other party, counting some twelve or fifteen against whom a vote of excommunication had been passed, advanced a similar claim, and invited the Consociation of Windham county to ordain Mr. Cogswell. This, it was understood, would bring the church under the jurisdiction of the Consociation, according to the Saybrook Platform. Among the opponents of Mr. Cogswell was a Mr. Cleaveland, who had two sons, John and Ebenezer, in college at New Haven. Being at home in September, while Mr Cogswell was preaching to the other party, they attended worship with their father, and one of them, who was a member of the church, partook of the Lord's Supper. On their return to college, they were expelled, November 19, for attending the meeting of the Separatists at Canterbury. In this expulsion, the Faculty declared that they acted in view of the advice given them by the legislature in May, 1742.

The facts became known, and produced a deep sensation throughout the colony. About this time, some members of the Senior class in college subscribed money for printing an edition of Locke's Essay on Toleration. The Faculty heard of it, called the offenders before them, and extorted confessions from all but one. Just before commencement, the obstinate senior found that his name was omitted in the list of those on whom degrees were to be conferred. He went to the Faculty, and told them that he was of age, and had property wherewith to defend his rights; and that, if his degree was withheld, he would apply to the King in council for redress. He then left them; but was soon informed that he might take his degree with his class.

December 28, the Consociation ordained Mr. Cogswell as pastor of the church at Canterbury. About fifty families refused to acknowledge him as their pastor, or the Consociation as a body authorized to act in the case; adhered to the Cambridge Platform, and maintained separate worship, at which "exhorters" were often, if not commonly employed, and which seems not to have been remarkable for sound doctrine, a Christian spirit, or decorousness of demeanor. Some of the "exhorters" were arrested, and as they refused to give the required bonds in the sum of £100, to cease from exhorting, were imprisoned. Some of the people had their property seized and sold by legal process, to pay Mr. Cogswell's salary; and others were imprisoned to compel them to pay. Others, Trumbull says, were arrested and imprisoned for not hearing him.

The effort to enforce the universal reception of the Saybrook Platform seems to have been vigorous and determined. A new church was formed at Salisbury, on the Cambridge Platform, and the Rev. John Lee was ordained as its pastor in 1744. The Association of New Haven county reprimanded the church for adopting that Platform, and suspended Messrs. Humphreys of Derby, Leavenworth of Waterbury, and Todd of Northbury, from the ministry, for assisting in the ordination. The ordination, however, could not be annulled. In 1766, Lee was still pastor at Salisbury, and preached the election sermon before the legislature. Humphreys was at one time expelled from the Association, for preaching to a Baptist church.*

* There were probably some circumstances which were thought to aggravate the offence; but Trumbull mentions none.

An attempt was also made to enforce the Saybrook Platform against the First Church in Branford, and its pastor, the Rev. Philemon Robbins. The Baptists in Wallingford, just after Mr. Bellamy had preached to them, as mentioned in the beginning of this chapter, obtained a promise from Mr. Robbins, to preach to them on the sixth of January, 1742. Before he went, he received a request from forty-two members of Mr. Whittelsey's church in Wallingford, to abstain from preaching there, and a line signed by two ministers of neighboring parishes, advising him not to go. Still, as he had promised, and as "it was a time of religious concern among them," he went, and preached two sermons, with good effect. For this, a complaint was entered against him at the next meeting of the Consociation, February 9. As his preaching was before the Act against Disorders, he could not be deprived of his salary for it; and as he and his church had never adopted the Saybrook Platform,* it was difficult to force him to a trial. The Consociation, however, continued to harass him till September, 1746, when, after an *ex parte* trial, and after hearing the charges and testimony against him, they pronounced him guilty. A year or two after, as he made no confession, the Consociation voted to depose him from the ministry. The act of deposition was never rescinded, but he continued to act as pastor of the church. In 1755, the Consociation invited him to take part with them in an ordination; after which he was treated as if these things had never happened.

The charges on which he was condemned, and his own statements concerning them, are instructive, as they show how men, at that day, first misunderstood and then misrepresented each other. Mr. Robbins, in arguing against the doctrine, "that the death of Christ not only satisfied for, but wholly took away, original sin from all persons," said: "Even infants were by nature children of wrath, and, while unsanctified, were as odious in the sight of God as snakes or vipers are to us;" adding, that serpents, when they first come into the world, are not odious on account of any mischief they have done, but because of their serpentine nature; and also, that "no doubt, multitudes of them [infants] are

* This was one of the churches which refused to send messengers to the convention which formed the Saybrook Platform. *Trumbull.*

sanctified and saved." On this was founded a charge, that he had "taken it upon him to determine the state of infants dying in infancy, declaring that they were as odious in the sight of God, as snakes and vipers were unto us; and left it wholly in the dark, whether there was any saved or not." He had taught, that "there is no promise of any saving good, in all the Bible, made to any unconverted man, or any sinner while in an unconverted state." He was charged with teaching, "that there is no promise in all the Bible that belongs to sinners;" and this was condemned as "Antinomianism." He had said: — "When a sinner is converted, he knows it. That is, he knows the change, though it may be he is not satisfied, or rather, does not then think, that it is conversion. — Yet, can a man be brought out of the kingdom of Satan into the kingdom of the Son of God; can a man be brought out of midnight darkness into noonday light, and not know there is a change?" This struck at the hopes of a numerous class, who were comforting themselves with the belief, that regeneration is to be expected by all who observe certain moral and religious rules, but takes place so quietly, and produces so little change at the time, that neither the person himself, nor his most intimate friends, can know any thing about it. He was therefore accused of teaching, "that it as easy for persons to know when they are converted, as it is to know noonday light from midnight darkness." He had said, "The most vicious person stands as fair or fairer for conviction and conversion, than the strictest mere moralist, that is settled upon his lees and built strong on his own righteousness. Publicans and harlots shall enter the kindom before such." He was accused of teaching, "That the most vicious or vilest person stands as fair or fairer for conviction and conversion than the strictest moral man; thereby making holiness and obedience to the law of God no way necessary to be found in men for their salvation." There had also been some disorderly proceedings introduced into meetings for worship by Davenport, Brainerd, and Buel. Some of these Mr. Robbins endeavoured to prevent at the time, and others he regretted afterwards. His real offence doubtless was, being a zealous, active and efficient promoter of the revival. For this, a member of the Consociation told one of his uneasy people, — "If you can get hold of Mr. Robbins, catch hold." That expression, the man said, opened his eyes, and he afterwards sustained his pastor.*

One charge against Mr. Robbins was, "his justifying Mr. Allen [Rev. Timothy Allen, of West Haven] in his comparing the Scriptures to an old almanac." On this, Mr. Robbins remarks: "I have no otherways justified Mr. Allen, than only by telling the answer he made to his charge, which was, as near as I can remember, thus: 'The reading of the Holy Scriptures, without the concurring influence and operation of the Spirit of God, will no more convert a sinner, than the reading an old almanac.' I have heard him lament the manner of expression, and he has offered to confess it to the Association of this county. But the news of a man's penitence seldom reaches so far as the sound of his crime."

This story of Mr. Allen circulated extensively, and was put into several shapes. Dr. Chauncy wanted it to put into his book against the revival, and wrote to Mr. Whittelsey, scribe of the Consociation, for an authentic statement. Whittelsey replied officially, after examining his documents: "I find one of the articles charged and proved against him was, that he had publicly said, that the word of God, as contained in the Old and New Testaments, is but as an old almanac; for which, and various other crimes proved against him, he, continuing obstinate, was deposed by the Consociation." The letter published in Scotland on the "State of Religion in New England," said of Connecticut: "The people in that colony are still wilder than these in Boston. The converts all pretend to a light within, without the direction of which they will not go about the ordinary offices of life. One of their ministers is dismissed from his people, for preaching that an unconverted man is not capable of understanding one word of the Bible, and that to a converted man it is no better than an old almanac, because he has a brighter light within him. But not many parishes would have turned away their minister for such an opinion as this." It underwent other equally gross perversions. According to Trumbull, Allen lamented the improper language in which he had expressed his meaning, when on his trial before the Consociation. Yet they deposed him, saying, that they had blown out one New Light, and would blow them all out. This was in

* Robbins' "Plain Narrative." O. S. Ch. Lib.

1741. In 1800, he was pastor of a church in Chesterfield, Mass., at the age of 85. His "other crimes" are not specified; but were probably indiscreet efforts for the conversion of men.

The case of the Separatists demands a distinct consideration; a matter of some difficulty, from the want of sufficient documents, and from the fact, evident from such documents as remain, that they neither clearly understood themselves, nor were understood by their contemporaries. Enough may be learned, however, to establish some important facts.

They prevailed mostly in New London and Windham counties. Here, notwithstanding legal enactments, they continued to grow, and even gained strength from opposition. Many of the clergy seem to have labored earnestly and with a good spirit for their recovery, but with little success.

December 11, 1744, the "Associated Ministers of the County of Windham" addressed a Letter* on this subject "to the people in the several societies in said county." They commence by expressing their conviction, that "there has been of late, in a few years past, a very great and merciful revival of religion in most of the towns and societies in this county, as well as in many other parts of the land." They also believe that the prince of darkness, unable any longer to destroy men by keeping them in a state of security and formality, was compelled to resort to a new device, "imitating, as nearly as he could, the work of the Holy Ghost, both by setting on imaginary frights and terrors, in some instances, on men's minds, somewhat resembling the convictions of the blessed Spirit and awakenings of the conscience for sin, and also filling their minds with flashes of joy and false comforts, resembling somewhat, in a general way, the consolations of the Holy Ghost. — This, in its beginning, was not so plainly discerned and distinguished, in many instances, from the work of the Holy Spirit, especially as there was sometimes a mixture of such things with the true experiences of the people of God; and it was also partly owing to the injudicious and violent opposition of some to this work, who, while they saw bad things attending it, and many people taken with them, boldly concluded it was all of a piece, and, with tremendous rashness, ascribed it all to the devil; while

* O. S. Ch. Lib.

others, on the other hand, looking on the good, and being persuaded that it was a day of God's wonderful power and gracious visitation, suddenly and weakly concluded, that there was little wrong in the appearances, besides mere human weaknesses and unavoidable infirmity." In the progress of the work, they believed Satan had succeeded in instigating some to provoke persecution, by which they were hardened more and more in their errors, "and many are drawn away after them, partly out of pity to them, and by wrong conclusions, that their sufferings are an evidence that they are right, and partly out of opposition to others, whom they think to be carnal and ungodly men." "Some of the most considerable" of the errors of the Separatists, the Association state to be,

"1. That it is the will of God to have a pure church on earth, in this sense, that all the converted should be separated from the unconverted.

"2. That the saints certainly know one another, and know who are Christ's true ministers, by their own inward feelings, or a communion between them in the inward actings of their own souls.

"3. That no other call is necessary to a person undertaking to preach the gospel, but his being a true Christian, and having an inward motion of the Spirit, or a persuasion in his own mind, that it is the will of God that he should preach and perform ministerial acts: the consequence of which is, that there is no standing instituted ministry in the Christian church, which may be known by the visible laws of Christ's kingdom.

"4. That God disowns the ministry and churches in this land, and the ordinances as administered by them.

5. That at such meetings of lay preaching and exhorting, they have more of the presence of God than in his ordinances, and under the ministration of the present ministry, and the administration of the ordinances in these churches."

Proof was then adduced of the errors of one of the exhorters, Mr. Elisha Paine, who had formerly been encouraged by some of the ministers, and who was "known to be of much superior ability to the others." It appears from the testimony, that for want of clear ideas concerning the Trinity, Mr. Paine sometimes used language tinctured with Sabellianism; and that he held saving faith to be, the persuasion of a sinner, that Christ died for him in particular. He held the doctrine of a particular atonement; that is, that Christ died for certain individuals, and not for others; and that in conversion, God reveals to the sinner the fact, that he is one of that number. He held, too, that the saints, by virtue of grace in themselves, know the certainty of grace in others; so that they need not mistake in distinguishing the converted from the unconverted. He had also declared, that "it was made manifest to him, that Christ was about to have a pure church, and that he had not done his duty in time past in promoting separations and divisions among the people, and that for time to come he should endeavour to promote and encourage separations; and that likewise Christ's own ministers would have their churches rent from them by reason of their not doing their duty in that respect." Being asked what duty they neglected, he replied, that "they did not separate those who were converted from the unconverted in the church."

About a year afterwards, (October 9, 1745,) a Separate church was organized at Mansfield, whose Confession of Faith throws clearer light on some parts of their belief. Among them are

"*Article* 15. We believe we are of that number who were elected of God to eternal life, and that Christ did live on earth, die and rise again for us in particular; that he doth now, in virtue of his own merits and satisfaction, make intercession to God for us, and that we are now justified in the sight of God for the sake of Christ, and shall be owned by him at the great and general judgment; — which God hath made us to believe by sending, according to his promise, (John 16,) the Holy Ghost into our souls, who hath made particular application of the above articles."

"18. That all doubting in a believer is sinful, being contrary to the command of God, and hurtful to the soul, and an hindrance to the performance of duty."

"20. We believe, by the testimony of Scripture and by our own experience, that true believers, by virtue of their union to Christ by faith, have communion with God, and by the same faith are in Christ united to one another; which is the unity of the Spirit, whereby they are made partakers of each other's gifts and graces, without which union there can be no communion with God, nor with the saints."

"21. That whoever presumes to administer or partake of the seals of the covenant of grace without saving faith, are* guilty of sacrilege, and are in danger of sealing their own damnation."

22. [This relates to the church, and has, among others, these particulars: —

"3. That true believers, and they only, have a right to give up their children to God in baptism."

"7. That at all times the doors of the church should be carefully kept against such as cannot give a satisfying evidence of the work of God upon their souls, whereby they are united to Christ."

"9. That a number of true believers, being thus essentially and visibly united together, have power to choose and ordain such officers as

* They did not profess to be inspired as grammarians.

Christ has appointed in his church, such as bishops, elders and deacons; and by the same power, to depose such officers as evidently appear to walk contrary to the Gospel, or fall into any heresy. Yet we believe, in such cases, it is convenient to take advice of neighbouring churches of the same constitution.

"12. We believe that all the gifts and graces that are bestowed upon any of the members, are to be improved by them for the good of the whole; in order to which there ought to be such a gospel freedom, whereby the church may know where every particular gift is, that it may be improved in its proper place and to its right end, for the glory of God and the good of the church.

"13. That every brother that is qualified by God for the same, has a right to preach according to the measure of faith, and that the essential qualification for preaching is wrought by the Spirit of God; and that the knowledge of the tongues and liberal sciences are not absolutely necessary; yet they are convenient, and will doubtless be profitable if rightly used; but if brought in to supply the want of the Spirit of God, they prove a snare to those that use them and all that follow them." *

In order to understand the true position of these Separatists, in relation to the churches and the ministry, the reader must recollect the position of their opponents. The practice of the "Half-way Covenant" had become general, and men joined the churches as a means of grace; as one of those performances by which, while yet unregenerate, they were to put themselves in a hopeful way for conversion. Against the doctrine, that "It is the will of God to have a pure church upon earth, in this sense, that all the converted should be separated from the unconverted," the Windham county ministers argue: "To separate all true believers from those who are only nominally, but yet professedly so, and by their outward works and doctrines not proved to be otherwise, is to set up two visible kingdoms of Christ in the world, and to take one of these visible kingdoms out of another." In opposition to the doctrine, that all are to be admitted to the church as believers, who are "not proved to be otherwise," the Separatists maintained, that "the doors of the church should be carefully kept against such as cannot give a satisfying evidence" of their piety. The ministers argued, that all who make "an outward, credible profession of Christianity," must be admitted to the church, because it is impossible for us to know who are converted and who are not. The Separatists held, that the saints have certain knowledge of

* See the articles, entire, in the Result of a Council of the Windham County Consociation, held at Scotland, January 13, 1747. Athenæum Library.

each others' piety. The ministers would bring unconverted men into the churches, that the "seals of the covenant" might be the means of their conversion. The Separatists pronounced such use of the "seals" to be "sacrilege." The ministers believed, that Christ has instituted certain rules concerning an "outward call" to the ministry, by observing which, a man, whether converted or not, may be made one of his true ministers, so that men are bound to receive him as such. The Separatists held, that an "inward call" was indispensable, and was sufficient. They were the ignorant and blundering, but zealous and conscientious advocates of some important truths, which they mixed with pernicious errors, but which their adversaries totally opposed. They denounced and separated from the churches, as made up, in part, of hypocrites; meaning, not intentional deceivers, but persons who professed religion while destitute of true piety. The ministers defended the practice of admitting such hypocrites into the churches, quoting, "The kingdom of heaven is like leaven, which a woman took and hid in three measures of meal, till the whole was leavened." "The kingdom of heaven," they say, "intends the church of Christ, with all the ministry and ordinances of his word.— The leaven is the gospel doctrine, and the holy influence of the true members of Christ. — But how can this mass and meal be leavened by it, when the leaven is taken away from it, and kept at a distance and never to touch it?" They quoted, too, "But in a great house, there are not only vessels of gold and silver, but also of wood and of earth, some to honor and some to dishonor." The vessels of wood and of earth, they maintained, are these hypocrites,* who, though unconverted, must be admitted into the church, and "be there, among the wheat and honorable vessels, — that they may be under proper ordinances for their conversion, and for the trial of his people."

But, in despite of all such reasonings, the zealous declaration of the exhorters, that hypocrites ought not to be in the church, would strike many of their plain, honest hearers with a very truth-like sound; and though they might not know how to dispose of the arguments on either side, they would say, "It stands to reason, that hypocrites ought not to be in

* They use this very word, in this very connexion.

the church." They would feel, too, that if religion be so great a matter as ministers pretend and conscience commands us to believe, the difference between a saint and a hypocrite must be such that they can ordinarily be distinguished from each other ; so that hypocrites, as a general rule, may be excluded from the church. In these thoughts lay nearly all the moral power of the Separatists. By the force of these, they maintained themselves against all the attacks of their adversaries, and what is more, against the influence of their own blunders and bad spirit, till Edwards published his treatise on the "Qualifications for Full Communion." That treatise took their best weapons out of their hands, and, by a judicious use of them, accomplished the work upon which they were bringing disgrace. The errors of both parties were vanquished by a clear statement of the truth.

On the question, whether the saints have certain knowledge of each others' piety, the Separatists had a less advantageous position. It is doubtless true, that men of congenial spirits soon feel their congeniality; and cases are not very uncommon, of hypocrites, who have lived for years so as to escape church-discipline, but for whom the truly pious were never able to work themselves into a feeling of brotherly love and Christian confidence. But there may be congeniality between bad spirits, as well as good, and a man may very naturally "feel his heart going out in love" towards another, when both are deeply tinctured with the same faults, and especially if both are sinfully bitter against the same enemies. This wonderfully sweet "communion between them in the actings of their own minds," when carefully analyzed by an accurate observer, with good specimens before him, sometimes yields very unexpected ingredients, the most abundant of which is mutual flattery. The flattery is commonly implied, rather than expressed. Each shows himself wonderfully pleased with whatever the other says or does. Each openly considers the traits of which the other is proud, as proofs of uncommon piety. Each calls wrath against the other's opponents, "holy indignation." In such ways, without ever expressing their opinions of each other directly, they flatter each other incessantly. Each sees his own image in the other, and they really have "certain knowledge," that they are very much alike ; but, unhappily, the traits in which they resemble each other are no part of Christian character, and therefore their congeniality is no proof that either is a converted man. And the same congeniality may be felt between the unholy affections of one who is sanctified in part, and the same affections in one who is not sanctified at all, and may be the means of deceiving them both. Among those who are thus bound together, party spirit naturally usurps the name and place of brotherly love; hatred of opponents passes for zeal for God ; and defamation and bitter railings are counted Christian boldness. It is a communion in evil, and gives activity and vigor to all the evil in which they have communion with each other. All this was strikingly exemplified by these Separatists ; and they were the more readily led into it, because the truth condemned so much that they hated.

The Separatists at Mansfield, in the beginning of the twentieth article of their Confession of Faith, appeal to their "own experience," as one of the grounds of their religious belief. On the same ground, they professed to know that God approved the labors of their exhorters. They asserted, that they enjoyed more of the presence of God in hearing them, than in hearing the regular clergy. The answer of the ministers to this argument is candid and conclusive.

"We were, divers of us, at the first appearance of these things, considerably at a loss, and rather inclined to think that God did own such mistaken zeal, so far as to awaken and quicken many souls and do them good, and might intend it as a means of humbling to us, for our carelessness and want of zeal in his service and love to souls. And though we know that God will never set aside his own ordinances, yet as to ourselves, we hope we can truly say, we are not only willing to be laid aside from our pulpits, but to be buried in our graves, and have our names forgotten upon the earth, if our blessed Lord may be glorified and souls saved through that means. And we did, several of us, set ourselves, with as much diligence as we could consistently with our other business, to examine into this matter. — Upon our best observation, so far as we can remember, when we have observed any pious souls, who have by means of such meetings and performances in them had a more passionate and affectionate outgoing of love to God and Christ, it has been generally attended with much corrupt mixture of carnal joy, or bitterness, or pride, more than usually attends the fruits of the Spirit with the pure institutions of the gospel. — People who are most zealously affected to these meetings, — do indeed often speak of wonderful discoveries of the gloriousness of God and the preciousness of Christ; but, for the most part, when they come to explain these discoveries, they give an account of some powerful sense of Christ's infinite and amazing love in dying and bearing hell for them in particular; and seem to have been filled with a strong and passionate love to him for what he has assuredly done for them, without any acting of faith in the veracity of God in the gospel offer of salvation. — And when they speak of the views of the terrible justice and holiness of God, it seems too often to direct them to personal applications, and to be terminated on particular objects whom they think to be opposers, and with vehemence to treat them as discovered to them to be the objects of the divine displeasure. The discoveries which many of them have at such times, are of the certainty that this is the work of God, and an assurance that he will carry it on in spite of earth and hell."

Thus they were led to ascribe to the Holy Spirit, views and feelings which in reality sprung from their own revengeful tempers; and some of them, whose subsequent lives evinced their piety, for a while behaved worse than a pious man, not awfully deceived, could be induced to behave.

The ministers concluded their letter with excellent advice, addressed in a good spirit, to all classes of men. One passage shows that they had learned one lesson, which some of their brethren in other parts of the colony did not yet understand. They say to the unconverted: "If private persons, who are not obliged by any oath or office, keep stirring up prosecutions, and promoting and furthering the corporal punishment of religious disorders, and driving on coercive measures to reclaim those that wander out of the way of understanding, this is not only the most effectual method to prevent *their* conviction, but is also like to be the occasion of neglecting your own souls, comforting yourselves with a false zeal for God and his cause, while you remain as great strangers to God as you were born." They must have had nearly the same opinion of the influence of prosecutions commenced by men in office; but this they respectfully left to be inferred.

The Separatists were neither deterred by penalties, nor won by persuasion. On or about October 9, 1745, several members of the church at Mansfield, and of neighbouring churches, met and organized themselves as a church. None of them had letters of dismission from the churches to which they belonged, and some of them were under censure, probably for ecclesiastical irregularities. They adopted the Confession of Faith, from which extracts have already been given. January 15, 1746, or near that day, they met, "under pretence of ordaining Deacon Thomas Marsh as teaching elder." Several ministers attended, to remonstrate with them. They were reviled, and, being unable to gain a candid bearing, they read a protest against their proceedings. For some reason, now unknown, the ordination was deferred. About a month afterwards, they met again, for the same purpose; but on that very day Deacon Marsh was arrested and imprisoned. They ordained John Hovey teaching elder; Thomas Denison, John Austin and Matthew Smith, laymen, imposing hands upon him. They then ordained Matthew Smith and Thomas Denison, ruling elders; and John Austin and Shubael Dimick, deacons. In July, Hovey, Smith, and Denison ordained Deacon Thomas Marsh, teaching elder, and the next day ordained Thomas Stephens to the same office at Plainfield. All these persons were supposed, by the neighbouring ministers, to be destitute of the necessary qualifications for their offices.

The members of the Consociation of Windham county assembled as an ecclesiastical council at Scotland, January 13, 1747, and having made arrangements for preparing their business, and recommended to the churches to keep days of fasting and prayer in the interim, adjourned February 11. At their adjourned meeting, after a careful inquiry into facts, they considered it their duty to bear solemn, official testimony against the errors of the Separatists. They decided, that there was no good reason for separating from the churches; and that if there was, the Separatists had not taken the regular gospel steps to reclaim their erring brethren before separating from them, but had separated in an uncharitable and unchristian manner. Therefore, they resolved, the churches ought to withdraw fellowship from them. Yet they were not to be given up as hopeless, but efforts ought to be made with them as individuals, to reclaim them from their errors.

As it had been asserted that some of the ministers of the county held, that the saints have certain knowledge of each others' piety, that illiterate and unauthorized men ought sometimes to preach, and that outcries and bodily agitations are evidence of the presence and influence of the Spirit of God, the council made careful inquiry, and found that not one of the ministers in the county held any of these opinions. Yet, they admitted, "some of us have been too unguarded, and missed it in our conduct in several things; and particularly have erred in too hastily passing judgment on persons as converted." Some of them had given occasion to think they were in favor of exhorters, by a letter to Elisha Paine, who, they hoped, might be useful; "but have since found abundant cause to alter our judgment, and lament our weakness, and the hurtful consequences of it to the interests of Christ's kingdom." The letter appears to have been written when Paine was in prison, and thought to be in danger of unusually severe treatment. *

There were churches of Separatists in New London, Stonington, Preston, Norwich, Lyme, Canterbury, Plainfield, Windsor, Suffield, and Middletown. Trumbull says, that the whole number in the colony, "first and last," was "ten or twelve." At Preston, Paul Parks was ordained as teaching elder, and was charged not to premeditate what he should say in his preaching, but to speak as the Spirit should give him utterance.

The condition of the Separatists in Connecticut excited a lively interest among some of the Dissenters in England, who appointed a committee to watch over their religious liberty. Dr. Avery, the chairman, wrote a letter on the subject, which was read in the General Assembly. Gov. Law, in reply, informed Avery of their errors and extravagances. Avery replied, that civil penalties were not the appropriate remedy, and could not cure them. What influence this correspondence had, is doubtful; but as the rigor of legal prosecution was relaxed, their zeal diminished, and they became gradually less irregular. When Edwards' treatise on the "Qualifications for Full Communion" had overthrown the Half-way Covenant, and the churches no longer justified the admission of "hypocrites," the Separatists ceased to be the representatives of any important truth not held by the regular churches, and the strong reason for their existence was at an end. By degrees, some returned to the communion from which they went out; but more generally, they united with the Baptists. In 1818, Trumbull believed the denomination to be extinct.

It is the united testimony of all witnesses, when speaking of New England in general, that New London and Windham counties were the principal seat of the evils produced by exhorters and separations. What and how great they were there, the reader has seen. From a candid consideration of the whole subject, it appears that some of their departures

* Trumbull, and the result of the Council, before quoted. Ath. Lib.

Your most respectfull
Humble Servant
T Prince

from truth, good order, and a Christian spirit, were really as gross as they have been represented ; but that they were betrayed into some of their errors, by their opposition to other errors, scarcely less pernicious, generally prevalent around them, and obstinately defended by the regular churches. It appears, too, that the prevalence of Separatism and its concomitant errors and evils was far less extensive than it has usually been represented ; that the amount of evil fairly chargeable to this source in the whole country, has been greatly overestimated, while the good which it aided to accomplish, has not been acknowledged. It must be admitted, too, that these disorders arose, in part, from the early errors of some of the most prominent promoters of the revival. This is unanswerably proved by their own confessions, made when the experience of three or four years had taught them wisdom. But it is equally certain, that a vast majority of the friends of the revival, both clergy and laymen, were, from the beginning, their steady and intelligent opposers ; and nothing can be more unjust than charging upon them, as a body, the peculiar errors of the Separatists.

---

## CHAPTER XVIII.

The Controversy in Massachusetts. — Whitefield's Second Visit to New England. — His subsequent Labors and his Death.

Some of the leading features of the controversy as it existed in Massachusetts, have already been exhibited ; especially in the account of the Testimonies, Chapter XVI. To give a minute history of all, even of what still remains in print, would be both tiresome and useless. Only some of the more important publications can be noticed, with such specimens of the remainder as may afford a fair sample of the whole. The giants in this controversy, beyond all dispute, were Edwards and Chauncy. These men seem well to have understood their relation to each other and to the contest. Chauncy sometimes appeared as the avowed antagonist of Edwards ; and though Edwards seldom, if ever, mentions either Chauncy or his publications, it is perfectly obvious to any one who reads them both, that he often had him distinctly in view, and wrote to oppose his influence.

Chauncy's first serious attack was the publication of "The Wonderful Narrative: or, a Faithful Account of the French Prophets, their Agitations, Ecstasies, and Inspirations. To which are added, several other remarkable instances of Persons under the influence of the like Spirit in various Parts of the World, particularly in New England: With an Introduction, directing to the proper Use of such Extraordinary Appearances in the course of Providence." The French prophets first appeared about the year 1700. For more than a century, persecution, sometimes resisted, with various success, by civil war, and sometimes endured with patient submission; royal promises, made in guile and broken in perfidy; unexpected massacres in times of peace; arrests, imprisonments, executions on the gibbet, on the wheel, or at the stake, had composed the external history of French Protestantism. Now, for the last time, a few thousands of them, in the almost inaccessible fastnesses of the Cevennes, rose in arms against their oppressors. The war raged for years. Often, in battle, quarter was neither given nor accepted by either party. At the beginning of the winter of 1703, Montrevel, the royalist general, ordered a country forty leagues in extent, to be laid waste, and the cottages to be torn down or burned. A famine followed, and meanwhile the gallows was always kept standing, and the hangman within call. It is not necessary to believe that, as has been asserted, some of the Huguenots were trained to imposture. They firmly believed that they were the Lord's people; and they had good reason to regard their persecutors as his enemies. They could not doubt that God would sustain his own cause; and when it became evident that nothing but miracles could save them, they expected miracles. Want of food and sleep and rest, disordered their bodies, and therefore intense thought, violent emotion, heroic hopes, and the sight and suffering of horrible wickedness more easily overpowered their imaginations. Some thought themselves inspired. They were seized with tremblings and convulsions. They spake, as was supposed, with other tongues than their vernacular. They professed to deliver messages from God, and to predict future events; and if a desperate attack on their enemies was made at their suggestion and proved successful, the event was received as evidence of their divine commission. The insurrection was brought to an end, partly by negotiation and partly by force. In 1706, three of the prophets, who are said to have had but little reputation among their own people, took refuge in England, where others appear to have joined them soon afterwards. Though their prophetical character was not acknowledged by the French Protestants already settled in London, they succeeded in gaining followers, even among the titled nobility, and what is more, among men of some education ; but after a few years, their attempts at working miracles, and especially the failure of their predictions, that certain of their company would rise from the dead, destroyed their credit. They seem at last to have lost all self-respect ; to have acquired the art of bringing on at will those mental and bodily paroxysms which had been mistaken for illapses of the Holy Spirit, and to have exhibited their prophetic gifts for gain. Chauncy's object was, to bring discredit upon the revival, on account of the involuntary outcries, faintings and convulsions that attended it, by showing that these were signs, not of the presence of the Holy Spirit, but of enthusiasm or imposture, as in the case of the French prophets. The work was regarded by the friends of the revival as a powerful and mischievous book. It was republished in Scotland.

The first publication of Edwards on this subject, was his sermon on "The Distinguishing Marks of a Work of the Spirit of God ; applied to that uncommon Operation which has lately appeared on the Minds of many of the People of this Land." It was preached at New Haven, September 10, 1741, and soon published, with a preface by Mr. Cooper, of Boston, and republished in England and Scotland. In this sermon he argued, first, negatively, that neither the work being carried on in a very unusual and extraordinary way, nor its being accompanied with effects on the bodies of men, nor its occasioning a great ado and much noise about religion, nor impressions on the imaginations of many of its subjects, nor the influence of example in carrying it on, nor the fact that many who seem to be its subjects are guilty of great imprudences and irregularities, nor the delusions of Satan that accompany the work, nor the falling away of some into gross errors and scandalous practices, nor the fact that the earnest preaching of the terrors of the law is a means of carrying it on, is any proof that the work is not of God; and secondly, he set forth the positive marks by which a real work of the Spirit of God may be distinguished from all counterfeits.

An answer to this sermon and its preface, by one who styled himself "A Lover of Truth and Peace," and who, if not Dr. Chauncy, thought and wrote very much in his style, was published at Boston. Of the positive marks of a genuine work of God, which Edwards had laid down, he says: "I acknowledge, that the rules and marks he mentions are good; but cannot join with him in explaining those rules, and applying them as he does." He might have made the same remark on the whole sermon; for he nowhere disputes the truth of a single principle for which Edwards contends, but spends his whole force in discussing their application to "the late religious commotions." Nor is there much, if any, express contradiction between them in respect to facts. Edwards fixes his attention mainly on the good which those commotions were accomplishing, makes that prominent in the discussion, and thence infers that the work was, "in the general," from the Spirit of God. His antagonist does not deny that many souls had been savingly renewed; but in his picture, the evil is always made prominent, and therefore the work "in the general" is condemned. And such was the prevailing style of the controversy.

In 1742, Edwards published his "Thoughts on the Revival of Religion in New England," which was the great work on that side of the controversy. The next year, Chauncy published his "Seasonable Thoughts on the State of Religion in New England,' which was the principal work on that side. These works are much like their predecessors, though on a larger scale. Edwards admits and censures the evils that prevailed, but dwells upon the good that had been accomplished, concludes the work to be from the Spirit of God, and encourages solicitude for its continuance. Chauncy admits that good had been done, but represents the evil as predominant, and wishes the "commotion" at an end. Neither of them, however, gives any definite estimate of the amount either of the good or the evil that had been done; so that, even on that point, there is no explicit contradiction between them. Nor is there any very important difference in the rules by which they would judge of the genuineness of a revival. The real parting point between them was never made the subject of discussion, and perhaps was not distinctly seen by either. Chauncy was shocked at the "censoriousness" of the revivalists. In his view, every man ought to be regarded and treated as a true Christian, as a really pious man and an heir of heaven, who did not prove the contrary by embracing some "damnable heresy," or by committing some scandalous immorality, even though no positive evidence of his piety could be found. He demanded for all such persons, a regular and unimpeached standing in the churches, and if regularly ordained, in the ministry also; for perhaps they were already regenerate, and if not, they were in the way of their duty, and might reasonably hope to be regenerated before leaving the world. The revivalists saw that these views were deceiving and ruining many souls. They preached to such persons, as under the wrath of God, and in the straight road to eternal perdition. This, in Chauncy's view, was shocking censoriousness. He could have no patience with it; for, as he thought, it disturbed the quiet of good men, or of those who were in a fair way to become good; it tended to excite the wrath of those who were thus denounced, and to fill families and communities with discord; it divided churches and parishes into parties, and destroyed the comfort and endangered the salaries of ministers. When Davenport condemned ministers by name as unconverted, and advised their people to separate from them, and some followed his advice, he saw in it only the carrying out of the principles of all the revivalists. He thought it the duty of all men to resist such a system, and do their utmost to make all things quiet again. Edwards, on the other hand, had not yet emancipated himself from the "half-way covenant" views in which he had been educated, and therefore was not yet furnished with the ideas which he needed, to meet this point as it ought to have been met. He correctly acknowledged censoriousness to be a great sin, which had been awfully prevalent; but he did not show, as was desirable, that much which had been condemned as censoriousness, deserved a better name. He contented himself with showing that, notwithstanding this evil, the work might be, and certainly was, of God, and that men ought to labor for its promotion, notwithstanding the imperfections and incidental evils with which it was attended.

In the conclusion of this treatise, Edwards recommends,

as a means of promoting the revival, "that a history should be published once a month, or once a fortnight, of the progress of it, by one of the ministers of Boston, who are near the press, and are most conveniently situated to receive accounts of it from all parts." Agreeably to this suggestion, the "Christian History" was established the next year. Similar publications were commenced about the same time in London and Glasgow.

Some of the minor controversies of the day show more precisely the form which some of these subjects took in many minds.

The Rev. Theophilus Pickering, pastor of the Second Church in Ipswich, wrote, February 3, 1742, to the Rev. Nathaniel Rogers, Junior Pastor of the First Church, and Mr. Daniel Rogers, who was then preparing for the ministry : * —

"I am at a loss to understand the distinction betwixt the ordinary and usual work of God in the conversion of sinners, and that work wherein you are engaged, which you emphatically call 'This Work — This Work of God.' And inasmuch as you have been mindful in your public prayers to beg of God that he would convince and stir up such ministers as are backward to that which you call 'This Work,' and have also, by expressions dropped in private conversation, led me into a belief that it would be very agreeable to you to see me disposed to encourage 'This Work,' as you call it; inasmuch as a good agreement among ministers is of great consequence to religion, and my coming into your sentiments and measures may as well happily tend to the advantage of my ministry in general, (if you are in the right,) as be well pleasing to some of my parishioners, who zealously affect you and are at the pains to ply me with their importunate solicitions: — Therefore I beseech you, brethren, by the mercies of God, that you would endeavour to resolve my doubts with respect to 'This Work' that you contend for, —

"1. By declaring what it is, and wherein it differs from the converting work of God that was carried on in New England from the days of our fathers.

* A communication in the Boston Evening Post of November 22, 1742, begins thus: "We lately heard from York, that on or about the 13th of July last, one Mr. D—l R—s summoned together a solemn (and we think an unlawful) assembly, consisting of the elders and pretended messengers of some of the neighbouring churches, to ordain the said R—s at large, to be a vagrant preacher to the people of God in this land : contrary to the peace of our Lord the King and Head of his church, and to the good order and constitution of the churches in New England, as established by the Platform. — In which transaction, we hear that the Rev. Mr. M—y, W—se, J. R—s and G—m resolutely proceeded, although some others of the neighbouring ministers justly bore their testimony against such an irregular action." — The Cambridge Platform allows no ordination, except as elder of some church.

"2. By showing, from the Sacred Scriptures, that those things (if such there be) in which it differs, are the work of the Spirit of God, and unexceptionable grounds for your terms of distinction."

The Messrs. Rogers answered, February 5:

"By the work we hope our hearts are engaged in, which, as you may have observed, we call 'This Work – This Work of God,' we mean God's work of convicting and converting sinners; and we do not mean to distinguish it from the convincing and converting work of God, carried on in New England in the days of our fathers, or anywhere else in any age of the Christian church; for we suppose God's work in convincing and converting sinners to be ever the same, as to the substantial parts of it. Nevertheless, as this is a work distinct from all the other works of God, it may surely be spoken of with various marks of distinction."

They then expressed their belief that this work had for some time been carried on with unusual power, and their desire that all ministers would coöperate in promoting it. This was not satisfactory. Pickering wrote again, February 15, and endeavoured to extort a confession, that by "This Work," they meant more than they were willing to confess, and that it included "some effects attendant, as visible signs or open discoveries" of the Spirit's operations. Receiving no answer, he wrote again, July 16, in the same strain. "That which I want to know," he says, "is, What and how much you take into that which you call 'This Work of God,' as grounds of distinction; and upon what authority you receive it. If there be a different manner of operation, or new evidences, — that have not been usual in the conversion of sinners in later times, — I pray you to enumerate and ascertain them; — to show me what Scripture warrant you have to expect such things in the present age of the church; and evince, by the word of truth, that those things are to be believed to be the work of God." He wished to get an acknowledgment, that the faintings, outcries, and other disorders were a part of the work itself, and not mere accidental attendants on it; for he could then prove that a part of the work was bad, and therefore not from God. He wrote again, August 18; but he received no answer, except that to his first letter.*

The same question was brought up in Turell's "Dialogue on the Times."

"*Neighbour.* Sir, the grand question I want to be resolved in is, What is the Work of God?

---

* See the Correspondence, in the O. S. Ch. Lib.

"*Minister.* There are many things which may be called the work of God, and are really so; as the work of creation, providence, redemption in general; and some eminent acts of mercy and judgment have had that name given them in particular; and our faith and obedience are styled so in the gospel. But that which is now called the work of God in the land, and appears so to me, is 'The work of his grace, wrought on the hearts of many by his word and Spirit.' It is past a doubt with me, that the blessed Spirit has been sent down to convict, convince and convert sinners, and to quicken, enliven and comfort the saints; and a conspicuous reformation is wrought in some places.

"*N.* But do you mean neither more nor less, Sir, by the work of God among us, or the outpouring of the Spirit, than this work of grace, in conviction, conversion, light, and comfort?

"*M.* I am persuaded it is safest and best to fix upon this only, as the present work of God in the land, and not to place it in uncertain appearances. I have good reason to think, (having had opportunity to converse with all sorts of persons,) that if ministers and Christians had thus fixed it, there would not have been that seeming opposition to it from good men; and that we should also have cut off occasion from those who are enemies to serious godliness, to scoff at it."*

He then goes on to show, that neither outcries, faintings, dreams, trances, visions, revelations or impulses are any part of "The Work," and that some of them are of very dangerous tendency. This Dialogue was published in the summer or autumn of 1742. The revival had been powerful at Medford, where he was pastor, and some of the first outcries in that region were among his own people, and under his own preaching. He believed that "some scores had been savingly wrought upon." In the preface to his "Directions to his People," published early in the spring of that year, he declares, "that of the many I have conversed with under the common impressions, two or three excepted, they have been all wrought upon in a way agreeable to the gospel, and just as I should have desired seven years ago." The "Directions" are in the same spirit with the "Dialogue on the Times," and were published, he tells us, partly to vindicate his character, which had been injured by a report that, from being a zealous promoter of the glorious work of God's grace, he had become an opposer; and partly, that the opposers and enemies of the work might no longer say that its friends swallowed down every thing, and attributed all appearances and imprudent management to the God and Spirit of order.

The reader will now understand why Dr. Colman, in 1744, was so scrupulous about the phraseology of Daven-

* O. S. Ch. Lib.

port's "Retractations." Davenport at first wrote: — "I am now fully convinced and persuaded, that several appendages to this glorious work are no essential parts thereof, but of a different and contrary nature and tendency; which appendages I have been, in the time of the work, very industrious in and instrumental of promoting, by a misguided zeal." At Dr. Colman's suggestion, that this might be misunderstood, he amended it, so as to read: — "Several things, which in the time of the work I was very industrious and instrumental in promoting by a misguided zeal, were no parts of it, but of a contrary nature and tendency." So careful were the leading promoters of the revival to have this matter understood. And with its friends, they were successful. "These extraordinaries" soon came to be regarded by all, as they had ever been by most, as "no parts" of the work, and they have long since ceased to appear in our congregations. With its opposers, they labored in vain. The argument for which Pickering made such persevering efforts to secure a foundation, was too convenient to be spared; the language of some exhorters and a very few ministers afforded some pretext for using it; the party clung to it pertinaciously, and handed it down to their successors; and to this day, many Unitarians, Universalists and infidels suppose that such things are really "parts" of a revival.

How much excuse the conduct of some zealous revivalists furnished for such a conclusion, it is impossible to ascertain, and difficult even to conjecture. Complaints in general terms, of horrible disorders all over the land, are abundant; but it is seldom possible to ascertain exactly what they were, or where they happened; and the proof of their existence is seldom any thing more than the assertion, that "they are notorious." All the "censorious," that is, all who required positive evidence of piety before admitting its existence, were counted as promoters of all disorders. Numerous friends of the revival, who were well acquainted with the facts, and whose testimony is unimpeachable, complained in express terms, "that disorders and errors had been both multiplied and magnified by unfriendly reporters;" and a careful examination of the documents of the day will convince any candid man, that they had reason to complain. Yet it is certain, that there were great errors and disorders, and that some persons, and even some ministers, condemned all who endeavoured to repress them, as opposers of the revival. Croswell* pronounced "the excellent Mr. Turell" an opposer, and thought his "Directions" to be "more infectious and poisonous than 'The French Prophets,' or the 'Trial of Mr. Whitefield's Spirit.'" Croswell may have been provoked to this, in part, by what he esteemed a personal attack. Turell had cautioned his people against certain itinerants, whom Croswell supposed to be Mr. Buel and himself. It is certain, too, that real opposers were sometimes exceedingly artful, and did the work of opposition so adroitly, that it was difficult to fasten the charge upon them. One noticeable instance deserves to be recorded.

The Rev. Jonathan Ashley, of Deerfield, being in Boston, Mr. Cooper, out of courtesy, and not because he needed assistance, invited him to preach at Brattle Street on the Sabbath, November 28, 1742. Mr. Ashley's text was, Paul's commendation of charity, 1 Corinthians 13: 1—3. He compared the state of the churches in New England to that of the church in Corinth, where there had been "a very plentiful effusion of the Divine Spirit." He mentioned many particulars in which the two cases resembled each other, the same faults prevailing in both. He set forth the excellence of charity, and proved that without it, all signs of piety on which men are disposed to rely, are deceptive. Considered in itself, the sermon was a good one. The faults against which he inveighed, were actually in the land; and he carefully guarded himself against the danger of contradiction, by not stating definitely how extensively they prevailed. It was a carefully guarded statement of some of the principal truths on which the opposers of the revival relied for the support of their cause, without any mixture of their usual misrepresentations. But the great practical question between the two parties then was, whether efforts ought to be made for the continuance of the revival, or for the restoration of universal quiet; and the general tendency of the sermon was, to leave an impression in favor of the latter. Everybody understood the preacher's aim. A few expressed their disapprobation by leaving the house. The opposers of the revival felt that they had gained a triumph, by having such a sermon preached in that place; and, to make their triumph com-

* Letter to Turell, O. S. Ch. Lib.

plete, the sermon must be published, "at the request of many of the hearers." This would make the impression far and wide, that Mr. Cooper and the church at Brattle Street had changed their minds, and instead of wishing still to promote the revival, were now wishing to put down all excitement. A copy was requested for the press. Cooper saw the bearing of these things, and wrote to Ashley, remonstrating against the unkind and unfair advantage taken of his ministerial courtesy, and urging him to withhold his sermon from the press. Ashley, however, furnished a copy, and it was published; and Cooper must submit to the virtual misrepresentation of his sentiments, or expose himself to ridicule. He was not the man to hesitate in such a case. Though fully aware, as he said, of the sneers he should encounter, he immediately informed the public, through the Boston Gazette, of the whole affair, and stated his objections against the publication of the sermon. This, as he had foretold, brought upon him a shower of newspaper wit and sarcasm, and among other things, a taunting letter from Ashley himself. He was ridiculed for thinking a correct knowledge of his opinions so important to the public, and for setting himself up as a censor of the press, and as a man whom ministers must consult, before publishing their sermons. Such was the position in which the opposing party had placed him, without violating the letter of any of the laws of courtesy. They had only exercised their undoubted rights. They had done like a merchant who gets another man's property so adroitly, that the law can take no hold of him. — There is some doubt how far Ashley was to blame in this affair. One of his letters, probably that to Cooper, afterwards published, was carried to the Boston Gazette for insertion, by Eliot, the publisher of the sermon. The editor of the Gazette refused to insert it, said that it had been altered, and offered Eliot ten pounds for a sight of the original. Eliot said that the original was not then in his possession, and refused to produce it.*

But, after all allowances for mistake and misrepresentation, testimony remains definite and conclusive, of sad disorders. One of the most remarkable instances was at Ipswich, in 1744. A particular account of it, signed by the Rev.

* The Sermon is in the O. S. Ch. Lib.; and all the pamphlets in the Athenæum Lib. See also, Boston Gazette for December 1742, and January 1743, in the Mass. Hist. Soc. Lib.

Messrs. Joseph White, Samuel Wigglesworth, John Webb, John Chipman, Joshua Gee, Joseph Emerson, William Hobby, John Warren, Jedediah Jewett, Simon Bradstreet, and James Chandler, most of whom were well known friends of the revival, and who visited Ipswich on purpose to investigate the affair, was published in the Boston Gazette of July 24, and copied into the Evening Post of July 30. It appears from their statement, that one Richard Woodbury, of Rowley, who had taken it upon himself to travel as an exhorter, had in the spring sent letters of reprehension and exhortation, "in a style presumptuous, if not blasphemous," to many ministers in the vicinity. The Rev. Nicholas Gilman assisted him in preparing these letters, and about the first of June, with the assistance of "several laics," privately ordained him as an evangelist. After his ordination, he went with Gilman to visit several of the ministers to whom the letters had been addressed, and came to Ipswich about the first of July. Here his language was blasphemous and profane, and his public and private conduct, ridiculous and absurd. He professed to come as a special messenger from God, authorized not only to teach, but to pronounce temporal curses on the rebellious. He told one who doubted his mission, that he should be convinced before they met again; and told another, that he should be dead and in hell in an hour or two. On one occasion, having asserted his power to bless and curse eternally whom he pleased, he said he was poor, and those present must give for the support of the gospel, or their money should burn with them in hell. He pretended to cast out devils and work other miracles; and sometimes he drank healths to "King Jesus," and to "the King of kings and Lord of lords." Woodbury received no countenance from any minister except Gilman, and one or two others, who are not named. The venerable senior pastor of the First Church in Ipswich, the Rev. John Rogers, testified, that notwithstanding the disturbance thus occasioned for a time, the good work of grace was still going on among his people.

A communication which immediately follows this statement in the Evening Post, is one of the most remarkable pieces of impudence extant. The writer says, he is glad that these "Rev. gentlemen have their eyes so far opened at last, as to declare publicly against such detestable things;"

and adds, "It were to be wished that they, and others of their brethren, had been earlier in their opposition." The eyes of these gentlemen had never needed opening to the detestable nature of such things. They had publicly declared against every thing of the kind, in the solemn "Testimony" of July 7, 1743. Some of them had declared publicly against Davenport and his disorders. As for "others of their brethren," Tennent had warned the churches against enthusiasm as early as 1741; Parsons had published his "Needful Caution" early in 1742; and many others had fully declared their disapprobation of all "such detestable things" in many ways, besides their united "Testimony" in 1743. All these things were quite as "public" as any disorders had been; and yet the writer would have men believe that these gentlemen and their brethren had always been blind to the evil nature of such things till now, and that their public declaration against them was something new. The fact that such an insinuation was thus publicly made, shows that there was a class of men who were ready to receive it as truth.

There were serious contentions and divisions in some of the churches, and separations from them; though there is no reason to believe the oft-repeated assertion, that the land was full of such cases.

A council from ten churches was convened at Exeter, January 31, 1743. It appears from their published result, that "a considerable number of the brethren" had withdrawn from the communion of the church, and had called a council, which had met, and sanctioned their proceedings; which, in the opinion of the council now called, ought not to have been done. The "dissatisfied brethren" assigned several reasons for withdrawing. One was, the refusal of the pastor to admit certain preachers into his pulpit; another was, the conduct of the pastor, in "discountenancing such as had been the subjects of a glorious work of grace." A third was, the settlement of the pastor, Rev. Woodbridge Odlin, whom they regarded as an opposer of the work of God, and the validity of whose settlement they disputed. A fourth was, the pastor's refusal to call a church meeting, except on certain conditions which the brethren thought objectionable, and which the usages of that church did not authorize him to require. The "dissatisfied brethren" refused to unite in calling this council of ten churches; and the council, after hearing an *ex parte* statement, sustained the pastor and "standing brethren."*

The Rev. Ezra Carpenter, pastor of the Church in Hull, was one of the signers of the "Testimony" of July, 1743; yet some of his people were dissatisfied, because, as they thought, he did not preach the doctrines of grace, and was an opposer of the revival. A council was called in 1743, which advised the church to remain at peace with its pastor, as there was no reason for dissatisfaction. This result procured only a partial and temporary peace. The discontent revived, and Mr. Carpenter was dismissed in 1746. Mr. Eells, of Hingham, was moderator of both councils.†

There were difficulties in the Second Church in Bradford; but the "Brief Narrative" of the aggrieved brethren, does not show what connexion they had with the revival. They accused Mr. Balch, their pastor, of Arminianism. He told Ichabod Cheney, "if you think my principles to be erroneous, you ought to prove them so." Cheney brought forward his charges in writing, March 10, 1744, with written testimony to support them; but some informality was alleged against his mode of proceeding, and he and his witnesses were put under censure. They proposed a mutual council. Mr. Balch objected, that a council would decide according to its party predilections. A council was called, selected by Mr. Balch and his friends. It sustained him and the church against the aggrieved brethren. They invited the First Church in Gloucester, who were thorough-going friends of the revival, to take up the subject; but the church in Bradford refused to hear them, and nothing was effected.‡ Mr. Balch, Tucker of Newbury, Barnard of Haverhill, and others in that region, were known as Arminians.§ In 1746, Balch was engaged in a public controversy in defence of Arminianism, against Wigglesworth of Ipswich and Chipman of Beverly. There can be no doubt, that the difficulties in Bradford were aggravated and hastened to a crisis, by the state of mind which the revival produced.

The troubles in the Second Church in Ipswich, of which the Rev. Theophilus Pickering was pastor, manifestly grew

---

* O. S. Ch. Lib † Boston Gazette, Dec. 16, 1746.
‡ "Brief Narrative." O. S. Ch Lib.
§ Historical Sketch of Haverhill, Mass. Hist. Soc. Col.

out of the revival, and ended in a division of the church. As early as the beginning of 1742, some of his people were dissatisfied with his conduct in respect to the revival, and wished him to engage in promoting it. Meetings were held in the parish, attended by the Rev. Messrs. White of Gloucester, Emerson of Malden, Nathaniel and Daniel Rogers, and probably by others. Pickering wrote to Nathaniel Rogers, and published his letters, complaining that they preached in his parish without his consent.* March 12, 1744, twenty-six members presented a remonstrance to the church against the pastor, containing fourteen specifications under three general heads; and on the 27th of April, a second was presented, containing eight new specifications. Not obtaining satisfaction, they separated from the church, and finally became the Fourth Church in Ipswich, over whom the Rev. John Cleaveland, whose expulsion from Yale College has already been mentioned, was settled in 1747. The twenty-two specifications were laid before a council called by the Second Church, which met May 20 and June 10, 1746. One of the charges was, "Your not being instant, in season and out of season, in the work of God; and that, when God's Holy Spirit hath so wonderfully been poured out upon many persons in many places, and in yours in particular, you did not close with its operations, and so be instrumentally a promoter of God's work upon the hearts of his people under your care; but contrariwise, so treated the work of God and the subjects thereof, styling it enthusiasm and imagination, as if it might proceed from a distempered brain, or conceit in the mind." On this the council judged, "That the Rev. Mr. Pickering has been wanting in his ministerial duty, in the late times, in his not early and thoroughly examining into the nature of the religious appearances among his flock, whereby he might have been better enabled to distinguish between things holy and profane; and that he has too much neglected the instructing and guiding the subjects of those operations, insomuch that, we fear, he is in some measure chargeable with the irregularities which have happened among them." Another charge was, "Your not examining into the experiences of those that have offered themselves to join with the church in full communion, as you ought." The council say, "We

* See the Correspondence, already quoted.

fear that Mr. Pickering in some instances has been negligent in his duty of examining persons in order to their admission to the Lord's Table." Several of the charges related to a transaction, of which the account is very imperfect. It appears, however, that, in April, 1744, during a conversation with some of his parishioners, something had been said of his "losing a parish;" that he took minutes of the conversation, complained of them to the Grand Jury, and urged their presentment; and that he demanded of them sufficient security, to refund all damages that might in any way arise to him in consequence of their conduct. The council judged that on this point the aggrieved had just cause of offence, and that Mr. Pickering had made Christian satisfaction. They judged also that the aggrieved had had "hard treatment," in respect to several applications for church meetings and councils. On other charges, affecting Mr. Pickering's orthodoxy and ministerial character, they found "no just cause of offence;" and on the whole, that he was "not guilty, in general, according to the tenor of the charges brought against him by his aggrieved brethren." They pronounced the conduct of the aggrieved, in withdrawing from the communion of the church, setting up a separate meeting, and inviting persons of doubtful character, coming to them in a disorderly manner, to teach them from time to time, unjustifiable, and worthy of the censure of the church; though they recommended "great tenderness, and even long-suffering," in dealing with them. One of the ministers, it was said, did not vote for this result, as he thought it too severe on Mr. Pickering; and three ministers and three messengers protested against it, as too lenient towards him, and too severe on the aggrieved; though they disapproved the separation. The venerable John White, of Gloucester, was moderator, and all the ministers, except two, were signers of the Testimony of July, 1743.*

In such a state of things as these specimens indicate, Whitefield returned to New England. After a voyage of eleven weeks, he arrived at York, in Maine,† October 19, 1744.

* See Pamphlets on the Chebacco Controversy, in the O. S. Ch. Lib. and Athenæum.

† Gillies says, "at New York, in New England." Philip, in his account of Whitefield's landing, gives the name correctly; but in another part of his work (p. 254) calls it "Toronto;" confounding the place with Toronto

Owing to some slight imprudence, he became unwell before landing, and violently and dangerously sick soon after. By the sedulous attention of his host, a physician, once a noted deist, but now one of his spiritual children, he obtained relief after four days, and from that time gradually improved. The good Mr. Moody called upon him, and said, "Sir, you are, first, welcome to America; secondly, to New England; thirdly, to all faithful ministers in New England; fourthly, to all the good people in New England; fifthly, to all the good people of York; and sixthly and lastly, to me, dear Sir, less than the least of all." The "Christian History" announced his arrival, and added, "that his intention was, to pass on to Georgia; and, as he goes on, to meddle with no controversies, but only to preach up the parts of vital piety and the pure truths of the gospel, to all that are willing to hear them." At Mr. Moody's earnest request, after some hesitation, he preached, and immediately went to Portsmouth, November 6. He preached that evening for Mr. Fitch, and was to have preached the next morning, but was too ill, and deferred it till afternoon. His audiences were large, attentive, and affected. In the evening, his malady returned,* and confined him at Portsmouth till November 24.

---

in Upper Canada, which was once called York. British poets, however, must bear the palm for blunders of this kind. See how Montgomery, in his "Greenland," describes the country on the St. Lawrence.

> "Regions of beauty there these rovers found,
> The flowery hills with emerald woods were crowned;
> Spread o'er the vast savannas, buffalo herds
> Ranged without master. ———
> Here from his mates a German youth had strayed,
> Where the broad river cleft the forest glade;
> Swarming with alligator shoals, the flood
> Blazed in the sun, or moved in clouds of blood;
> The wild boar rustled headlong through the brake."

*Alligators* in the St. Lawrence! and *buffaloes* feeding in the *savannas* on its banks! He might as well confound England with Egypt; fill the Thames with crocodiles, and make the hippopotamus feed on its shores among the papyrus Campbell, who says, that Americans cannot write poetry, is quite as bad. In his "Gertrude of Wyoming," he makes the Oneida Indians, in Western New York, hunt not only the alligator, but the condor, which is found only on the Andes, in South America. He is equally wrong, though more excusable, where he makes his Oneidas call a spirit, "Manitou," like their more northern neighbours. The Iroquois have no labials in their language. They think it ridiculous for a man to "shut up his mouth when he goes to talk."

* Shurtleff, Chr. Hist. II. 320. Whitefield's own dates, here, seem to be in peculiar confusion; owing, perhaps, to his sickness.

It must have been of his second day at Portsmouth, that he wrote: "My pains returned; but what gave me most concern was, that notice had been given of my being to preach. I felt a divine life, distinct from my animal life, which made me, as it were, laugh at my pains, though every one thought I was 'taken with death.' My dear York physician was then about to administer a medicine. I, on a sudden, cried out, Doctor, my pains are suspended; by the help of God, I will go and preach, and then come home and die. With some difficulty I reached the pulpit. All looked quite surprised, as though they saw one risen from the dead. I, indeed, was as pale as death, and told them they must look upon me as a dying man, come to bear my dying testimony to the truths I had formerly preached to them. All seemed melted, and were drowned in tears. The cry after me, when I left the pulpit, was like the cry of sincere mourners, when attending the funeral of a dear departed friend. Upon my coming home, I was laid on a bed upon the ground, near the fire, and I heard them say, 'he is gone.' But God was pleased to order it otherwise. I gradually recovered."

The day before he left Portsmouth, Shurtleff wrote: "The prejudices of most that set themselves against him before his coming, seem to be in a great measure abated, and in some, to be wholly removed; and there is no open opposition made to him. I have frequent opportunities of being with him, and there always appears in him such a concern for the advancement of the Redeemer's kingdom and the good of souls, such a care to employ his whole time to these purposes, such sweetness of disposition, and so much of the temper of his great Lord and Master, that every time I see him, I find my heart further drawn out towards him."

"Saturday, November 24," says the "Christian History" of December 15, "the Rev. Mr. Whitefield was so far revived as to be able to take coach, with his consort, and set out from Portsmouth to Boston; whither he came, in a very feeble state, the Monday evening after: since which he has been able to preach in several of our largest houses of public worship, particularly the Rev. Dr. Colman's, Dr. Sewall's, Mr. Webb's, and Mr. Gee's, to crowded assemblies of people, and to great and growing acceptance. At Dr. Colman's desire, and the consent of the church, on the Lord's day after his arrival, he administered to them the holy communion. And last Lord's day he preached for the venerable Mr. Cheever, of Chelsea, and administered the Holy Supper there. The next day preached for the Rev. Mr. Emerson of Malden. Yesterday he set out to preach at some towns to the northward ; proposes to return hither the next Wednesday evening, and, after a few days, to comply with the earnest invitations of several ministers, to go and preach to their congregations, in the southern parts of the province.

"He comes with the same extraordinary spirit of meekness, sweetness, and universal benevolence as before : in opposition to the spirit of separation and bigotry, is still for holding communion with all Protestant churches. In opposition to enthusiasm, he preaches a close adherence to the Scriptures, the necessity of trying all impressions by them, and of rejecting whatever is not agreeable to them, as delusions. In opposition to Antinomianism, he preaches up all kinds of relative and religious duties, though to be performed in the strength of Christ ; and, in short, the doctrines of the Church of England, and the first fathers of this country. As before, he first applies himself to the understandings of his hearers, and then to the affections : and the more he preaches, the more he convinces people of their mistakes about him, and increases their satisfaction."

The administration of the Lord's Supper by a priest of the Church of England in the Congregational Church at Brattle street, gave offence. Some said, that the consent of the church was neither given nor asked, and Dr. Colman was blamed for introducing Whitefield by his own authority. Dr. Colman's defence was, that as it was customary for pastors to invite the assistance of other ministers on such occasions, he thought it unnecessary to call for a vote of the church ; that he plainly intimated his intention in his prayer after sermon, and then, on coming to the table, said, "The Rev. Mr. Whitefield being providentially with us, I have asked him to administer the ordinance ;" and that, by the countenances of the people, it seemed to be universally agreeable to them, which he supposed to be all the consent which the case required. Certainly Dr. Colman was not to be severely blamed for such a proceeding ; and the account fully exonerates Whitefield from the charge afterwards brought against him, of violating ecclesiastical order on this occasion. He had a right to consider Dr. Colman's invitation as sufficient proof of the orderliness of the service.*

Meanwhile, opposition had been showing itself, and preparing to act publicly and officially. The propriety of inviting him into the pulpit had been discussed in private correspondence, and anonymously in the newspapers. A writer in the Boston Evening Post, of November 19, insisted, that before being invited into any pulpit, he should be required to show himself penitent for his itinerancy, to retract his slanders, especially against Archbishop Tillotson, to acknowledge his injurious treatment of the Boston ministers, especially in sending Mr. Tennent to insult them, and to render a fair and just account of the money he had received for his orphan house. Some of the articles were evidently malicious, and even mean. One of them upbraided Whitefield with his wife's non-attendance at a certain lecture, at which, however, as it afterwards appeared, she was present. One of the most respectable was in the Evening Post of December 17. The writer says of Whitefield: "Indeed, he seems to be more cautious than formerly, and so refrains his lips from speaking all the gross things, which were so shocking to all serious and thinking persons; and he insists something more upon the substantial and useful doctrines and duties of religion. But an express and full acknowledgment of his faults, and an honest testimony against bad principles and uncharitable speeches and disorderly walking, is still altogether wanting, and therefore every thing else he says or does can have little or no good effect: the evil will still remain the same that it was." Such was the general strain of the more serious and gentlemanly writers. They maintained, that the whole tribe of itinerants, exhorters and Separatists still claimed him as on their side; and they demanded some public declaration from his pen, which should compel them to abandon that claim. He, however, relied on the effect of his present unobjectionable labors, and no such declaration appeared.

At length, organized opposition commenced. First appeared "A Letter from Two Neighbouring Associations of

* President Quincy, in his History of Harvard College, represents Dr. Colman as one of the "Liberal" party in the ministry of that day, in distinction from the "high Calvinists," who invited and sustained Whitefield. He nowhere intimates that Colman and Whitefield had any intercourse.

Ministers in the Country, to the Associated Ministers of Boston and Charlestown, relating to the admission of Mr. Whitefield into their Pulpits." * It was dated December 26, 1744. The members of the first of the two associations were Caleb Cushing, of Salisbury; Joseph Whipple, of Hampton Falls; John Lowell, of Newbury; Pain Wingate, of Amesbury; Jeremiah Fogg, of Kensington; Nathaniel Gookin, of North Hampton, N. H.; Elisha Odlin, of Amesbury; Peter Coffin, of Kingston; William Parsons, of South Hampton, N. H.; and Samuel Webster, of Salisbury. The members of the second were John Barnard, of Andover; Joseph Parsons and William Balch, of Bradford; James Cushing, of Haverhill; Christopher Sergeant, of Methuen; William Johnson, of Newbury; John Cushing, of Boxford; Thomas Barnard, of Newbury, and Edward Barnard, of Haverhill. They disclaim all desire to dictate to the Boston ministers what preachers they should receive, and justify their public remonstrance on this occasion by saying, that the consequences of Mr. Whitefield's admission would not be confined to the churches whom he was permitted to address, but would be public and extensive, affecting the interests of other ministers and churches. They assume, as an undisputed truth, that great and grievous disorders had prevailed among the churches, through the influence of itinerants. They ask: "Brethren, are you satisfied Mr. Whitefield approves not of these disorders? Is he against separations? Is he an enemy to enthusiasm?—And why have you not imparted the grounds of your satisfaction, if you have received any, to the public?—Do you find in him a disposition to the most plain Christian duty, of humbly confessing and publicly retracting his wicked and slanderous suggestions concerning the ministry, and concerning our colleges, so much our glory? Have you prevailed with him to make full satisfaction to the injured? Has he done it, or is he doing it? Do you find him inclined to heal the unhappy divisions occasioned by his former visit? Can you learn whether we are to be united in affection and Christian communion, or whether some one party is not, if possible, to prevail upon the ruin of the rest?" They avow their belief, that his former visit had done more harm than

* O. S. Ch. Lib.

good. They inquire, "Have you not, by opening your pulpit doors to this gentleman, encouraged and spirited up the weaker sort of people to expect the like of their ministers? — And can any thing perplex their conduct, more than yours, in asking Mr. Whitefield to preach; as it must undoubtedly create much disaffection to them, in many of their people, for refusing him?" They urged, that as countenancing Mr. Whitefield would have an extensive influence, and greatly affect ministers and churches throughout the land, it ought not to have been done without previously consulting, by some general meeting or method, those whom it must affect; that it was wrong for a few thus virtually to determine for all, in a case of common and universal concern; and that, even after consultation, he ought not to have been admitted, unless there was a prospect that it could be done without endangering the peace of the churches. And finally, they besought all who had not taken this step, seriously to consider the dangers and mischiefs to which it might lead, and to present an unshaken opposition to the solicitations of those who should urge them into it.

To this was appended an extract from the records of another Association, which met at Cambridge, January 1, 1745: —

"Present, the Rev. Messrs. John Hancock, of Lexington; William Williams, of Weston; John Cotton, of Newton; Nathaniel Appleton, of Cambridge; Warham Williams, of Waltham; Seth Storer, of Watertown; Ebenezer Turell, of Medford; Nicholas Bowes, of Bedford, and Samuel Cook, of Cambridge.

"The Rev. Mr. Appleton having applied to his brethren of the said Association for our advice, relating to a request which hath been made to him by a number of his church and congregation, that he would invite the Rev. Mr. George Whitefield to preach in Cambridge: — After supplications to God, and mature consideration of the case proposed, and the several pleas made in favor of said request, and the state of the town, as also the many weighty objections which lie against the said Mr. Whitefield with respect to his principles, expressions and conduct, which are not yet answered, nor has any Christian satisfaction been given by him for them: considering also how much the order, peace and edification of the churches of this land are endangered, together with the divided, unhappy state of many of them,

"It was unanimously voted, That it is not advisable, under the present situation of things, that the Rev. Mr. Appleton invite the Rev. Mr. Whitefield to preach in Cambridge.

"And they accordingly declared, each of them for themselves respectively, that they would not invite the said gentleman into their pulpits."

This advice was signed by each member of the Association, and attested by John Hancock, Moderator.

Of the signers of the letter to the Boston pastors, several appear to have been decided opposers of the revival, in all its stages, and the name of no one of them is found among its friends. The Association which gave advice to Appleton was, at least in part, of a different character. The part acted and the declaration made by Williams of Weston at the General Convention in 1743, should certainly rescue his name from the list of opposers. Appleton's sermon on the same occasion shows where he stood.* Cotton and Turell were signers of the Testimony of July, 1743, and Appleton sent in his Attestation, to be published with its doings. Turell was an early and influential promoter of the revival, and the first "outcries" in the region around him occurred among his own people, under his own preaching. Cotton's character is also fully vindicated by his "Earnest Exhortation to seek the Lord while he may be found, and call upon him while he is near;" being "Two Sermons, delivered at the Lecture in Newton, April 29, and May 8, 1741, when many were seeking for direction and assistance under their convictions from the Spirit of God striving with them." † In a note appended to these sermons, he states, that more than three hundred young people of his charge, besides many advanced in years, had lately visited him as serious inquirers. In the close of the second sermon, he bears decided testimony in favor of the revival, as it existed in neighbouring towns, and in other colonies; and the sermons themselves were wise and able efforts to promote it. They were delivered a little more than seven months after Whitefield's first arrival in Boston. — Such were four out of the nine, who subscribed the advice and pledge at Cambridge.

The "Testimony" of the Faculty of Harvard College, "against the Rev. Mr. George Whitefield and his conduct," was dated December 28, 1744.‡ The Faculty say: "We look upon his going about in an itinerant way, especially as he hath so much of an enthusiastical turn of mind, utterly inconsistent with the peace and order, if not the very being, of these churches of Christ. And now, inasmuch as, by a certain faculty he hath of raising the passions, he hath been the

* See Chapter XVI. † O. S. Ch. Lib. ‡ O. S. Ch. Lib.

means of rousing many from their stupidity, and setting them on thinking, whereby some may have been made really better, on which account the people, many of them, are strongly attached to him, (though it is most evident that he hath not any superior talent at instructing the mind, or showing the force and energy of those arguments for a religious life which are directed to in the everlasting gospel,) therefore," to meet prejudices in his favor, they give the reasons for their Testimony.

First, they charged him with "enthusiasm;" meaning by an enthusiast, "one that acts either according to dreams, or some sudden impulses and impressions upon his mind, which he fondly imagines to be from the Spirit of God, persuading and inclining him thereby to such and such actions; though he hath no proof that such persuasions or impressions are from the Holy Spirit." This they sustained by numerous quotations from his journals and other writings. Some of their proofs were unanswerable. Others were made by putting a worse construction upon his words than was necessary, though not worse, perhaps, than had been put upon them by some of his admirers. For example, they quoted from his sermon on the "Indwelling of the Spirit," the words, "to talk of any having the Spirit of God without feeling it, is really to deny the thing." This, they express their fear, "has led some to take the expression literally, and hath given great satisfaction to many an enthusiast among us since the year 1740, from the swelling of their breasts and stomachs in their religious agitations, which they have thought to be *feeling the Spirit*, in its operations on them." There is no reason to suppose that Whitefield understood the word in that sense, or to doubt that it was so understood by some of his enthusiastic followers.

They next charged him with being "an uncharitable, censorious and slanderous man." In proof, they refer to "his monstrous reflections upon the great and good Archbishop Tillotson," and quote from his Journal, where he says he was obliged to tell Commissary Garden he believed he was an unconverted man. "But what," they ask, "obliged him to tell all the world of it in his Journal?" They refer to his "reproachful reflections" on Harvard College, in his Journal, "where are observable, his rashness and his arrogance. His rashness, in publishing such a disadvantageous character of us, because somebody had so informed him. Surely he ought, if he had followed our Saviour's rule, to have had greater certainty of the truth of what he published of us to the whole world. But his arrogance is more flagrant still; that such a young man as he, should take upon him to tell what books we should allow our pupils to read. But then he goes further, when he says, of Yale College as well as ours, 'As for the universities, I believe it may be said, their light is now become darkness, darkness that may be felt.' What a deplorable state of immorality and irreligion has he hereby represented us to be in! And as this is a most wicked and libellous falsehood, (at least as to our College,) as such we charge it upon him." They finish this head of his censoriousness, by quoting what he had said of the clergy; that he was "persuaded the generality of preachers talk of an unknown, unfelt Christ;" and "Many, nay, most that preach, I fear, do not experimentally know Christ." In view of these things, they pronounce him "an uncharitable, censorious, and slanderous man; guilty of gross breaches of the ninth commandment of the moral law, and an evident disregard to the laws of Christian charity, as they are delivered to us in the New Testament. And now," they ask, "is it possible that we should not look upon him as the blamable cause of all the quarrels on account of religion, which the churches are now engaged in? And this, not only on account of his own behaviour, but also as the coming in of those hot men* amongst us afterwards, (who, together with the exhorters that accompanied them, cultivated the same uncharitable disposition in our churches,) was wholly owing to his influence and example."

They next bear testimony against him as "a deluder of the people," in the affair of contributions for the orphan house. He had made the people believe, that the orphans were to be under his own immediate instruction, and encouraged them to expect that some of them would in time preach the gospel to the people here, or to their children, and this made them willing to contribute; but "he has scarce been there for these four years; and besides, hath left the care of

* "The Tennents," Philip says, in his "Life and Times of Whitefield;" but only one Tennent came, and he was not accompanied by exhorters. The allusion is not to Tennent, but to such men as Davenport, and Croswell, and Buel, and others of less character, who are deservedly forgotten.

them with a person whom these contributors know nothing of, and we ourselves have reason to believe, is little better than a Quaker." This person was Barber, Davenport's early friend, who met Whitefield at Newport. They thought him "little better than a Quaker," because he followed impressions instead of the written word of God. They pronounced Whitefield's account of disbursements unsatisfactory, because several charges of large amount were "for sundries, no mention being made therein what the sum was expended for, nor to whom it was paid."

Such were their objections against the man. They also bore testimony "against his manner of preaching."

First, they thought his extempore manner of preaching "by no means proper," because extempore preachers are, of necessity, less instructive, the greater part of the sermon being commonly "the same kind of harangue which they have often used before, — so that this is a most lazy manner" of preaching; and because it exposes the preacher to utter rash expressions, and even dangerous errors, as Whitefield had done in several instances, probably from that cause.

"But lastly," they say, "we think it our duty to bear our strongest testimony against that itinerant way of preaching, which this gentleman was the first promoter of amongst us, and still delights to continue in. — Now, by an itinerant preacher, we understand one that hath no particular charge of his own, but goes about from country to country, or from town to town in any country, and stands ready to preach to any congregation that shall call him to it. And such an one is Mr. Whitefield; for it is but trifling for him to say, as we hear he hath, that he requires, in order to his preaching anywhere, that the minister also should invite him to it; for he knows the populace have such an itch after him, that when they greatly desire it, the minister (however diverse from theirs his own sentiments may be) will always be in the utmost danger of his people's quarrelling with, if not departing from him, should he not consent to their impetuous desires." An itinerant, too, must be an exciting preacher, or he would not find employment; and when he has excited the passions of his hearers, can instil into them almost any doctrine he is pleased to broach, however erroneous; as had been done by the itinerants who followed Whitefield, "and thrust themselves into towns and parishes, to the destruction of all peace and order." "But which is worse, and is the natural effect of these things, the people have thence been ready to despise their own ministers; and their usefulness among them, in too many places, hath been almost destroyed." Nor could Mr. Whitefield pretend that he was acting in the scriptural office of an evangelist; though he seemed to prepare the way for it, where, in his journal of his voyage to England after his former visit, he said, "God seems to show me it is my duty to evangelize, and not to fix in any particular place." For, they argue, "the duty of that officer certainly was not to go preaching, of his own head, from one church to another, where officers were already settled, and the gospel fully and faithfully preached;" and to suppose that such an officer was needed to labor among churches supplied with faithful and able pastors, would be to suppose that Christ, through incapacity or unfaithfulness, had failed to appoint the necessary officers in the ministry.

They conclude, by recommending to pastors, "to advise with each other in their several Associations, and consider whether it be not high time to make a stand against the mischiefs which we have here suggested as coming upon the churches."—This was signed by the President and whole Faculty.

What the greater part of the Faculty thought of the revival at first, is not known. Wigglesworth, Hollis Professor of Divinity, was a thorough Calvinist, and probably favored it. The feelings of the President, Holyoke, were unequivocally expressed in his Convention sermon,* May 28, 1741. "And though religion is still in fashion with us, yet it is evident that the power of it is greatly decayed. Indeed, those two pious and valuable men of God,† who have been laboring more abundantly among us, have been greatly instrumental, in the hands of God, to revive this blessed work; and many, no doubt, have been savingly converted from the error of their ways, many more have been convicted, and all have been in some measure roused from their lethargy. But the power of religion had been greatly weakened, and hath for a long time been too much in show and profession only." He had then seen the revival in progress for more than eight

* O. S. Ch. Lib.

† "Mr. Whitefield and Mr. Tennent," is Prince's marginal annotation.

months. He had also read Whitefield's Journal, and alludes to what he said of the College, in these words: "I can, from my own examination of things, assure this venerable assembly that that society hath not deserved the aspersions which have of late been made upon it, either as to the principles there prevalent, or the books there read; and though such as have given out a disadvantageous report of us in these respects, I doubt not, have done it in a godly jealousy for the churches of Christ, that are to be supplied from us, yet, blessed be God, they are at least mistaken herein; nor has that society been in so happy a state as to these things, from the time that I was first acquainted with the principles there, which must be allowed to be the space of four or five and thirty years at least, as it is at this day."

These passages show, that Holyoke did not sign this "Testimony" because he was a "a cold man," or an enemy to the revival, or out of revenge for Whitefield's remarks on the College. Those remarks, though he felt their injustice, he forgave, in consideration of the good motive which he ascribed to their author, whom he still regarded as a "pious and valuable man of God." The secret of his change can be explained.

When Whitefield first arrived at Boston, he came at the invitation of several of the leading pastors and others, to labor a few weeks with them and for them. This kind of "itinerancy," if it might be called by that name, had always been practised and approved in New England. It continued to be practised, without objection, during this revival, by Edwards and others. After Whitefield's return to England, he published the declaration already quoted from his Journal: "God seems to show me it is my duty to evangelize, and not to fix in any particular place." At first, partiality for its author prevented any unfavorable interpretation of this language; but experience at length taught the public what it meant. The evangelizing was to be performed, not in regions where Christ had not been named, or where there was a destitution of the means of grace, but among old and established churches, even if supplied with able and faithful pastors. A divine command to evangelize in such places, evidently implied a divine command to pastors and people in such places, to welcome his evangelical labors; so that whenever he should come, none could refuse him without being guilty of rebellion against God. Whitefield may not have been fully aware of the import of his claim ; but Davenport and his associates understood it, and felt equally sure that God had called them also to evangelize in the same style. They went forth accordingly, and demanded admission into churches where they had not been invited. If the pastor refused to welcome them, they appealed at once to his people, denounced him as an enemy of the work of God and a child of the devil, who was leading them blindfold to hell, and called upon them to separate from him. Regard for ecclesiastical order being thus trampled under foot, there was nothing to hinder laymen from receiving and obeying the same "impressions." A swarm of unordained exhorters accompanied and followed the ordained itinerants, and penetrated into still other parishes and neighbourhoods, spreading enthusiasm and confusion wherever they went. And for all this, both the itinerants and exhorters quoted Whitefield's authority. This led to a reconsideration of the whole subject. It was found that Whitefield's language and conduct would bear the construction which his enthusiastic friends had put upon them. His extravagant commendations of Davenport were remembered. His regard for dreams and impulses were called to mind. And then, he was a clergyman of the Church of England, and could not be supposed to have any special regard for Congregational church order. Though he must have been informed of the disorders committed under the sanction of his name, he had never denounced them, or authorized any of his correspondents to do it for him ; and since his return, though frequently called upon to speak, he preserved an unbroken silence, and even allowed the "Christian History" to announce, that he intended to take no part in any of these controversies. From all this, many inferred that he approved the disorders that had been committed, and would labor to promote them ; and others believed that they grew naturally out of faults of which he had been guilty, so that he was, in an important sense, "the blamable cause" of their occurrence ; and that, as he intended to continue the practice of the same faults, his labors would promote the same evils.

The next publication, January 3, 1745, was a letter from the Rev. Nathanael Henchman, pastor of the First Church in Lynn, to the Rev. Stephen Chase, of Lynn End, giving his reasons for declining to admit Mr. Whitefield into his pulpit.* Though the work of an individual merely, it deserves notice, as a specimen of the thorough-going opposers of the revival. He speaks of the time, as one " wherein were never more lectures, prayers and sermons, with high pretences to extraordinary light and devotion, and, it may be feared, never less vital religion. I confess, Sir," he says, " it is not a little satisfaction to me, that, while I am a sorrowful spectator of the divisions, separations and confusions which took their origin from this gentleman, I have never timorously secreted myself, nor betrayed the cause of Christ, by giving place to strolling itinerants and swarms of mean animals called exhorters, who are protected by their notorious ignorance and brazen impudence, with the countenance of some." His first objection against Whitefield was, his want of good standing in the Church of England, where he had not settled his affair with Commissary Garden, and where many refused him their pulpits. The second was, his " slanderous treatment of our colleges." The third was, " the insufferable pride and vanity of the man, with his intemperate, glowing zeal. Who ever equalled him in vain-glorious boasting ! — How frequently doth he publish his peculiar intimacy with heaven !" Fourthly, " his sermons are mostly one set of expressions, from variable texts, addressed more to the passions than the nobler powers of the reasonable mind ; which, if gravely delivered by another, Mr. Whitefield's admirers would not account fit to entertain Christians." Fifthly, " his frequent changing sides, — (in one country he is a true son of the Church of England, in a second a staunch Presbyterian, and in a third, a strong Congregationalist,) is one argument with me, that his honesty is not to be relied on." — "Sixthly, his listening to dreams, impulses, impressions, inward feelings and secret whispers, as though religion was all extasy, is dangerous to the church of God." — " Seventhly, his industrious and officious crowding himself into other men's labors, I account a great disorder. Had he a special commission from God, to be a universal and general visitor of the whole church militant, and Christ's vicegerent to determine all ecclesiastical matters, and could he prove his mission and produce his credentials, the case would be different. But sure

* O. S. Ch. Lib.

I am, our Bible knows no such spiritual overseer and surveyor-general of the churches; nor will his pretences to uncommon sanctity, and fancying he is exalted above the ordinary clergy, convince the world that Christ hath subjected all his ministers to Mr. Whitefield's authority, and by him to be killed and made alive at pleasure." — Eighthly, he suspected that Whitefield came to prosecute two grand designs. The first was, "to make a purse for himself, by begging with great solemnity for his poor little ones at the orphan house in Georgia, — the most ill projected scheme since darkness was on the face of the deep, to found an orphan house in an infant and expiring colony, and in the heart of an enemy's country; though it answered well his mendicant intention." This design he inferred, partly from his neglecting to publish a full account of his disbursements, though often called upon to do it. In the postscript, written after the account had been published, he objected to it, because he "omitted saying for what and to whom large sums had been paid, and hath offered no vouchers," so that the whole was merely "an abuse on mankind." And he inferred the same design "partly from his preaching mostly in our large towns, and slighting the lesser parishes, where souls are as precious, but ready money not so plenty." The second grand design imputed to Whitefield was, "to raze the foundation of our churches, and change the religion of New England." This design, "to destroy our ecclesiastical constitution," was inferred "from his striking immediately, and with a bold face, at our standing regular ministry, without regard to their public character and extensive usefulness. — Had Mr. Whitefield been employed by a secret hand behind the curtain, I cannot readily conceive he could have embraced a more probable method to subvert our church constitution." As to the pleas, that Whitefield had done much good, and that he was changed for the better, Henchman replied: "I scruple his having done good, but as God may have brought good out of evil; and at the same time, I believe God hath permitted him to do vastly more evil than good. Nor can I look upon Mr. Whitefield as changed for the better, while the Separatists are sweetly hugged by him, and he continues in the neglect, as hitherto he hath done, of what the plain laws of Christ require of him; to repair, to the utmost of his power, in a plain, explicit and public manner, the great injuries he hath offered to religion, to our colleges, and the character of many valuable gentlemen with us; and as an honest and upright clergyman of the Church of England, that he make his peace at home, and steadily adhere and preach agreeable to the Thirty-nine Articles, which, he saith, he proved true from the word of God, before he subscribed them." To "make his peace at home" as the Church of England then was, Whitefield must have preached baptismal regeneration, and justification by decent morals; and nothing but that, or something equally quieting, would have satisfied Henchman.*

Next came "The Sentiments and Resolution of an Association of Ministers, convened at Weymouth, January 15, 1745, concerning the Rev. Mr. George Whitefield."† It is in a better spirit, or at least in a better style, than any of the preceding, and has some additional thoughts. Having declared their concurrence with the Faculty of Harvard College and the three Associations already mentioned, in the articles exhibited against Mr. Whitefield," they add: "Whatever charity may prompt us to think of the honesty of his design, yet we cannot but disapprove of him as an itinerant preacher. We know not any such officer appointed by Christ, the Head of the church, nor what warrant Mr. Whitefield can plead, besides his own impulses and impressions, for his acting in that capacity." They bear testimony "against his enthusiastic spirit," and then proceed to notice some things that had occurred lately. One was, "Mr. Whitefield's conduct with respect to those

* The History of the First Church in Lynn is instructive. Its quiet, if it had ever been disturbed, became as profound as Henchman himself could wish. It was perfectly free from "intemperate, glowing zeal." It was agitated by no feeling about religion that could cause the least disturbance. As a consequence, there was no anxiety about soundness of doctrine, but rather a disposition to receive without questioning the most quieting doctrines that could be preached. The quiet grew deeper and deeper, under a succession of Unitarian ministers, till there were but three male members in the church, and the people were left without a pastor, because there was not feeling enough about religion to raise a minister's salary. While thus destitute, some theological students from Andover visited them, and occasionally performed such labors as the rules of the Seminary permit. The agitating doctrines of grace soon began to produce feeling. Increasing numbers began to care about religion. At length, by the aid of the Massachusetts Missionary Society, an Orthodox pastor was settled, under whom the quiet of others still was disturbed, and the church grew, till they were again able to support a pastor without aid. The minutes of the General Association for 1840 inform us, that it has 166 members, of whom 42 are males, and 250 children and youth in Sabbath School and Bible Class.

† O. S. Ch. Library.

persons who cry out in the public assemblies, and are supposed to be religiously affected by the preaching of the word. This gentleman has said, in one of his journals, that 'he believes these things come from the devil.' Accordingly at his first preaching in Boston, in this visit, he spake openly to a woman that cried out, desired her to refrain, and added, that 'such things are not for the glory of God.' And several times since, he has in words borne testimony against this disturbance, calling it a stratagem of Satan. But it has been observed, especially while he was preaching in the country towns, that upon such an incident he would at once raise his voice, as if he was trying to vie with them in screaming ; and by these means others are affected in the like manner, and the cry waxes louder and louder, till the assembly is thrown into confusion ; and afterwards a pompous account is published to the world, of the power of God, and the visible tokens of his presence in that congregation. — And how much worse is it, if at such a time public thanks have been given to God for the effects of his power and grace, before he has had any opportunity to converse with the persons thus affected, to know their state of mind." — They were "surprised and grieved," that he, a priest of the Church of England, should administer the Lord's Supper in Congregational churches. — They testified against his preaching, "as having a tendency to promote a spirit of bitterness. He is often crying out of persecution ; and has said, that if it were not for the restraints of human laws, the streets would run down with the blood of the saints. At the same time the people think, and perhaps are taught to think, that few or none are saints, but those who adhere to him and his cause. What must be the effect of this, but to raise the most virulent enmity and malice in the hearts of his followers, against those who are called opposers, and to dispose them to treat one another as the most inveterate enemies ? " — They condemn his practice of singing hymns in the public roads, when riding from town to town; and finally remark, that in almost every town where he had preached, the consequence had been, more or less alienation between the minister and people ; sometimes the minister and sometimes the people being for him, and the other against him ; whence came contention, and the obstruction of the pastor's usefulness. "Wherefore," they say, "we now declare, each one for himself, that we cannot with a good conscience, and therefore will not, directly nor indirectly, encourage Mr. Whitefield to preach, either publicly or privately, in our respective parishes."

Of themselves they say : "We are free to acknowledge that some of us, a few years ago, pleased ourselves with the hopeful prospect of an happy state of the church. But, alas, the many sad effects of an enthusiastic, erroneous and divisive spirit, which have appeared since, chiefly promoted by Mr. Whitefield's itinerancy, and the other gentlemen who followed his steps, now afford a melancholy proof that this judgment was formed too suddenly, and upon too weak evidence. Whatever pleasing scenes the fancies of any of us might then paint to ourselves or others, yet now we are all filled with fearful apprehensions, from the black and thick cloud which hangs over our churches, and threatens their ruin, unless the Sun of Righteousness mercifully appears to dissipate it." They then exhort all "to examine, how far they have been accessory to the present difficulties and confusions," and "beg that none may mistake a party spirit for the spirit of the gospel, or imagine that religion consists in either an obstinate attachment or violent opposition to Mr. Whitefield."

This was signed by Samuel Niles, of Braintree, Moderator ; Nathanael Eells, of Scituate; Samuel Brown, of Abington ; Ebenezer Gay, of Hingham ; Daniel Perkins and John Angier, of Bridgewater ; John Taylor, of Milton ; Samuel Dunbar, of Stoughton ; Jonathan Bowman, of Dorchester ; William Smith, of Weymouth ; John Fowle, of Hingham ; and Philip Curtis, of Stoughton. They were, as their own statement implies, of different opinions concerning the revival from the first, and in all probability, differed now concerning its character at the beginning. Eells and Fowle were signers of the Testimony of July, 1743. Perkins invited Tennent to his pulpit in 1741, which was a principal means of promoting the revival in Bridgewater. The cautious part acted by Eells, as moderator of the General Convention in 1743,* shows something of his views ; and he soon found occasion to express them very definitely. To counteract the influence of all these testimonies against Whitefield, the names of the signers of the Testimony of July 1743 were published in the newspapers, as witnesses to his great usefulness.

* See Chaper XVI.

Eells explained himself thus, in the Evening Post of February 4: "I have been, and still am, of the opinion that there hath been, in several towns in New England, within a few years past, a great revival of religion; but never was of the opinion, that 'Mr. Whitefield was, under God, the principal means' of reviving it. — Possibly he may have been an instrument of doing good to some particular persons that have heard him; but, according to the best observation that I have been capable of making, I never found reason to think that God made him the principal means of its revival. He hath, if I am not much mistaken, been the means of much censoriousness, confusion and disorder, in one place and another; and I verily believe that God, in judgment, and not in mercy to this people, hath sent him again into this country."

To the publication of this Association was added a note, in which the Rev. Messrs. Nehemiah Walter, of the First Church in Roxbury; James Allen, of the church in Brookline; and Nathanael Walter, of the Second Church in Roxbury, express their approbation of what had been published by the College Faculty and the three Associations; and their determination not to invite Mr. Whitefield, or any other itinerant, into their pulpits. Nehemiah Walter was the venerable Puritan, the successor of Eliot, whom Whitefield visited at Roxbury, soon after his first arrival at Boston. According to his Journal, the interview was highly satisfactory to both. Allen of Brookline signed the Testimony of July, 1743, and sent an account of the revival among his people to Cooper, which was published in the "Christian History."

It was impossible for Whitefield to keep silence, as he had intended. He had inflicted injuries, which justice required him to repair; and while he neglected it, his enemies took advantage of the neglect, and good men were becoming disaffected. His private correspondence shows what he thought of the charges against him. January 18, he wrote to a friend: "Some occasions of offence had undoubtedly been given whilst I was here and preached up and down the country. Nothing, however, appeared, but a pure divine power, working upon, converting and transforming people's hearts of all ranks, without any extraordinary phenomena attending it. Good Mr. Tennent succeeded me. Numbers succeeded him. Lecture upon lecture was set up in various places. One minister called to another to help drag the gospel net. And by all accounts I can have from private information, or good Mr. Prince's weekly History, one would have imagined the millennium was coming indeed. But in this mixed state of things, wild fire will necessarily blend itself with the pure fire that comes from God's altar. This the enemy long waited for. At last, it broke out and spread itself, and it must be confessed, by the instrumentality of many good souls, both among clergy and laity, who, mistaking fancy for faith, and imagination for revelation, were guilty of great imprudence. All is laid to me, as being the *primum mobile ;* though there was not so much as the appearance of any thing of this nature, when I left New England last." February 19, he wrote : " Some unguarded expressions, in the heat of less experienced youth, I certainly did drop. I was too precipitate in hearkening to and publishing private information, and, Peter-like, cut off too many ears." This is certainly not very far from the truth. Yet there is reason to suspect that he still thought too favorably of the " disorders" and their authors. In a letter dated February 6, he informs a friend, that " the high sheriff, who was once most foremost in persecuting the good Mr. Davenport," was " a little convinced." Davenport, at that time, would hardly have called his treatment at Boston, persecution. His " Retractation " was dated July 28, 1744.

Whitefield began by publishing a letter to Dr. Chauncy, dated November 19, 1744, and written while he was sick at Portsmouth. In his " preface to the reader," dated January 18, 1745, he says, " I should have published it much sooner, had I not hoped that the manner and method of my preaching would, by the blessing of God, have rendered it needless. But being called upon from different quarters to give an account of my conduct and some part of my writings, I now think it my duty to publish the letter."

It was in reply to some parts of Chauncy's " Seasonable Thoughts on the State of Religion." Its temper, Chauncy, in his answer, dated January 31, acknowledged to be unexceptionable, though its substance failed to remove his objections.

Chauncy's leading objection was against itinerant preaching. " This," he said, " had its rise, at least in these parts, from Mr. Whitefield ; though I could never see, I own, upon what warrant, either from Scripture or reason, he went about preaching from one province and parish to another, where the gospel was already preached, and by persons as well qualified for the work as he can pretend to be." Whitefield replied: "But did I come unasked? Nay, did not some of those very persons who were as well qualified for the work as I can pretend to be, send me letters of invitation? Yes, assuredly they did, or otherwise, in all probability, I had never seen New England." This was certainly a sufficient justification of his first visit, if he came merely as an invited minister, to render occasional assistance to those who requested it; but it did not touch the question, by what warrant he set up as an itinerant for life. On this point, he only referred to a former promise to inform the world at some future time, how he "was led out into" his "present way of acting." Chauncy had intimated, that Whitefield's itinerating had not been to his temporal disadvantage. "He has certainly made large collections; and if, in doing this, he had a fellow-feeling with the orphans, it is no more than might be expected." Whitefield understood "fellow-feeling" to mean "fellow-sharing," of such a kind as would prove him "a consummate villain." He felt hurt by this imputation upon his honesty, and pronounced it "ungentleman-like, as well as uncharitable." Chauncy, in return, felt hurt by this interpretation of his words, and protested that such a thought never entered into his heart. Chauncy, though incapable of appreciating such a man as Whitefield, was too good a judge of character to suspect him of intentional dishonesty. Another charge was, that "the spirit of rash, censorious and uncharitable judging" of ministers "first appeared in Mr. Whitefield, who seldom preached but he had something or other to say against unconverted ministers." He replied, "Was there any harm in this? Are not unconverted ministers the bane of the Christian church?" It did not occur to him, that preaching against that "bane" in almost every sermon, implied that the bane was very plenty, and that a great deal of such preaching was needed; in other words, that he thought a great part of the ministers unconverted, and the people willing to have it so. Of the offensive sentence near the close of his New England Journal,—"Many, perhaps most that preach, I fear, do not experimentally know Christ,"—he said: "I confess, this was too unguarded; for whether in fact it was true or not, that most that preach in

New England did not experimentally know Christ, yet I ought to have taken more time before I delivered my judgment. I thank you, Rev. Sir, for pointing out this fault to me. But that I had a design, either in preaching or writing, to alienate people's minds from their standing ministers, I utterly disavow. My whole design in preaching was, to show the unspeakable danger of persons taking upon them to preach Christ to others, till they are acquainted with him themselves; and in my writings, to give an impartial account, as far as I was informed, how affairs which concern the kingdom of God, stood in New England." This is doubtless an honest account of the matter, as it lay in his own mind. But to many, it was not satisfactory. They could not believe that so eloquent a man could be so short-sighted. They thought he must have designed to produce the effects which followed so naturally from his words. But this was a topic, on which universal satisfaction ought not to have been given. There were those whom nothing would satisfy, but an abandonment and condemnation of the truth.

Of his treatment of Archbishop Tillotson, Whitefield said: "I acknowledge that I spoke of his person in too strong terms, and too rashly condemned his state, when I ought only to have censured his doctrine." As to his regard to impulses and impressions, he showed that some passages quoted from his writings admitted a safer sense than had been ascribed to them; but it was plain from his arguments, that his views were not, even yet, entirely correct.

Next, and before this could have gone into circulation, came a pamphlet containing the Testimony of an Association convened at Marlborough, January 22, 1745, and that of a number of ministers in the County of Bristol. These were in a worse spirit than any public body had yet exhibited. The first endorses the Testimony from Harvard College, and that of "some of our Rev. fathers and brethren in the ministry." It denies, that Whitefield had "come with another spirit than before," as he still adhered to the same errors, and as he published no confession of his faults. It was signed by John Prentice, of Lancaster; Israel Loring, of Sudbury; Job Cushing, of Shrewsbury; John Gardner, of Stow; William Cooke, of Sudbury; Nathan Stone, of Southborough; John Swift, of Acton; Aaron Smith, of Marlborough; Ebenezer Morse, of Shrewsbury; Thomas

Goss, of Bolton; Elisha Marsh, of Narraganset, No. 2; Joseph Davis, of Holden, and John Mellen of Lancaster.

The other is remarkable only for this passage: "When Mr. Whitefield first came among us, he used his utmost craft and cunning, to strike the passions and engage the affections of the people; and when he had wrought them up into a fond opinion of his excellencies, and they began to look upon him as one endowed with an uncommon measure of the Spirit, he continued to insinuate that unconverted ministers could do little or no good to souls; that dead men might as well beget living children. Having thus prepared the way, he leaves the country with this most vile insinuation: 'That many, nay, most that preach, I fear, do not experimentally know Christ, and the universities are become dark, darkness in the abstract.' Well, what is the language of all this? He that runs may read. Dead men may as well beget living children, as an unconverted minister do good to souls. The most of your ministers are unconverted. You must, then, if you have any regard to your souls, separate from them, and seek better help. But what will you do? You can't have any help from the colleges. *There* is nothing but darkness,—darkness that may be felt. You must then content yourselves with some illiterate exhorters, until you can have a supply from the Shepherd's Tent, the Orphan House, or elsewhere. It appeareth to us, that the devil, with all his cunning, could not take a more direct step to overthrow these churches, hurt religion and the souls of men." This was signed by Joseph Avery, of Norton; John Greenwood and David Turner, of Rehoboth; Ebenezer White, of Norton; Solomon Townsend, of Barrington; and John Burt, of Bristol. No proof has been found that any whose names are on these papers, were ever friends of the revival.

This, so far as appears, was the last of the associated ministerial Testimonies against Whitefield, as well as the least creditable to its authors. The number of pastors who signed them was sixty-three. Of these, nine are known to have been early friends and promoters of the revival, and it is probable that others were on the same side; but concerning the early sentiments of the greater part of the sixty-three, there is no proof, while it is certain that some of them were opposers from the beginning.

The next day, January 23, 1745, was the date of Whitefield's reply to the Faculty of Harvard College. It is one of his most finished productions of the kind, and that on which he mainly relied for the defence of his conduct in New England.

In defending himself against the charge of enthusiasm, he is partially, and but partially, successful; for, while he had never been so bad as they represented him, he was not yet wholly recovered from his early mistakes. He justifies what he had said of Archbishop Tillotson's works; but says, "This does not prove that I cast reflections, which you call monstrous, upon Archbishop Tillotson, as to his personal character." How this is to be reconciled with his previous concession to Dr. Chauncy, that he had done wrong in judging "his state and person," he does not explain. He asks whether what he wrote of the College, was not true when he wrote it; says, that he had no idea of representing their character to be so bad as they seemed to understand, but only that there had been a great religious declension, such as the President, in his Convention sermon, acknowledged to prevail throughout the land. He adds: "However, I am sorry I published my private informations, though from credible persons, concerning the colleges, to the world;" and assured them he should be glad to find that the President's testimony, in his Convention sermon the next spring, was correct. Whitefield's testimony concerning his own meaning is to be admitted. Yet, if he meant in his Journal, only what he asserts in this explanation, his language was blamably strong, and naturally had the effect of slander. And yet it is certain, from the testimony of Edwards and other contemporary evidence, that the colleges did need admonition. Some, well acquainted at Cambridge, asserted that Whitefield's statements were none too strong. The fact, that two of the Faculty had lately been deposed for gross immorality, was quoted as evidence on both sides; by one, as evidence that immorality was found there, and by the other, as evidence that it was not allowed. Both inferences were probably correct.

As to the orphan house, Whitefield asked, could it be proved that the contributions made for its support, were not faithfully applied for that purpose? Did he promise to be always there? And if providentially absent more than he expected, could he help it? And did the people know nothing of Barber, who was with him in his tour through New England; and who, whatever might have been reported of him, was a good man? The published accounts, he said, were satisfactory to the contributors; and indeed, they would have been satisfied without any, for they had confidence in his honesty. But did the Faculty ever see any that were more particular? Were those of the Society for Propagating the Gospel more so? If money were entrusted to them, for the College, would they publish a more particular account? Here, Whitefield judged incorrectly. His account was, as his enemies said, "general and lumping," not audited, and without vouchers,—such as ought to satisfy none, except those who had other reasons for confidence in his honesty. It was much more severely handled in Scotland, than here.

Extempore preaching, he decidedly preferred to any other. Yet he did not preach, or pretend to preach, without previous study. His sermons cost him as much previous labor, as if they were written; so that this way was not a lazy manner of preaching. The dangerous errors, which they said he had uttered, were mere slips of the tongue, and had been retracted as soon as he was informed of them.

Itinerancy he defended, as scriptural and right. Understanding an evangelist to be, what they say an itinerant is, "one that hath no particular charge of his own, but goes about from country to country, or from town to town in any country, and stands ready to preach to any congregation that shall call him to it." For the divine command, "Go ye into all the world, and preach the gospel to every creature," he argued, "authorizes the ministers of Christ, even to the end of the world, to preach the gospel in every town and country, though not 'of their own head,' yet whenever and wherever Providence should open a door, even though it should be in a place 'where officers are already settled, and the gospel is fully and faithfully preached.' This, I humbly apprehend, is every gospel minister's indisputable privilege." He asked, "Was not the Reformation began and carried on by itinerant preaching? Were not Knox" and other reformers, "itinerant preachers?" He then quoted from the appendix to Baxter's Reformed Pastor, a plan which had been adopted in some parts of England, for circular lectures, by settled ministers selected for the purpose, and with the consent of the pastors. As to the "hot men" that came after him, he knew not who they were, and ought not to be held accountable for their conduct. He then quoted from Holyoke's Convention sermon, and from their Testimony itself, evidence that his labors had been useful. His eloquent conclusion must be given entire.

"Gentlemen, I profess myself a Calvinist as to principle, and preach no other doctrines than those which your pious ancestors and the founders of Harvard College preached long before I was born. And I am come to New England with no intention to meddle with, much less to destroy, the New England churches, or turn out the generality of their ministers, or settle them with ministers from England, Scotland or Ireland, as hath been hinted in a late letter written by the Rev. Mr. Clapp, Rector of Yale College. Such a thought never entered my heart; neither, as I know of, has my preaching the least tendency thereunto. I am determined to know nothing among you, but Jesus Christ and him crucified. I have no intention of setting up a party for myself, or to stir up people against their pastors. Had not illness prevented, I had some weeks ago departed out of your coasts. But as it is not a season of the year for me to undertake a very long journey, and I have reason to think the great God blesses my poor labors, I think it my duty to comply with the invitations that are sent me, and, as I am enabled, to be instant in season and out of season, and to preach among poor sinners the unsearchable riches of Christ. This indeed I delight in. It is my meat and my drink. This I think I may do, as a minister of the King of kings, and a subject of his present Majesty, King George, upon whose royal head I pray God the crown may long flourish. And as I have a right to preach, so, I humbly apprehend, the people, as Christians, as men, and New England men in particular, have a right to invite and hear. If the pulpits should be shut, blessed be God, the fields are open, and I can go without the camp, bearing the Redeemer's sacred reproach. This I am used to, and glory in; believing that if I suffer for it, I shall suffer for righteousness' sake. At the same time I desire to be humbled, and ask public pardon for any rash words I have dropped, or any thing I have written or done amiss. This leads me also to ask forgiveness, Gentlemen, if I have done you or your society any wrong. Be pleased to accept unfeigned thanks for all tokens of respect you showed me when here last. And if you have injured me in the Testimony you have published against me and my conduct, (as I think, to say no more, you really have,) it is already forgiven, without asking."

This by no means satisfied the Faculty. It was soon answered by Prof. Wigglesworth; and even as late as November, 1754, when Whitefield was again in the country, and preached at Cambridge, Wigglesworth followed his preaching with two lectures, on "The Ordinary and Extraordinary Ministers of the Church," in which, and in the notes appended, the same doctrines are advanced and the same charges are brought as in the Testimony; and what is still more, the charges of bad intentions, brought by the Faculty of Yale College, are endorsed. Yet his persevering kindness was at length acknowledged. In 1764, he solicited donations of books for their library, lately destroyed by fire. Four years afterwards, while Holyoke was still President, the following minute was entered on their records:

"At a meeting of the President and Fellows of Harvard College, August 22, 1768, the Rev. G. Whitefield having, in addition to his former kindness to Harvard College, lately presented to the library a new edition of his Journals, and having procured large benefactions from several benevolent and respectable gentlemen; *Voted*, that the thanks of the Corporation be given to the Rev. Mr. Whitefield, for these instances of candor and generosity."

The "Declaration" of the Faculty of Yale College was dated February 25, 1745. After endorsing the Testimonies of the Faculty of Harvard College and of four Associations near Boston, they "think it proper more largely to insist upon two things."

"First, it has always appeared to us, that you and other itinerants have laid a scheme to turn the generality of ministers out of their places, and to introduce a new set, of such as should be in a peculiar manner attached to you; and this you would effect by prejudicing the minds of people against their ministers, and thereby induce them to discard them or separate from them. And this appears to us, I. Because the principles which you and the other itinerants laid down, did naturally and necessarily produce this effect; which are these:

"1. That the generality of ministers are unconverted. 2. That all unconverted ministers are half beasts and half devils, and can no more be the means of any man's conversion, than a dead man can beget living children. — Upon the publication of these principles, people are filled with the greatest prejudices against their ministers, and a multitude of separations immediately and necessarily followed.

"II. This consequence, that people should discard or separate from their ministers, not only necessarily and in fact follows from the foregoing principles, but it was also intended and designed. These two principles, that the generality of ministers are unconverted, and that they are such baneful and pernicious men as you have declared, when discharged among the multitude, and received into their minds, do as naturally and necessarily tend to make them discard their ministers, as a brace of bullets discharged into their hearts has to take away their natural lives. It is utterly inconceivable to us, that men should from time to time zealously propagate such principles, and yet never design or think that they should have any such effect."

They quote his solemn declarations to Dr. Chauncy and the Faculty of Harvard College, that he had no such design; but they tell him plainly that they do not believe him, and that fairness and consistency require him freely to own his design. Then they infer, that if all unconverted ministers are to be discarded, a new supply must be introduced. This supply cannot come from the colleges, because "the light in them is but darkness." It must therefore consist either of exhorters, or foreigners.

"You publicly told the people in New England, that they might expect, in a little time, some supply from your orphan house; and you told the Rev. Mr. Edwards, of Northampton, that you intended to bring over a number of young men from England, to be ordained by the Tennents. Whether any were to come from Scotland or Ireland, we think, is not material. And it has been the constant practice of the Tennents, and their Presbytery, of late years, to send ministers to supply the separations in New England; particularly Messrs. Finley, Sacket, Blair, Treat, and sundry others, to preach to the separations at Milford, New Haven, &c., and some of them showed written orders for it, from that Presbytery. Yea, so violently were they engaged to supply us with their ministers, that they would do it in direct opposition to the civil and ecclesiastical government. Thus the scheme appears to us evident in every part of it, both from the principles you have laid down, and by the constant endeavours from time to time to put it in practice."

The other thing which they thought proper "more largely to insist upon," was his supposed "scheme to vilify and subvert our colleges, and to introduce a set of ministers into our churches by other ways and means of education." In proof of this, they quote his description of the state of the colleges, and Gilbert Tennent's assertion, that the public academies were "corrupted," and recommendation of private seminaries, "under the care of skilful and experienced Christians." They assert, that "soon after the publication of these slanders upon the colleges, this was upon several accounts in a worse state than it was before. Sundry of the students ran into enthusiastic errors and disorders, censured and reviled their governors and others; for which some were expelled, denied their degrees, or otherwise punished; and some withdrew to that thing called "The Shepherd's Tent."*

* Backus, (Eccl. Hist. N. E. Vol. II. page 145,) after giving an account of Davenport's arrest in Connecticut, his examination at Hartford, and his expulsion from the colony, adds: — "Separations were hereby caused at New London, New Haven, and Milford." "And it was impressed on sundry minds, that they must go forth their way, and erect a Shepherd's Tent at New London, to educate persons in for the ministry. Such a school was therefore opened, to which a number resorted, wherein Allen presided." This Allen was the same who had been censured for comparing the Bible to an old almanac.

They quote another of his solemn disclaimers in his letter to Dr. Chauncy, say plainly that they do not believe it, and conclude by exhorting ministers and churches to avoid him, as one of those that "cause divisions and offences."

Meanwhile, Whitefield was preaching at Boston, and making excursions in the vicinity. The Evening Post of March 11, said, "Prince, Webb, Foxcroft and Gee are the directors of Mr. Whitefield's public conduct, as he himself has lately declared at Newbury." He had other powerful friends among the clergy, and still more among the laity, who invited him by vote into some pulpits, where the pastors were "shy" of him. His friends in Boston offered to build for him "the largest place of worship ever seen in America," but he declined. Lectures were proposed at six o'clock in the morning. He complied, and had audiences of two or three thousands. There were "movings" and "meltings" under his preaching as formerly, and some interesting cases of conversion; but there was no revival, in the present technical sense of that word. People heard, and were affected; but there was no spreading among the impenitent, as if by sympathy, or by a simultaneous impression on all, of those views which constitute conviction of sin. Nor ought any thing else to have been expected. Both ministers and people were thinking too much about the man, to profit by his preaching.

February 7, he was at Ipswich, where he spent some days. Mr. Pickering, of the Second Church, declined admitting him to his pulpit, and assigned his reasons in a letter, which was published. It contains the usual objections set forth in the various "Testimonies," and is remarkable only for one convenient metaphor. The Bishop of London had published something concerning "Lukewarmness and Enthusiasm." Whitefield had said in reply, "all ought to be thankful to that pilot, who will teach them to steer a safe and middle course." Pickering asks, "But what if the pilot should take the vane for the compass?"

Early in March, he made another excursion to the East, as far at least as Berwick, in Maine. About the middle of the month he was at Exeter. Here some of the more zealous members of the church had withdrawn, and formed a new church. As already related, their act had been sanctioned by one council, and censured by another, the last of which met in January, 1743.* Whitefield preached to them twice, though Mr. Odlin, the pastor of the church from which they had withdrawn, "solemnly warned and charged him against preaching in his parish."† In the newspaper account, those to whom he preached are called "Separatists." Odlin evidently claimed a right to control their hearing the gospel, and the Evening Post sustained his claim. The Post ‡ was the favorite organ of the party opposed to the revival. The affair throws some light on the character of the "separations," and of the complaints concerning them.

This spring the celebrated expedition against Cape Breton was undertaken. Col. Pepperell, a devoted friend and constant hearer of Whitefield, was chosen to the command. Mr. Sherburne, another of his friends, at whose house he often lodged, was appointed commissary. Sherburne said that Whitefield must favor the expedition, or the serious people would not enlist. He also requested a motto for his flag. This Whitefield refused to furnish, as it would be out of character. But Sherburne's importunity finally prevailed, and he gave, "*Nil desperandum, Christo duce*;" *Fear nothing, while Christ is leader*; upon which great numbers enlisted. Some of the "aggrieved brethren" at Chebacco, who separated from Mr. Pickering, seem to have been among the number. Whitefield preached to the troops before their departure; but he excused himself from going as their chaplain, by saying he thought he might be more useful by stirring up the people to pray for their success. In about six weeks, news came that Louisburgh had surrendered, and Whitefield preached a thanksgiving sermon for the victory. The fall of Louisburgh, "the Gibraltar of America," astonished Europe; and the boldness, the persevering energy and military talent displayed by this little army of the Colonies, in doing, without the aid they had requested, what the most able warriors thought scarce possible to be done by any force, procured the honor of knighthood for the commander, and the most lavish commendations for all engaged in the enterprise. Whatever may be thought of their views of

* Result of Council at Exeter, O. S. Ch. Lib.
† Eve. Post, March 25, 1745.
‡ "Tom Fleet's paper," as Fleet said the revivalists called it, by way of contempt.

Christian duty in respect to war, the result shows that the subjects of this great revival were not weak-minded men, even after their conversion.

After a visit to the south, Whitefield was again in Boston in July. In August, he was again at Philadelphia. He remained in the Middle and Southern Colonies, till he embarked, March 15, 1748, for Bermuda, which he left early in June for England. He visited New England again in 1754, again in 1764, and finally in 1770, when he died, on the Sabbath morning, September 30, at Newburyport, and was buried, according to his own desire, in front of the pulpit of his friend Parsons, formerly of Lyme, but now pastor of a church here, which the revival had called into existence.

An encomium on his virtues and his labors, his piety and his eloquence, would be in place here, but is needless. They are well known to all men. It is more to the purpose of this work, to transcribe the testimony which convinced the Synod of Glasgow, in Scotland, October 6, 1748 ; supposed to have been published originally by Dr. Erskine of Kirkintillock, but preserved and endorsed by Gillies.

A motion had been made, tending to prohibit or discourage ministers from employing Mr. Whitefield, and some speeches were made in its support. It was said in reply, among other things, that "with regard to his imprudences, there is a great difference between blunders owing to a bad heart, and those that are owing only to a misinformed judgment ; especially when the mistakes that occasioned them, have misled several great and good men. Whether Mr. Whitefield's scheme of an orphan house be prudent or not, it is demonstrable that it was honestly meant. The magistrates of Savannah published, three years ago, in the Philadelphia Gazette, an affidavit that they had carefully examined Mr. Whitefield's receipts and disbursements, and found that what he had collected in behalf of the orphans, had been honestly applied, and that besides, he had given considerably to them of his own property. As to his maintaining that assurance is essential to faith, encouraging an unwarrantable regard to impressions, and being too hasty in pronouncing men carnal or converted, his sentiments in these particulars have been altered for upwards of two years ; and now he scarce preaches a sermon, without guarding his hearers against relying on impressions, and telling them that faith and a persuasion that we are justified are very different things, and that a holy life is the best evidence of a gracious state. These retractions are owing to a real change of sentiment. Letters from correspondents in New England show, that this change is at least of two years' date, and that ever since it happened, he has preached and acted with remarkable caution." The motion was rejected, by a vote of forty-seven to thirteen, and such as chose to invite him into their pulpits, never afterwards met with any molestation.

This witness is true, and is confirmed by other testimony. Gillespie, of Carnock, wrote to Edwards, September 19, 1748: "I was glad to hear you write, that he [Whitefield] labored with success in New England, in rectifying mistakes he had favored, about intimations made by the Lord to his people, &c., and heartily wish he may be directed to apply an antidote here, where it is also needed." Though right in the main from the beginning of his ministry, his early errors had been great, and nowhere had they shown themselves more prominently, or produced more injurious effects, than in New England. His second visit, in 1744, was made while he was in the process of recovery from them, and was doubtless a means of hastening its completion. The perfect vindication of his character for pecuniary honesty, furnished by the magistrates of Savannah, came out in 1745, — after that visit. For the remainder of his life, the faults of his character were like the spots on the sun; detected, without much difficulty, by the cool and careful observer who takes pains to look for them; but, to all practical purposes, lost in one general and genial effulgence.

---

## CHAPTER XIX.

The Revival continued at the South. — The Presbyterian Synods. — The Rise of Presbyterianism in Virginia. — Whitefield's labors in the Southern Colonies. — The healing of the "Great Schism."

The protest of 1741,* failed entirely to answer its most important purpose, — that of preventing the intrusions of Tennent and his friends into the congregations of their op-

---

* See Chapter V.

posers. As should have been foreseen, they felt that, having been cast out of the communion of the Synod, they were no longer under any kind of ecclesiastical obligation to regard the ministerial authority of those who had excluded them; but were at perfect liberty to preach the gospel to all who might apply for it, without the least regard to the Synod or its members. The same impression was made on all who desired their labors; and on the second day after the schism, the Presbytery of New Brunswick received applications for supplies of preaching from eighteen or twenty places, most of which were beyond their bounds, and from fragments of old congregations, under the pastoral or presbyterial care of their opposers. It was resolved to send preachers to them all, as far as practicable.* They divided their Presbytery into two, which held a united meeting annually, by the name of the "Conjunct Presbytery." They were joined by several who had not been excluded by the "Protestation." It is evident from the results which appeared in subsequent years, that they continued their efforts for the diffusion of piety; though little is known of the details of their labors and success, beyond what is contained in the letters of the Tennents, Blair and Dickinson, which have been given in a preceding chapter, and their labors in Virginia, which will soon be noticed. A church was formed in Philadelphia in 1743, and Gilbert Tennent became its pastor. At its first communion, in May, 1744, the number of communicants was more than one hundred and forty, nearly all of whom were fruits of the revival.

The members of the Presbytery of New York refused, from the first, to acknowledge the legality of the Protest by which the New Brunswick brethren had been excluded from the Synod. After several vain attempts to have it set aside, they withdrew from the Synod of Philadelphia, and formed the Synod of New York, which held its first meeting at Elizabethtown, September 19, 1745. It included the Presbytery of New York, and all the members of the "Conjunct Presbytery," and was decidedly superior to the Synod of Philadelphia, not only in active piety, but in numbers, talents, and weight of character.† What the New York brethren thought of the revival, may be gathered from the fact,

* Prof. Hodge, Const. Hist. Vol. II. page 197. † Ibid. 254.

that Dickinson and Pemberton were leading members; and still further from the following passage in their Protest to the Synod of Philadelphia, May 29, 1742.

"We protest against all those passages in any of the pamphlets which have been published in these parts, which seem to reflect upon the work of divine power and grace which has been carrying on in so wonderful a manner in many of our congregations; and declare to all the world, that we look upon it to be the indispensable duty of all our ministers to encourage that glorious work, with their most faithful and diligent endeavours. And in like manner, we protest and declare against all divisive and irregular methods and practices by which the peace and good order of our churches have been broken in upon."

At their first meeting, the Rev. William Robinson was appointed to spend some months in missionary labors among the rising congregations in Virginia. As these had been brought into existence by this revival, a brief account of their origin will be in place. It is taken from a letter written, June 28, 1751, by the Rev. Samuel Davies, afterwards President of the College at Princeton, to the Rev. Mr. Bellamy of Bethlem, Ct., who had requested the information.*

"I hope I may observe without the umbrage of calumny, what glares with irresistible evidence on the eyes of the serious of all denominations among us, that religion has been, and in most parts of the colony still is, in a very low state. A surprising negligence appears in attending on public worship, and an equally surprising levity and unconcernedness in those that attend. Family religion is a rarity; and a solemn solicitude about eternal things is still a greater. Vices of various kinds are triumphant, and even a form of godliness is not common. The clergy universally, as far as my intelligence extends, have embraced the modish system of Arminian divinity, (though I allow myself the pleasure to hope there are sundry conscientious persons among them,) and the Calvinistic, or rather Pauline articles of their own church are counted horrendous and insufferable. But I suppose that universal fame has superseded my information; and therefore I willingly exempt myself from the disagreeable task.

"I cannot find there has been a dissenting minister settled in Virginia, till lately, since its first plantation. You no doubt remember what Dr. Mather, and Mr. Neal from him, relate of the sending of Messrs. James, Knowles and Thom-

* O. S. Ch. Lib.

son into it from New England, at the invitation of sundry of its inhabitants, above a hundred years ago; and of their being compelled to depart the colony by the Governor's order, after preaching a few sermons: since which there have been hardly any attempts made to obtain such ministers till a few years ago; and many of the populace knew little or nothing of any denomination, but that in which they have been educated.

"I have reason to hope, Sir, there are and have been a few names in various parts of the colony, who are sincerely seeking the Lord, and groping after religion, in the communion of the Church of England; which I charitably presume from my finding there were a few of this happy character in and about Hanover before the late revival of religion. Such were awakened, as they have told me, either by their own serious reflections, suggested and enforced by divine energy, or on reading some authors of the last century, particularly Bolton, Baxter, Flavel, Bunyan, &c. Some of them were wont to attend on public worship in the established church, without much murmuring at the entertainments there; though they were sensible these were vastly inferior to what past ages were favored with, and often wondered if there were such doctrines taught any where in the world at present, as they found in the writings of these good men. Others of them, though they had no objections against the ceremonies of the Church of England, except a few, who were shocked at the impracticable obligations imposed upon the sponsors in baptism, were utterly dissatisfied with the usual doctrines taught from the pulpit. Though these were generally true, and would have been useful, in their connexion with the scheme of evangelical doctrines; yet so many necessary truths were neglected, as rendered those that were inculcated of very little service. The whole system of what is distinguished by the name of experimental religion, was passed over in silence. The depravity of human nature, the necessity of regeneration, and its prerequisites, nature and effects, the various exercises of pious souls according to their several cases, &c. these were omitted; and without these, you know, Sir, the finest declamations on moral duties or speculative truths will be but wretched entertainment to hungry souls.

"The few that professed a dissatisfaction with the general strain of preaching in church, and therefore either absented themselves, or attended with murmuring and reluctance, were generally counted whimsical creatures, and hypocritical affectors of singularity. And indeed they could not but own their sentiments singular; for they knew of none in the present age of the same mind with them; and therefore had no prospect of obtaining a minister to preach to them those doctrines they thirsted for. Their notions, as far as I can learn, were sound in the main, though intermixed with some corrupt notions verging towards Antinomianism, the opposite extreme to that they had left. And though this rendered them more odious to their adversaries, and furnished them with occasions more plausibly to expose them; yet, considering their circumstances, as being destitute of a judicious minister to instruct them in the doctrines of the gospel, and caution them against mistakes; and as laboring under the prejudices of education, and transported with the sallies of their first zeal, which is generally imprudent and wild; I am more surprised at their soundness and regularity in most things, than at their mistakes and extravagances in a few.

"In this case about ten or twelve persons, who are now members of my congregation, had been for some time before the revival of religion which began in the year 1743. One Mr. Samuel Morris, (for I am not ashamed publicly to mention his name, notwithstanding the calumnies flung upon it by many,) a person of a forward, sociable spirit, who had for some time been extremely anxious about his eternal state, and unweariedly seeking relief by all means within his reach, at length obtained a discovery of that glorious method of salvation through Jesus Christ, to which sinners from all the ends of the earth look, and are saved, and where they universally agree to fix all their hopes, notwithstanding the great diversity of their circumstances as to situation, education, outward instruction, &c. The distinct relation he has given me of his exercises at that time and since, and the prevailing piety of his common behaviour, leave me no room to be anxious about the sincerity of his religion; though, as it is common in such cases, his former pious zeal to do good, with a few very pardonable imprudences that attended it, have fixed an indelible odium on his character among many who opposed the religious concern he attempted to promote. After this discovery of the gospel, his soul was anxious for the salvation of his neighbours, and inflamed with zeal to use means to awaken them. This was the tendency of his conversation; and he also read to them such authors as had been most useful to him, particularly Luther's Comment upon the Galatians, which first opened to him the way of justification through Christ alone, and his Table Discourses; sundry pieces of honest Bunyan's, &c. By those means, a few of his neighbours were made more thoughtful about religion than usual, and doubtful they had lived till then in a careless ignorance of it; but the concern was not very extensive.

"I have prevailed, Sir, on my good friend before mentioned, who was the principal private instrument of promoting the late work, and therefore well acquainted with it, to write me a narrative of its rise and progress from this period till my settlement here; and this, together with the substance of what he and others have told me, I shall present to you without any material alterations, and personate him, though I shall not exactly use his words.

"'The Rev. Mr. Whitefield had been in Virginia, I think, in the year 1740, and at the invitation of the Rev. Mr. Blair, our late Commissary, had preached in Williamsburg, our metropolis, about sixty miles from Hanover. His fame was much spread abroad, as a very warm and alarming preacher; which made such of us in Hanover as had been awakened, very eager to see and hear him; but as he left the colony before we heard of him, we had no opportunity. But in the year 1743, a young gentleman arrived from Scotland with a book of his sermons preached in Glasgow, and taken from his mouth in short hand, which with difficulty I procured. After I had read it with great liking and benefit, I invited my neighbors to come and hear it; and the plainness, popularity and fervency of the discourses being peculiarly fitted to affect our unimproved minds, and the Lord rendering the word efficacious, many were convinced of their undone condition, and constrained to seek deliverance with the greatest solicitude. A considerable number convened every Sabbath to hear these sermons, instead of going to church, and frequently on week days. The concern of some was so passionate and violent, that they could not avoid crying out, weeping bitterly, &c., and that when such indications of religious concern were so strange and ridiculous, that they could not be occasioned by example or sympathy, and the affectation of them would have been so unprofitable an instance of hypocrisy, that none could be tempted to it. My dwellinghouse at length was too small to contain the people; whereupon we determined to build a meetinghouse, merely for reading; for we knew of no minister in the world whom we could get to preach to us according to our liking; and having never been accustomed to social extempore prayer, none of us durst attempt it in company. By this single mean, sundry were solemnly awakened, and their conduct ever since is a living attestation of the continuance and happy issue of their impressions. When the report of these, sermons and the effects occasioned by reading them was spread abroad, I was invited to several places to read them, at a considerable distance; and by this means the concern was propagated.

" 'About this time, our absenting ourselves from church, contrary, as was alleged, to the laws of the land, was taken notice of; and we were called upon by the court, to assign our reasons for it, and to declare what denomination we were of. As we knew but little of any denomination of dissenters, except Quakers, we were at a loss what name to assume. At length, recollecting that Luther was a noted reformer, and that his doctrines were agreeable to our sentiments, and had been of special service to us, we declared ourselves Lutherans; and thus we continued till Providence afforded us an unexpected opportunity of hearing the Rev. Mr. William Robinson.'

"Here, Sir, it may be proper for me to lay aside the person of my informer for a while, and interrupt the connexion of his relation, to give you some account of the travels and successes of that zealous, faithful and laborious minister of Christ, the late Mr. Robinson, whose dear memory will mingle with my softest and most grateful thoughts, as long as I am capable of reflection. He was in the ministry about six years, and never took the charge of a congregation till a few months before his happy and triumphant exit. The necessitous circumstances of many vacancies, and the prospects of more extensive usefulness, engaged him to expose his shattered constitution to all the hardships and fatigues of almost uninterrupted itinerations; and it has been my lot to trace his travels in sundry parts of Pennsylvania, Maryland and Virginia; and I cannot recollect one place in which he had officiated for any time, where there were not some illustrious effects of his ministry. He had a noble, disinterested ambition to preach the gospel where Christ was not named ; and therefore, by the permission of the Presbytery, he took a journey through the new settlements in Pennsylvania, Virginia and North Carolina, in which he continued about two years, oppressed with the usual difficulties a weakly constitution finds in travelling a wilderness, and animated only by his glorious successes. He continued for some time in Lunenburg, a county about one hundred miles southwest of this, where, (as I shall have occasion to observe more fully hereafter,) a small number of Presbyterians from the northern colonies were settled, intermixed with a number of loose Virginians ; and there he was the happy instrument of reclaiming many thoughtless creatures, and founding a flourishing congregation. In Amelia also, a county somewhat nearer this than the former, his labors were extensively blessed ; and while he was there, or near it, some of the people in Hanover, having had some imperfect information of him, sent him an invitation to come and preach to them, though they knew very little of his character or method of preaching, only that it was uncommon, and tended to awaken people. They ventured to make an appointment for him to preach at their reading house (if I may so call it) before they received any promise from him by their messenger ; and with much difficulty he came against the day appointed. Some of the people were anxious to discover his principles privately, in the morning, before he was to preach ; but knew not how, till they fell upon the device of asking his opinion of some books they approved of. Upon his declaring his approbation of these tests of orthodoxy, they were transported with the most pleasing expectations, and with eager impatience, attended him to the place where he was to preach.

"I shall now reassume the person of my informer, and proceed in his narrative, 'On the sixth of July, 1743, Mr. Robinson preached his first sermon to us, from Luke 13 : 3, and continued with us preaching four days successively. The congregation was large the first day ; and as the report of him spread, it vastly increased on the three ensuing. It is hard for the liveliest imagination to form an image of the condition of the assembly on these glorious days of the Son of man. Such of us as had been hungering for the word before, were lost in an agreeable confusion of various passions, surprised, astonished, pleased, enraptured! so that we were hardly capable of self-government; and some could not refrain from publicly declaring their transport. We were overwhelmed with the thoughts of the unexpected goodness of God, in allowing us to hear the gospel preached in a manner that surpassed even our former wishes, and much more our hopes. Many that came through curiosity, were pricked to the heart; and but few in the numerous assemblies on these four days appeared unaffected. They returned astonished, alarmed with apprehensions of their dangerous condition, convinced of their former entire ignorance of religion, and anxiously inquiring, what they should do to be saved. And there is reason to believe there was as much good done by these four sermons, as by all the sermons preached in these parts before or since.

"'Before Mr. Robinson left us, he successfully endeavoured to correct some of our Antinomian mistakes, and to bring us to carry on the worship of God more regularly at our meetings. He advised us to meet to read good sermons, and to begin and conclude with prayer and singing of Psalms, which till then we had omitted.* When we next met, we complied with his directions; and when all the rest refused, I read and prayed with trembling and diffidence; which method was observed in sundry places, till we were furnished with a minister. The blessing of God remarkably attended these more private means; and it was really astonishing to observe the solemn impressions begun or continued in many, by hearing good discourses read. I had repeated invitations to come to many places round, some of them thirty or forty miles distant, to read; with which I generally complied.

---

* When Mr Robinson took his leave, the people offered him a considerable sum of money, as a reward for his services He refused it, lest the purity of his motives should be suspected; which, in view of the circumstances of that whole region, was probably judicious. At his first stopping-plrce, he found the money in his saddle-bags. He immediately returned to Mr. Morris, to restore it. His friends were mortified that he had come solely to bring back the money, and urged that they knew not what to do with it, as it had been collected in small sums from many donors, and could not well be returned. A new thought seemed to strike him. He proposed to take the money, and give it to a very promising young man, who was studying divinity at the north, and who greatly needed assistance; adding, that when licensed, he should come and be their minister. The proposal was accepted, and the money was given to Samuel Davies. The sense of obligation for this assistance was what determined Davies, when licensed, to go to Virginia. *Am. Quart. Reg.* IX: 307.

Considerable numbers were wont to attend, with eager attention and awful solemnity; and sundry were, in a judgment of charity, thoroughly turned to God, and thereupon erected meetinghouses, and chose readers among themselves, by which the work was more extensively carried on.

"'Soon after our father, Mr. Robinson, left us, the Rev. Mr. John Blair paid us a short visit; and truly, he came to us in the fulness of the gospel of Christ. Former impressions were ripened, and new formed on many hearts. One night, in particular, a whole house full of people was quite overcome with the power of the word, particularly of one pungent sentence that dropped from his lips; and they could hardly sit or stand, or keep their passions under any proper restraints, so general was the concern during his stay with us; and so ignorant were we of the danger persons in such a case were in of apostasy, which unhappy observation has since taught us, that we pleased ourselves with the expectation of the gathering of more people to the divine Shiloh, than now seem to have been actually gathered to him; though there be still the greatest reason to hope, that sundry bound themselves to the Lord in an everlasting covenant, never to be forgotten.

"'Some time after this, the Rev. Mr. John Roan was sent by the Presbytery of Newcastle (under whose immediate care we had voluntarily placed ourselves) to supply us. He continued with us longer than either of the former; and the happy effects of his ministrations are still apparent, in many instances. He preached at sundry places at the earnest solicitations of the people, which was the happy occasion of beginning and promoting the religious concern, where there were little appearances of it before. This, together with his speaking pretty freely about the degeneracy of the clergy in this colony, gave a general alarm, and some measures were concerted to suppress us. To incense the indignation of the government the more, a perfidious wretch deposed, he heard Mr. Roan use some blasphemous expressions in his sermon, and speak in the most shocking and reproachful manner of the established church. An indictment was thereupon drawn up against Mr. Roan, (though by that time he had departed the colony,) and some of the people who had invited him to preach at their houses, were cited to appear before the General Court, (which, in this government, consists of the Governor or Commander-in-chief, and His Majesty's council,) and two of them were fined twenty shillings sterling, besides the costs, which in one of the cases would have amounted to near fifty pounds, had the evidences demanded their due. While my cause was upon trial, I had reason to rejoice that the throne of grace is accessible in all places, and that helpless creatures can waft up their desires unseen, to God, in the midst of a crowd. Six evidences were cited to prove the indictment against Mr. Roan; but their depositions were in his favor; and as for the evidence mentioned just now, who accused him of blasphemy against God and the church, when he heard of Messrs. G. Tennent's and S. Finley's arrival, he fled, and has not returned since; so that the indictment was dropped. I had reason to fear being banished the colony; and all circumstances seemed to threaten the extirpation of religion among the dissenters in these parts.

"'In these difficulties we lay, without any person of a public character to appear in our favor; whereupon we determined to acquaint the Synod of New York with our case; hoping that a synodical representation of it to our worthy Governor, the Hon. Sir William Gooch, might free him from the misinformations under which he labored, and procure us the liberties granted to Protestant Dissenters by the Act of Toleration. Accordingly, four of us went to the Synod, May, 1745, when the Lord favored us with success. The Synod, being informed of our difficulties, and presuming they might be removed by an impartial representation of our affairs, drew up an address to our Governor, and sent the Rev. Messrs. G. Tennent and Samuel Finley to wait on his honor to present it, and to officiate a few days among us. Sir William received them with condescension and respect, and granted them liberty to preach in Hanover. By this means, the tremendous cloud that hung over us was dissipated for a time, and our languid hopes were revived. Mr. Tennent and Mr. Finley continued with us about a week; and though the deluge of passion in which we were at first overwhelmed, was by this time somewhat abated, yet much good was done by their ministry. The people of God were refreshed, and sundry careless sinners were awakened. Some that had confided before in their moral conduct and religious duties, were convinced of the depravity of their nature, and the necessity of being renewed in the spirit of their mind; though indeed there were but few unregenerate persons among us at that time, that could claim so regular a character; the generality of professors indulging themselves in criminal liberties, and being remiss in the duties of religion; which alas! is too commonly the case still in such parts of the colony as the late revival did not extend to.

"'After these gentlemen had left us, we continued vacant for a considerable time, and kept up our meetings for reading and prayer in sundry places; and the Lord favored us at these occasions with his gracious presence. I was again repeatedly presented and fined in court for absenting myself from church, and keeping up unlawful meetings, as they were called; but the bush flourished in the flames.

"'The next that were appointed to supply us, were the Rev. Messrs. William Tennent and Samuel Blair. They waited on the Governor, and readily obtained his permission to officiate among us. Their labors were not in vain in the Lord. They administered the sacrament of the Lord's Supper among us before their departure; which was the first administration of that heavenly ordinance among us since our dissent from the Church of England; and we have reason to remember it till our last moments, as a most glorious day of the Son of man. The assembly was large, and the novelty of the mode of administration did peculiarly engage their attention. The children were abundantly fed, and others were brought to hunger and thirst after righteousness. It appeared as one of the days of heaven to some of us; and we could hardly help wishing we could, with Joshua, have delayed the revolutions of the heavens, to prolong it.

"'Messrs. Tennent and Blair continued with us about a fortnight; and immediately after their departure, Mr. Whitefield came and preached four or five days in these parts; which was the happy means of giving us further encouragement, and engaging others to the Lord, especially among the Church people, who received his doctrines more readily than they would from ministers of the Presbyterian denomination.

"'After his departure, we were destitute of a minister, and followed our usual method of reading and prayer at our meetings, till the Rev. Mr. Davies, our present pastor, was sent by the Presbytery to supply us about six weeks, in spring, Anno 1747, when our discouragements from the government were renewed and multiplied: for on one Sunday, the Governor's proclamation was set up at our meetinghouse, strictly requiring all magistrates to suppress and prohibit, as far as they lawfully could, all itinerant preachers, &c., which occasioned us to forbear reading that day, till we had time to deliberate and consult what was expedient to do; but how joyfully were we surprised before the next Sabbath, when we unexpectedly heard that Mr. Davies was come to preach so long among us; and especially, that he had qualified himself according to law, and obtained the licensure of four meetinghouses among us, which had never been done before! Thus, when our hopes were expiring, and our liberties more precarious than ever, we were suddenly advanced to a more secure situation. Man's extremity is the Lord's opportunity. For this seasonable instance of the interposition of divine providence, we desire to offer our grateful praises; and we importune the friends of Zion generously to concur in the delightful employ.'"

Such was the rise of Presbyterianism in Virginia. In 1748, Davies obtained licenses for three more meeting houses, and thenceforth divided his time among the seven. Notwithstanding many troubles from the partisans of the Church of England, who had the government of the colony in their hands, Presbyterianism continued to gain strength, and even when this letter was written, the revival was still in progress.

Meanwhile, Whitefield was laboring in other regions, especially Pennsylvania and Maryland. His course, and the general results of his labors, as he estimated them at the time, may be learned from his letters. He wrote;—

"*Bohemia, Md., October* 8, 1746.—I trust the time for favoring this and the neighbouring southern provinces is come. Everywhere, almost, the door is opened for preaching, great numbers flock to hear, and the power of an ascended Saviour attends the word. For it is surprising how the Lord causes prejudices to subside, and makes my former most bitter enemies to be at peace with me."

"*Annapolis, Md., November* 8, 1746.—Lately I have been in seven counties in Maryland, and preached with abundant success."

"*Charleston, January* 23, 1747.—The Lord Jesus is pleased to give me great access to multitudes of souls." He wrote from the same place, March 15, that Bethesda was never in a better condition; that he had opened a Latin school there during the winter; that the Spirit was striving with several of the children, and that he hoped yet to see ministers furnished from Georgia. April 28, he wrote from Bohemia, of the success of Davies in Virginia; but a proclamation had been issued against itinerants, so that the door was shut against Whitefield.

"*Wicoacomico, Md., May* 16, 1747. — Maryland is yielding converts to the blessed Jesus. The gospel seems to be moving southward."

"*Near Newton, Md., May* 21, 1747. — I have been now a three hundred miles' circuit in Maryland, and through one or two counties in Pennsylvania. Everywhere the people have a hearing ear, and I trust some have an obedient heart."

"*Philadelphia, June* 1, 1747. — At present I have full work here. The congregations yesterday were evidently large, and for this month past I have been preaching to thousands in different places."

He soon went to New York, and then to Newport, Boston, and Portsmouth. On his return, he wrote to Gilbert Tennent:

"*New York, August* 29. — My reception at Boston, and elsewhere in New England, was like unto the first. Arrows of conviction fled and stuck fast. Congregations were larger than ever, and opposers' mouths were stopped. Will you now take another trip?" Tennent was not at liberty to comply, even if he desired it.

After short visits to Philadelphia and Bohemia, Whitefield, according to previous arrangements, went to spend the winter in North Carolina. His letters from Bathtown continually express hopes of a revival, but none of them record its existence. Yet his labors doubtless prepared the way for those of the Synod of New York, which were successfully carried on a few years afterwards. In May, 1748, he embarked for Bermuda, whence, after some weeks, he continued his voyage to England. His subsequent visits to these colonies were much of the same character, though at times, as at New York in 1764, attended with remarkable success.

To provide a supply of ministers for carrying on the good work extensively and permanently, the Synod of New York procured, in 1746, the first charter for the College at

Princeton. The Rev. Jonathan Dickinson was chosen its first President, and continued in that office till his death, in 1747. Mr. Burr, the son-in-law of Edwards of Northampton, succeeded him. The charter was unacceptable, and in 1748, another was granted by Governor Belcher, who was Governor of Massachusetts at the time of Whitefield's first arrival. For many years, this college received a large proportion of its students from New England, where many of the pious had more confidence in it, than in Harvard or Yale. Among its later Presidents were Edwards, who succeeded his son-in-law, Davies and Finley, — all ardent and successful laborers in this great revival. In 1753, Gilbert Tennent and Samuel Davies made a successful visit to England and Scotland, by appointment of the Synod at the request of the Trustees, to procure funds for its support.

Twenty-two ministers were present at the formation of the Synod of New York in 1745. Eight others attended in 1746; nine others in 1747; three others in 1748; five others, besides the whole Presbytery of Suffolk, on Long Island, in 1749. Six new members were reported in 1750; nine in 1751; three in 1752; five in 1753; six in 1754; three in 1755; six in 1756; three in 1757; and one in 1758. The whole number reported as belonging to the Synod that year, was seventy-two. The Synod of Philadelphia, meanwhile, received twenty-two members; but, owing to deaths and other causes, had only about the same number of members which the division left, — a little more than twenty. They had made some efforts to build up new churches in Virginia and elsewhere, but with rather moderate success.

It is evident from these facts, that the impulse given to the progress of religion in 1740, was still felt. With occasional visits from Whitefield and the constant labors of the Tennents and their allies, the revival continued for many years, — not always in the same place, or the same form, but substantially existing and efficient in increasing the number of the pious. In no other way can we account for the fact, that the number of ministers in the Synod of New York was more than tripled in seventeen years.

Notwithstanding repeated efforts at reconciliation, in which the members of the New York Presbytery usually took the lead, the schism continued till May 29, 1758. Gilbert Tennent had long been anxious for a reunion. In 1749, he published his *Irenicum Ecclesiasticum*, for the purpose of promoting it. In this and other writings, he argued powerfully against several sentiments and practices which had been ascribed to him, and even against some which he had apparently held. The parties became convinced that there were no differences between them sufficient to justify their separation. All felt the need of union, in order to the greatest prosperity of the cause of religion. The Synod of Philadelphia, too, must have perceived that they were steadily losing their importance, and could escape becoming an insignificant sect, only by uniting with that body which would certainly become *the* Presbyterian church in America.

In arranging the terms of union, the Synod of Philadelphia declared, that the "Protestation" of 1741 had never been judicially adopted, and was not accounted a synodical act, but only the act of those who signed it; so that there was no need of revoking it. As to "rash judging" and "intrusions," it was agreed, "That it shall be esteemed and treated as a censurable evil, to accuse any member of heterodoxy, insufficiency or immorality, in a calumniating manner, or otherwise than by private brotherly admonition, or by a regular process according to our known rules of judicial trial in cases of scandal. And it shall be considered in the same view, if any presbytery appoint supplies within the bounds of another presbytery without their concurrence; or if any member officiate in another's congregation without asking and obtaining his consent, or the session's, in case the minister be absent. Yet it shall be esteemed unbrotherly for any one, in ordinary circumstances, to refuse his consent to a regular member when requested." The whole subject of licensure and ordination was left to the presbyteries, without interference from a Synod's committee. Congregations which had become divided during the schism, were to be united where it could conveniently be done; but where both parties had settled ministers, should be allowed to remain as they were. The Synod of New York declared its belief unaltered concerning the revival; and the united Synod declared, that a change to penitence, faith and a holy life is to be ascribed to the Spirit of God, even though attended with "bodily commotions" and other irregularities; and that persons who, without such a change, fancy themselves converted because they have had visions, or trances, or faintings, or the like, are "under a dangerous delusion."

The number of members of this united body, which was called "The Synod of New York and Philadelphia," was ninety-six.* Of these, seventeen are known to have been graduates from Princeton, three from Harvard, and twenty-three from Yale. Others of them, as the Tennents, had been educated in this country, and many were from Europe.

In the Presbyterian Church, after the union, the friends of the revival had an overwhelming preponderance on account of their numbers, and still more on account of their activity, energy, and weight of character. They imparted their spirit to the church itself, when acting as a whole; to the young men who entered its ministry, and to the new congregations that were added to its communion. And thus the Synod of Philadelphia were saved from following their allies in New England, in Scotland, in Ireland, and in England, into the dead sea of Arminian inefficiency, and the bottomless gulf of Unitarianism. Had the Synod of Philadelphia been strong enough to stand alone, its history would have been like that of Henchman's church at Lynn. It would have kept all its congregations still and quiet. It would have repressed all strong feeling about religion. It would have induced a general apathy in people and ministers, in which neither would have cared much for any thing but the privilege of remaining undisturbed. Consequently, all disturbing doctrines would have been first neglected, and then disbelieved, and the truly orthodox "standards" of the church would have been either altered, or regarded as a dead letter.

---

## CHAPTER XX.

### THE RESULTS.

THE first inquiry of most readers will be, How many were truly converted during this revival? A precise answer to this question is impossible. Whitefield's records of his own success scarcely form a basis for a conjecture. As has

---

* Prof. Hodge's List, Const. Hist Pres. Styles says, "above 100;" and adds, 41 destitute congregations in Pennsylvania and Delaware alone.

been shown, he immensely overrated the numbers of his hearers; and he had very little opportunity to ascertain how many of them received any saving benefit from his labors. When he saw hundreds or thousands at a time melted by his eloquence, he called it a "gracious melting," thanked God for the display of his power, hoped they would prove true converts, and hurried away to preach the gospel to other thousands. Multitudes of cases answered to his hopes. Other multitudes were only made to weep by his eloquence, without being converted, convicted, or even alarmed. The same is true, to a less extent, of other itinerants of the day.

Various estimates have been given, of the number added to the churches. Dr. Cogswell * thinks it probable, that twenty-five thousand were added to the churches in New England. Trumbull † estimates the number of converts in New England in two or three years, at thirty or forty thousand. Others place the number as high as fifty thousand. To these must be added the numerous accessions to the Presbyterian Church, which we can only conjecture from the rapid increase of settled pastors. Where so many new congregations were formed, we may be sure that many old ones were enlarged.

The number of Congregational churches, too, was increased. The Rev. Ezra Styles, of Newport, afterwards President of Yale College, in his sermon on "Christian Union," published in 1760,‡ states that since 1740, "an augmentation of above 150 new churches has taken place, founded not on the separations, but natural increase into new towns and parishes," making the whole number of Congregational churches 530. If, by this "augmentation," the number of churches only kept pace with the increase of population, it shows the influence of the revival; for without that influence, a greater proportion of new settlements would have remained without churches. But doubtless it was otherwise, and many of them were established in the older parts of the country, by the peaceable division of towns and parishes, to meet the increased desire for religious privileges. For instance, a revival began at Leicester, about the commencement of the year 1742. Edwards, as has been mentioned, spent several weeks there, laboring with great success. In May, 1744, a

* Christian Philanthropist, p. 392. † History Ct. ‡ O. S. Ch. Lib.

new church was organized in the west precinct of Leicester, and, in November following, the Rev. Joshua Eaton was ordained as its pastor.* Nor may we suppose, that all the churches which were "founded on the separations" were useless. In some instances, they were founded on separations from degenerate churches and an unconverted ministry, as even charity must admit, and were the means of establishing and preserving gospel ordinances in their life and power, where otherwise there would have been only the dead form of religion. Some of them occurred where the Christian population was large enough to justify division. Though all or nearly all of them were more or less disorderly at first, and some of them too disorderly to be capable of long life, some of them became regular and orderly churches, and subsist as useful institutions to this day. President Clapp, who in 1742 forbade his pupils to attend the Separate meeting at New Haven, became an attendant there himself in less than ten years.† Still more of the Separatist churches became Baptists, and still subsist; and the older Baptist churches were considerably increased during the revival, and especially after 1745. Their increase is not included in the estimate of Dr. Styles.

We have, then, these elements of conjecture: 1. The estimates of the number of converts during a few years in New England, by men who were active in those times or remember them, vary from twenty-five to fifty thousand. 2. One hundred and fifty Congregational churches were regularly formed in less than twenty years, including the years in which the country was distracted and its growth impeded by the "old French wars." 3. A considerable number of Separatist churches was formed, which really added to the strength of the Redeemer's kingdom. 4. There was an increase of strength, known to be considerable, to the Baptist churches in New England. 5. The number of Presbyterian ministers had increased from forty-five or less, before the schism, to more than one hundred; and Presbyterian congregations had increased, so that there were forty-one desitute, in Pennsylvania and Delaware alone. — The growth of the country, notwithstanding the wars by which it was retarded, accounts for some part of this increase; but after all due allowance

* Boston Gazette, Nov. 27, 1744. † Backus, Eccl. History N. E.

on that account, it is evident that the revival had done much to enlarge the number of the pious and extend the influence of religion.

But the increase in the number of churches and church members is a very inadequate measure of the increase of piety. Great numbers of church members were converted. We must remember that the practice of admitting to the communion all persons neither heretical nor scandalous, was general in the Presbyterian church, and prevailed extensively among the Congregational churches. In consequence, a large proportion of the communicants in both were unconverted persons. Multitudes of these were converted. Of course, there was no census of the unconverted members of the several churches, or of the conversions among them; nor would any of them be counted as additions to the churches. In some cases, the revival seems to have been almost wholly within the church, and to have resulted in the conversion of nearly all the members. A large addition ought to be made, on this score, to the estimated number of conversions.

No considerable deduction is to be made from these estimates, on account of the supposed converts who in the end "fell away;" for the estimates rest mostly on facts of a later date than their apostasy. At the commencement of the revival, the practice of attempting to distinguish between the converted and the unconverted was for the most part obsolete, and, except among the Separatists, there was little thought of reviving it. Any manifest approach towards it was condemned by the majority, even of the pious, both in the ministry and out of it, as "uncharitable," "censorious," and "divisive." Very naturally, therefore, they counted and reported the number of the "awakened," including church members and others; and thus the impression was very extensively made, that the "awakened," generally, were expected to prove real Christians. It was to estimates formed under the influence of such habits of thought, that Edwards alluded, in his letter to Dr. Erskine, of June 28, 1751. "I cannot say that the greater part of supposed converts give reason, by their conversation, to suppose that they are true converts. The proportion may, perhaps, be more truly represented by the proportion of blossoms on a tree, which abide and come to mature fruit, to the whole number of blossoms in the spring."* The result would be much the same now, if all whose attention is aroused during a revival, were at first counted as "supposed converts." The estimates already given, are founded on facts and opinions gathered after the false blossoms had fallen off.

The value of these conversions must not be estimated by their number alone. Their proportion to the population of the country must be considered. Dr. Styles supposed the number of inhabitants in New England, in 1760, to be 501,-909; and fifteen years afterwards, at the commencement of the war of the Revolution, the population of all the colonies was supposed to be three millions, at the most. He approves the statement of Franklin, that the population of New England doubled in about twenty years; so that in 1740, it could not have been much over 250,000; and for the other colonies a similar reduction should be made. Suppose, however, the whole population of all the colonies to have been 2,000,000. It is now about 17,000,000, or more than eight times as great. Suppose the whole number of converts to have been 50,000, which seems quite low enough. They would bear as great a proportion to the whole number of inhabitants, and would do as much towards changing the relative power of the religious and irreligious, as the conversion of 400,000 would do now.

We should remember, too, that many of these converts were already, and had long been, church members, and, from their want of piety, were at best dead weights to the churches. They now became active and valuable members. There was a twofold gain. In every such instance, the church felt its encumbering burden diminished, and its strength increased. Almost every church has its dead weights, and knows what an impediment they are to its usefulness; but few in this day are able even to imagine the condition of a church, where a large part of the members give no evidence of piety, except that they are neither heretical nor scandalous; still less, the condition of a church, composed almost entirely of dead weights, all supposing that God looks upon their membership with approbation. What must be the value of a revival, in which the members of such a church are converted into active Christians? What

* Dwight's Life of Edwards, p. 460.

shall we say of a revival, which works such a transformation of churches throughout the length and breadth of the land?

And what shall be said of ministers, who are mere dead weights? Whitefield was rash, and Tennent was severe, in their judgments of the number of unconverted ministers. They were probably fewer than these men supposed, especially in New England. Still, it is useless to deny their existence. When the colleges received young men without even the appearance of piety, to prepare for the ministry; when, if graduates were found to possess competent knowledge, and were neither heretical nor scandalous, their piety was taken for granted and they were ordained of course; when the doctrine that unconverted ministers, though orthodox in doctrine and regular in their lives, were "the bane of the church," gave offence, we may be sure that unconverted ministers existed. And such, not universally, but to a lamentable extent, was the case in all the colonies. There can be no doubt, that a considerable number of ministers were converted during the revival. Such was their own judgment concerning themselves; and in the opinion of others, their previous and subsequent lives showed its correctness. Of nearly equal importance was the conversion of a considerable number of students, preparing for the ministry. At the time of Whitefield's third visit to America, from 1744 to 1748, there were not less than twenty ministers in the vicinity of Boston, who considered him as the means of their conversion.* Those who owed their conversion to the revival, in the whole country, must have been considerably more numerous. The value of such an infusion of life into the ministry was incalculable. Every such conversion relieved the church of a "bane," and gave her a blessing. Nor was this all. Many truly pious ministers had a very low standard of duty, of hope, and of effort. They were scarce aware that any thing was required of them, besides the conscientious performance of a certain round of official services. These being performed, they trusted that God added his blessing, whether they could see any signs of it or not. Believing that all orthodox and moral men ought to be in the church, they felt no practical need of any evidence, by which those who were merely such, might be distinguished from the truly

* Philip's Life and Times, p. 311.

regenerate; and feeling no need of it, they ceased to look for it, or expect it. They regarded the new birth as an imperceptible inward work, which they hoped was going on among their people. Many such pastors were awakened to new views of ministerial duty, learned to be no longer satisfied without manifest evidence of usefulness, and thenceforth labored to produce ascertainable changes among the people of their charge. On the whole, the beneficial influence of the revival on the ministry was immense.

But this was not all that the revival did for the ministry. It fully and finally killed the doctrine, that an unconverted ministry might be tolerated. At its commencement, opinions on this subject were in a state not easily understood by men of the present day. Parents felt that they were doing a worthy deed, by consecrating their unconverted sons to the ministry, and sending them to the colleges to be prepared for it. The colleges felt that it was their business to take such youths and prepare them; and to doubt the fitness of those whom they had trained to the profession, seemed to be an attack both upon their reputation and their income. The extensively prevailing view of regeneration, as a work attended by no ascertainable evidence, discouraged all questioning concerning a minister's spiritual state. There was a dread, too, of the Popish doctrine, that the word and sacraments derive their efficacy from the minister, and not from Him who instituted them. It was very natural, therefore, that Dr. Chauncy, in reply to Whitefield's question: "Are not unconverted ministers the bane of the Christian church," should write: "If they appear to be unconverted, by a conduct visibly contradictory to the gospel, I own they are a plague to the church of God, as well as the greatest scandal to religion. Nor is it a hurt, but a service to the interest of Christ, to expose their character, and lessen their influence to do mischief. But the case is widely different, where, so far as appears to the world, they are the men their profession obliges them to be. If, by unconverted ministers, you mean those who appear to be so by a faith or life visibly contradictory to the gospel, I entirely agree with you. But if you intend, by unconverted ministers, those whom God knows to be so, though from what outwardly appears they ought to be well thought of, I doubt not but you are under a great mistake."* And again: "Conversion does not appear to be alike necessary for ministers in their public capacity as officers of the church, as it is in their private capacity."† Who would write so now? Who now would condemn as erroneous in doctrine, a single sentence in Tennent's Nottingham sermon? What theological seminary would open its doors, or what education society would supply funds, to a young man not supposed to be regenerate? The false doctrine of that day was not, even then, firmly established, especially in New England. Men still remembered the old Puritan doctrine and practice, that none should be ordained without a satisfactory examination in respect to their Christian experience. Every body felt, that calling a minister unconverted, would have the effect, among his people, of calling him unfit for his place. The error was mostly a practical one, consisting in a lax administration, and a false theory, partially and hesitatingly adopted, to justify it. When a bold and vigorous attack was made, it fell at once. The demand, that a minister should be a converted man, was felt to be reasonable, and when public attention was once strongly fixed upon the question, the churches and the community soon settled it correctly. And the correct settlement of this question is a permanent good, of inestimable value. It has practically reached all evangelical denominations in the United States, so that no leading man in any of them would dare to write now, as Chauncy wrote, or even as "the venerable Stoddard" had written before him. This permanent good result infinitely outweighs all the temporary evils, great as they certainly were, produced by the Separatists and other enthusiasts during the contest. The revival not only furnished many converted pastors then, but secured a converted ministry for coming times.

Of the progress of truth on this subject in the Presbyterian Church, there are some interesting records. In 1761, three years after the union of the two Synods, an overture was introduced to the following effect: "As holiness is a qualification requisite in a gospel minister: Quere, whether it be the duty of a Presbytery, or possible for them, to make candidates give a narrative of their personal exercises, and upon this form a judgment of their real spiritual state towards

* Letter to Whitefield. O. S. Ch. Lib. † Seasonable Thoughts.

God, as the ground of admitting or rejecting them?"* The question was deferred till the next year, when its authors gave an explanation of its meaning. They stated, that all were agreed as to the duty of obtaining satisfactory evidence of the candidate's experimental acquaintance with religion, "excepting that some insist on requiring and using an account of the candidate's personal exercises and experiences in religion, as a means of a judicature's satisfaction and ground of their proceedings with him; which we disallow. So the case to be resolved seems only, whether a candidate's declaration of his own personal experiences and exercises in religion, given in the way of narrative of these, or in answer to questions put to him concerning them, should be required by a judicature, as one appointed, warrantable and useful means of forming a judgment of his experimental acquaintance with religion, according to which judgment they are to receive or reject him."† There was no difference of opinion as to requiring "a serious profession and godly life." After each member had expressed his views, the Synod voted, that a declaration of the candidate's personal experience should be required, as a proper means of forming a judgment of his experimental acquaintance with religion. Forty ministers and twenty-three elders attended this meeting. Only thirteen voted in the negative, and one was doubtful. If all voted, there were forty-nine in the affirmative.

The question then arose, whether this vote was not a violation of the sixth article of the agreement by which the Synods were united, by which both Synods were allowed to act according to their own judgment on this subject; "for it was well known to the Synod of New York, that the presbyteries belonging to the Synod of Philadelphia did not examine a candidate's experiences." The question being put to each member, it appeared that the members of the Synod of New York who were present at the union, generally understood the sixth article to require a relation of experiences, but the members of the Synod of Philadelphia understood it otherwise. To avoid another schism, the Synod declared that the vote just passed was to be understood only as an expression of opinion, and not as a law, binding upon such as thought differently.‡ Even this failed to give uni-

* Prof. Hodge. Const. Hist. II. 394, from "Minutes, p. 50."
† Ibid. 396. "Minutes, pp. 64, 65." ‡ Ibid. 399. "Minutes, p. 73."

versal satisfaction; and Messrs. Robert Cross, Francis Alison, John Ewing, John Symington and James Latta were formed into a Presbytery for one year, to be called the Second Presbytery of Philadelphia.* The question whether this Presbytery should be allowed to remain in being, was deferred from year to year till 1766, when it was voted in the affirmative, several of the New Brunswick ministers protesting against it.

In the Presbytery of Donegal, the troubles on this subject were still greater. To terminate them, the Synod divided the Presbytery in 1765. This gave dissatisfaction, and various expedients were proposed to make peace. A protest, entered in 1766, declares, that the "distressed brethren could not in conscience submit to the examination of the hearts or experiences of candidates in the way voted by the Synod, as they esteemed it contrary to the word of God, to common sense, and the uniform practice of the Protestant churches." Two ministers, Joseph Tate and John Beard, formally withdrew from the communion of the Synod, and several others appear to have been on the point of doing it. In 1768, the dissatisfied were distributed among the Presbyteries of Donegal, Newcastle, and the Second Presbytery of Philadelphia, where views similar to their own prevailed; and thus this schism was healed.

The difference of opinion respecting experiences, though not formally made prominent, was at the bottom of the controversy which produced the schism of 1741, when the Tennents and their friends were in the minority, and were excluded. In 1762, their majority was about forty-nine to fourteen, or seven to two.

The revival also did much to furnish means of education for the ministry, and for all the learned professions. The reader has already seen that it produced the College at Princeton, and thus prepared the way for the Theological Seminary there. It was also the parent of Dartmouth College. Among the Mohegans converted in 1741, was Samson Occum, then seventeen years of age. In December, 1743, Wheelock of Lebanon, whose labors in the revival have been repeatedly noticed, received him as a pupil, and he pursued his studies in the family for several years. In

* Const. Hist. II. 377. This was probably the first instance of an "elective affinity" Presbytery.

1748, Wheelock determined to commence a school for the education of Indian preachers, and a donation from Joshua Moor, a farmer in Mansfield, in 1754, gave it a permanent foundation. The influence of the revival on several Indian tribes helped to furnish him with pupils, and in 1762, he had more than twenty under his care. In 1766, the Rev. Nathaniel Whitaker and Occum, who had become a preacher of some distinction, went to England to solicit funds for the Institution. Occum attracted unusual attention, Whitefield aided them, and a large amount of funds was obtained. The school was afterwards removed to its present location, in Hanover, N. H., and Dartmouth College was added to it.*

The influence of this revival on the cause of missions to the heathen ought not to be overlooked. The New England Pilgrims had set the Protestant world the first example of such labors, and they and their descendants had sustained the work for more than a century. Societies had been formed in Great Britain to aid them; and at a later day, some kindred movements had been commenced on the continent of Europe. Within a few years, several missions had been established among the American Indians, but few conversions had followed them. The most prosperous was the Stockbridge Mission, under Sargeant. The revival gave an impulse to the work at nearly all the stations. On Long Island, thirty-five adults and forty-four children were baptized by Mr. Horton, in two years from his arrival in 1741. Soon after, there were numerous conversions among those near Stonington; and a visit from them was the means of awakening those in Westerly, R. I. An account of this last awak-

---

* It may be proper to mention, that with the founding of Dartmouth College, in 1770, a series of revivals commenced, which continued for several years, and spread over several towns in that vicinity. They were evidently a result of the revival of 1740, and possessed many of its leading characteristics. There may have been no outcries or convulsions; but there were remarkable dreams and visions, and wonderful experiences, which, in the minds of the judicious, even then, betokened future apostasy. The author of this history has known several of the converts as Universalists and infidels, and well remembers the excommunication of some of them. He has known others as stable and consistent Christians Several of them became eminent ministers of the gospel; and to the influence of one of them, — the Rev. Asa Burton, D. D., for more than half a century pastor of the church in Thetford, Vt., — more than to any other man, the extensive prevalence of sound religion in that part of New England must be ascribed. It is certain, that spurious conversions were much more numerous then, than in late revivals in the same region.

ening, from the pen of Mr. Parks, the missionary, is given in the preceding pages. Heathenism seems to have been extirpated from that whole region. In 1743, Brainerd began his missionary career at Kaunaumeek. In 1745 he removed to New Jersey, and commenced his labors at the Forks of the Delaware and at Crosweeksung. His first visit to the latter place was attended with the evident presence of the Holy Spirit in the awakening and conviction of his hearers. When, after two weeks, he left them for a season, William Tennent was sent for and came to supply his place. The work went on under Tennent's preaching, and received still a new impulse on Brainerd's return. All Christendom knows the glorious scenes that followed. These dates, and the name of Tennent, and the history of Brainerd while at New Haven, show that Brainerd's triumphs were a part of this great revival. He soon died ; but he " yet speaketh," and his influence is felt wherever there are missions. Wheelock's Indian School has already been mentioned. In 1763, it had three missionaries and eight school-masters laboring among the Indians ; and from this school and from conversation with Whitefield, the Rev. Samuel Kirkland went forth, in 1764, on his mission to the Oneidas. Whitefield visited and encouraged both this Indian School and Brainerd's mission. And finally, the Concert of Prayer for the Conversion of the World was first suggested by the leading revivalists in Scotland, in October, 1744 ; and the influence of Edwards and their other American allies gave it prevalence here.

But there were results of another kind, no less important than these ; results bearing directly on the constitution of the churches, and on the principles which animated and governed them.

The revival set bounds to the progress of heresy. That a cold and formal Arminianism extensively prevailed, is too notorious to be questioned. The decided Calvinists of that day asserted, that Socinianism also was making progress in the land. Though the charge was denied for many years, Unitarians now maintain that it was true, and in this they are probably correct. The growth of Unitarianism was doubtless modified by the revival, but did not originate in it ; for it was already in the land, and growing in secret, when the revival commenced. A contemporary document will here be in place.

In the summer of 1745, Prince, Webb and Gee of Boston, and Hobby of Reading, published an invitation to the friends of the revival, to meet at Webb's, on the last Wednesday in September.* The meeting was attended by Prince, Webb and Gee of Boston, White of Gloucester, Rogers of Kittery, Bailey of Weymouth, Leonard of Plymouth, Rogers of Ipswich, Owen of Groton, Ct., Hobby of Reading, Parker of Plympton, Jewett of Rowley, Cotton of Halifax, Hemenway of Townsend, Bliss of Concord, Porter of Bridgewater, Ellis of Plymouth, Crocker of Taunton, Rogers of Gloucester, and Conant of Middleborough; and their "Testimony" was afterwards subscribed by Campbell of Plympton, Shaw of Bridgewater, Goddard of Leicester, and Hovey of Rochester; in all, twenty-four. No reason is assigned, why it received so few signatures; as the friends of the revival generally are known to have entertained similar views. Probably, the greater part of them thought it inexpedient to agitate the country by a "Testimony" just at that time, when the angry controversies occasioned by Whitefield's return had not subsided, and when the itinerants would take unfair advantage of every thing that could be pressed into their service. In their "Testimony" they say:—

"We cannot but also observe that the principal means of the late revival were, the more than ordinary preaching up such Scripture and most important doctrines as these, namely: The all seeing eye, purity, justice, truth, power, majesty and sovereignty of God; the spirituality, holiness, extent and strictness of his law; our original sin, guilt, depravity and corruption by the fall; including a miserable ignorance of God and enmity against him, our predominant and constant bent to sin and creatures above him; our impotence and aversion to return to him; our innumerable and heinous actual offences, and thereby our horrid, aggravated guilt, pollution and odiousness in his eyes; his dreadful and efficacious wrath and curse upon us; the necessity that his law should be fulfilled, his justice satisfied, the honor of his holiness, authority and truth maintained in his conduct towards us; our utter impotence to help ourselves, and our continual hazard of being sent into endless misery; the astonishing displays of the absolute wisdom and grace of God in contriving and providing for our redemption; the divinity, mediation, perfect holiness, obedience, sacrifice, merits, satisfaction, purchase and grace of Christ; the nature and necessity of regeneration to the holy image of God by the supernatural operation of the divine Spirit; with the various parts of his office in enlightening our minds, awakening our consciences, wounding, breaking,

* Evening Post, Aug. 19, copied from Boston Gazette, July 3.

humbling, subduing and changing our hearts, infusing his saving graces, exciting and helping us in the exercise of them, and in all obedience, witnessing with our spirits that we are the children of God, and raising his consolations and joys in us; the difference between his saving graces and merely moral virtues without sanctification, whereby multitudes are deceived to their eternal ruin; in special, the nature and necessity of receiving Christ, so as to be actually united to him and have entire and everlasting interest in him, to be forthwith justified by his imputed righteousness, adopted into the number of the children of God, entitled to all their privileges assured in the covenant of grace, have Christ as our mediatorial and vital Head of all good, with his constant dwelling and acting by his Spirit in us; and then, in continual acts of faith, deriving from him fresh supplies of spiritual liveliness and comfort, as also light and strength for every duty and to carry on our sanctification; the nature of gospel obedience and holiness, and their necessity, not as the matter of our justification, but as the fruit and evidence of justifying faith, and to glorify God and enjoy him the principal end both of our creation and redemption: and lastly, the sovereignty of the grace of God in this whole transaction, from its original, in the decree of election, to its consummation in glory.

"And as the more than ordinary preaching up these great truths of revealed religion and experimental piety, being the same which were so successfully preached by the first sound and pious fathers of New England, have been the principal means of the late revival; we are sorry to see, that under the name of New Light, many of the preachers of these most important truths, and especially those which concern the office and operation of the Spirit of grace in bringing lost and perishing souls to Christ, are by many run down and ridiculed; as those our pious forefathers were in their day, under the same or alike reproachful terms, by many on the other side of the water; and they who preach the same truths of the gospel and experimental piety as those great divines, Hooker, Cotton, Shepard, Goodwin, Owen, Flavel, the Mathers, Willard, Stoddard, are represented by some as New Light, Enthusiastical or Antinomian preachers; whereby the awful danger grows, of banishing even the faith of the glorious office of that divine Agent in the work of conviction, conversion, sanctification and comfort, first out of our pulpits, and then out of the land. Yea, to so deplorable a pass have some traducers of this revival brought us, that if any of the young generation begin to leave off their cursing, swearing, immoderate drinking, obscene discourse, grow concerned for their souls, and repair to the word; they are immediately branded and vilified by their vain companions with the name of New Lights, and efforts are made to laugh them out of their serious concern for their souls and eternity; which we fear has been the ruinous case of many.

"In such an awful situation of things as this, we cannot but apprehend that the divine Head of the church now loudly calls us, and all others who seriously believe and are deeply concerned for those great truths of the gospel as collected in the above said Catechism and Confession of Faith, with the interest of vital piety; without imposing in the least on others, or assuming any authority over the conscience of any, which we utterly abhor, as directly contrary to the very nature of religion itself; to unite our resolutions and endeavours, by all proper means, consistent with liberty of conscience, to maintain, encourage and promote the same."

They then copied an act of the General Assembly of the Church of Scotland, in 1736, recommending the faithful preaching of the doctrines of grace. This they approved, as the best way of guarding against errors of all kinds, "in particular the Socinian, Antinomian and Arminian;" and concluded by urging all ministers, whatever they might have thought of the revival, to unite in maintaining and promoting "the said important truths, and the power of godliness."

The revival was, in all its valuable features, a manifest example of the power of those doctrines. Those who received benefit from it, knew that those doctrines were the means of conferring that benefit upon them. The whole multitude of converts regarded those doctrines as the means of their own salvation, and as the indispensable means of the salvation of others. Thus a great company of orthodox preachers and many tens of thousands of orthodox Christians were raised up, whose own experience forbade them to doubt the importance of doctrinal truth. Otherwise they might have gone on, like the mass of those whom the revival failed to reach, into the abyss of open and undisguised Unitarianism. In this respect, even the bitterness of controversy was overruled for good. It made men sensible that there were important differences of opinion among them, and that the defence of the truth was committed to its friends, and not to the public generally.

The Baptist churches also shared, both in the danger and the deliverance of that day. Their own historian, speaking of the revival in its earlier stages, says:

"A measure of it was granted to the Baptists in Boston, Leicester, Brimfield, Newport, Groton and Wallingford; but as the work was begun and carried on almost wholly by Pædobaptists, from which denomination their forefathers had suffered much, most of the Baptists were prejudiced against the work, and against the Calvinian doctrine by which it was promoted."*

With the Separatists, they had more sympathy. Both agreed in rejecting the whole Halfway Covenant theory, and all its consequences. Both entertained the same views of ordination, and of Christian liberty. Both had the same opponents, and to a great extent, for the same reasons. It

* Backus, Eccl. Hist. N. E., Vol. II. page 134.

was natural, therefore, that they should first love each other, and afterwards unite ; and thus the influence of the revival was carried into the Baptist churches, especially in Rhode Island and its vicinity, in 1749 and afterwards.*

Another result of the revival was, a better knowledge of the nature of religious experience. Without great ignorance on this subject, many of its worst disorders would have been impossible. Edwards wrote to Gillespie of Carnock, in 1751, concerning his dismission :

"Another thing that has evidently contributed to our calamities, is, that the people had got so established in certain wrong notions and ways in religion, which I found them in, and could never beat them out of. Particularly, it was too much their method to lay almost all the stress of their hopes in religion on the particular shape and method of their first work; that is, the first work of the Spirit of God on their hearts, in their conviction and conversion; and to look but little at the abiding sense and temper of their hearts, and the course of their exercises and trials of grace, for evidences of their good estate. Nor had they learned, and many of them never could be made to learn, to distinguish between impressions on the imagination and lively spiritual experience. And when I came among them, I found it to be too much a custom among them, without discretion or distinction of occasions, places or companies, to declare and publish their own experiences, and oftentimes to do it in a light manner, without any air of solemnity. This custom has not a little contributed to spiritual pride, and many other evils. When I first settled among the people, being young and of little experience, I was not so thoroughly aware of the ill consequences of such a custom, and so allowed, or at least did not testify against it, as I ought to have done.

"One thing that has contributed to bring things to such a pass at Northampton was, my youth and want of more judgment and experience at the time of that extraordinary awakening about sixteen years ago. Instead of a youth, there was want of a giant in judgment and discretion, among a people in such an extraordinary state of things. In some respects, doubtless, my confidence in myself was a great injury to me; but in other respects, my diffidence of myself injured me. It was such that I durst not act my own judgment, and had no strength to oppose received notions and established customs, and to testify boldly against some glaring false appearances and counterfeits of religion, till it was too late. And by this means, as well as others, many things got a footing, which have proved a dreadful source of spiritual pride, and other things that are exceedingly contrary to true Christianity. If I had had more experience and ripeness of judgment and courage, I should have guided my people in a better manner, and should have guarded them better from Satan's devices, and prevented the spiritual calamity of many souls, and perhaps the eternal ruin of some of them."

---

* Backus.

If Edwards made such confessions, what might have been made by others? Their own accounts of the revivals in their parishes, copied into former parts of this work, show in part. The want of discrimination between true and false experiences must have struck every reader. And yet these are favorable specimens, such as were published for edification, and are almost wholly free from the grosser errors, which prevailed extensively among the Separatists and others. In fact, false experiences were so prominent, that they were supposed by many to constitute what was called "the work" and "this work of God;" and under this delusion, some industriously promoted them, while others made the most extravagant of them a ground of reproach against the whole revival. Many of the more judicious protested against this error, but were unable so to set forth the difference between true and false experiences, as to disabuse the public mind.

Edwards first took up this subject among his own people, in a course of sermons, delivered, probably in 1742 and 1743.* The substance of these sermons was afterwards thrown into the form of a "Treatise concerning Religious Affections," and published under that title early in 1746. It was immediately republished in England and Scotland, and from that time to the present, has been the standard work on that subject, both there and here; nor is there any reason to suppose that it will ever be superseded.

Some may think it a fault in this excellent work, that so much of it is occupied in refuting errors that are too absurd to be entertained, even by the weakest and most ignorant minds. But when the work was written, those errors, even the most absurd of them, actually prevailed, and were working mischief extensively; and it is by the light which that work shed on the Christian world, that we now see their absurdity so clearly. Errors concerning the "Witness of the Spirit," texts of Scripture impressed upon the mind, and the nature of saving faith, are common, even in the writings of good and sober men of that day; † while the most extravagant notions

* Dwight's Life of Edwards, p. 223.

† The Rev. Jonathan Dickinson, of Elizabethtown, N. J., was one of the greatest and safest men of that age. Yet, in his "Display of Special Grace," his true convert is made to tell how he first received comfort by a text of Scripture, which came to his mind in a new light; and no intimation is given that comfort does not always come to the convert in that way, or that persons may deceive themselves by taking comfort in that manner.

of comfort being given by impressions on the mind ; by seeing Christ on the cross, or smiling from the judgment-seat ; of assurance of acceptance with God conveyed in dreams, or by effects on the body ; of the value of religious loquacity, and of feelings that are irrepressible, or that come strangely and unaccountably, and are not made on purpose by him that feels them, with other errors of the kind, were rife and highly esteemed among the Separatists and exhorters. The Rev. Andrew Croswell, already repeatedly mentioned, who was one of the most powerful of the itinerants, and who had much about him that was good and needed at the time, published a book entitled, " What is Christ to me, if he is not mine? Or a Seasonable Defence of the Old Protestant Doctrine of Justifying Faith ; " in which he maintained that saving faith consists in " a man's believing, this moment, that God doth, for Christ's sake, forgive his sins, and that Christ, with all his benefits, belong to him, notwithstanding his unworthiness." This faith he held to be produced in the sinner's mind by the immediate influence of the Holy Spirit, revealing the fact that he is one of those for whom in particular Christ died ; contrary to what Edwards maintains, " that no revelation of secret facts by immediate suggestion is any thing spiritual and divine, in that sense wherein gracious effects and operations are so." Indeed, a list of the errors confuted in the " Treatise on Religious Affections," would form a very perfect summary of the false Calvinism of the day.

This treatise conferred a double benefit upon the churches. In the first place, it destroyed confidence in false experiences, so that men were no longer deceived with respect to their own piety, or that of others, by many things which had formerly deceived them ; and thus the number of false hopes and consequent apostasies has been vastly diminished, many souls have been saved from deluding themselves to their own destruction, and the cause of Christ has been saved from much reproach. And secondly, as a consequence of this, false experiences have in a great measure ceased ; for when certain states of mind are understood to be worse than worthless, men are no longer tempted to work themselves into them, or ministers to produce them ; and, satanic agency apart, a false experience is always the work of man. To estimate the amount of good achieved by this work, consider what the state of religion would be, if all the errors against which Edwards contends, were zealously urged and extensively prevalent in the churches.*

The restoration of the true doctrine concerning church membership was another important result of the revival: and this, too, was produced through the mind of Edwards. He must have seen the stupefying influence of the prevailing practice on the unconverted, who supposed that, as they were in the church according to God's appointment, their course of life was in some respect acceptable to him; and that, being in covenant with him, they were in little danger of dying till prepared for death. It is certain that the conduct of the Separatists received his anxious attention. He must, therefore, have seen their arguments against the admission of hypocrites into the church; and it was not in his nature to cast arguments away through prejudice, without ascertaining what mixture of truth there might be in them. He must have seen, too, how closely the practice of receiving unconverted members was connected with the cant about "censoriousness," and the demand that no orthodox and moral man should be considered, addressed, or in any way treated, as an unconverted person. In short, the revival must have shown him how the prevalent usage, in many ways, took off the edge of divine truth, and shielded men from its assaults.

Dr. Hopkins says, that Edwards had scruples on this point at the time of his ordination, but not such as to prevent his adopting the practice with a good conscience; "but at length his doubts increased; which put him upon examining it thoroughly. The result was, a full conviction that it was wrong." He does not tell when this change of opinion took place; but it was evidently before his Treatise on the Affections was published;† and Dr. S. E. Dwight intimates, that

* The authority of this Treatise has been sustained, mainly, by the evident wisdom of its practical conclusions, which commend themselves to every man's conscience, while the philosophy which runs through it has not been generally understood. Edwards derives all gracious affections from "a new simple idea," which is different, in its very nature, from any idea received through the bodily senses, and "which could be produced by no exalting, varying or compounding" of any ideas thus received. But according to the philosophy which has generally prevailed for many years past, man can have no ideas but such as are received through the bodily senses, or are formed from those thus received; and of course, the "new simple idea" of which Edwards speaks, is impossible. If the doctrine of that Treatise is right, the intellectual philosophy which has usually been taught in our colleges is wrong.

† Edwards' Works, 4: 361. Worcester's edition Dwight's Life of Edwards, p. 305, 314.

it was communicated to some of his people still earlier. But it was not till December, 1748, that he had occasion to act officially on his new principles, by telling a young man who offered to join the church, that he could not be active in admitting him, without a profession of piety. In February, 1749, he communicated his views to the committee of the church, and proposed to preach on the subject; for, though he correctly claimed it as his undoubted right to select the subjects of his sermons according to his own discretion, he thought it not proper to bring that agitating topic into the pulpit, without the express approbation of his people. They were unwilling that he should preach on it; but, as the church ought to be informed of his opinions and his reasons for them, they proposed that he should do it in print. Accordingly, he prepared his "Humble Inquiry into the Rules of the Word of God, concerning the Qualifications requisite to a Complete Standing and Full Communion in the Visible Christian Church." It was printed at Boston, under the supervision of Foxcroft, and with a letter from him to Edwards, as an appendix, proving, by a multitude of learned quotations, that the Protestant churches of Europe had always held saving grace to be an indispensable qualification for acceptably partaking of the Lord's Supper. They did not, however, touch the question, whether the church ought to exclude those who give no evidence of saving grace, or whether the question of fitness, except in cases of heresy and scandal, should be left wholly to the communicant. They did not touch the conclusion against which Edwards was arguing, but they demolished one of its chief supports.

"Mr. Edwards was sensible," his biographers tell us, "that his principles were not understood, but misrepresented through the country;" but they do not tell us what principles were imputed to him. We may learn it, however, from a consideration of the circumstances.

The practice introduced by Stoddard had become general in New England. The old churches which had never adopted it, kept on their way quietly, and their dissent attracted no attention. The Separatists, however, had been loud in their denunciations of churches which admitted "hypocrites" to their communion, and were the only body then before the public, as opposers of the church membership of unconverted persons. The strength of their system, that which gave it any hold on the consciences of men, lay in the very doctrine which Edwards had now avowed. What could be more natural than a cry, that he was going over to the Separatists, or perhaps, that he had actually adopted their views?

The Rev. Solomon Williams, of Lebanon, whose influence in reclaiming Davenport was well known, and who had published a reply to Croswell's book on "Justifying Faith," and who had thus become prominent as an opposer of the Separatists, answered Edwards' work of the Qualifications for Communion. Edwards, in his rejoinder, which finished the controversy, as it left nothing more to be said, complained that Williams had misrepresented his views. Among other "misrepresentations," he charged Edwards with holding, that the church should require a relation of the candidate's "inward experiences." For this, the Separatists were distinguished. He charges Edwards with insisting on "an account of such inward feelings, as are by men supposed to be the certain discriminating marks of grace." This, again, likened him to the Separatists; and he himself remarks on this imputation, "Mr. Williams knew that these phrases, 'experiences' and 'inward feelings,' were become odious of late to a great part of the country." He represented Edwards' principles to be "such as suppose men to be searchers of others' hearts;" a standing reproach against the Separatists. Another misrepresentation was, that Edwards would attempt, as if it were practicable, to exclude all unsanctified persons from the church. This also was like the Separatists. In a note appended to his Reply, Edwards says, "Many reports spread about the country, that I insisted on perfection as a term of communion." Perfectionism had appeared among the Separatists. About the time of his dismission, some of the Separatists wrote to him, claiming him as one of their number;* and doubtless they had advanced similar claims at an earlier date.

But we need not rely on inferences. Edwards himself sums up these misrepresentations, in the preface to his Farewell Sermon, in these words: "That I insisted on persons' being assured of their being in a state of salvation, in order

* Backus' Eccl. Hist. of the Baptists in N. E. Backus was first a Separatist, and became a Baptist about this time.

to my admitting them into the church; that I required a particular relation of the method and order of a person's inward experiences, and of the time and manner of his conversion, as a test of his fitness for Christian communion; yea, that I have undertaken to set up a pure church, and to make an exact and certain distinction between saints and hypocrites, by a pretended infallible discerning of the state of men's souls; that in these things I had fallen in with those wild people, who have lately appeared in New England, called Separatists; and that I myself was become a grand Separatist."

The Separatists had now made themselves even more odious than they were when Davenport was their leader. Some of them had become, in their own esteem, too holy to receive the ordinances from any such minister as was then on earth, and therefore baptized each other. Some of them had risen above the obligation of their marriage covenants, and the scandalous fruits of their unlawful intercourse had become notorious.* Their progress, and the mischiefs they wrought, had been sufficiently alarming, before such scandalous immoralities had appeared among them, and while Davenport was their greatest man. What, then, might be expected if Edwards, with his gigantic power and immense personal influence, should put himself at their head? When we consider also, that, as related by his biographers, several leading men had previously become disaffected, and were ready to believe the worst concerning him, and to propagate their belief, it cannot appear strange that Northampton was in commotion, that his people refused to hear him preach in defence of his supposed Separatism, and that the greater part of them were dissuaded from reading his book.

The final council on this subject was held June 22, 1750. There were present, ten pastors and nine delegates. On the question of his dismission, the pastors were equally divided. Each of the delegates voted as his pastor did; and as the Rev. Mr. Billings, of Cold Spring, had no delegate, there was a majority of one in favor of his dismission. Four pastors and three delegates of the minority published their pro-

* Backus gives particular instances, with the recital of which it is better not to stain these pages. He says, however, and doubtless with truth, that such things were not chargeable on the Separatists generally.

test, for several reasons; one of which was, "his sentiments being, as we apprehend, perfectly harmonious with the mind of our Lord Jesus Christ, and strictly conformable with the practice of the apostles, and that of the Reformed Church in general throughout the world." Four of the majority published a reply to the Protest. This called forth a Vindication of the Protest, by the Rev. William Hobby, of Reading, one of the protesters. This provoked, from the same members of the majority, "A Letter to the Rev. Mr. Hobby, in answer to his Vindication." This letter contained statements which Edwards was obliged to "nail to the counter," in a letter to Hobby, through the press. It was now June, 1751. His Reply to Williams was not published till November, 1752; about three years and a half after his first publication on the subject.

The influence of these proceedings and publications could not but be great. The name of Edwards was enough to rally all who had still held to the primitive constitution of the New England churches; and when called forth, they were far from being contemptible, either in numbers or in weight of character. His influence was enough to recommend the doctrine to all the friends of the revival. The revival itself, by reviving the belief that the unregenerate ought to be treated as unregenerate, in order to their conversion, prepared and predisposed the minds of its friends to receive his doctrine. His dismission produced a deep feeling of astonishment, of sympathy for him, and of indignation against his opposers, not only throughout New England, but in the other colonies, and even in Great Britain. All these things drew attention to this controversy, and disposed the pious to be on his side. Half the ministers of the council that dismissed him, declared, in their protest, that they believed his doctrine to be according to the Scriptures, and one of them, Billings of Cold Spring, was dismissed in the spring of 1752 for his adherence to it; but, as few churches could be willing to place themselves by the side of that in Northampton in the public estimation, it is not known that any other minister was dismissed for the same cause.

A full account, in detail, of the spread of Edwards' doctrine concerning church membership, would be interesting and instructive; but materials for it could be found, only by examining the records of the several churches that acted upon it; and those records, in most cases, were badly kept, and a great part of them have been lost. We know, however, the general result. Every Congregational church in New England, probably, has either adopted that doctrine,* or become Unitarian. The future destiny of each of the churches seems to have depended more on its treatment of this question, than on any other single event. Those that were friendly to the revival, generally, but not universally, returned with Edwards to the ancient doctrine and practice, were thenceforth composed of members who made a credible profession of piety, and are saved. Those hostile to the revival, regarded that doctrine and practice as "divisive," as "uncharitable," as "censorious," as "an invasion of God's prerogative, to judge the heart." They continued the practice of making no discrimination between men as converted or unconverted, and in most, but not all cases, the result is, that now, no man is excluded from their communion for any error in doctrine, or any immorality in practice;† and in some of them, even the form of church membership is given up; the churches, as distinct from the congregations, no longer exist, and the ordinances are administered indiscriminately to all who will receive them.

This revival of the ancient doctrine produced other important consequences. It destroyed the power of the Separatists. They had lived and increased by the power of the truth, that churches ought to be composed of pious men. For a time, they alone had attracted attention as its advocates. It had now a more conspicuous advocate. The man to whom all eyes were turned as its chief defender, was not one of their number. Their weapon was taken away, and wielded by a mightier hand. The host that rallied under him, out-numbered them immensely, surpassed them still more in talents, in learning, and in Christian character, and

* In some, — the Old South Church in Boston, for example, — the Half-way Covenant system has never been expressly abrogated, but only fallen into disuse.

† At least, the most extensive inquiries which the author has been able to make, have led him to the conclusion, that no such thing as discipline exists in the Unitarian churches. Some of their leading publications have submitted in silence to the charge of its entire absence, when they might be expected to deny it if they could. All their language concerning excommunication and exclusion, strengthens this belief. This is a sufficient reason, and should be urged as the prominent reason, why membership in a Unitarian church cannot be a passport to our communion tables.

was not justly chargeable with their offensive irregularities; still less with the immoralities which had begun to appear among them. The adoption of this doctrine, too, shielded a multitude of churches from their most dangerous attacks; for they could no longer plausibly denounce them as churches that knowingly admitted hypocrites. Thus disarmed of its strength, the sect ceased to grow, and soon began to decline.*

The influence of this change on other communions has been important. The doctrine that churches ought to be composed of pious men, so appeals to the conscience, that none who hold to a discoverable difference between the pious and the impious, can wholly withstand it. In the United States, its power is felt in every sect, where experimental religion is not condemned as a delusion. There is nothing in the "Standards" of the Presbyterian Church, which

---

* They seem to have been increasing and organizing rapidly about this time. Backus (Vol. 2, page 175) gives the following list of Separatist ordinations; —

"Solomon Paine, at Canterbury, Sept. 10; Thomas Stephens, at Plainfield, Sept. 11; Thomas Denison, at Norwich Farms, Oct. 29; Jedediah Hyde, at Norwich Town, Oct. 30; *Matthew Smith*, at Stonington, Dec. 10; John Fuller, at Lyme, Dec. 25; Joseph Snow, at Providence, Feb. 12, 1747; Samuel Wadsworth, at Killingly, June 3; Paul Park, at Preston, July 15; *Elihu Marsh*, at Windham, Oct. 7; Ebenezer Frothingham, at Wethersfield, Oct. 28; Nathaniel Shepherd, at Attleborough, Jan. 20, 1748; — *Isaac Backus*, at Bridgewater, April 13; John Paine, at Rehoboth, Aug. 3; *William Carpenter*, at Norton, Sept. 7; *John Blunt*, at Sturbridge, Sept. 28; *Ebenezer Mack*, at Lyme, Jan. 12, 1749; — Joshua Nickerson, at Harwich, Feb. 23; Samuel Hyde, at Bridgewater, May 11; John Palmer, at Windham, May 17; *Samuel Hovey*, at Mendon, May 31; Samuel Drown, at Coventry, Oct. 11; Stephen Babcock, at Westerly, April 4, 1740. [probably a misprint for 1750:] *Joseph Hastings*, at Suffield, April 7; Nathaniel Ewer, at Barnstable, May 17; Jonathan Hyde, at Brookline, Jan. 17, 1751; Ezekiel Cole, at Sutton, Jan. 31; Ebenezer Wadsworth, at Grafton, March 20; Nathaniel Draper, at Cambridge, April 24; Peter Warden. May 17." — To these he adds an "&c." Not improbably, the punctuation is erroneous, so as to throw some of them into the wrong year. Those in italics became Baptists.

He also informs us, that Elder Moulton baptized thirteen members of the Separatist church in Sturbridge, in 1749, and soon after, all its officers and most of its members, more than sixty in number. They were taxed, to support the minister of the Congregational church. In Framingham, a church was organized by a council in 1747. It seems to have been at least tinctured with Separatism. Its members were taxed for the support of the minister of the town, and became Baptists. In Titicut, between Bridgewater and Middleborough, where a revival had commenced in 1741, some parish difficulties ended in the establishment of a Separatist meeting in December, 1747; a church was organized in February, 1748; its members were taxed, as usual, and became Baptists.

requires evidence, or even a profession, of personal piety, as a condition of membership; and yet it is very generally required. The written law of the Wesleyans is as Wesley left it; admitting all "who have the form, and are seeking the power, of godliness," with such a seeking as the unregenerate are capable of; but they are generally unwilling to admit, that they receive unconverted men to their communion. In the Protestant Episcopal Church, there are multitudes who regard "confirmation" as a profession of piety, such as is made by those who join Congregational churches, and who are grieved if it is not so understood by others. In all these communions, the influence of this great idea on the members and on the public around them, doubtless enforces a stricter discipline, and makes membership without apparent piety more uncomfortable and less common. It does much to keep unfit members out of those communions, and to secure regularity of life among those that are within. The influence of the revival in this respect can scarce be estimated too highly. It brought out and presented in bold relief, the idea, that conversion is a change, ordinarily discoverable by its effects, so that he who exhibits no evidence of it, may with propriety be regarded as an unconverted man; and then it created a demand in the public conscience, for evidence of conversion in church-members; and the beneficial influence of this demand is felt in all evangelical churches.

It would be curious, and might be instructive, but it would require a volume, to trace out the influence of this great awakening on what has been called "New England Theology." Its great names are, Edwards, who was the great man of the revival; Bellamy, his pupil, a younger but scarcely less powerful laborer in it; and Hopkins, who was converted during the revival, and also studied theology with Edwards. The revival could not fail to exert a powerful influence on their theological inquiries; and there is abundant evidence, in the style of reasoning which they introduced, that it did not. From beginning to end, it all looks at practical results; it seeks to produce the phenomena of a revival; it aims to work a change in the sinner's mind, of which he will be sensible, and which others may observe. For this purpose, it addresses him as a sinner, as an unbeliever, over whom proof-texts, even from the word of God, have no controlling power. It aims to show him the reasonableness of the constitution under which God has placed him, and of the demand, that he should immediately "repent and be converted;" and to make him feel his entire dependence on God, and at the same time, his entire responsibility for his moral state. Its defects sprung from the same source. It too much neglected whatever in theology did not bear, obviously and directly, on these favorite points. It paid too little attention to Biblical proof, the force of which the impenitent and unbelieving would not feel. And in the hands of some men of a later day, it was too much biased in favor of whatever scheme promised to work well in bringing sinners under conviction. In other words, its continual regard for practical utility led some to embrace doctrines which they judged to be convenient, instead of doctrines which they had proved to be true ; or more accurately, perhaps, to take their own opinion of the convenience of a doctrine, for proof of its truth.

Something was accomplished, too, in the cause of religious liberty, in various parts of the country ; but as the mode of operation was not everywhere the same, they must be considered separately.

In New England, it gave a mortal wound to parish despotism. The idea of religious liberty which the Puritans brought with them to New England, was correct so far as it went ; and it went far in advance of their age. They held that each duly organized "congregation of faithful men" is a church, an entire church, having full power to manage its own religious concerns, and not subject, in spiritual matters, either by appeal or otherwise, to any larger body, or to any man or body of men ; being under no religious obligations to other Christian communities, except those of Christian kindness, confidence and respect. Even those of them who were called Presbyterians, held to a presbytery of elders in each congregation, elected by the brethren, and not to a presbytery composed in part of the representatives of other churches ; for it was a fundamental principle with them, that no Congregational church could rightfully be subjected to any earthly jurisdiction out of itself. In each church, every question was to be decided by a majority of votes, or by the elected presbytery. There were two guards against the despotism of the majority. First, the church had no jurisdiction over any but its own members, and no one became a member except by his own request. Secondly, every member in regular standing, had a right to transfer his membership to some other church, whenever he judged it necessary "for better edification." A system of religious liberty so perfect as this, the modern world had never seen, and few of its wise men had ever thought of; and it would not be easy, even now, to tell what important addition has been made to its principles.

But their system was in danger. Except themselves and a few bold, truth-trusting brethren in England, nobody had any respect for it, or would hesitate to demolish it in a moment, at the call of a slight temptation. The "no-human government theory" of modern days was then rife among the Quakers, some of whom reduced it to practice more revoltingly than any have done of late. The German Anabaptists had claimed authority from heaven, to overthrow all government but their own, by force of arms. The Puritans saw, or thought they saw, confusion coming in from both these sources. They knew that they must maintain good order in their colony, or the English government would put it in order for them without ceremony, and probably in a way which would not spare their system of religious liberty. They thought it necessary, therefore, to repress Quakerism from the beginning; and when, after some years, their Baptist brethren began to adopt the German doctrine of close communion, to denounce their churches as no churches of Christ, and to gather others in utter disregard of them, they thought the whole brood of errors which had desolated Germany with civil war, was coming in upon them, and that this heresy also must be repressed. It was doubtless a false alarm; but it was natural and honest, and soon gave way to the force of evidence. The Church of England, too, or some of its members, as soon as the colonies began to rise in importance, wished to subject them and all their inhabitants to Episcopal jurisdiction;* and the plan was not aban-

* Probably many, and perhaps most, of the Episcopalians in the colonies, were innocent of any such design, and merely desired liberty to enjoy such forms of worship as they preferred; but the hopes of some of the leaders were avowed without disguise, and those of others were plainly visible through the disguise they threw over them; while the whole party were in favor of a system, which would in the end have subjected all the colonists to the dominion of bishops.

doned, till the establishment of Independence rendered it hopeless.

Though each particular form of danger had not been foreseen, the Puritans had been aware from the beginning, that their system of religious liberty would be assaulted by various forms of anarchy on the one hand, and of despotism on the other ; and they felt obliged to guard vigilantly against the approaches of both. They allowed the formation of no church, nor any preaching that might lead to the formation of a church, on any anarchical or despotic principles. They required every church member to submit quietly to the majority of his brethren ; or to transfer his membership, peaceably and regularly, to another church "for better edification ;" or to unite with others of his own mind, in peaceably and regularly forming a new church, which should be free from any principles of anarchy or despotism ; and to do this publicly, under the eyes of the rulers of the land, so that the safety of their proceedings might be known to all.* That compelling all men to receive freedom with its necessary safeguards, even against their will, may itself be a species of despotism, seems not to have occurred to them ; or, if it did, they knew not how to avoid it. The whole country was divided into parishes, in each of which a church was organized and a pastor settled according to law, with whose rights none were allowed to interfere. Almost universally, those members of a parish who were not members of the church, regarded its pastor as their religious teacher, and were active in his selection, settlement and support. He was the minister of that parish. He was held responsible for the religious instruction of its inhabitants. The idea grew up very naturally, that those who held him thus responsible, should not put themselves under other teachers without his leave, and that other teachers ought not to derange his plans of usefulness, by breaking in upon his parish contrary to his judgment ; and

---

* If those who held to the baptism of believers only, and that by immersion, had been willing to form their churches in this way, it is by no means certain that they would have met with any opposition. It is quite certain, that they were not "persecuted" for their belief concerning baptism, or for acting according to it, till they became close-communionists, and set at nought the established ecclesiastical order. Then their principles, as they believed, forbade them to recognise the standing churches as churches of Christ, by taking letters of dismission from them; and the natural result,—natural in that age of the world,—soon followed.

thus it came to be extensively felt, both by ministers and others, that a pastor had at least a moral right to control the giving and receiving of religious instruction within the geographical bounds of his parish.

There would be no valid objection against this system, if we could only secure, in every parish, a pastor who would supply all the spiritual wants of every one of his parishioners; or if every pastor would be aware of his own deficiencies, and supply them by procuring such assistance as he needs. But as the world is, it exposes the parishioners of a worldly, a heretical, an indolent or an incompetent pastor, to spiritual starvation; and that, nothing can bind them to endure, or other ministers to allow. People have a right to such preaching as they need; and the ministers of Christ have a right to preach his gospel to all those who need their labors; and no minister whose people are perishing through his deficiencies, can possibly have any Christian right to interfere.

This truth, the revival made to be deeply felt. There were many pastors, whose people needed other preaching than theirs. Their people became convinced of it, and would hear other preachers. Zealous ministers became convinced of it, and would preach to the perishing, wherever they found them. The solemn claims of eternity, deeply felt, overcame all regard for parish lines and the official authority of ministers.

This point was vigorously contested; as appears by the whole warfare against itinerants, and in much of that against the Separatists. The reader has already seen how it was assailed by Testimonies in Massachusetts, and in Connecticut by legislation. Ministers not only refused to open their pulpits to itinerants, and cautioned their people against hearing them, — which they had an undoubted right to do, if the itinerants were dangerous men, — but in some instances, that of Odlin, at Exeter, for example, forbade itinerants to preach within certain geographical limits. They laid the hand of authority, also, on members of their churches. Dr. Chauncy, in his Convention Sermon in 1744, urged a bold and vigorous use of church discipline, as a means of repressing disorders, and building up the churches "in peace and holiness." Though he spoke in general terms, he alluded very distinctly to the "exhorters," who "left their own business, and took upon them the work that was proper to ministers," and to the disorders which attended their meetings; though he also intimated that others, who "walk in a disorderly manner," needed discipline. In the Convention Sermon of the next year, the Rev. Peter Clark spoke still more plainly. He proposed the inquiry, "Whether the disorderly separations, that have so greatly prevailed in the several churches of the land, have been duly animadverted on in the way of ecclesiastical discipline." This, he thought, "the most likely method of putting a stop to it, by keeping up the reverence of order in the church of God; by representing the beauty and majesty of Christ's spiritual government; by letting men know that the church of Christ is not a confused rout, or like 'a city broken down, and without walls,' leaving men at their liberty to go and come without control." This advice was followed, probably, in many places. The historian of Chelmsford states, that all Separatism, and all following after itinerants and exhorters, was effectually repressed there by church discipline. In many places the Separatists, not having organized their churches regularly, according to law, were harassed by taxation for the support of the ministers from whom they had seceded, of which several instances have been mentioned. At last this system of annoyances became too odious to be continued, and fell into disuse; but the contest never ceased, till the law enabling towns to settle ministers was repealed, and every citizen was left to do as his conscience or his covetousness might dictate, about supporting the gospel. It is well known that the Unitarians, who are the ecclesiastical successors of the disciplining party, defended that law to the last; and that the Baptists, and all who are descended in whole or in part from Separatism, were ever its uncompromising opponents.

In New York, New Jersey and Pennsylvania, the operation was different. Here was the principal seat of the Presbyterian Church. The agreement by which the two Synods were united after the schism, bound each minister to open his pulpit in ordinary cases to any brother who desired it. This was evidently intended to secure to the friends of vital piety the privilege of preaching to all Presbyterians, and to all Presbyterian congregations the privilege of hearing good preaching. But the greatest danger there was from episcopacy. Under the administration of Lord Cornbury, in 1707, the Rev. Francis Makemie, the patriarch of Presbyterianism, had been arrested and imprisoned for several months, for preaching in New York; and there is little doubt that on his discharge, he was obliged to repair to Boston, to get the account of his trial and imprisonment printed.* And when the First Presbyterian Church in New York, some years after, applied to the king for a charter, that they might be enabled to hold their own house of worship and burying-ground, instead of vesting them in the Church of Scotland as trustee, the Episcopalians for some time successfully resisted the application. The Episcopalians then claimed to be the established church in New York, to which all but the Dutch, whose right of dissent was secured by treaty, owed ecclesiastical obedience. Indeed, some of them advanced the same claim, in respect to all the colonies. The great increase of strength which the revival gave to Presbyterianism, was a powerful element of resistance to that claim.

In Virginia, Episcopalianism was as rigidly established and enforced by law, as ever Puritanism had been in New England. All were taxed to support the clergy, and compelled by fines to attend worship. In the preceding century, missionaries from New England had been arrested and sent home. The account already given from the pen of Davies, concerning the origin of Presbyterianism in Virginia, shows the want of religious liberty at that time, and what was the first efficient agency in promoting it. Presbyterianism continued to grow, and to struggle for liberty and equality of rights, till, being joined by the increasing power of the Baptists † and by other influences, it overthrew the spiritual despotism which had subsisted from the planting of the colony.

The establishment of religious freedom in Virginia was perfected by the aid of that political party, of which Jefferson was the leader. Jefferson, in his youth, had gained his first clear idea of a republican government, from seeing the Congregationalism of a Baptist church in his vicinity. Though a French infidel in respect to religion, he was in favor of liberty everywhere. It was good policy, too, for him and his party to strengthen themselves by an alliance with the friends of religious freedom. Their writings, speeches and votes on this subject procured them favor with

* See the account, in the O. S. Ch. Lib. with Ms. annotations by Prince.

† The First Baptist Association in Virginia was formed in 1766.

all the Baptists, Methodists, and other opponents of the Church of England at the South, and with the members of the same sects generally throughout the country ; while it threw all the friends of universal taxation for the support of the gospel, and all whose dread of French infidelity was their strongest religious feeling, into the opposite party. Thus the influence of the revival in Virginia reacted upon New England, and aided in the complete establishment of religious fredom.*

It would be saying too much, to ascribe to the revival any appreciable influence in producing the independence of the United States ; though the waking up of mind among men of all classes, the revival of those truths in which the free spirit of Puritanism had its origin, the earnest discussion of the principles of freedom and human rights, and the habit of contending for rights sturdily and with religious zeal, which was nourished among men of all orders, were doubtless useful in preparing many minds for the questions that awaited them. The causes of resistance to British aggression, however, were older and more general than the influence of the revival, and operated strongly in the minds of families and classes that opposed it, such as the Hancocks of New England, and the Episcopalians of Virginia. But the revival, commencing when the mature men of the Revolution were in their youth, was evidently a merciful provision against the dangers of that day. The demoralizing influence of war awaited the land. The political writings of Thomas Paine, through all of which there runs a secret vein of infidel metaphysics, were to become popular. The country was about to be brought into close alliance and friendly intercourse with France, where infidelity was already rife, and was soon to be openly predominant. The French republic was to dazzle the world with promises of freedom more perfect than the world had ever seen, but of which infidelity was an essential constituent, and this country was to be under peculiar temptations to be deluded by them. The religious principles of the country needed to be strengthened in advance, against all

* This was not the principal cause which produced the old Federal and Democratic parties, and determined the character of each ; but its influence was too important to be overlooked, and must be duly appreciated by every one who would understand their history. The political affinities then formed, continue still to operate in some parts of the country ; though the cause which produced them has long ceased to exist.

these dangers. With all the accession of strength that religion received from the revival, it did but just stand the shock; and for a long time, many of the pious feared that every thing holy would be swept away. Strengthened by so many tens of thousands of converts, and by the deep sense of the importance of religion produced in other tens of thousands, both in and out of the churches, religion survived, in time rallied and advanced, and is marching on to victory.*

This great revival should teach the Christian world some salutary lessons, which it would be improper to close this work without mentioning.

It should teach, that there is a proper sphere for the labors of itinerant evangelists, and where it may be found.

That a pastor may sometimes, with propriety, leave his own flock for a season, in the care of a substitute, or even without a substitute, to labor where his help is needed and desired, no one, perhaps, has ever doubted. The utility of this practice is too manifest to be called in question. Such labors were often performed by Edwards and others in New England; and by the Tennents and others in New Jersey and Pennsylvania. Such was Tennent's visit, and Whitefield's first visit, to Boston. But this is not itinerant evangelism. Nor is there any good reason why a licentiate, or an ordained minister temporarily without charge, should not assist a pastor who needs and desires his assistance. The question relates not to these. It relates wholly to itinerant evangelists by profession; to those who, like Whitefield, deem it their "duty to evangelize, and not to fix in any particular place." It can scarce be any man's duty to resolve that he will continue in such labors during life; for he cannot know what the calls of duty shall be on the morrow; but there is a proper field for such labors, and some ought to engage in them.

Such a field was presented by Great Britain and her

* Notwithstanding all that is said of the "degeneracy of the age," and notwithstanding all the lamentable facts which give it plausibility, the author is fully convinced, as the result of the best induction from facts within his power, that this country, as a whole, has been steadily advancing in religion, in good morals, in regard for law and order, and in rational, Christian ideas of liberty, almost if not quite from the beginning of the present century. That Scripture is fulfilled, which declares, that "the memory of the wicked shall rot" The faults and follies of former years are to a great extent forgotten, and therefore the past looks better than it really was.

American colonies in the time of Whitefield. In all parts of the kingdom, there were churches which had a name to live, but were dead. Many pastors, in various parts, were loose in their lives ; many in all parts were unsound in doctrine ; and still more were, — to use Tennent's language, — "contentedly unsuccessful." They were unwilling to be roused, or that their people should be roused, from their slumbers. They must be suffered to lead their people down to perdition, or some evangelist must break in upon them and rouse them against their will. It was so in New England ; though, in Whitefield's judgment, less so than in any other part of the world. The best men of that day were perfectly aware of it ; though, for various reasons, they did not proclaim it without reserve. The "contentedly unsuccessful" were in regular ecclesiastical standing, and generally free from any such overt act of sin or avowal of heresy as would furnish grounds for deposing them ; and the cases of many were so doubtful, that a good man would not dare to accuse them, lest he should do them injustice ; while an accusation against the whole body, as containing unsound members, would be met, as it was in the Synod of Philadelphia when Blair and Tennent made it, by a challenge to point out and convict the guilty. They therefore brought no accusations ; but they silently assumed the need of itinerant evangelists, and acted accordingly. This may have been a blamably timid course, but it was perfectly natural. Its character was well understood at the time. Tennent was questioned in the newspapers, whether his coming to New England was not prompted by the belief, that the settled ministers there were insufficient for their work. Chauncy, in his letter to Whitefield, put the same interpretation on Tennent's visit. To this question, no inoffensive answer could be returned, and it was not answered ; though Tennent answered distinctly all the other questions that accompanied it. The same censure on the ministry was implied in the arguments by which the employment of itinerants was defended. It was said that no great reformation had ever been effected without such labor ; that the Reformers in Germany, and Knox and his coadjutors in Scotland, and even the apostles themselves, were itinerants. Prince said, that Jesus Christ was an itinerant preacher. This argument was to the purpose, only on the supposition that here, as in the cases referred to, people were led astray by false or incompetent guides, who ought to be converted, or displaced by a reformation. Whitefield himself gave his opinion without reserve in his Journal, that "many, perhaps most that preach," were unconverted men; and though he afterwards justly condemned his rashness, in saying this with so little opportunity to know the facts, he never retracted his opinion. Other itinerants, besides Davenport, were still more reckless, and attacked individual ministers by name, as unconverted, and wrote them letters of admonition and warning accordingly. Tennent's "Nottingham Sermon" was republished at Boston, and extensively circulated. Every thing, in short, implied the belief, that there was an extensive deficiency in the ministry, and that a reformation was needed. The sounder part of the ministers and churches could not, for many reasons, proclaim that they were too good to need the remedy which they insisted on administering to their brethren. If itinerants were to be employed, they must be encouraged to go through the land, and preach to all indiscriminately, wherever they could. Thus, and thus only, could the hearers of "contentedly unsuccessful" ministers be effectually reached. It was done. The state of the country demanded and justified the doing of it. Whatever language of general approbation may have been used concerning the employment of itinerants, the controlling motive for employing them was evidently drawn from the existing need of their labors. Among the Presbyterians, and in England, the same motives were avowed with less restraint.

The ministry for whose reformation such a system is adopted, cannot be expected to submit to it quietly. It begins with an implied declaration, that they are unfit for their places, and unworthy of the confidence which is reposed in them, and of the emoluments they receive; and it threatens to reduce them to their proper level. A few may be compelled, by their own consciences, to admit the truth of the charge, and may reform; but generally, they will resent and repel the attack. The evangelist will often be compelled to violate ecclesiastical order and ministerial courtesy; for he goes where that order is made a wall of defence against saving truth, and where that courtesy would require him to honor the unfaithful. If successful, he will divide churches and unsettle ministers. He may wish and seek to avoid it as far as possible, by the conversion of whole churches with their pastors; but such will not be the usual result of his labors. He brings "not peace, but a sword," and sets neighbours, friends and families "at variance," and will be condemned as a disturber of the peace of society and of the churches; as an "uncharitable," "divisive" and "slanderous" man. Unpleasant as such things are, he should be prepared for them, and meet them without disappointment, and without irritation. If he is a suitable man, and performs the labors and endures the trials of his vocation with a right spirit, the result will be, as it ever has been, good.

The events of that day, however, give no sanction to the employment of itinerants, where there is no such need of them. How could they? How could the usefulness of evangelists, in breaking in upon degenerate churches in despite of unfaithful pastors, prove that they must be useful in a community of sound churches under faithful pastors? The experiment was not tried; for there was no considerable region on earth, in which to try it. Some things were said, indeed, in favor of employing itinerants irrespective of any fault in the ministry or the churches; but they were said under the influence of strong temptation. Men must say them, or own that the employment of itinerants implied an accusation, which they were unwilling to bring. They were the mere speculations of tempted men, concerning what would be proper in a state of things that did not then exist, and who were mainly led to employ itinerants by other motives. They are therefore of little weight.

It is true, that itinerants labored in some of the soundest churches, under some of the best pastors, in the land; and that good results followed. It is equally true, that evil results followed their labors in such places; and it is not possible to ascertain how much of the good, or of the evil, was fairly chargeable to their influence. It must be remembered, that the revival was not commenced by the labors of itinerants, but of settled pastors; of Edwards and others in New England, and of the Tennents, Blair, and their coadjutors in New Jersey and Pennsylvania. It commenced even before Whitefield began to preach in England. Or if we, most unphilosophically, leave the "Surprising Conversions" at Northampton and other places before 1739 out of the account, still the revival had commenced and been spreading in New England, under the labors of the pastors, for nearly a year before Whitefield arrived; and there was every encouragement to hope, that it would be more extensive, powerful, and fruitful of good, than any that New England had ever witnessed. In its progress, some of the richest harvests were gathered in towns where itinerants never labored; and in some places where the best results attended their labors, the awakening had commenced before their arrival, and the results would have been good, perhaps equally good, and possibly even better, without their assistance.

The history of that period, therefore, furnishes no decisive answer to the question, whether itinerant evangelists ought to be employed among sound churches having faithful pastors; though it furnishes an abundance of facts, from which a partisan may construct a plausible argument on either side. But it shows that churches may be so degenerate, and pastors so unsound, unfaithful, or "contentedly unsuccessful," as to justify and demand their employment. If any attempt to embarrass, and practically to nullify, this conclusion, by asking who is to judge where evangelists are needed, and whether every evangelist is to judge for himself, and go wherever his own vanity prompts him, the answer is ready. The right and wrong of every case depend upon its circumstances, and not upon any man's judgment concerning it. The evangelist must inquire, and consult, and judge correctly, and act accordingly, or take the consequences of doing wrong. Neither his office, nor his erroneous opinion that he is doing right, nor the approbation of any man or body of men, can justify him in intruding his services upon those who would be better without them, or can bind any to receive his labors, who do not need them. As the majority of the signers of the Testimony of July, 1743, correctly thought, "this liberty cannot be invaded or denied without inhumanly invading the essential rights of conscience; so it must be left to the *serious consciences* both of ministers and people," whether they will admit an evangelist among them. In like manner, the "serious conscience" of the itinerant must decide, to whom he will offer his services, and how strenuously he will seek access to those who reject him.

Another lesson is one of admonition, concerning the dangers that attend a revival. Human beings, while on earth, are always in some danger of doing wrong things, and of acting in a wrong spirit. The spirit of a revival gives them an impulse towards that which is good, but by no means makes them infallible ; while, in many cases, the consciousness that they are moving mainly in a right direction, diminishes their sense of liability to error. Those whose humility and self-distrust are too weak in proportion to their zeal, naturally become obstinate in their errors, and condemn all who hesitate to embrace them. When the most zealous leaders have at length placed themselves clearly in the wrong, the common sense of mankind revolts against them, their influence for good ceases, and the revival ends in a quarrel. In time, passion subsides ; those who have quarrelled are assailed by remorse ; they become penitent ; they seek and obtain pardon for their sins ; another revival commences, and, if they have not learned humility and a teachable spirit, ends like the former. Instead of moving steadily onward in the straight line of duty, they move in a circle, which at first touches that line, and varies from it, as they advance, only by an almost imperceptible difference, which no man can notice without seeming censurably cold ; but which gradually diverges, and at length carries them away at right angles from their proper course, and then backward, and round again to the point from which they started.

When a revival is very powerful and very general, so that, to those within its influence, the whole world seems to be awakened, they are very apt to talk of "the spirit of the age," to take that spirit for their guide, and to condemn or approve of men, in proportion to the entireness with which that spirit governs them. This is "mistaking the vane for the compass," and is sure to end in evil. The spirit of any age is the spirit of the men of that age ; the spirit of men either wholly sinful, or sanctified but in part. It is, therefore, either wholly or in part, a wrong spirit ; and whoever gives himself up to be led by it without reserve, will inevitably be led into sin and folly. Such persons, "measuring themselves by themselves, and comparing themselves among themselves, are not wise." The spirit of the purest revival has in it a mixture of error and of evil, and must be often corrected by a standard more perfect than itself, or it will bring itself to an end by its own faults. Detecting the faults of a revival, therefore, and correcting them, is a work of the first importance.

On this subject, the history of the "Great Awakening" is full of instruction.

Consider the temptations and errors of Whitefield; his letter to Pemberton of New York, asking pardon for his arrogant treatment of him, when "puffed up" with success; his letter from Savannah, full of thanks for reproof, and entreating forgiveness of all his friends for his "too imperious carriage;" his dictatorial letter to Wesley, written while "puffed up" by his first triumphs at Boston, which every writer on his character mentions to this day, — his friends with regret and his enemies with triumph; the self-complacent vanity with which he told how well he preached whenever the governor heard him; and the rash and indecent haste, with which he condemned the majority of New England pastors as graceless men, when he had not had time to form even a probable conjecture of their character. Think of the half holy, half ambitious aspirations of Barber and Davenport, for a great revival, which should do great good and make them great men; and how Davenport, more and more deceived, continually rising in his own esteem, and mistaking the unhealthy stimulus of a fever for the illapses of the Holy Ghost, became an obstinate and wrathful fanatic. To say nothing of multitudes of weak and ignorant men, who, moved by the spirit of the age, gave themselves out for great ones, and went about zealously doing mischief where they meant to do good, — think of saner men than Davenport; of Allen, comparing the Bible to an old almanac; of Wheelock, raising his voice, so as to increase the confusion, when his hearers cried out, pushing the most exciting exercises to the most exciting extent and duration, and recording in his journal before he slept, that so many "were converted" that evening; of Brainerd, thinking, feeling, speaking and acting with such "indecent heat," for months, that he himself condemned his journal for that period to the flames, and began anew by recording its condemnation. The proof is conclusive, that leaders in a revival are in special danger of becoming proud, arrogant, rash and unsafe men. Nothing but exemplary watchfulness over their own spirits, aided by faithful admonitions and rebukes from those who see their faults, and attended by the special grace of God, can prevent it. The proof is conclusive, too, that the itinerant revivalist is in peculiar danger. As he naturally soon leaves a place where he is unsuccessful, he spends most of his time where his own power over the minds of men is the most conspicuous object in his sight, and where he is delighted with the visible proofs of his own eminent usefulness ; and he is evermore surrounded by those who, either through design or indiscretion, act the part of flatterers, even otherwise than by their presence and interested attention to all he says. He has abundant reason to know, with Whitefield, "how difficult it is, to meet with success, and not be puffed up with it," and to say with him, "my corruptions are so strong, and my employ so dangerous, that I am sometimes afraid."

The itinerant's danger is the greater, from the improbability that he will receive such admonition and reproof as he needs. If he has habitual attendants, as Whitefield had, they will mostly be his devoted friends, who admire all his errors. Much the greater part of his intercourse is with comparative strangers, who are aware that they do not know him well enough to admonish him judiciously, and that he does not know them well enough to appreciate their admonitions, and who therefore excuse themselves from the task. Opposers will speak of his faults ; but his friends will pronounce their censures unjust, and will be indignant ; and he will see that they are exaggerated, and perhaps malicious, and will probably give no heed to them ; or perhaps he will think, that what "the enemy" hates, must be right ; and, as he finds numbers ready to sustain him, will go on in his errors. What good man ever needed checking in his career, more than Davenport, when he came to Boston ? And yet what an outcry was raised, because the pastors protested against his errors, while they avowed their hope, that God had used him "as an instrument of doing good unto many souls !" "And why," exclaimed Croswell, in his published reply, "are they not willing that God should use him as an instrument of doing good unto more souls ?" And numbers of zealous men were found, to echo the reply ; Boston was filled with angry controversy, and the awakening there was at an end. Even such faults as his could not be reproved, without bringing such rebukes upon the reprovers. The preacher and his partisans grow wild together ; and whatever be his faults, no one can mention them, without being denounced as an opposer of the work of God.*

* For a further illustration, see Turell's Directions to his People, and Croswell's Answer.

Almost inevitably, therefore, the itinerant will become an obstinate man; obstinate in his errors, and obstinate in proportion to his errors. Of all the itinerants of that day, Whitefield is the only undoubted exception. Davenport, indeed, was said to be reclaimed by the labors of Williams and Wheelock; but it was not till his bodily fever subsided. While that continued, no reproof had any effect upon him, but to bring down upon the reprover a sentence of condemnation, as an unconverted man, and an opposer of the work of God; or at best, as "Jehoshaphat in Ahab's army." As to the rest, scarce an instance can be found, in which any one of them profited by admonition or reproof. Some of them at length became pastors of churches as excited as themselves, and both grew sober together. Others sunk into insignificance and are forgotten. But Whitefield profited by reproof. Sometimes, when more than usually "puffed up," as on his visit to Northampton, he suffered in this respect like other itinerants, and pointing out his errors rather alienated him than reformed him; but very generally, he was thankful to friends who reproved him, and candidly considered the rebukes even of his enemies, and, if they had convicted him of real faults, confessed them and reformed. Witness his treatment of Dr. Chauncy, and of the Faculty of Harvard College.* This trait in his character saved him; and he continued to be useful, and to rise in public estimation, to the end of his life. Had he been obstinate, like others, he would have sunk, like them, into obscurity after a short career, and been long since forgotten by the world at large, as they have been. Whitefield was not more distinguished from other itinerants by his surpassing eloquence, than by his readiness to be corrected; and this, without which all his other gifts would have been worse than lost, should receive the special attention of those who think of making him their model.

It is, however, of little use to give advice to men who are vain and ignorant enough to entertain such a thought. Make Whitefield their model! What would you say to a man who

---

* Doubtless, "Prince, Webb, Foxcroft and Gee," who, it was said, "directed all his public conduct" during his second visit, were of use to him in this respect; but his letter to Chauncy was written while he was sick at Portsmouth, before he met them; so that, though it was probably improved by their suggestions before publication, the honor of originating it is clearly his.

should seriously propose to make Samson his model, in feats of bodily strength? You would say *of* him, that his egregious over estimate of himself renders him unfit to be reasoned with. A man of sufficient power to be a Whitefield, would be incapable of forming himself after a model. He must, from the nature of his own mind, strike out a course for himself. Whitefields cannot be made by imitation; and he who is not aware of it, is incapable even of understanding the character that he would assume. It is of little use to argue with them. Though it is lamentable that any thing of the kind should occur in the history of religious effort, they must be left to realize what Pollock says of those who would ape Lord Byron:—

> "Many, that aimed to imitate his flight
> With weaker wing, unearthly fluttering made,
> And gave abundant sport to after days."*

But they will not merely make sport. They will do positive injury. All religious effort which does not commend itself to the understandings and consciences of men, brings discredit upon religious effort in general, and upon all who are engaged in it, and thus destroys their power to do good. The bad behaviour of itinerants, the avowed imitators of Whitefield, from 1742 to 1744, furnished the enemies of the revival with an excuse for shutting the whole class, including Whitefield himself, out of their pulpits; and such an excuse that their people very generally sustained them, and many who were friends and efficient promoters of the revival at first, were compelled to unite with them. Nor was this all. The enemies of the revival were furnished with means of blackening the reputation of the whole work. They were able to make many believe that those errors and their bad fruits were essential and main parts of what was called "this work," and "this work of God;" and thus, that the work, as a whole, was a bad work from the beginning, and ought

---

* It is often said, that Whitefield cannot have been a very great man, because his sermons contain only plain, common thoughts, such as men of ordinary minds habitually use. But what made those thoughts so common? They were not common when he began to utter them. In England especially, and to a considerable extent, here also, they astonished his hearers by their strangeness. What is more common, than a voyage across the Atlantic? But was Columbus, therefore, only an ordinary man? The case of Copernicus is more nearly parallel. He reasserted a truth which had been uttered, repudiated and forgotten. That truth is now common, even among schoolboys. But was he, therefore, only a child in intellect?

to be opposed. Evangelism tempted the itinerants into errors, and into obstinacy in error; and their errors furnished materials for a wall, which effectually stopped the progress of the revival.*

And finally, the Great Awakening should teach a lesson of faith, of encouragement, of cheerful hope, even in the darkest times. We are too apt to be thrown into despondency by every departure from our own notions of order and propriety, and to think that when every thing does not move exactly as we would have it, every thing is going to destruction. We forget the inspired sentiment: "The wrath of man shall praise thee, and the remainder of wrath thou shalt restrain." We forget, that all the powers of darkness are entirely under the control of the Father of light, and are permitted to make no movement, which he will not overrule for the advancement of his cause. Irregularities may work evil,

* It is surprising, that the enemies of the revival were so generally able to hold their places. By the outcry which they raised, one would think that a great part of them were driven from their parishes, and that the rest were in imminent danger; whereas, in fact, the increase of dismissions was very little more than in proportion to the growth of the country, and the increase in the number of pastors; as will appear by the following table, constructed from several volumes of the American Quarterly Register.

*Dismissions in nine Counties in Massachusetts, from 1731 to 1760, inclusive.*

| *Counties.* | 1731 to 1740. | 1741 to 1750. | 1751 to 1760. |
|---|---|---|---|
| Suffolk, | 0 | 2 | 1 |
| Middlesex, | 3 | 2 | 2 |
| Norfolk, | 2 | 2 | 3 |
| Essex, | 4 | 4 | 3 |
| Worcester, | 3 | 4 | 5 |
| Plymouth, | 1 | 5 | 4 |
| Hampshire, (now Hampshire, Hampden and Franklin,) | 1 | 4 | 6 |
| Bristol, | 1 | 0 | 3 |
| Berkshire, | 0 | 0 | 1 |
| Total. | 15 | 23 | 28 |

The causes of the dismission of Edwards at Northampton, in 1750, and of Billings of Cold Spring, soon after, have already been stated. Maccarty, of Kingston, was a friend of the revival; and the opposition of its enemies among his people led to his dismission in 1745; after which he spent the long remainder of a useful life at Worcester. Burr, of Worcester, was dismissed in 1745; and Lincoln's History of Worcester suggests, that probably the "New Lights" were in part the cause of it. There may have been other cases of the kind, but no intimation of them has been found. Considering how many of them were worthy to be dismissed, such could not have been the result, had not the faults of the itinerants and their partisans enabled them to enlist the consciences of men on their side, against the revival, after it had become degenerate.

and it may be our duty to resist them; for our resistance may be the appointed means of restraining "the remainder of wrath." But God will surely produce an overbalance of good, and will bring good, even out of the evil. Our system of forms and opinions may be the best the world ever saw, and better than any other that we can conceive; but God's time may have come to make the world wiser, and introduce better forms and opinions even than ours. In such revolutions, the human understanding seldom goes intelligently foremost, clearly comprehending the good to be accomplished, and the means of attaining it. Oftener, God stirs up the hearts of men to an irrepressible longing for something better than their minds clearly conceive; society is agitated by their well-meant but ill-directed efforts, like those of the Separatists, seeking a pure church; till at length, some giant mind, like that of Edwards, or more often, the common sense of the community of the pious, discerns the rising truth which is to enlighten the world. In the church, as in the natural body, painful and alarming symptoms are generally the struggle of the vital powers against some latent cause of disease; but, as the church cannot die, the struggle ends in the victory of the vital powers, and the establishment of more perfect health.

When did appearances ever justify more gloomy forebodings, than from 1742 to 1745? The whole land was full of angry controversy. Pastors were divided against pastors, churches against churches, and the members of the same church against each other, and against their pastor. The established rules of ecclesiastical order were set at defiance, and openly trampled upon in the name of God; and numbers were everywhere found to justify and adhere to those that did it. Ignorant and headstrong men were roaming at large, pretending to be under the immediate guidance of the Holy Ghost, and slandering the best men in the land, and multitudes believed them. Religious meetings were often attended with disorders, from which the most reckless "new measure man" of the nineteenth century would shrink back in absolute dismay. Conversions, most evidently spurious, were proclaimed as real, and God was publicly praised for them; and supposed converts, concerning whom even the judicious had hoped favorably, were falling away by thousands. One system of false theology was gaining favor, as a means of opposing these evils ; and another system, equally false and more directly pernicious, was mingling with the revival itself, and spreading as it advanced. Why should not good men be alarmed ? Select, from the preceding accounts, ten places, where the revivals were the most pure, and orderly, and unexceptionable. The occurrence of ten such revivals now, in orthodox churches under the guidance of pastors of good repute, would fill the land with consternation. It is no wonder, that good, judicious, sober men were alarmed ; that they thought the conversion of some hundreds or thousands had been purchased at too dear a rate ; that they pronounced the revival a source of more evil than good, and on the whole, itself an evil ; that they joined its opposers, and ever after kept as far as practicable from every thing of a similar appearance. Now, when the lapse of a century has shown to what those things were tending, we see clearly enough that the fears of those good men deceived them, and that those only were in the right, who adhered to the revival, while they contended against its errors.

There was, indeed, abundant cause to apprehend evil, and to be active in opposing it, and setting bounds to its progress. In this work, Edwards lamented that he had not dared, in the earlier stages of the revival, to do what he afterwards saw to have been his duty, lest he should do mischief; and others had much more reason than he had, for the same lamentation. But there never was any reason to fear that God would not take care of his own kingdom, or to forget that by those very commotions, he was working out the best interests of his church and of the human race. We can see that it was so ; and they ought to have believed that it would prove so. They could then have labored with cheerful hope, with courage, and therefore with effect, in promoting the good and diminishing the evil. We should profit by their history, and, in the midst of commotions which threaten the stability of all that is good on earth, should remember, that the great Disposer of events is only exchanging what is imperfectly good for what will be better, and is, with an infinite calmness, working out results, which, though now beyond our comprehension, will minister to our everlasting joy.

THE END.